DAWN

DAWN

ONE HELL OF A LIFE DAWN FRASER

HODDER

A Hodder book

Published in Australia and New Zealand in 2001
by Hodder Headline Australia Pty Limited
(a member of the Hodder Headline Group)
Level 22, 201 Kent Street, Sydney NSW 2000
Website: www.hha.com.au

Reprinted 2001

**National Library of Australia
Cataloguing-in-Publication data**

Fraser, Dawn, 1937- .
  Dawn : one hell of a life.

  Includes index.
  ISBN 0 7336 1342 X.

  1. Fraser, Dawn, 1937- . 2. Swimmers - Australia -
  Biography. I. Title.

797.21092

Design by Gayna Murphy, Greendot Design
Typesetting by Bookhouse, Sydney
Printed in Australia by Griffin Press, Adelaide

For Mum, Pop and Donnie, who anchored the past.

*For my brothers and sisters, Rose, Joyce, Ken, Chookie,
Heather and Alick, who are always there for me.*

And for Dawn-Lorraine, the future.

I think you will all know how hard it has been to write this book.

CONTENTS

FOREWORD

In many, many ways our Dawn *is* our Australia. To those who neither know nor understand either, both can appear hard, remote, inhospitable, rough, ready, frightening and even dangerous. But for those who really know our Dawn and her country, both are beautiful beyond belief; both are incomparable.

The real story of our Dawnie, as only she would dare to tell it, is of a little girl from a big and happy Aussie family. But a family from the wrong side of the tracks in an era when folk were supposed to know their place and stay there. No one told Dawn this, or she didn't understand, or more likely she instinctively knew, rebelled and set out to do what no one had ever dared before—in life, especially in the pool.

From her first competitive swim our Dawn was a natural champion. And from her first competitive swim victory (from which she was disqualified for being a 'professional' at age twelve) the Establishment sought to put our Dawn back where she belonged. But swimming with a chip on her shoulder that would have been an anchor for a lesser mortal, Dawn won and won and won again and again and again, and achieved what no Olympian had done before and few are likely to repeat.

Even as her country and the world stood in awe of our Dawn, the Establishment struck back in 1964 and celebrated her third consecutive Olympic gold with a ten-year ban; effectively a lifetime disqualification—for what?

For a while it appeared the Establishment had had their dirty, born-to-rule way. Our Dawnie lost business, money, partner, health and phony friends. But never ever her self-respect or determination and will, because just when our Dawn had been written off by almost everyone, she came back: to health, financial independence, even a seat in the New South Wales Parliament.

The whole of ordinary Australia stood as one and acclaimed our Dawn as Australia's greatest female athlete during the bicentenary in 1988. Then in Atlanta at the Olympic Games of 1996 she was honoured as one of the greatest Olympians of all time. And finally, in 1998, even the Australian Government could not stand in her way and, thirty-four years after her name had first been submitted, our Dawn was awarded the Order of Australia (at least it wasn't posthumous).

In 2000, as if it were meant to be, her country and the world again stood to honour our Dawn as the special guest of the President of the IOC, and later as she triumphantly took part in the greatest Olympic opening ceremony ever, in her home town. Our Sydney. Our Dawn.

There has only ever been one Dawn Fraser and I, for one, thank God for that. Our long friendship and love for one another has never been in doubt; we have had some wonderful and some tough times together. In fact, sometimes we spent so much time with each other that many people thought it would make more sense if we just moved in together. Certainly, if we had and had produced kids, they would have swum like fish and drunk like fish! Having Dawn's friendship, love and respect has been one of my life's great good fortunes.

Her story, her life, her book is one of amazing and rare frankness and insight. Funny, sad, hilarious, tragic, thought provoking.

When you have read and thought about our Dawn's life story you too will know her better, love her even more. Without even knowing it you will also have become a better and more tolerant human being.

Our Dawn has earned the love and respect of all Australians. Except a few. And who wants to have a beer with them anyway?

With love, respect and adoration to my beautiful friend Dawn Fraser from her mate always and forever.

John Singleton

1

THE ONE THAT CAME
THE LONGEST WAY

As I heard my name being announced in the grand Vienna State Opera House on the night of November 19th, 1999 I thought I would never be able to stand up. The edited version on video makes it look easy, as if I almost jumped from my seat without a second thought, but that was far from the case. The MC's actual words were:

'It is the one that came the longest way. Dawn Fraser.'

Michael Gross, a guest presenter for the night and the great Olympic butterfly champion known as 'the Albatross', had spoken. But I couldn't move.

I was completely numb. I sat for what seemed like five minutes and tried to force myself to stand but I simply couldn't respond to what was happening. To my mind it was supposed to be either Kristina Egerszegi or Janet Evans from among the five nominated women. How could it be me? I was aware of my daughter sobbing next to me and still I sat there without moving. Eventually my friend Carl Lewis turned around from the row in front and said, 'Dawn, it's you. Congratulations,' which thankfully prompted Dawn-Lorraine to take control. Grabbing my elbow she pushed me forward: 'Mum, get up, it's you. Get up, Mum. It's you.' Finally I stood.

Walking down the aisle I couldn't think of anything other than managing the steps up to the stage and not dropping the magnificent crystal trophy that was about to be handed to me as the newly announced World Female Swimmer of the Century. Those few steps seemed almost impossible to take, even though I had taken so many difficult steps in the spotlight during my life.

Somehow I made it onto the stage. At first I couldn't speak. I hadn't prepared a speech because I have never been presumptuous about anything. I had never expected to win, let alone to be named an Athlete of the Century at the World Sports Awards. After I had taken a firm hold of the 7.8 kilogram Swarovski crystal trophy that Michael handed me, a trophy that I still think is one of the most beautiful things I have ever seen, I tried to compose myself. All I could manage was 'Ladies and Gentlemen' before stopping. Fortunately a round of applause filled the silence before I went on.

'There are many great athletes in this room tonight. And I'm very proud to be one of them. I'm sorry, I'm very emotional…' Another round of applause. I rarely show my emotions in public. My father always taught me never to cry in front of others or to show what's going on inside and now I was just barely stopping the tears from flowing. After thanking those who had nominated me and voted for me around the world I went on to thank my mother and father for having me. Pop would surely have understood such an outburst on an occasion like this.

'...I guess we all have a story to tell to the children of the world and yes, like Carl, I came from a very working class family. But I loved my sport. I could have taken up horse riding but that was too expensive. So swimming was the next best thing because I only needed one pair of bathers and a towel...

'...may I just say how grateful I am to be in the room tonight...with all you great athletes. Thank you for making my life a wonderful life...'

Later that night, lying in bed in my luxurious hotel suite, I thought about how I had really meant what I'd said onstage and how far I had come from the streets of Balmain to the grand city of Vienna and its beautiful Opera House. I marvelled that I'd been chosen from among my peers, the athletes I loved and admired, to be honoured with such an amazing title. I thought about how Nana and Pop Fraser would have been so very proud of me and I hoped that somehow they knew what had happened. Mostly though I thought about the cheeky little girl at Balmain Baths in her baggy hand-me-down swimsuit with her threadbare towel, and how people had tried so hard to stop her from pursuing a swimming career. It occurred to me that I might not have survived until now if I hadn't been raised to be so resilient and—yes—thick-skinned.

Well Frase, I thought, it's been a long battle but I guess you've made it. Then I slept like a baby.

2

WE'VE GOT
A SWIMMER HERE

I was born on September 4th, 1937 in the main bedroom of my parents' little terrace house. I still live in that house in the inner-Sydney suburb of Balmain. It's a classic two-storey Victorian with iron lace in the pattern of Scottish thistle. People would give their eyeteeth and plenty more for houses like it now but back then it was definitely on the wrong side of the tracks. There were up to thirteen of us living there in three bedrooms at one stage. Like nearly everyone else in the area we didn't have any money and we rented our house, but we had all the love in the world and a strong sense of belonging to the family and the neighbourhood.

The youngest of Rose and Kenneth's eight children, I was named after the dawn that was breaking over Cockatoo Island as I first came into the world. When Mum's waters broke, according to my brothers and sisters, there was so much fluid that Dad kept calling out, 'We've got a swimmer here, it's coming out swimming!' My eldest sister, Rosie, who was twenty-one at the time, swears to this day that she named me but none of the rest of them remember it like that. My father told me before he died that they'd run out of names so he chose Dawn when the midwife pointed out the time of day I'd been born. I've been called a lot of things since being named Dawn—both good and bad—but when I was growing up my nickname was Trill. No one can clearly recall why but I think it was because I was always trying to do a really loud whistle with my fingers in my mouth but never could. These days friends and family mostly call me 'Frase', 'Aunty Dawn' and 'Dawnie'.

What everyone does agree on about my birth is that Rose said 'Shove her back! We don't own her' when Nurse Walker ran downstairs to tell everyone they had a little sister. She was embarrassed that her mother was having a baby when Rose was old enough to be dating boys herself. Rosie says she was relieved that Mum 'carried herself well' and that you couldn't really tell she was pregnant with me at Rosie's twenty-first birthday party, towards the end of the pregnancy.

My brother Ken was boiling up the copper while Mum was in labour with me and he had to run up and down the narrow stairs with hot water in Mum's big pink dish, which I still have. Nurse Walker kept asking for more and more hot water and Ken had to keep bringing it to Dad at the bedroom door. Kenny began to worry about where all the water was going. Eventually Dad told him he'd been throwing it over the front verandah onto the street after the nurse had finished with it, 'to clean the footpath up'.

I joke with my daughter that my parents kept going until they had perfection. And Dawn-Lorraine always adds that I achieved perfection the first time round by having her and didn't need to keep going. Rose is the eldest and named after Mum, then Joyce, and Kenneth named after Dad, John Hugh (or Chookie, as he is still known, after the great Balmain Rugby League player Chook Fraser), Heather, Donald, Alick and me. We're pretty evenly spaced with just a few years in between each. Everyone was still living at home when I was born. The four boys shared a bedroom upstairs while Rosie, Joycie and Heather shared the downstairs bedroom. I slept in a cot in my parents' room until I was old enough to move in with Donnie and Alick, who had moved to the upstairs covered verandah after some in-laws had moved in too. The arrangements changed a few times over the years as my sisters were married and their husbands came to stay, and some of my brothers moved out.

We're a very close family but when I was growing up I was closest to Donnie and Alick. We three were more or less brought up together, with Alick just eighteen months older and Donnie seven years older than me. I was included in everything the boys did. I was a real tomboy and ran wild with them all over the district. That was the beginning of my love of the company and conversation of men and my great friendships with strong larrikin types. Although I also have some terrific friendships with women, I get bored with the things some women talk about. And I can't stand gossip. Perhaps I've been on the receiving end too often. To this day I'd rather work on my farm than shop and I'd rather talk about football than clothes. I put it down to those childhood days of running wild with a gang of boys in Balmain.

Balmain, on a peninsula in Sydney Harbour, was a tough, working-class suburb when I was growing up. Now it's mostly populated with well-off professionals instead of wharfies and you're more likely to see BMWs than bicycles on its narrow streets. From the last part of the nineteenth century, though, Balmain was known as a maritime centre, and the local heavy industry of building and repairing ships meant it wasn't thought of as a nice place to live.

There were also lots of factories operating in the area when I was a kid, although all have now been closed and many converted into expensive apartments. It's taken a long time for Balmain to become a suburb that people respect but I've loved it all my life.

I don't remember there being cars in Balmain when I was very young. In fact I didn't see a car in our street until I was about eight years old. There was a tram running down some of the major streets and we kids would jump on occasionally and go for a ride. It was quite a tricky thing to do and we'd practise on the hill where the street runs steeply down to the Darling Street Wharf. There the tram would travel very slowly using a unique system of a counterweight running on rails in a tunnel beside the tramline. The counterweight was connected by cable to a special buffer car at the front of the tram—what we called the 'dummy'. The dummy offered resistance as it was pushed by the tram, making it move very slowly down the hill. It was the perfect place to learn the skills before scaling faster moving trams back up the road. Of course I'd tell Mum I was just going fishing down at the wharf.

Almost everything was done by horse and cart. The ice, milk and fruit were all delivered that way. There was also a dunny run. The only toilet for our household was a tin that sat under the wooden seat in a brick and corrugated iron outhouse in the back-yard. The tin had handles on it and once a week Alick and I would carry it out for the dunny man to replace. It was a disgusting job and probably needs no more explanation to give you the picture.

We had a proper bath once a week in a room at the back of the house which didn't resemble a modern-day bathroom at all. It was, in a word, 'basic'. There were certainly no tiles or porcelain basins. The copper was boiled and we'd take buckets from the copper to the tin tub. We'd all use the same water, emptying the cold and adding more hot as we went. It was never very hot by the time I got in last with Alick. Later Pop got hold of a chip heater which had a pipe coming up the middle of it with a tap connected at the end over the bath. If you weren't paying attention the water would sometimes boil up and spit at you. Being the youngest I was usually put at the spitting end of the bath. To this day I prefer a cold shower because I got used to washing with cold water in my child-hood as well as swimming in cold water at the pool when I started training.

Opposite our house was a local primary school, Birchgrove Public, and next door to the school there was a coal mine which had been established in 1897 to tap the seam of coal that runs along the coast between Newcastle and Wollongong. It was an ideal site for a mine because the water there was deep close to the shore-line and Balmain was already a maritime centre near the city. Although it was thought at the turn of the century the coal supply would last for more than two hundred years, most of it is still under the ocean as the mine was closed for the last time in 1945 after a sad history during which many men were injured or lost their lives.

The mine was last used in 1942 when natural gas, which was in demand as a substitute for petrol during World War II, was drawn off from old underground tunnels. After the mine was found to be unsafe it was sealed, but even this involved tragedy when an explosion in 1945 during the sealing killed two men and injured more. I was roaming around with my gang of friends after the explosion and we found a hand still in a glove in nearby Water Street. I will never forget how it looked: bloody and gory. I've been told that over the years parts of bodies were found washed out at Bondi Beach after explosions in the mine.

So while it was an ideal site for a mine it was not so great for the school and the neighbourhood kids. I am sure my asthma and bronchial problems were made worse over the years by playing in the deserted mine, and of course the gas leaks weren't the best either. We were forbidden to play there by our father and by the caretaker appointed by the Department of Mines because the gas was still escaping long after the closure, with the highest reading as late as 1954. Before it was sealed my mother went on a walking tour of the mine as far as the heads of Sydney Harbour. When my brothers and sisters came home from school they found her covered in soot. I've heard that some of the tunnels are still there today although they are supposed to have been flooded, filled and sealed. New housing was built over the top in 1987 and I know there have been complaints of subsidence since then. I've always had my doubts about the area and I joined residents' action groups calling for further investigation at the time when the new housing was proposed.

•

My beloved father, Kenneth Fraser, was the first strong man in my life. When I was growing up he worked at Cockatoo Island as a shipwright. At 18 hectares, the island is the largest in Sydney Harbour and can be seen from the front balconies of my house. It was used from the 1830s as a prison, later becoming a women's reformatory and a site for the mooring of school ships for destitute and delinquent boys. Eventually the island became a shipyard and my father worked there during World War I when it was a Commonwealth Government defence installation. Pop Fraser, as he was known, arrived in Australia in approximately 1910 at the age of twenty, having worked his way here on a ship from Scotland. He was born in the Sutherland Shire and he never lost his broad accent. I can still hear his voice as he'd arrive home: 'Dawnie, where's my slippers?' When he was angry none of us could understand a word he was saying.

Pop was always home around 6.30 p.m. after the pub had closed. They worked hard back then and the pub was the place to go at the end of the day. They'd knock off work by 4.00 p.m. and get in an hour and a half's drinking before tea. It was mostly at the Riverview when I was growing up, a pub I later owned for several years. Those were the days of the 'six o'clock swill' and early closing.

The schooners were lined up on the counter at six o'clock and by ten past they'd be saying 'Close the doors, close the doors!' and the men would have to get their beers down and be out of there. Everyone knew everyone else in the district and some of the men had their special places in the pub. Pop had 'Ken's Corner'. Just before he was due to arrive at the pub the barman would yell out, 'Kenny Fraser will be here in a minute,' and by crikey if someone was sitting there when he came in he'd be yelling at whoever it was to 'Get out of my bloody corner!' Nearly everyone did.

From the time I was about six years old, if I had finished all my jobs after school, I'd meet Pop at the Cove Street ferry wharf and walk up to the pub with him. I'd have to wait outside but I could usually get Pop to buy me a juice: he practically always gave in to the blue eyes of his little Dawnie. Other nights Pop used to call to me when he came home and I'd have to take his lunchbox so that my mother wouldn't see what was in it. 'Be a good girl, Dawnie, and take it up to the toilet.' I'd remove the little square bottle of rum and hide it for him in the top of the toilet cistern in the back-yard so he could sneak a drink out there. When I was very young I'd have to stand on tiptoes, tilt it over the side and drop it in. I don't know who Pop thought he was kidding because you could smell the rum on him a mile away. I still hate the smell of it, and have only ever drunk rum myself in the days when I was running the pub and couldn't afford to take time off work with the flu. I'd have a beer with a rum chaser. I used to say to my customers, 'This is what my dad drank.' I guess by today's standards he'd be classi-fied as an alcoholic being at the pub every night but everyone did it then. He used to say the rum was good for his asthma. My father was very protective of my mother and one of the only things that led to a fight between them was the rum. She hated it.

I guess you could describe Pop as a hard man, but he was a good father and I adored him. He was very strict, especially with the boys. Kenny had Mum set his place at the other end of the dinner table one night just to get a break, but Pop wouldn't have it because Kenny was the eldest son and his place was next to him at the top of the table. We all sat on stools that Pop had made and he used to check that our hands and faces were clean and our ears washed before we sat down to tea. He could tell if we'd been disobeying him and playing in the mine because of the soot in our ears.

We were all kept in line with a razor strap. Heather remembers we'd get ten whacks per cheek on the bottom if we were bad and a tablespoon of castor oil for playing up. Castor oil was also the remedy for any sickness.

From the time he came out here from Scotland, Pop was rarely out of work; he was such a skilled shipwright he was constantly in demand. Even when lots of men were laid off from Cockatoo Island during the Depression, Pop kept working. In fact during both world wars he was considered more valuable working as a shipwright on the island than he would have been at the front, which is why he didn't join the forces.

Pop Fraser even made all our school cases out of wood with dovetailing and he didn't use a single nail; even the handles were attached with screws. Looking back they were extremely beautiful cases and I wish I'd kept one. My brother Chookie is the only one of my brothers who followed Pop in his trade and he also became a highly sought-after shipwright.

Various brothers and cousins of Dad would come out from Scotland on ships from time to time. That's how there came to be vodka in the house, which my brothers mixed into my lemonade when I was ten years old. I gulped it down—just as my brothers had told me to—right before I ran up the stairs to change for school sport one Friday afternoon. I fell back down the stairs, passed out and later became violently ill. Donnie and Alick really got into trouble over that one.

There were a few uncles on Dad's side who stayed in Australia. Uncle George, one of his brothers, came here and ended up becoming a tramp. Dad used to pick him up from Belmore Park, a little reserve opposite Central Railway Station, where he mostly slept. Pop would bring him home, make him have a bath and give him clean clothes. The old rags would be stoked up in the copper. Uncle George had a swag on a big pole with a billy at the end of it. He never stayed with us for long and in a month or so he'd be gone again. The first time my brothers ever saw my dad cry was when he picked Uncle George up from the park. We never knew Pop's parents and to this day none of us really know much about his family or his childhood. I visited his sister Mary on my way back from Rome in 1960 but have had no contact since.

For a relatively short man—he was only five foot seven—Pop was big chested. In fact he had a huge chest at forty-nine inches. He was extremely strong too, although he suffered from bronchial complaints and asthma, two things he passed on to me. Although it has been reported many times that Pop was so ill during my childhood that we all gradually went out to work to help run the household, he actually rarely missed work even when he was terribly sick. We all went to work early because that's what working-class kids did back then when there was little encouragement and less opportunity to finish school, let alone go to university. Pop had a bottle of red medicine next to his bed that he'd inhale through a tube at night. I'd lie in the dark and listen to his rattling wheeze and hacking cough. Of course his problems weren't helped by smoking but everyone smoked back then, and Pop rolled his own with Log Cabin tobacco completely unaware of the damage he was doing.

My dad was a bit of a leader in the area and started the crib games and dominoes in the pub. These would be played at different houses around the neighbourhood every weekend as well. People played for money but the amounts were very small as we were all poor. It was more about the company and socialising than the money. And of course there was no television in the early days, so dominoes in the pub was the height of entertainment.

The card games often took place at our house and I would be the one to serve the beers. As a seven-year-old I already knew how to fill up the quarts through a funnel from the jugs so I didn't take too much gas out of the beer before Sunday. On Sunday the Codocks football team would come back to our place after the game for a drink. Codocks was formed by the men who worked on Cockatoo Island Docks, and the team and their supporters would fill our backyard. Once again I'd be carrying heavy beers up and down the back garden and I loved it. I was a hardworking and outgoing child and I loved having a part to play.

Pop was an excellent soccer player and when he arrived in Australia he joined a team in the Balmain district. Mum's brother also played for the team and we think that's how my parents met, but as Mum's father was a sailor perhaps Cockatoo Island was the connection: no one in the family is sure any more. We do know that they married in 1914 and that put an end to any thoughts my dad had about returning to Scotland to live. My mother, Rose Christina Miranda, and her brothers and sisters were born here and grew up in Balmain but her father was from Peru. It was a favourite family story that his distant cousin was Carmen Miranda, but as Carmen was Brazilian and our Mirandas were Peruvian, it seems pretty unlikely. As with Pop's family, none of us really knows much about Mum's background or how her father came to be here. Nana Miranda is remembered by my older brothers and sisters as being able to cut the top off an apple, scoop out the flesh with a teaspoon, and place the intact skin back on the table as if it had never been touched. That's how she ate apples. They say she was a wonderfully warm, loving woman, although my memories of her are hazy at best. My mother, or Nana Fraser as she was known to us, must have taken after her mother because she was loved by everyone. Pop used to sing *Rosie O'Grady You Are My Posy* to her. She was an unassuming woman and extremely hardworking. At five foot ten she was taller than Dad and as a young woman had dark good looks that came out in about half my brothers and sisters and also in my daughter, Dawn-Lorraine. Donnie was especially good-looking. I suspect I have more of my father's genes and also his temperament, although there's no mistaking I'm my mother's daughter as I get older.

I remember a time when my mother's usually calm temper erupted and she chased my father up the stairs with a carving knife. My father kept saying in his Scottish brogue, 'Put the knife down, Rawsie. Give me the knife, Rawsie. Jesus Bloody Christ, Rawsie, give me the knife!' I was hiding in the cupboard under the stairs at the time which is where I'd always go when I was frightened. On that occasion I think Dad had been on the rum.

Mum was always washing and ironing, right up to the end of her life. It wasn't only our clothes she looked after; to make ends meet she took on other people's too. At times it seemed she laundered for almost everyone in Balmain. If a bachelor moved into the neighbourhood to work on Cockatoo, people would say, 'Mrs Fraser will do your washing for you.' I can remember her ironing eighty shirts one night. My father had to build her a special clothes horse to hang them from and we had to make sure the wire part of the wooden coat hangers she used didn't rust and mark the shirts. We kids would collect the washing in the barrow that Pop had made us. Nana Fraser was a wonderful housekeeper and kept everything tidy, although our furnishings were very simple. The linoleum floor always shone and when Mum had finished using the copper for washing the clothes it was up to us kids to polish it until we could see ourselves in it.

On any day of the week you could see my mum hanging over the front downstairs balcony speaking to passers-by or to our neighbours on either side, the Bakers and the Lloyds. The mothers congregated in the ladies' parlour of the pub on Friday nights and Saturday afternoons and they'd sit and shell the peas or string the beans for dinner while they had a chat. The first time they went there it was like a women's uprising. They were sick of the husbands being up there every night so they decided to surprise them one day. The men were shocked when they were told they had visitors in the ladies' parlour. 'What are youse doing here?' they wanted to know. 'We're having a beer just like you,' the women chorused. And that was that.

Mum was Catholic and Pop was Presbyterian. Pop always said that the Presbyterians had been slaughtered in the highlands of Scotland by the Catholics and he'd never forgiven them. He taught us that religion was nothing to fight over and said that as long as we were baptised and married in a church of our choice, that was all that was required of us in the area of religion. We'd put Pop's teaching into practice at Sunday School whenever one of the kids was having a birthday cake after the scripture lesson. We'd get the word and the Frasers would be there mixing it with whatever denomination, eating the cake and having a great time.

After Sunday School we'd go home to a roast dinner before the football game in the afternoon. That was the best meal of the week. Dad would slaughter a chook and it would be hung out on the clothesline to drain. In the meantime the copper would be boiled so the bird could be plunged into hot water before being plucked. When I was a bit older, say ten or eleven, Donnie would let me help kill the bird for lunch, and I would be thrilled and horrified at the same time to see it running headless around the yard, blood spurting from its neck. Food was pretty scarce in those days, and there were lots of Frasers to feed. During the middle years of my childhood, with World War II not long finished, we were all on rations, which meant buying eggs, butter, bacon, sugar and other staples with coupons. These lasted only a short time in our big family, and many a time we would have dripping on bread. Breakfast was usually porridge soaked overnight in a big pot, sometimes toast but mainly fried bread, especially on Monday after the roast when there was plenty of dripping for frying.

Mum tried to keep us kids in line so that Pop didn't get stirred up. She tried to keep us on the right side of him. Kenny can remember her coming to him after he got a belting and giving him a cuddle: 'She was a great old girl.' She was good to all of us and never showed she had a favourite, although everyone says I was spoiled by Pop. I guess I was spoiled by the standards that applied to my older brothers and sisters but not in the way kids are today. We all had to pitch in and work from the age of about six. Mum used all sorts of home remedies and handed-down wisdom in bringing us kids up. I can remember her wiping wet nappies over the faces of her grandchildren to help keep freckles away and I'm told she did it to us too.

I was always strong willed. When Joycie married her husband, Billy, I was their four-year-old flower girl. I carried out all my duties perfectly at the church but when it came time for them to leave for their honeymoon I had packed my bag ready to go too. I was clinging to Joycie and when it finally sank in that I wasn't included in the holiday I kicked Billy in the shins and screamed the house down. I've always wanted to travel.

I followed in my brothers' and sisters' footsteps across the road to Birchgrove Public School when I started in the infants as a five-year-old. Donnie and Alick were at school with me but the others had left by the time I started. I went to school with the neighbourhood kids, who happened to be mostly boys. I had a uniform because my sisters sewed, and there were lots of hand-me-downs. I also had shoes but plenty didn't. I can still remember being very excited when I was given my first long-sleeved white blouse, tunic and tie. By then I was in the primary school and all the girls wanted to be in Mr Forster's class. He was very handsome. One day my teacher was away and the partitions between the two classes were pulled back—and there was Mr Forster. I still remember my excitement. I had such a crush on him.

The first time I went to school sport, at the age of six, Alick was playing in the grand final of the school football competition. Donnie had come along to watch too. One of the boys on the team was hurt and couldn't play, so I was fitted out with a pair of football shorts and a jumper, boots and socks. The only problem was my long hair; it was so long I could sit on it. The boys got hold of a pair of scissors and cut it off straight across the top of my plait. They put me on the wing and told everyone on the other side: 'Stay away from our winger. If you touch him we'll kill you.' We won the game and no one on the other side ever knew our secret.

Pop Fraser loved my long hair and on that particular Friday I was too scared to go and meet him at the ferry wharf after work. Even though we had won the game, the reality of how Pop would react to my haircut had begun to sink in. Down at the wharf Pop asked where I was and Alick told him I had to go and run some messages for Mrs Lloyd next door. They walked up to the Riverview and in the meantime I helped Mum clean up, cook dinner and set the table. She still wouldn't talk to me she was so mad about my hair.

When Pop came home at 6.30 with Alick we were all sitting at the table waiting for him. When he saw my hair he blew up. He was speaking so quickly in that thick Scottish accent that no one could understand him. He started to swear and speak Gaelic and the only clear words were things like 'I'll belt the !@*# pants off you.' And he did. He belted the boys so hard they had to stand at the mantlepiece to eat their dinner. I got a whack too, but not as hard as the whacks Donnie and Alick copped because Pop said they were older and should have had more sense. It took him a month to get over my hair and he didn't speak to me for at least a week.

It was clear to me even at the age of seven that my teacher, Mrs Rose, didn't like me because I was thought to be a bit of a naughty girl. One particular day I was sitting in the front row of the classroom and I really needed to go to the toilet. I kept saying 'Mrs

Rose, please may I go to the bathroom? Please Mrs Rose may I go to the bathroom? Mrs Rose, may I go to the bathroom? *Pleeeeeeease* Mrs Rose, I'm wetting myself!' And I peed my pants right there in front of everyone and I was made to stand up at the back of the room in the corner with wet pants and urine dribbling down my legs. At lunchtime I ran home and told Mum what had happened. Even though Mum was a pretty quiet person she was definitely coming over to the school to pull Mrs Rose's nose off. I don't know what was said but Mrs Rose was a bit nicer to me from then on.

My hair had fully grown back by the time I was nine: around the same time that we started to use pen and ink for our writing. Like all school children then, we had nibs and inkwells. Two boys from my gang of street kids, Georgie Baker and Freddie Fields, used to sit behind me and every now and then they would put the end of my plait in the inkwell. Then one of them would say my name at the right time and I would swing around, spraying ink all over the teacher. Jeez I would get into strife, even after Mum's little meeting with Mrs Rose. To this day that's one of the reasons why I dislike having long hair, along with the trouble it used to be when I started my swimming training.

Whenever I went to school with wet hair after morning training Mrs Rose would be furious. She used to hit us over the knuckles with a metal-edged ruler if she thought we were misbehaving and that happened to me many times when my hair was wet. Still, we got our own back often enough. In those days women wore bloomers that came down to the top of the knees. Mrs Rose used to sit with her legs open and the whole class could see straight up the bloomers. We'd all sing out: 'Close your legs, we can see your powder puff up there.'

When I was eleven my gang and I decided to wag school for the day and go down to the Balmain Baths, the harbour swimming pool right at Elkington Park near my house, which was later renamed the Dawn Fraser Baths. What I hadn't thought about that day was that my brothers Donnie and Ken worked next door to the baths at the National Box Factory. Donnie was the 'dogman' and Kenny was the crane driver. The job of the dogman was to stand on the crane hook, keep watch and blow the whistle to direct the crane driver. With his bird's-eye view of the area he spotted us wagging school, and when morning-tea time came he raced over to the baths, grabbed Alick, Tommie O'Neil, Georgie and Freddie and dragged them all home. He was gone before I was seen; at least I *thought* I hadn't been seen. I ran down to the point at Elkington Park near the baths and hid in the air-raid shelters. I thought it would be safer to sit there and eat my lunch. Just as I was congratulating myself on how clever I'd been, Donnie's head popped over the top of the shelter and he grabbed my pigtail. Then I was dragged home too. After getting into enormous trouble from Mum I was sent back to school. I said I'd been sick in the morning which is why I was late but my hair was wet from swimming so I ended up being caned at school too. Being caught out twice was very humiliating for a cocky eleven-year-old.

I really hated school but I always wanted to learn. When I was nine years old Donnie gave me a pencil sharpener in the shape of a globe for Christmas and I wanted to go everywhere on that globe. I used to daydream about travelling and finding out about Australia and all the places on the globe. It remained in the back of my mind from then on through my teenage years that somehow I was going to do that, to travel and see the world. When I started swimming well and winning competitions one of the things that drove me on was the chance of travel that it offered. I wanted to go anywhere and everywhere and the more I saw, the more my eyes were opened to life's possibilities. I wanted to have the things and the way of life that I was seeing others living. While I wasn't a well-behaved student at school, when I paid attention and the lesson was inter-esting I had no trouble absorbing the information. I was never a poor student; I just didn't seem to get enough of the things that interested me. We never really thought about getting an education. It was more about survival, feeding the family and having fun.

Friday was the best night of all in the neighbourhood when I was growing up. The miners, the wharfies, the milkmen, boat-builders, shipwrights, engineers and all the workers would be in the Riverview. We kids would sit outside on the back of the coal truck putting the leftover coal into hessian bags for our father to take home to feed the fire. Whoever had the most coal in their bag when Dad left the pub would get a nice treat after tea: either a packet of chips or peanuts. The coal man would leave the bags and leftover coal for us and he might be bought a beer or two in return. We used the barter system most of the time back then. The bags would be returned the next day via the pub.

We all had our jobs to do as kids to make sure the family got by and to give Mum some extras. Donnie helped the iceman take his horse and cart around the streets selling ice for the ice chests that we used in those days before refrigerators. Alick and I some-times helped him do the ice run by chipping off the ice with him but the two of us also looked after the council horses that were kept behind the Balmain Town Hall. When I turned seven I began to clean the horses and muck out their stables. On the weekends we also made sure they were fed. Sometimes I'd collect the manure and sell it to people in the area for their vegetable gardens for about a shilling a bag, and occasionally do the spreading too.

We had our own horses because sometimes an underfed stray was found in the streets and if no one claimed it in a week the police allowed us to keep it. Alick kept his horses at the mine until one got into the caretaker's prized flowerbed and ate everything. All hell broke loose that day.

I loved the horses and riding. From the age of eight I'd ride with the boys all the way to Epping on Sydney's upper North Shore to stay overnight with Mum's relatives. It probably seems a long way to ride these days but back then, across paddocks and bushland, it only took us about two hours. We'd take off over the Iron Cove Bridge and then travel across country via the Field of Mars cemetery. That part scared me. I remember Mum would always say not to canter through the cemetery and disturb the graves. We'd canter elsewhere, though, and were quite fearless on horseback. Epping in those days was more of a farming area, with lots of bush and market gardens. We didn't often have saddles or any fancy equipment but we taught ourselves to ride well. Ever since then I've had a strong connection with horses and a continuing interest in them.

Another job we all did at some point was to go down to the National Box Factory, or the 'Boxie' as it was known around the district, and collect woodchips for the fire. I can remember doing this after dark and sneaking in through a hole in the fence, although Alick says there was a sympathetic caretaker at one stage who'd let us Fraser kids in through the gate. We'd load the woodchips into our barrow and take it proudly home for the copper, the chip heater or the fireplace. At different times Ken, Alick and Donnie all worked at the Boxie.

When I was about nine I became a 'runner', and my working life became a lot more interesting. The job involved going around to the houses in the district and collecting people's bets, which I'd then take down to an SP shop in East Balmain run by Harry Hardin and Lenny McPherson. Lenny later became a well-known Sydney underworld figure but he was great to me throughout my life. My brothers Ken and Chookie knew Lenny too and have good memories of him, but my sister Rosie, who was the same age as Lenny, says he was really mean to her. Lenny used to punch her in the stomach on the way home from school, and in the end the teachers had to keep him in until she got home safely. So it's no surprise she doesn't remember him fondly. She said to me once, 'When his name came up in the paper in later years I thought to myself: "That bastard used to punch me".'

My job as the runner came about because I was already working occasionally cleaning floors in the local milk bar which was owned by Harry Hardin. I also knew the district like the back of my hand and I was a pretty skinny kid who could get in and out of tight places, which was essential for the job. I'd get in through the bars at the local hospital, sneak into the wards and take bets from the patients. I liked talking to all the old people. In those days we didn't have TABs, so SPs were the only way to have a bet away from the track. It was illegal but everyone in Balmain used SPs. It was like two-up back then, when you could walk into any pub and they'd be playing: the police mostly turned a blind eye. Now of course two-up is strictly policed and you only see it being played openly in the pubs on Anzac Day, while the days of the SP bookmakers are gone forever.

I worked for Lenny and Harry for about five years but because I was a runner I wasn't allowed to bet myself. I sometimes used to put one on in a false name but usually I would just write on the packet 'bet for Mrs Fraser', and if I won I would take a little out for myself and give the rest to my mother. I was aware from an early age that we all had to do our bit. It was as much a part of who we were as going to the pub on Saturday and watching the football on Sunday. We were workers. I was also brought up with the 'old school' belief that as long as you didn't hurt anyone or dob anyone in, it was generally all right to be doing what you were doing. So I went along doing my job as a runner, minding my own business, and I suppose that's how I've lived my life, too: don't tell and don't ask. I'm not sure that code has always served me well but it's part of who I am.

I loved Saturday mornings because I got a kick out of knowing that Mr Hardin and Mr McPherson trusted me with such a big responsibility. When there was a lot of money involved, Lenny would drive me around to pick up the bets, but I'd still go in and collect. I enjoyed the feeling of power, having been the youngest of eight and the least powerful person in my family. Running gave me a place and a role that was all my own. The fact that everyone knew I was 'Lenny's little girl' made me feel special, perhaps for the first time in my life. I was always loved but I was also just a little part of a big clan. Mum didn't really know what I was up to back then. I'd pretend any winnings I made came from other work. Dad knew but he turned a blind eye until the day he saw Lenny dropping me off on the corner of our street. He was waiting on the front verandah and he told me I was never to be seen in Lenny's company again. I kept running after that but I became more careful. I'd line up in the betting shop on Saturday and take my pay. No questions asked.

Alick and I had a barrow run and our barrow was the best in Balmain. Pop Fraser had put expensive ball-bearing wheels on it. We'd run all sorts of messages for people in the district, picking things up and dropping them off. Alick once saved enough from the barrow run to buy a special bike, unlike the rusty things we usually tore around on put together by Pop from bits and pieces. But he wouldn't let me ride it because it was a man's bike and because it had cost so much. When he wasn't around I'd get on it even though it had the bar across the middle. I'd put my legs through the middle and lean across the bar because my legs were too short to straddle the bar. Once I became so frustrated by the bar that I tried to get rid of it with a hacksaw. When I couldn't saw through the steel I panicked and tried to fill in the cuts I'd made with some sort of glue. Alick found out and I really copped it. After that I went back to riding with the bar over my shoulder. That went on behind his back until one day I was riding down Macquarie Terrace, around the plantation and into my street. I went to put the brakes on when all of a sudden they fell off and went through the spokes of the wheels. Naturally I fell off too and smashed the bike to pieces. When my brother saw the bike he was heartbroken and knew instantly it was me, even though at first I tried to pretend I hadn't done anything by saying, 'Look what someone's done to Alick's bike! They've stolen it and wrecked it. How terrible!'

One of my strongest memories of growing up is the way people used to share with each other. You'd look out for your neighbours and help each other along. It was what people today long for in a community. If a job came up for one of my brothers and they knew a married man needed it more, they'd hand it over and find something else for themselves. One day when rationing was on I found a box of butter in the middle of the street and very proudly took it home to Mum. She could have sold it and made quite a bit of money but instead she gave most of it away to the neighbours. If you gathered some coal from the mine in two bags you'd give one bag away. We took what we needed but were never greedy.

We lived through some difficult times together in Balmain. The Depression hit the docks and Cockatoo Island hard and lots of the local men were out of work. I also remember the houses being blacked out during World War II. We'd even take rolls of tar paper and cover the windows. After the Japanese submarines got into Sydney Harbour you would hear the air-raid siren going off which meant you had to turn out all the lights, and I was instructed by my parents to hide. I used to get into the cupboard under the stairs with a little candle and my marbles. The wardens would be walking around the streets checking for any lights left on and people all around seemed to be singing out, 'Get that light off. Turn that light out.' I was only a little girl and I remember being terrified.

It is true that I was a wild child. There were very few girls of my age in the neighbourhood so I ran in my gang with all the boys from the streets around ours. We were into everything. I didn't like to be controlled. It was as if there was something inside me urging me to take things on. I was also a fearless child as I grew older. Harry Gallagher, my swimming coach, said I was a 'den-smart child', meaning that as the youngest in a large family I had to fight for everything, but I would describe myself more as a street kid. The streets I grew up on were of course very different from those that so-called 'street kids' grow up on today, nevertheless I spent most of my time roaming around the district. Just as Harry said, I did feel from a very early age that I had to fight for things—no fisty fights or anything like that, because I loved my family, but just making sure I was heard and had a place. I had very poor health, I was extremely skinny and often just breathing was a struggle. At one stage it was thought that I had tuberculosis and might have to go to an infirmary but the diagnosis was eventually chronic asthma. I wanted desperately to belong and be a part of things and so I found myself the leader and daredevil in my gang.

One of the games my gang used to play in the neighbourhood after dark was 'Nick Nock'. You needed a cotton reel to play this game and I would always get one from my sister Joycie who worked at Larco, a factory on Darling Street which made uniforms and tracksuits. I suspect she thought I was borrowing the cotton reel to copy her, but we had other plans. Once we had the reel of cotton we'd draw a name out of whatever was available. I could never understand why mine was drawn so often. I was usually the one chosen to quietly open the gate of a selected house a few streets from home, sneak up to the front door and tie the cotton onto the knocker before sneaking back out the way I had come in, unravelling the cotton as I went. When we'd all hidden ourselves from view I'd pull the cotton as hard as I could to make the doorknocker work. Of course when the person opened the door there was no one there. Then our poor neighbour would close the door and we'd wait a minute before knocking again. Once again there'd be no one there when the door was answered. A few giggles would escape into the street and a third tug usually achieved the effect we were after: a red-faced neighbour angrily scanning the street for the culprit.

Much to my amazement on one occasion the neighbour yelled, 'I'm going to tell your pop on you Dawnie Fraser.' That gives you some idea of my reputation at the ripe old age of eleven. I tore the cotton from the doorknocker and I started to furiously rewind while all the kids were whispering, 'How the hell did he know it was Dawnie?' We were all shocked and scared, and for a few days after that incident I'd meet Pop at the Cove Street Wharf after work to try to find out if the man had said anything to him. Much to my surprise and relief he never did. When I say I was fearless, Pop was a different story. I was always pretty scared of him when he was angry.

But this didn't stop me taking risks. When everyone was asleep at night I would creep into Mum and Dad's room, urged by my brothers, sneak some tobacco and papers out of Pop's tobacco pouch and then hide them underneath my pillow. Friday night was good for this caper because it was pay day and that meant a new pouch of tobacco. Pop's Log Cabin came in strips so I could take two or three and no one would ever know. We'd mash it with choko leaves from the vine in the backyard, then we'd take it down to the school to smoke it. I didn't really enjoy smoking but there I was at the centre of anything that was going, being the ringleader and bravest of all the kids.

One particular weekend when I was about ten we were at the school smoking our homemade cigarettes when Mum and Mrs Baker came across; they had seen the smoke rising up from the school. There were about twenty kids all in a huddle and me in the centre sitting on my little stool. I turned to see my mother and Mrs Baker walking down the stairs. As I went to hide my cigarette Mum grabbed me by the plait (that bloody plait!) and said, 'You get home, Dawnie.' Mum told Dad all about the smoking but much to our surprise he didn't say anything that night. Instead, he kept us back from going to the football the next day—which was punishment enough—and made Alick and me sit in the backyard and smoke a cigar each. At first we thought, 'Gee, this is great, Dad's going to have a smoke with us.' We soon worked out what he was doing and were as sick as dogs. I vomited all over the yard and the chooks ran out and ate it up. Dad cured me for a long time, and although my brothers wanted me to steal more tobacco I never did. That's not to say that I didn't smoke from then on because I did. Although I never liked smoking, as a kid and later as a teenager I smoked as an act of defiance and toughness. And when I owned the Riverview I smoked because it became a habit to smoke with the clients at the bar.

Donnie was my childhood hero. He was very athletic and it seemed he could do anything he turned his hand to. Donnie always included me in his life, which to me was a constant adventure. He was also my protector. As he got older he even took me to the local cinema when he dated girls. It must have been annoying having a smartypants little sister tagging along, especially when I'd see him sitting with his arm around a girl: 'Donnie, I'm going to tell on you unless you buy me an ice-cream.' Or I'd squeeze in between them. He never showed that he minded though, and I worshipped the ground he walked on.

Of all the wonderful things Donnie gave to me, he was actually the first one to ever make me swim. Most of the family were swimmers and Mum swam at the Balmain Baths every day right up until she was nine months pregnant with me. Perhaps this made an impression on me even before I was born. We'd often go on family outings to the baths and have a picnic in the park. It was a cheap outing, as only the kids would go into the pool while the adults would wait in the park with the picnic. There were plenty of ways of getting in free but with Mum and Dad we always paid. I actually thought we owned the swimming pool when I was growing up and it took a long time for me to understand that although it was right near our house and various relatives had lived in the pool caretaker's cottage at different times, we didn't own it. Even at thirteen, around the time I met my swimming coach, Harry Gallagher, I still took a proprietary interest in the pool.

I first started to swim on one of our family outings to the baths when I was about four years old. Alick and Donnie used to jump from the high tower at the baths with me, the baby, on their backs. They were actually brilliant divers who later became part of the well-known Harry Tickle Diving Troupe. One day at the pool Donnie said it was about time I learned to swim and he jumped in as usual, but he let me go right there in the middle of the deep end. I had to get myself to the side of the pool so I just started a sort of swimming dog paddle and managed to reach the edge. I was quite scared and didn't talk to Donnie for the rest of the day. What he had done, though, was force me to start swimming. I was literally thrown in at the deep end and the rest, as they say, is history.

3

FINDING A COACH
AND LOSING A GOD

I am terrified of heights so when I think back to the times that I used to cling to my brothers' backs at the top of the 30-foot diving tower at Balmain Baths I am amazed at my bravery as a four-year-old. Of course it was really due to my complete and utter faith in Donnie and his ability to protect me from everything and everyone. He was the perfect big brother who'd even settle Alick's and my fights with other kids, which happened pretty often because I'd always be giving cheek.

By chance rather than by good planning I grew up in a very encouraging household. With both Pop and Donnie including me in all their activities I felt there was nothing I couldn't do. Nor were there restrictions because I was a girl or because I was the youngest. I just had to muck in along with everyone else and I think it was this that made me tough, so I was already a keen competitor from about the age of four. Pop Fraser showed me how to use a hammer when I was five and together we'd make things like the school cases and the barrow. I might as well have been a son to him for all the distinction he made between what was and wasn't considered appropriate activity for a girl. We were a very physical, lively and sometimes chaotic family.

Most of the Frasers had strong sporting ability. My father played soccer and all my brothers played football and swam, with Donnie and Alick in particular becoming great footballers, swimmers and divers. My sister Heather played vigoro and hockey too, although it must be said that of all of us she is the homebody. Heather can remember trying to catch me down at the baths after I'd dive-bombed her or grabbed her legs under water but I'd just slip away because I was so quick. She says that even my skin felt more slippery than anyone else's.

The Balmain Baths is a harbour pool at the bottom of a sweeping public park shaded by magnificent Moreton Bay figs. The caretaker's cottage sits on the edge of the park just above the path that leads down to the baths. The pool itself is an odd shape, longer on one side than the other, and it juts out into the Parramatta River. For some reason the water around there has always been dark and murky and I have never seen the bottom of the pool from above. Often I would swim out into the river by diving down and swimming underneath the wall through a hole. At high tide the sea water would sometimes sweep in right over the boards around the edge of the pool. It was a fair training pool at 73⅓ yards long but very crowded in summer. There weren't any roped-off lanes back then; it was everyone for themselves. I mostly went in free, either by scaling the fence, climbing in through a hole in it, manoeuvring through the turnstyle without paying or being favoured by the caretaker after I had begun to do well at my swimming.

We spent a lot of time on all sorts of water activities. Donnie, Pop and Mrs Lloyd next door taught me how to fish when I was very young and to this day I enjoy it—I'm not bad at it either. My mother was more of a homebody like Heather but Mrs Lloyd loved the outdoors and fishing, so together we'd go down to the edge of the mine or to Cove Street Wharf. We'd use lines and catch leather jacket, bream and blackfish for dinner. The river was relatively clean back then, although there was sometimes a lot of oil on top from Cockatoo Island.

One day Mrs Lloyd and I were fishing together on the edge of the mine wall when we saw two men coming down the hill with a sugar bag. Out on the river a small boat chugged towards the edge of the mine wall and we assumed the men were going fishing because most people carried their fishing gear in a sugar bag. As they came towards us one of them handed me the bag while he clambered aboard the boat. I remember asking what was in the bag because it was so heavy. About an hour later I had the answer when the police came down to us to ask if we'd seen any men. It turned out they had just held up and robbed the Morts Dock payroll. The heavy bag they'd been carrying apparently contained a rifle.

Donnie also let Alick and me make canoes with him which we'd row around the pylons of the local wharves gathering mussels and oysters for Mum to make into a soup. Our homemade canoe was made from scraps from the Boxie, and Pop helped us put it together. We kept it well repaired, plugging holes with tar that we'd prise up from the road on hot days, and we stored it down at the Boxie. Sometimes on a Saturday morning Alick and I would get up very early and go as far as the famous Doyle's fish and chip shop at Watsons Bay. We'd paddle ourselves into the harbour and then get a tow from the launch drivers at Cockatoo Island. They'd drop us off at Parsley Bay and we'd paddle around the headland to Watsons Bay. We knew the Doyle boys quite well and we always told their parents, Jack and Alice, that we'd paddled all the way. They would sell us a whole basket of prawns from their trawlers for next to nothing and then we'd paddle back round to Parsley Bay and hitch a tow back to Balmain. We'd always give the launch men a parcel of prawns and then sell the rest.

Another member of the family who encouraged me and greatly contributed to my swimming success was my cousin Ray Miranda, known to everyone as 'Chut' or 'Chutney', although I can't recall why we called him that. In many ways he really launched my career. At the age of twenty-one he became my coach because he saw some potential in my eight-year-old style when I swam with the other kids at the baths. He was a coach to several of us kids but I think he took a special interest in me because we were related. He was great fun and looked exactly like my mum and Donnie with those dark Peruvian looks. A lot of the Mirandas lived around the Balmain area, and Chut, who was a very good swimmer himself, took over as caretaker at the baths when I was ten. This only helped to confirm my impression that our family owned the pool.

Chut first started to train me by correcting my style. He showed me what to do and what not to do in the water and we did all the usual laps and races. We learned the different strokes from Chut and although I could do them all quite well I always liked freestyle the best. One of the places Chut took about twenty of us for training was the White Bay Power Station. This had been built on the edge of Balmain in 1913 to provide additional power for the ever-expanding suburban tram system. Every Saturday a gate would be opened and all the cooling water that had been used by the station would gush out into a large canal about four swimming lanes wide. The warm water flowed at a fairly fast rate down the canal, before forcing its way out through a grille at the end and into the harbour. This rush of water was known as the Swifty Canal or, to the initiated, 'the Swifty'. It was the only really warm water we ever swam in and we'd have to swim really hard against the flow to get to the other end. We had to be careful, though, because the sides of the canal were covered in barnacles which could cut us badly. The flow of water lasted for about two hours every Saturday afternoon and the men in charge at the station allowed Chut to take us there. Each time we got to the top of the canal we'd let the water push us back down to the grille at the edge of the harbour where we'd start all over again. We'd be scared to have our feet poking through the grille because we were told the warm water attracted sharks, and just the thought of it made us swim very hard to get up the Swifty and away from the grille. I must have become very strong from swimming there because it was at least 130 yards long and it took an enormous effort to swim from the grille to the top. It was great fun though, and quite a ride on the way back down.

•

Donnie and Alick belonged to the Leichhardt/Balmain League of Swimmers and Chut encouraged me to join too. It's important to note here that this was considered to be a professional body. I had no idea what that meant back then and I don't think I ever heard the term until it was too late. Basically it meant that all those members over the age of sixteen, like Chookie and Kenny at the time, could win money as prizes. Not a lot mind you. About ten pounds for a big win. All of us who were under sixteen, which included Donnie, Alick and me when I first joined the League, would receive points for races we won and each point was worth something. Instead of receiving money on the presentation night we'd be able to choose a trophy to the value of our points and that was presented to us instead.

I was soon winning quite a bit, so I could choose good trophies. I got Mum and Pop a mantelpiece clock with a big face and I won them a nice wireless. Plus I won knives and forks and plates, which were nice things for my parents. I felt that they'd put a lot of time and effort into me and I wanted to repay them. I still have the first trophy that I won. It's about the size of an egg cup and was awarded for the 33 yards 'tiny tots' race I entered as an eight-year-old. I was very proud of that little cup and still treasure it.

The swimming helped stave off my asthma and I instinctively knew it was doing me good, although I didn't understand exactly why it helped my lungs back then. Unfortunately I often ended up with earache from swimming and I'd be crying in pain and have to go to Mum and Pop's bed at night. I'd put my hand on Mum's shoulder and she'd say, 'Come on, Dawnie.' I'd climb in and put my ear on Mum's breast and try to keep it warm. Pop would go off: 'Oooh, has she got bloody ear trouble again? No more swimming, no more swimming. She'll have to give the swimming away. That's it, she's not swimming any more.' He'd still let me get into bed, though.

Despite my ear problem, from about the age of eight I started to participate in carnivals. That was a wonderful thing for me because it meant travel. On my first trip away, at the age of nine, we went to compete at Broken Hill. We played cards all the way there on the train and by the time we arrived I'd won all the other kids' money. I'd been taught to play cards by Pop and I'd watched the adults carefully in the pub and in our backyard. Pop had also taught me to play dominoes. We'd travel like that once, maybe twice, a year. I'd have to save up my weekly pocket money to be able to go and when we got to our destination we'd be billeted with local families. It gave me a glimpse of how other people lived.

Other weekend activity continued to revolve around Codocks Football Club. Every Sunday my family went to Birchgrove Oval to watch them play before coming back for beers at our house.

One Christmas, when I was eight, all the neighbourhood kids went along to the annual Codocks Club Christmas picnic at the Hollywood Picnic Grounds near Lane Cove National Park. There were sack races, egg and spoon races and of course swimming races and all of the children were given two shillings as a Christmas present at the end of the day.

Gradually I realised I was becoming quite a good swimmer. By the age of ten I was winning all my club and district races. Although I had asthma I had built up stamina by running my barrow everywhere, riding bikes and roaming around the Balmain district as a runner. And swimming allowed me to harness my wilful streak and my naturally competitive spirit. When I turned twelve and began to show quite a bit of promise by beating all the other kids of my age in the League, Chut suggested I join the Balmain Amateur Swimming Club which was based at the baths. This was the path to glory and recognition rather than money, but it didn't mean anything to me at the time. I was only twelve years old and basically did what I was advised to do by my older relatives.

I continued to swim well in the amateur club and Mr Miles, a neighbour up the road who ran the corner shop and could afford a car, would take his daughter Jennifer and some others of us to compete with clubs in other suburbs. Soon I was able to see how well I went as a swimmer in a bigger pond, but, although I was competitive and didn't like to be beaten, this was much more about social activity—just as it is for kids who play weekend sport today. I didn't really think about my swimming between races. I was more interested in having fun and very much going along for the ride.

One day we all squeezed into Mr Miles' car and went to Granville Pool, a freshwater Olympic-size pool, to compete in the Western Suburbs District Carnival. I was in a handicap race and was the back marker over the 55 yards. I dived in, swam as I usually would and came first by a narrow margin, which was not a particularly astonishing result for me at that stage. However, there was another girl in the race by the name of Lorraine Crapp who was already rightly regarded as the golden-haired girl of amateur swimming in our age group. She had already competed interstate and was beginning to rival older champions like Marjorie McQuade. I didn't know any of this at the time but I was soon to learn a whole lot more about the sport I had taken up. Lorraine, who later became a good mate, came second that day and the Secretary of the Amateur Swimming Union of Australia (ASU), Mr Bill Berge Phillips, and other officials walked around the pool immediately after the race to find out who I was. I certainly had no idea who they were and I wasn't concerned when they asked Chut where I'd come from. Frank Guthrie, Lorraine's coach, was also curious about my identity. 'Her name's Dawnie Fraser and she comes from Balmain. Watch out for her.' I didn't understand the reason for all the fuss but I did like the compliments and the attention.

Some weeks after the race Coral Macintosh, one of the officials at the Balmain Amateur Swimming Club, addressed us after training. Apparently someone had found out that I had been a member of a professional body of swimmers, and that I had taken two shillings from Codocks for swimming. As a result I had been officially banned by the ASU from taking part in amateur races for two years. This was completely confusing to me as a twelve-year-old. I had no concept of amateurism and professionalism and remember turning the words over in my mind and talking to my brothers about their meaning. To me it meant not being able to belong to the club and not taking part in all the activities I was enjoying so much. I had no idea what I'd done wrong but it hurt me deeply because I felt excluded and singled out at a time when I desperately wanted to be included. I have no idea to this day how the ASU found out about the two shillings, although I believe Frank Guthrie made it his business to find out more about me after the handicap swim.

Chut tried to explain to me what had happened and that I would have to stand down for two years to regain my amateur status. He wanted me to go with him to explain to Bill Berge Phillips that all the kids had been given two shillings for Christmas and that I had only ever won trophies and not money from the League races. Chut sensibly believed that once it was properly explained the ban would be automatically lifted. And naturally I believed Chut.

I didn't have a clue at that age what the ASU was. I was quite nervous because I'd never been to an office to speak to someone behind a desk. Chut did most of the talking. I'd been taught not to interrupt my elders and betters and even though I was usually cheeky in my own environment I felt out of place in that office so I sat quietly. Chut explained my situation but Bill Berge Phillips would have none of it. I felt anger welling up inside me and I wanted to spit in his face but I sat there as he thumped his fist down on the table and said I would never swim for Australia and that the ban would remain in place because those were the rules. Even though it had never occurred to me that I would swim for Australia, I looked Bill Berge Phillips in the face and said, 'Yes I will and not you or anyone else will stop me.' Then Chut grabbed me by the hand and we left. After the meeting I thought no more about this crazy idea but somewhere deep down I believe the seeds had been sown. I did not like to be told what I couldn't do.

Naturally my parents didn't step in. It just wasn't their place to do so. Although they were well respected in our community and we were all fiercely proud of our background, we knew our place. We didn't feel inferior but we just got on with it and accepted the way things were. We lived by the code of getting on with our business and not getting involved in areas that didn't concern us. Even later when I competed in national swimming races it was very, very rare for my parents to be able to watch me. We didn't have the money to buy tickets and they weren't handed out either. It wasn't a big issue in my family when I was banned so I carried the hurt inside me.

Back at the pool after meeting Bill Berge Phillips I felt very emotional and churned up but didn't fully understand why. I jumped into the water and swam myself to calmness. From that day Coral Mackintosh and Chut fought very hard to have my amateur status restored. It has been written several times that Bill Berge Phillips was my saviour and that he was the one who fought for me, but that simply isn't true. I still believe that swimming at that time was very much a silvertail sport and I was the girl from the wrong side of the tracks who said what she thought. In the 1950s I began to be taken to North Sydney Swimming Pool beside the Sydney Harbour Bridge at Milsons Point. This was like going to Disneyland. The Olympic-size pool seemed so glamorous and I was starry-eyed on the few occasions we competed there. As I thought about my situation I began to realise I had probably come along like a bolt from the blue and upset the natural order of things at the ASU. The ban remained in place for eighteen months and all the while I just kept training.

We had three cinemas in Balmain when I was growing up. There was Hoyts, the Kings Picture Show, and what we called 'the old bug house', for obvious reasons, although it was officially known as the Amuse-U. Nearly a year and a half after the ban had been placed on me I was at the Kings Picture Show sitting with a boy I really liked. My brothers were there too with their girlfriends when my name came up on the screen: MISS D FRASER COME TO THE MANAGER'S OFFICE. I was scared because I'd been holding hands with the boy and I thought someone had seen us: maybe they'd told my mother and she was waiting for me. So I decided not to get up. My brothers were singing out in the dark for me to go but I sank further down in my seat and refused to budge. Next the ushers started coming through shining their torches on our faces. 'I know where she's sitting,' I heard someone say, and next thing the torchlight was directed straight onto me. Everyone was cheering and calling out, 'Get the torch off. Get out of it!' I was so embarrassed and humiliated. I staggered over everyone's legs to get out of my row and into the foyer, where I saw Coral Mackintosh standing talking with the manager. She'd been to my house and was told I was at the cinema.

'I've come to tell you first-hand the good news. You've been reinstated.' She was beaming at me and clearly expected a reaction but because of my embarrassment and lack of real understanding of the ban I didn't show any excitement. I was less than thrilled really and wished that she hadn't made such a spectacle of me. I thanked her quickly and ran off. Looking back in later years when I again struck trouble with the ASU I really understood what she'd done for me and appreciated it much more than I did then as a thirteen-year-old.

While the ban had been imposed on me before I had even left primary school, it was to have an enormous effect on the way I approached my swimming career in later years. Back then I was still the tough little twelve-year-old living my life on the surface and concealing the hurt beneath. I was still running for Lenny, watching Codocks on the weekend, helping my mum with household work, sneaking into the baths with my gang of neighbourhood kids, training with Chut and competing again with the swimming club. Life couldn't have been better as far as I was concerned.

I was a very good marbles player as a kid and because we couldn't afford very many marbles Pop used to make them for me from clay found in our backyard. He used to take them to work and put them in the furnace so they'd be unbreakable. I'd hide my marbles from my brothers in the little cupboard under the stairs so they wouldn't pinch them. On my last day at Birchgrove Public at the age of twelve I held a marble scramble by dropping all my marbles over the top of the balcony. All the little kids came running from everywhere to grab them. It was a very funny sight and the last memory I have of those carefree days in the school playground opposite our house. I didn't go back there for several years but when I finally did, it was quite a triumphant homecoming.

By the time I left Birchy to go to high school, Alick was already at Rozelle High and Donnie had finished school and was working at the Boxie as the dogman. I had been worrying for quite some time that I would have to go to an all-girls school and wasn't looking forward to being separated from my brothers and my many male friends. My sister Joyce was working at Larco, and Heather and Rosie were training as dressmakers elsewhere. I had quite good marks at the end of primary school so I was given the opportunity to go to a high school called Riverside, a few suburbs away in Gladesville. My parents were very pleased that I'd been selected for Riverside and were happy to find the extra money for the return tram fare each day. They were always proud of our achievements even though education was never really discussed at home. Riverside was considered a better class of school because it was in a smarter suburb, slightly more academic but basically still a home science school that prepared its students for the trades or working in the home. Tertiary education was never on my agenda, or on anyone else's around there. It was still the 1950s and women were mainly prepared for a life of domestic bliss—or at least a life of domestic duty—be they rich or poor. I had an idea that I could be a doctor and looking back that's what I would like to have been, if not a swimmer, but it was never really a possibility.

All my girlfriends from primary school had gone to Leichhardt Home Science School in the next suburb and I felt lonely. I had to catch two trams to get to Riverside, one out of Balmain up to the main thoroughfare, Victoria Road, and another one down Victoria Road to Gladesville. I knew no one and that was very different for me having been king of the kids in a very close-knit neighbourhood.

My time at Riverside was not a success. I didn't like the head-mistress because I felt she looked down on me and disapproved of my swimming and arriving at school with wet hair. There was never any encouragement and at times there was a none too subtle discouragement. The headmistress was very strict and I didn't like authority—all in all I found the school a bit too snooty. After only six weeks I was transferred to Leichhardt Home Science School to be with my friends. I'd complained so much that my parents had been prepared to say they couldn't afford the tram fares in order to get me transferred. The new school was next door to Leichhardt Boys and some of my best friends. Even though we didn't see the boys because segregation was pretty strict back then, we would often talk to them through a doorway between the two play-grounds. A favourite trick was to push a girl through the gate into the unknown and strictly forbidden boys' territory.

When I was at Leichhardt Home Science School I was still running wild with my gang in Balmain after school and on week-ends. By this time I didn't like being called a tomboy because I felt I was better than the boys. Of course I was already feeling a little different from the boys and when we stripped down to our costumes at the baths it was clear we were all getting bumps in different places. For the first time I felt a bit self-conscious. No one ever spoke about sex in our household and I was never fore-warned about having periods. For my siblings it was still very much taboo to mention what's 'down there'. The closest I ever came to sex education—or should I say sex misinformation—as a young teenager was when my brothers warned me that if I ever touched a boy I would have a baby. I used to think about how my father would kill me if that happened. I knew it was the ultimate shame for a girl to have a baby when she wasn't married and the thought of it terrified me. My family was very strict about such things and they instilled the fear of God in me about the dangers of boys. Lucky for them, I was a pretty naive kid even in my early teens. I was young for my years and much more interested in sport and my swimming than in chasing boys. My neighbourhood friends were still mainly boys, but they were definitely playmates not boyfriends.

I did, however, notice the male swimmers with the smooth-looking coach who one weekend appeared at my pool to train. When they arrived I was, as usual, hanging around the baths with my gang. They looked like rich kids to me and I didn't like the way the guy instructing them was taking over my territory. We watched for a while from the tower and the verandah at the side of the pool and I made fun of how the kids would do whatever the older bloke told them, swimming up and down in a boring regimented way at his every command. Training with Chut was much less formal and much more fun. I told my friends I thought the swimmers were sissies. They would change from their street clothes into one of several swimming costumes while all I had was a single threadbare swimsuit handed down from my sister, plus a towel and a football jumper. As far as we were concerned the changerooms were where you went to smoke. But although I thought they were sissies, I was also curious about the swimmers and their coach. I think a part of me didn't want those kids learning more than me. Little did I know then that among the swimmers I was watching was Jon Henricks, who later became my training partner and an Olympic champion. Secretly I liked the look of them; especially a boy called Bruce Livingston who I much later tried to kiss, despite my brothers' warnings about babies. However he was too shy to join in.

I wasn't about to tell anyone about my feelings that day. Their coach, Harry Gallagher, seemed a smart alec, too smooth and too suave for his own good, and I pegged him as a rich guy. When I found out from Chut that they came from the toffee-nosed Drummoyne Pool, just over the Iron Cove Bridge from Balmain but on the 'right side' of the Parramatta River, I was very angry. They had come to train at the Balmain Baths because their own pool had been flooded and the pumphouse ruined by the rising water. I organised my gang to dive-bomb and yell abuse at them whenever they were training or racing. As we landed on the swimmers we would yell out, 'Go back to brummy Drummie. Go back to crummy Drummie.' We completely disrupted their training and I was very pleased with myself.

We went on hassling them for about a week before they returned to their own pool but by then Harry Gallagher and I had exchanged words. I was coming up from the baths after a day of attacking his swimmers, and Harry was sitting in his car waiting for me to appear. I had an eye out for him and wasn't sorry to see him there. He leaned out of his window and said, 'You should get a light for that bike.' I told him to mind his own bloody business and who did he think he was anyway? First they invaded our territory and now he was trying to tell me what to do. I dismissed him abruptly and walked on, but secretly I liked the attention.

About four months later Harry Gallagher came back to our baths with his swimmers and my gang was ready for them. This time I told the girls in his squad about our pet sharks and eels in the pool and later I gave the order for some of my gang to swim in under the water and touch the Drummoyne swimmers' legs as they swam past. This sent them screaming from the pool.

By now Harry was really angry and approached me again to tell me how I'd ruined his session. I matched his aggression and told him I was pleased that I'd managed to achieve what I'd set out to do. So he tried another tack, saying I should learn to swim properly because he thought I was a good swimmer with potential. He also suggested that he could teach me at his pool. I couldn't believe what I was hearing and once again had to put him in his place. I told him I already knew how to swim and could beat any of his swimmers any day. We had a better pool for a start since his was only 50 yards long and the water had to be pumped in and out. The pump didn't always work and that's why they kept coming to Balmain. Just who did this pretender think he was? I told him my cousin Ray was the best teacher and that there was nothing I didn't know about swimming already. With that I walked away, but by then I was drawn to the idea of learning what he could teach me— if I could just get past the chip on my shoulder.

Not long after that I cycled over to Drummoyne one day when I should have been at school. Harry was there with his mother who helped him run the pool and Mrs Gallagher was very nice to me; I liked her immediately. As it happened, their pool was shut for cleaning but I helped them clean it out and lime-wash it. I was used to hard cleaning work and I really got stuck into it. Later they fed me and gave me a swimming costume from lost property. I was pretty pleased with the outcome and jumped on my bike and rode home over the Iron Cove Bridge in the dark.

One Saturday night Harry turned up at our house to ask my parents if I could join his squad. He'd clearly been thinking about me and I had thought a bit about him and his training too. Mum and Pop were at the Riverview but I told him I didn't think they'd agree to letting me join because Chut was my coach and we didn't have any money for lessons anyway. I went on to tell him that another coach, Frank Guthrie, had tried to have me banned after I'd beaten Lorraine in a race and that's why Pop didn't like other coaches. Harry then told me how he had coached Lorraine before he'd lost her to Guthrie. We seemed a good match. As we sat chatting on the front doorstep one of my gang called by to pick me up but I told him I couldn't go out because I was talking to my swim coach. Already I was showing off and letting people know that I had something special going here. Harry in turn told me he thought I could become a champion if I did what he said. I know now that he didn't really believe it but he did feel I had something and he had started to believe in that something. Eventually he made me believe too, although it took him a long time to gain my trust. I was naturally wary of people who seemed to be in authority. Neither did I like sharp clothes, corrugated hair and cologne. I had become especially distrustful after meeting Bill Berge Phillips and I thought Harry might be like him. I didn't know for a long time if he was going to help me realise my dreams or take them away. I told him I wasn't going to train with the stuck-up college girls in his squad but I'd train with Jon Henricks who I only knew as 'Spook' at that point. I had a long list of other things I would and wouldn't do and that he could and couldn't get me to do. I wouldn't do breaststroke and he wasn't to throw kickboards at me. From then on he became Mr G to me.

Eventually Harry Gallagher approached my pop through Chut. Chut convinced Pop to at least hear what this new coach had to say. So Mr G came to dinner and gently persuaded Dad that I could manage two training sessions a day, one before and one after school. Pop thought it was a lot of extra work for me and I still had to help Mum as well but I said I thought I could do it. By then I really wanted to get involved in what seemed like a whole new world and a chance to learn new things. Harry had planted the idea that I could become a champion. He waived his fee for the first time ever, in return for my helping Mrs G in the kiosk, because Pop had no way of paying. And so I became the very unlikely new member of Harry Gallagher's toffee-nosed swimming squad, the Golden Dolphins.

There was a third major upheaval in my life during this period that helped shape the swimmer and fierce competitor I eventually became. All through my training with Chut, and later when I made the decision to join Harry at Drummoyne and then complained about the early starts and endless laps, my brother Donnie always encouraged me. He was still living at home, working at the Boxie and doing the ice run. He was also playing football for a junior side of Codocks that had more or less started in our backyard. Donnie was the star of the team.

When he was twenty Donnie had two of his wisdom teeth removed because they'd been causing him trouble. The following week he went out and played football but was kicked in the throat, which started his gums bleeding again. The bleeding wouldn't stop and eventually, when Donnie was quite weak, Mum brought his bed into the lounge room downstairs to save him walking up to his bedroom. It also meant he was near the fire through the winter of 1951. Donnie kept on bleeding and no one seemed to know what was wrong with him. I certainly didn't know anything. I was thirteen, still at school and only just thinking about leaving to join Joycie at Larco. It scared me to see my brother like that and in this one instance no one explained anything to me or included me in the adult conversations about Donnie. I still didn't have any idea how sick he really was and at that time I don't think anyone else did either.

I used to sit on his bed in the lounge room and we'd read comics together and talk. He'd say to me that I should keep going with my swimming because I was becoming very good and if I worked hard I could become a champion. That was still a new idea to me because even though I had started at Drummoyne with Harry I couldn't really think that far ahead. I had my private thoughts about wanting to travel and I didn't focus on being a champion swimmer for the glory, I focused on how I could get to see the world. Gradually, with Donnie's encouragement, I began to think I really could do it through swimming. Don had helped me get a girl's bike to cycle to Drummoyne Pool for my training and I remember him saying how well the bike had worked out for me. I found our talks while he was lying in bed inspiring and I took his encouragement very seriously.

Eventually Donnie was moved to Balmain Hospital and after a while his problem was diagnosed as leukaemia. It was early days for such a diagnosis and Balmain Hospital was no leader in the field. They gave him transfusions but it didn't help. The white blood cells were eating the red cells and he just grew thinner and thinner. Nothing would stop his bleeding. I used to sneak down to the hospital with a little bucket of ice blocks from our ice chest. Then I'd climb through the bars on the windows, just as I did as a runner, and put the ice blocks into Donnie's mouth. He loved that. The last time I went to the hospital to see him, one day after training, I took my bucket of ice blocks as usual but found the curtains were closed around him. He wasn't able to do anything more than just lie there and he was frothing at the mouth. I was suddenly filled with fear and ran home and told Mum that Donnie was really, really sick.

The next day when I came home from training the house was strangely empty and quiet. Mrs Lloyd and Mrs Baker, our next door neighbours, were sitting in the front room. They told me to wait there but didn't tell me why. They didn't really have to. I knew the truth in my heart. Then I heard Mum and Dad coming in the front door and I ran into the backyard and locked myself in the toilet and wouldn't come out for a very long time. Donnie had turned twenty-one on September 8th, four days after I turned fourteen, and he died on September 26th.

The funeral was held a couple of days later but I wasn't allowed to go because in this, of all things, I was considered to be too young. I was told that Donnie had gone to heaven and that's all that was ever said to me. I found out from kids on the street what was planned. They gave Donnie a guard of honour with all the players from the Codocks football team standing on Victoria Road as the cortege went past. I hid myself on a corner outside the Bridge Hotel to watch the procession and I cried like I would never stop.

It devastated me to lose him. I had him on such a high pedestal and had no idea how I could go on without him. He was a god to me. His death was also a difficult concept; it seemed in some way that he was still in hospital and that I would see him again at any moment. At night I could hear my mother crying in bed and Dad consoling her. Then she'd be saying her prayers. Religion was to become a bigger part of our lives because Mum turned to prayer and the church after Donnie died.

I became a much more introverted person overnight. I was immensely lonely and didn't cope well with all the pain I now had inside. I didn't go back to training for a while because I couldn't face anyone telling me how sorry they were to hear my brother had died. My funny, handsome, athletic brother.

Finally Harry came over to see me and said I really did have to get back into training because we were aiming for some scratch races that were coming up as well as the winter championships in Melbourne in mid-1953. I listened to what he had to say but I didn't go back to Drummoyne straightaway.

At four o'clock in the morning I'd be lying in bed listening to the rain on the roof and thinking, 'Christ, I've got to ride over to Drummoyne to train and I can't be bothered because Donnie is gone.' Then I'd think about how he'd done the ice run in all types of weather and how much he'd wanted me to go on with my swimming. And of the girls bike he'd bought me to get to training.

Eventually I did go back to training and I used the physical punishment of swimming three miles twice a day to thrash out my emotions. I felt at that time, and later in big races, that I was doing it for Donnie.

4

THE WILD
ONE WINS

I stayed on for another two years at Leichhardt Home Science School before being granted a special leave pass to go and study a trade. I was fourteen and a half when I left school, which was not unusual for girls from Balmain and other working-class suburbs at the time. Everything seemed to have changed for me overnight. Donnie was gone; Pop wasn't very well and getting older. He was heading towards retirement by then at the age of sixty-two and his working hours were being gradually cut back. Given the tough life he had led, with the drinking and smoking thrown in, he was a good age for a man and, despite his lung complaints, still getting by.

I was keen to earn some money to help Mum and escape the boredom of school life. I hadn't been attending school regularly anyway. All my brothers and sisters were either married or working and only Alick and I were still at home. Up to a point, Dad's retirement contributed to my decision, but the main reason for leaving was to get out and pursue a swimming career. I had begun to think that I might really become someone through my swimming now that I had joined Harry.

When I left school for good I began working with my sister Joyce at Larco where my name had been down for some time to learn the trade of dressmaking. Larco's owners, Mr and Mrs Lavecky, taught me the whole trade just as they had Joyce. They had big industrial sewing machines which I learned to use as well as to dismantle and reassemble. Then I was taught to cut patterns and lay them over fabric before marking them up. Even now I sew well from that training, although I've never had much time to make my own clothes. I enjoyed the factory work; we were always busy and I like to be busy. There were about twenty employees there at the time and I got to know everyone well. I was earning two pounds seven shillings and sixpence per week when I started and my hours were 7.30 a.m. to 4.00 p.m., five days a week, with swimming training squeezed in before and after. I'd arrive on my bike, usually with wet hair which, depending on Mrs Lavecky's mood, either was or wasn't tolerated.

One day at Larco when I was about fifteen and a half I was working away at my bench when I felt something running down my leg and thought 'God, I have to get to the toilet.' I went in and found my pants were full of blood. It was a terrible shock and I screamed for Joyce. When she came into the cubicle I told her in a panic to run home and get Pop because I was bleeding to death. But she just looked at me calmly and said, 'Don't worry, you'll bleed like that for seven days every month from now on and it's nothing to be concerned about.' She gave me an old-fashioned rag to wear because there was no such thing as a sanitary pad as far as we knew. This was one of the worst things that had ever happened to me and I was very upset. Since I swam every day this was a major complication and I went home that night to Mum full of questions about these things called 'rags'. 'Never mind,' she said. 'It will only last for seven days.'

No one at home would tell me what periods were, so I had to ask a few girlfriends. 'Do you bleed from you know where?' They all said 'yeah' but none of them could tell me anything useful about why it happened. Soon after that I became aware of boys saying, 'Watch out the girls have got their rags.' We used to hang the cotton rags on the clothesline at home after washing the blood out of them and I felt deeply embarrassed about the whole business.

Periods were difficult to manage for swimmers back in the 1950s. These days swimmers manage their periods with tampons and the pill, but back then you just bled. Imagine being a teenage girl who has just started her periods, training in the water every day with boys and knowing that blood might be flowing into the water at that time of the month. I often missed training just to avoid any possible problems (although I must admit that sometimes I pretended I had my period just to avoid training and go and watch the football).

In order to train with Harry I had to leave home every morning at 4.30 a.m. It was always dark and for much of the year it was freezing cold too. Remember, there were no heated pools then. Added to this was the fact that early on I wasn't entirely happy to be there. There were good and bad aspects of what I was doing and for some time I wasn't quite sure how I felt. Certainly I liked the attention Mr Gallagher showed me. I liked beating the other kids and I liked the boys on the team. If I'm honest I probably had a bit of a teenage crush on Harry too, because he seemed interested in me and very sophisticated compared to the people I usually mixed with. I thought he was from a wealthy family and only found out much, much later that he had a similar background to mine. That's why he understood me so well. He recognised me for what I was.

Harry was interested in art and writing and he opened my eyes to a whole new world. I was eager to learn and he took me and other swimmers to the Art Gallery and exhibitions, and out to dinner in cafes and restaurants. Harry showed me how to eat politely, because at home it had been simply a matter of eating as quickly and efficiently as possible. In that sense Harry was ahead of his time. He looked after the whole person and recognised that there was more to having a successful swimming career than just doing laps. He really helped educate me, and that meant I could go out in public and travel with more confidence and have an understanding of how to behave.

All of these things drew me to Drummoyne Pool, as well as my burning desire to get out and see the world. On the other hand I didn't like being told what to do and I didn't want to show that I liked the other trainers in the squad who were all from good schools and wealthy homes. There were also plenty of distractions in Balmain, where I had friends who smoked and stayed out late and I was still a part of my gang. I wasn't a completely dedicated swimmer then. Sometimes I didn't turn up or, on occasion, I'd retire to the toilets for a smoke just to annoy Mr Gallagher and show him who was in charge. It was just devilment and attention seeking. He'd run in and say, 'Put that out and get back in the pool.' I had got the reaction I was after. He later described me as a nightmare to train and I guess I was. Often though, I was just plain sick with asthma and bronchitis.

When I trained properly I really trained hard. That's what made me cross when journalists wrote that I was slack at training. Difficult? Yes. Misbehaving? Yes. Defiant? Yes. But never, ever lazy.

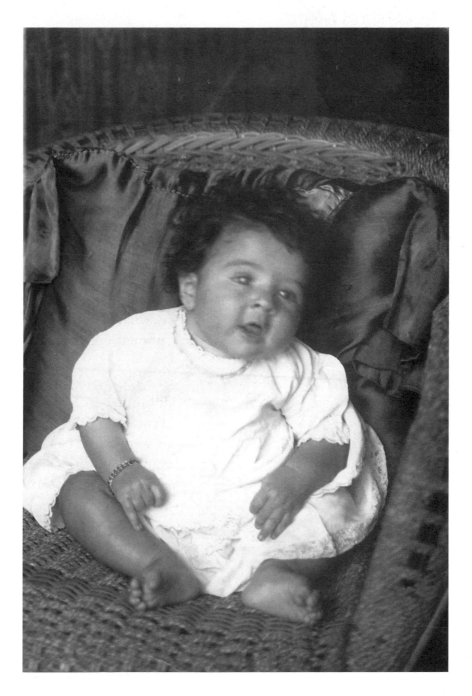

The earliest photo I have of myself at about eight months,
taken with the Box Brownie.

About five years old with my first doll—a rare shot in pink bows and a dress.

Mum and Pop in Martin Place, Sydney, early 1940s.

Our neighbour Mrs Lloyd, me and Mum in Pitt Street, winter 1940. My favourite childhood photo.

The angelic bridesmaid at Joycie and Bill's Balmain wedding just before my gale-force tantrum.

Cockatoo Island shipworkers in the 1940s (Pop is circled smoking Log Cabin).

The East Balmain tram with the 'dummy' where we used to practise scaling.

The coalmine in Birchgrove Road opposite our home on the Parramatta River.

Darling Street Balmain in the 1950s.

Our home
in Balmain.

Chookie outside Mrs
Lloyd's house with our
pet cocky.

oycic, Bill, Mum and Pop on the balcony at home,
te 1950s.

Pop and Joycie's husband, Bill, in 'Ken's Corner' at the Riverview.

One of the last pictures of Donnie.

Chookie surrounded in the ladies parlour at the Riverview, Mum on far left.

Aged thirteen with my gang, in the Lane Cove National Park.

My attractive new haircut, Adelaide circa 1957.

With Evening Peal just after it won the Melbourne Cup in 1956. I'm wearing my South Australian State uniform.

Getting ready to compete at the North Sydney Olympic Pool.

At North Sydney Olympic Pool, 1956, after breaking my first world record.

Anyone doubting it should take a look at my logbooks recording the thousands of miles I swam in training. I have been a worker all my life. It's part of my breed and I've worked from the age of six. I ultimately became such a dedicated swimmer under Harry that I sometimes had to be restrained from overdoing it. Eventually I realised that Harry and I were heading down the same path and while at first I thought he might be using me, I soon realised that we both wanted to make history and could only do it as a team.

I became friends with the squad, too—some of us are still close today. Harry had a knack of making us feel like a cohesive group. Straightaway he tried to draw me in. When we went to a meet he'd always look around the pool for the best place to set up camp to watch the swimming. He'd tell us that we had the advantage over the others because we had the best possie out of the wind. Cleverly Harry would give me extra responsibilities and soon I found myself telling the younger girls not to give Mr G cheek, which was the height of hypocrisy. Another trick of Harry's was to pin up pictures of our main opposition and get us to throw darts at them. It gave us that feeling of 'us against the world'. And it was Harry who organised some of the mums into making silk swimsuits for us with the Drummoyne logo on the back. They'd pin the silk fabric on for size and then sew it with elastic to make the suits tight fitting. Looking back on it, the costumes were pretty awful but we all matched and they helped us feel part of a team.

Clive Henricks, Jon's father, used to come to Balmain to pick me up in his Hillman truck and all of us kids would sway along in the back. That was well before the days of seatbelts and other safety restrictions. Later he drove a Studebaker, which I loved, and he'd take me along with everyone else to swimming carnivals. They never excluded me from the group even though I couldn't pay. There was no obvious snobbery towards me and although I used to see these kids arriving with three pairs of bathers I was never jealous. I wanted these things and I just had to work out how to get them. Swimming was always the answer. If I was embarrassed I would never show it because I was so proud of my home and family.

Although to me Drummoyne Pool represented the wealthy classes it was still, as I had called out to Mr G from the Balmain diving tower two years earlier, pretty crummy. It's still there today but is now a very different place. Back then when Harry was the caretaker and resident coach, the water had to be pumped in from the river, unlike our tidal pool at Balmain. We were always catching things from it because it wasn't chlorinated and so became stagnant during the weeks between pumping the water in and out. And there was often rubbish like banana skins, lolly papers, drink bottles and industrial chemicals in the pool. When the pool was empted it would be lime-washed. The kids suffered from ear infections, colds, flu, sore throats and more. You name it, we caught it. The concrete lining of the pool meant the water was even colder than in the harbour. Usually it was about 64 degrees Fahrenheit (18 degrees Celsius) but sometimes got down to 60. Nobody wore goggles at that time and as I used to swim with my eyes open they were often sore. As there were no starting blocks, Harry made us dive from the third step of the ladder down into the pool. This led to years of grazed and bruised toes but it also made me a bloody fast diver off the blocks.

We did very little water work in winter because it was far too cold but we still had to train in the clubroom doing our weights, pulleys and callisthenics. Sometimes Harry couldn't afford to pay the bills so we didn't always have lights in the clubroom. We'd resume training in earnest in September but it was still pretty cold. Every day there were standard sets to do. First up we'd kick on the boards, still wearing our T-shirts because of the cold. We used the boards because we didn't wear bathing caps and once our heads got wet we became too cold to continue. We'd kick up and down the pool until Mr Gallagher thought we were ready for the main training. That consisted of three miles in a session but sometimes I was too tired after a day's work to complete the afternoon session.

Eventually some of the fathers went down to an old marine shop and bought a second-hand boiler, and Mr Gallagher got permission from Drummoyne Council to stick it in a room at the pool. Then they built a little wading pool about ten feet square and the water used to get very hot. We'd get in there and warm up—almost boil really—between training sets and then jump straight back into the cold water. No wonder I had earaches and colds and problems with periods.

Mr G was a disciple of Professor Cotton at the Physiology Department of Sydney University, who had played a major part in the change that was going on at the time in Australian swimming. Harry was learning the scientific side of the sport along with other Australian coaches. We were more or less guineapigs but we didn't know it at the time. I never realised he was experimenting with us and just accepted that he knew exactly what he was doing because I was always improving. So we were exposed to all sorts of new training methods apart from swimming the usual endless laps. We'd be doing exercises with weights; experimenting with the intake of extra oxygen before swims; taking vitamins; working on depth of kick, underarm pull, breathing only when necessary and a general economy of style. We also did what I always called 'silly training'. That included swimming miles with our ankles tied together to strengthen our arms, or dragging half-full four-gallon drums behind us tied on with rope. Jon would go up and down for hours kicking his little sister along on a board. It made us very strong and fast when we were able to sprint unimpeded.

In 1952 when I first started with Harry we weren't training for anything in particular but I was doing time trials against the other kids in the squad and also competing in district carnivals. We didn't sit around talking about the Olympics and I can honestly say that it never occurred to me even then that I would one day go to the

Olympics. But even though my goals weren't very clearly defined, I came to realise that I needed to be consistent and work hard to keep ahead of the others and that's when things really started to fall into place. I was being drawn more and more towards the hard training and even began to look for it.

Jon Henricks and I were the sprinters on the team so we always worked together and raced against each other. Harry would give me a start and Jon would have to try to catch me. So I gradually became used to training with men and aiming for the men's times instead of the women's. I believe training with Jon made all the difference in the world to my performances because it gave me a different mindset, based on male performance. Jon and I also became like brother and sister over our training years and to this day can resume bantering with each other without missing a beat.

Halfway through 1953 the Winter Championships took place in Melbourne and some of my squad, including Jon, were going down to participate. I really wanted to go because Melbourne seemed so exotic to my sixteen-year-old mind. Harry tried to talk me out of it, suggesting I would benefit more from staying in Sydney and continuing with my current training program, but I wouldn't be held back from travelling. I ended up becoming extremely ill with pleurisy and asthma two days before my race. I suspect that I hadn't dressed warmly enough for the Melbourne winter. I was put into hospital to stabilise and later carried out to the plane on a stretcher and flown home. The plane was a DC3 and a fierce electrical storm struck on the way back. From my stretcher I watched in horror as the lightning seemed to bounce from one wing to the other and back again. The plane rolled and pitched and my fear of flying was born. Safely back in Sydney I was put to bed for five weeks to recover, bitterly disappointed that all my hard work seemed to have been for nothing. I reluctantly returned to training in October only to find that I was still doing well and all of those long, cold miles I'd swum the year before were now paying dividends.

In the summer of 1953/54 I went to my first State Championships which were held at North Sydney Pool. It was always known as 'the pool near Luna Park' and the place all swimmers aspired to, so it was thrilling to be competing there at last. There was the added bonus that you'd get to go to Luna Park afterwards. I was to compete in the 110 yards and 220 yards sprints. I won the 220 yards only one tenth of a second outside the Australian record of 2:29.6, although Lorraine hadn't been available for the swim. Most importantly, though, I'd won a trip to Melbourne for the 1954 national titles to be held the following February.

I was an unknown at the Australian Championships in Melbourne that year. Lorraine, Jon and Murray Rose were the ones receiving all the attention while I was a newcomer, still in awe of what was going on around me. Being part of the New South Wales team was a great milestone for me and I found it very exciting. One night I sneaked out of the Victoria Palace Hotel in Little Collins Street with a boy called David who was there competing for Tasmania. We went to Luna Park in St Kilda without telling anyone and had a wonderful time trying all the rides. The problem was that my chaperone, Aunt Mary Chambers, was waiting in the hotel foyer when we returned just after midnight. She quietly but firmly explained that I was part of a team and a team had rules and I had broken those rules. She didn't humiliate me in front of anyone else, though. She just said her piece and sent me to bed. It was never reported and never mentioned again and I am very grateful to her for that.

I was competing in the 110 yards championships, what is now the 100 metres freestyle. A win would mean a ticket to Vancouver for the Empire Games being held later that year and I swam out strongly into the lead in the first 75 yards. The plan was to go out hard first and then try to hang on to my lead in the second lap through sheer doggedness. I was struggling a bit to get my breath but my major problem was period cramp. Lorraine Crapp overtook me on the second lap and then Marjorie McQuade, leaving me to take third place. When I emerged from the pool there was blood running down my legs, I was miserable, and I felt I had let everyone down because Jon Henricks and Cyrus Weld from Drummoyne had both done so well. It has been reported that I lacked competitive experience, ran out of puff and just wasn't ready for big races but in fact I had been struck almost useless by the cramps.

Lorraine and Marjorie were selected for the Vancouver Games but my name was not on the list when the announcements were made. Once again I returned to a Sydney winter to read about Jon and Lorraine winning their races in Canada. I was extremely upset and very frustrated. Lorraine was even younger than me and I wondered when it would be my turn. But deep down I knew that I had it in me. In Melbourne I had almost earned that seat on a plane overseas. I felt I still had my best swimming ahead: I was only a stroke or two away from my prize.

After that loss I took some black paint and made a four-step chart on the back of my bedroom door with all my goals on it. It showed the various State and National Championships all the way up to the Olympics, and one by one I ticked off my goals as I reached them. Pop was furious that I'd made such a mess of the door but it was worth it for the physical reminder of what I had to achieve and why I was working so hard. It also reassured me that there were reasons for missing out on dating boys, going out with girlfriends and all the fun that most teenagers have at that time. Of course my swimming set me apart from most of my friends and sadly I lost touch with many of them.

For my next trial Mr Gallagher invited the New South Wales Ladies Swimming Association to come to the pool at Drummoyne because Dawn Fraser was going to attempt to break the New South Wales record of 60 seconds for the 100 yards. The 100 yards race was rarely swum but Drummoyne was ideal for it because it was a 50-yard pool as opposed to the usual 50-metre pool, a much longer swim. Anyway, I raced off but just failed to break the record so it was decided I would have a half-hour rest and try again. Once more I failed and took another half-hour rest before trying again. I tried and failed a third time and the ladies went home. Feeling hopeless and dejected I saw this as a major disaster but Harry told me the practice was good for me—and what's more I'd swum it in about 60.8 seconds.

In the following summer, 1954/55, I didn't win anything at State level but I came fourth in the 110 yards, which was enough to gain me a place on the team for the Nationals in Adelaide, and I was listed as a reserve in the 220 yards having swum fourth in the State Championships. Once again I failed and had the feeling that I was never going to get anywhere. My placing in the 110 yards at the Nationals was worse than the previous year when I'd placed third. This time round, Faith Leech from Bendigo in Victoria took first place, and Jan Munro from Queensland was second. I came fourth but felt as if I'd taken it far too easy and was a long way from exhausting myself. Not surprisingly, Harry Gallagher wasn't at all happy with the outcome. Miraculously, though, I ended up in the 220 yards championships because Lorraine withdrew with ear trouble. How strange that the illness that had plagued me and made my life a misery now overcame my toughest opponent. This was my chance to break through and I was determined not to miss out again.

In the afternoon leading up to the swim I met someone who was to become one of my lifelong friends. Adele Price was a diver representing Victoria at the Nationals and she was training with her squad at the pool. I was supposed to be resting and preparing for the race but as usual I was doing my own unique preparation by hanging around the pool. Adele and her squad were practising and of course I couldn't resist. Soon I was diving off the tower too, as well as dive-bombing them. Adele and I started talking and she was surprised to learn that I was swimming that night in the 220 yards because I was just mucking around as if I didn't have a care in the world. Gradually we got to know each other after that and began writing to each other before meeting up again at the 1956 Nationals.

When it came time for my race I went like the clappers from the starting blocks and no one came near me. I won by seven yards and in the process set a new Australian record of 2:29.5 seconds. My first gold medal! My first record! I felt as if jumping over the moon wouldn't be a problem. A window had opened and I realised I'd reached a very important point in my life. There were other successes for me during the 1955 Nationals, including seconds in the 110 yards butterfly and 220 yards medley. My view of the world had changed overnight and now all I could think of was the 1956 Melbourne Olympics. Still, in the back of my mind was the memory of how badly I'd swum in the 110 yards freestyle and I wondered how I could have done so differently in the 220. I knew I had a lot to learn and Mr G was the one to teach me.

When I returned to Sydney after the Nationals I was determined, fired up and excited about the future. My parents never really discussed my swimming but I knew they were proud of me, and my brother told me how excited they'd get when listening to my races on the wireless. Mum also told me she said prayers for me whenever I was racing.

After we'd been back in Sydney for a short time a complete bombshell turned my life upside down. Mr G called me into his little office after training and told me he was going to Adelaide to take over the City Baths where we'd swum for the Nationals. He'd made casual enquiries when he was there and found out that the current lessee was prepared to sell. This was wonderful for

Mr G but very complicated and troubling for me. He said he would have to lose his swimmers and start all over again but he wanted to take Jon Henricks and me with him. The Olympics were coming up the following year and he thought we both had a good chance of making the Australian squad. He pointed out that we would have to be there at least six months before the South Australian State Championships so we could register and compete for South Australia. I thought he was crazy and I was certain Pop would never allow it. I was only seventeen years old and still very much the baby of the family. My parents were proud of my swimming but family and home life still came first. I was helping out a lot at home because Mum and Pop had both been unwell. I'd had an inkling Mum wasn't terribly well but she covered, as mothers often do, and because I was the youngest and no one confided in me, I had to rely on sensing things.

As usual I was torn between family and neighbourhood ties, and my desire to travel and have a swimming career. Nevertheless there was no avoiding the fact that I wanted to go. Mr G explained that his parents were going with him to help run the pool; I could live in the flat above the baths with his parents, and his mother would look after me. I was still sure Pop wouldn't hear of it and I was right. He simply refused. He couldn't even believe that I'd asked. In the end Harry came over for dinner several times to talk him round. Pop was proud of my medal in the 220 yards but he had never let any of his daughters leave home unless it was to marry and he preferred the boys to be there too. To Pop, swimming was still just sport and he couldn't understand why I had to leave home for another State to do it.

Mum kept saying, 'Whatever you decide Pop, but I don't want my daughter to go.' I kept pleading and pleading even though I knew my heart would break when I finally left. Eventually after three meals at home with Harry gently persuading and my non-stop pushing at every opportunity, Pop very reluctantly agreed to give me six months. 'If you do what you think you can, you can go, but if you don't improve and do well at the Nationals then you come home.' My parents knew what I was like, that I was a pretty wild kid, and they made it very clear that I had to take this move extremely seriously or not at all. In fact I took my swimming far more seriously than they could have known. The Nationals in Sydney in February would be the trials for the Olympic squad and I wanted to be there more than anything in the world.

My brother Alick was showing great promise as a footballer by then and had moved to Queensland to play for a first-grade League side, Wynnum Manly. Mum and Pop couldn't manage on their own by now so they asked Alick if he would give up football to allow me to go to Adelaide. Alick basically sacrificed his career for me which made me even more determined to treat this opportunity very, very seriously. At the same time Pop explained that I was being given 'special privileges' and none of my brothers or sisters had ever been given the same.

One morning in July we set out very early to drive to Adelaide. My whole family stood on the steps of the house at Birchgrove to wave us a teary goodbye. Harry's fiancée, Jill, was with us, which was one of the major reasons I was allowed to go at all. Jon Henricks was going to join us at the end of the school term after he'd represented New South Wales in the State Championships. Harry sent him letters outlining the work he had to do.

Once we reached the highway Harry made me take over at the wheel. I had never driven before and didn't have any kind of licence but Harry was determined that I would learn, and so I did over the two days it took to travel to our new home at the City Baths in Adelaide. On that journey I did almost all the driving and finally got my licence the following year.

With my father's ultimatum ringing in my head I knew I had just six months to do well. If my times did not improve—they were then about 66 to 68 seconds for the 110 yards sprint—I would have to return to Pop and Mum in Sydney. I also knew Alick's sacrifice would have been for nothing.

It was freezing cold, windy and raining when we reached Adelaide. The City Baths were pretty impressive after Drummoyne but the fact remained that I lived in a room above the changing rooms. This meant that I had to share a stairwell with all the old men who came in from the streets for a hot shower as well as with the general public who came to swim. On nights when Harry's parents weren't there I was often scared. Harry was always out and about and so I found myself alone in a strange city where I didn't know anyone, in a huge complex full of noises and imagined danger. At the same time I had difficulty adjusting to cooking many of my meals, washing and caring for my own clothes, working during the day as well as training morning, lunchtime and night.

Those first six months were a testing time for me and I gave Harry a fright by deciding to go back to Sydney. Letters from my family had made me so homesick I just couldn't stand being away any longer. Harry helped me onto a plane and soon I was back in Balmain. But despite Pop's worries about me going away in the first place he now said to me, 'Dawnie, you went away to do something; do you want to fail at it?' I explained that I just couldn't stand being away any longer but eventually returned to Adelaide with my parents' encouragement, determined to stick it out. Once with Harry I threw myself into training with even greater determination.

Every Friday night a lady in the shop up the road from the house in Balmain let me make a reverse-charge call to her number because Pop and Mum didn't have a telephone at home. I'd have to book the call because it would take someone ten minutes to walk down the road to get Mum. At first I'd be told I couldn't get through and that I'd have to call back but in the end the switch operators would be saying, 'Is that Dawnie Fraser?' And after that they'd always book me in at six o'clock on a Friday evening. The phone calls helped enormously and made the distance between me and the people I loved just a little less.

Downstairs at the pool was a Turkish bath run by a lovely Yugoslavian man, an ex–soccer masseur called Alex. He became both my friend and my masseur after hard training sessions. One night I was alone in the flat above the pool when I heard a noise in the stairwell. It sounded like a person in trouble and I opened my door to hear better—keeping the screen door locked. I worked out the noise was someone snoring so I went back inside and called Alex. He discovered that even though we'd always been assured that every shower stall was checked before the complex was locked at night, one old man had been left in there. Alex, who was a huge man, swiftly dealt with the situation but it left me feeling even more paranoid.

Harry helped me find a job in a big Adelaide department store called Charles Birks. Over the next few years I worked in many different departments and continued there even after it was taken over by David Jones. They were good to me and the Managing Director, Mr George, tolerated my training and my need for extra leave for competitions. At one point I worked in the 'After 5' Department which sold glamorous evening wear. Often I'd be standing there with my hair still wet from swimming and my boss would say, 'Miss Fraser, get off the floor.' Then I had to go into the office or the back dressing-rooms to clean up until my hair dried. Mrs Ballantyne would sometimes whisper that over there by the evening gowns was so and so, a society matron, and I'd just bowl up to whoever it was and say 'Can I help ya?' Adelaide was pretty conservative in the 1950s and I was really very rough when I arrived so I was rarely allowed onto the floor to sell. I didn't speak properly and I was boisterous and really knew no boundaries. That was good for my swimming but disastrous for the After 5 Department at Charles Birks. Eventually I went to Mr George and told him After 5 was not the right place for me, so he transferred me to Sportswear and I learned all about buying, which I enjoyed. I also found casual work in a coffee lounge at Norwood, which was only fifteen minutes from the pool, and I worked the pumps at a local petrol station on Saturday and Sunday afternoons when they had a vacancy. In this way I began to earn quite good wages and my rent above the pool was low.

The first aim when we arrived in Adelaide was to win the State Championships in the summer of 1955/56. To my delight I won the 110, 220, 440 and 880 yards against some strong competition, which meant that I was on my way to the Nationals in Sydney where the Olympic squad would be selected. After arriving at Sydney airport we went straight to the Continental Hotel where the South Australian team would be staying. Of course I really wanted to go home and, after our workout, was given permission to stay at home for the night and catch up with my folks.

By this time swimming had become such a popular spectator sport that the queues for tickets stretched well beyond the end of the North Sydney Pool. There was no preferred seating then and I was sure Mum and Pop wouldn't be there. In fact, they'd been given tickets by Chief Justice Sir Leslie Herron, the President of the New South Wales Swimming Association, and he'd also organised a car to pick them up. They were in heaven. I had rarely seen them so excited. Sir Leslie Herron seemed to take a special interest in me and this wasn't to be the last time he showed such thoughtfulness and kindness towards my family.

Leading up to the Sydney Nationals, Lorraine Crapp was still very much favoured to win the 110 yards. It was known that I was swimming well but I was still an outsider, whereas Lorraine had smashed several world records coming into the competition. She easily came first in the 440 yards championship but I was close behind and equalled the world record in the time of 5:07.9. In my 110 yards heat I swam the fastest time at 65.5 and was pretty excited but Harry wisely told me not to get too cocky. Then, on the following night, just before the final, he told me he thought I'd set a world record. I told him he was full of it and then naively asked, 'What's the record, anyway?'. I still wasn't caught up in the business of records and mostly just worked to better my own times. Harry told me the world record was 64.6 seconds and had been held for twenty years by the Dutch swimmer Willie den Ouden. I looked at Harry as if he'd lost his marbles: the record had been in place since 1936 and now Mr G was saying I was going to break it.

Lorraine got off to a better start than I did and was in front at the 25 yards mark, but by the time we reached the end of the pool to turn I was ahead. From then I drew on everything I had and won in 64.5, a tenth of a second inside the twenty-year-old world record.

That night I cried with happiness when I found my parents in the crowd after the medals had been handed out. Then we all headed back to Balmain for a party even though I had to swim again the next day in the 220 yards freestyle championship. In the middle of the party I decided to bake a chocolate cake but every time I turned my back on the mixture someone would put some-thing into it, like egg shells or beer bottle tops. Nevertheless, the cake rose well and tasted great and I didn't go to bed until well after midnight. I felt really happy to be back home. The next night I broke the eighteen-year-old world record for the 220 yards. I'd made sure Alick's sacrifice had been worth it and I'd also proven myself to Pop. I was on my way to the 1956 Olympics.

•

After the Nationals we kept on training in Adelaide but in the summer months the pool was often too crowded to get a real go in the lanes. Apart from this, Harry's reputation had grown and now he had more than a hundred swimmers in his squad. As winter closed in, it became too cold to swim but Harry had heard about a small heated pool about 25 yards long in Broken Hill that was owned by The Zinc Company. Somehow he arranged for us to move to Broken Hill for a couple of months in mid-1956 to get us ready for the Olympic training camp. There had been plenty of press publicity and great predictions for our medal hopes at the Olympics so we were warmly welcomed in Broken Hill. Jon and I drove there in Harry's car because Harry had already left to get everything ready for us. During the journey the rain was terrible and the car slid all over the road before eventually blowing a tyre. We changed the wheel and ended up covered in mud which we also got all over the inside of the car. Not surprisingly, Harry wasn't happy with the state of his car when we arrived. We were all billeted out with different families in the area and began using the little pool. It was great for us sprinters and we really improved our tumble-turns, but it was a drag for Murray Garretty who was a distance swimmer.

Before going to Broken Hill, Mr G had pruned his main training squad to just six names who he thought might qualify for the Olympics. During the summer all the others in the squad had been forced to train in the crowded lanes while we six had the luxury of clear ones. Gradually Harry lost most of his other swimmers because of that decision. Apart from Jon and me, the other four were Margaret Gibson, Murray Garretty, Dale Krieg and Cyrus Weld. I made Harry's life hell mucking around with Dale, who was also a great practical joker.

Broken Hill was great fun as well as hard work. We had a wonderful time really with plenty of social life in between training. We did demonstration swims for the crowd as well as appearing onstage in the town's theatre. One of the stunts Jon and I pulled was to set up a race very seriously, with an announcer saying that for the first time Jon and I would sprint against each other. Then when the starter said 'Go!' Jon would swim as fast as he could while I'd run like crazy along the deck to the other end of the pool, touch the wall, run back down and jump in, making it look as if I was kidding Jon that I'd won. The audience loved it. All we swimmers signed autographs to earn an extra bit of money to help keep us going. Back in Sydney, though, rumours were spread, yet again, that we were paid swimmers and therefore professional. Nothing came of it except Harry's even greater determination that we would succeed. Harry also recalls that Bill Berge Phillips was quoted in a Sydney newspaper at the time as saying that if I trained hard enough I might be a chance for the women's relay team. Naturally Harry ignored that comment as we worked towards a whole lot more than just the relay.

The Olympic squad, which was to attend a special training camp in Townsville, consisted of thirty-four swimmers, all selected after the Nationals. Three coaches were appointed to train the swimmers and, amazingly, given his very rocky relationship with the Amateur Swimming Union, Harry was one of them. Other coaches who hadn't been named were also there with their swimmers, including Forbes Carlile. Back then coaches were not well regarded by the Amateur Swimming Union and they had to scrape their own money together first to go to Townsville and later to attend the Games. They were not welcome at major competitions, and even though Harry was an approved coach it would take all his shrewdness to be on the pool deck in Melbourne when we swam at the Games. He found out while we were in Townsville that the ASU had appointed an official coach, Bill Holland, who had never coached in his life. This meant that Harry would not be accommodated and looked after in Melbourne and nor would he be marching with the team or officially recognised. That honour would go to Bill Holland, an official from the ASU.

The coaches back then were paid by their swimmers and therefore regarded as professional by the ASU. The stupidity of this situation was that none of us would ever have made it without the coaches, so they were tolerated to a point but not as far as the pool deck during serious competition. I actually think Australian swimming did so well during this period because of the rivalry between the coaches. I was to battle several times during my career, as did Harry, to have him by my side at the most important moments. It is unthinkable today but that is how it was back then.

The Olympic squad was to train in Townsville for the twelve weeks leading up to the Games, and then the final group to compete would be announced after trials in Sydney and Melbourne. The coaches ended up in competition with one another and we didn't train as a group at all. Instead, the coaches fought, spied on each other's swimmers and ended up training at different times in the Tobruk Memorial Swimming Pool. Ricksie (Jon) actually stayed at the pool thanks to the Pool Manager Stumpy Lawrence—Laurie's father—who found him a room there. That meant Jon and I could sit on his balcony and spy on the other swimmers.

By the time I went to the training camp my new world record of 64.5 seconds for the 110 yards sprint had been broken by a Dutch swimmer, Cockie Gastelaars. Just a few weeks after my record-breaking swim at North Sydney Pool, Cockie swam the distance in 64.2 seconds in Amsterdam, and then a month later she lowered her time to 64 seconds flat. When I went to Townsville, even though I was swimming well and improving every week, I knew I had my work cut out for me.

Townsville was an exciting part of my life as I was beginning to see the first real rewards for my work. The Tobruk Memorial Pool was just a short distance from the sea and surrounded by coconut palms. We'd walk along the white beaches in wonderful tropical weather and were billeted out with great families all over Townsville. For the first week there were about nine of us all staying with one family; we were sleeping in hammocks and double beds and it was a bit of a squash. Fortunately I found a different family, the Bartletts, who I met at the pool where their daughter learned to swim. Maude and John had two younger children, Meryl and Davey, who I'd babysit in return for my board. The ASU did pay a certain amount and we had an allowance for toiletries and other bits and pieces, but it was very little.

The Bartletts lived halfway up Castle Hill, the mountain that overlooks Townsville, and there were lots of tiny green snakes and pythons in the bush around their house which John would some-times put through my window to scare me. He'd also throw water through the louvres to wake me up in the morning. I enjoyed being back with a happy, rowdy family, and despite my age I regarded the Bartletts as parent figures. Once a week the entire squad would have a barbecue down on the beach at Cape Pallandra and John Bartlett would help out by letting us drive his old jeep out there as well as around Townsville. At eighteen and a half I was older than a lot of the swimmers and I seem to remember being a bit of a ringleader in the social department. I still keep up with the Bartletts and counted Stumpy Lawrence among my friends for many, many years. In fact Stumpy, of all people, was to help me through the worst crisis in my life in later years.

A swimming carnival was held in Townsville in late August during which I broke Cockie Gastelaars' record for the 100 metres. I clocked in at 63.3 seconds and, as was the system then, I also broke the 100 yards record on the way at 56.9 seconds. Back in 1956 the two times could be recorded in one race as a rope would be hung over the pool at the shorter distance in yards and swim-mers breaking a world record would be clocked at both the shorter distance and the longer distance in metres when they touched the end. It is also important to note that while my favourite distance was the 220 yards, or 200 metres, swim, this was only a national and not an international event. FINA, the international body that governs swimming, felt at the time that although the 200 metres and 800 metres swims were appropriate for the men, the women could only swim 100 metres and 400 metres races. We were considered the weaker sex and it was thought that a sprint over more than 100 metres or a distance swim over more than 400 metres was beyond us. It took a long time before this changed and my favourite distance, the 200 metres sprint, only became part of international competition after my Olympic career was over.

In October we started to make our way to Melbourne via Brisbane and Sydney. First of all we went to Mackay to give an exhibition swim and already you could feel the excitement building up. The press had been reporting our records all over Australia so there was great anticipation about what we might achieve. The squad included Lorraine and me, Jon Henricks, Murray Rose, Terry Gathercole, Faith Leech, John Devitt and even a thirteen-year-old called John Konrads who came along for the experience. When we left Mackay we were supposed to go via Rockhampton and give another exhibition but one of the engines on the plane caught fire and we ended up returning to Mackay while it was fixed. This only increased my fear of flying. Next we went straight to Brisbane for a few days to swim before very large crowds and it was there, on October 1st, that I beat Lorraine by one-tenth of a second in the 100 metres freestyle at the Valley Baths

The trials to select the final swimmers to compete in the Games were held in Sydney and Melbourne and I was very nervous. Even though we'd broken world records we weren't guaranteed a place in the team, but Harry kept reassuring us by saying they weren't about to let us go. In Sydney you could hardly walk on the pool deck for the crowds that had gathered. Nobody told us the method of selection; all we knew was that we had to keep swimming fast and hope that we were chosen. I was staying at home during this stopover but my mind was really at the pool.

To make my nerves worse, Lorraine broke every record before her in Sydney prior to the final trials in Melbourne. She broke my 100 metres record with a time of 63.2 seconds and by the time we left for Melbourne she also held records for the 200 metres, the 400 metres and the 800 metres. I could claim only a part in the record for the freestyle relay in which Lorraine, Margaret Gibson, Barbara Jackson and I came together to clock in at 4:22.0.

In Melbourne up to ten thousand people a day were coming just to watch us practise. Swimming was undergoing a popularity boom due to the many world records we were breaking. The trials for final selection were to be held on October 25th, 27th and 30th. On the first night Lorraine and I swam in the 100 metres freestyle together, and though I beat Lorraine's world record with a time of 63 seconds flat, Lorraine swam the race in 62.4 to beat my record yet again. I still felt I could do better than her but exactly when that would happen was beginning to play on my mind. Harry had a reputation for bringing his swimmers to their peak at exactly the right moment and I placed my trust in him. He was unconcerned about Lorraine's times as he felt she was already performing at her best while he insisted that I could still do better. Lorraine beat me in the 400 metres on the second night of the trials, and on the third night we were purposely put in separate sections of the 100 metres freestyle and we both won: Lorraine in 63.7, while I swam the fastest time I had ever swum at 62.8.

In the end everyone who had gone to the trials was selected, and it seemed that the so-called 'trials' had been a ploy by the ASU to keep us all in line leading up to the Games.

Television had only just become available in Australia and the 1956 Olympic Games was the first big event to be televised. It was not uncommon to see one small black-and-white television set in a department store window with hundreds of people crowded around watching it. That's how many people got to watch the Games because the tickets were completely sold out and very few people owned their own television sets.

About three weeks before the opening ceremony we moved into the women's village in Heidelberg, a suburb of Melbourne. All around it there was a six foot high fence for security with barbed wire on top. There was a guard on the gate twenty-four hours a day and we used to say that our pole vaulters would do well because they practised by going over the fence into the women's compound. In 1956 the athletes' march into the stadium for the opening ceremony was a very serious business. Although medals weren't awarded, a team was selected and acknowledged as the winner and it was considered an honour to win. Every day the Australian team had marching practice and we'd be drilled by a major general at the training oval. We had a great time practising and thought it was a hoot, but at the opening ceremony, wearing our blazers with the Australian coat of arms on the pocket, we were very proud and serious.

Something very funny happened just before the Games when we were all in Melbourne. Ricksie was in the men's village and Harry was staying in Richmond with a freelance photographer and journalist called Ken Rainsbury. Ken took almost all the classic shots of me as an Olympic swimmer and soon became a good friend. We would come together to train and every time we did, the Russian swimming coaches and some of their swimmers would be watching our every move. They even filmed us. Eventually Harry said he'd had enough and took us off to train at the Richmond Baths instead. But he had told a journalist where we were training and he in turn told the Russians, and so in next to no time they were at the Richmond Baths too. Harry decided it was time to play a few games of his own and organised Jon and me to swim really slowly for several laps. He would then come over and give us some Smarties and suddenly we'd swim brilliant times. The Russians went to a lot of trouble to find out what Harry had given us—they even invited Harry and Jon out to dinner on the last night of the Games in order to quiz them.

There wasn't really any major talk about drugs in sport in 1956. There was no drug testing and although there were rumours that some people were taking something to help them out it wasn't a major consideration. We did follow the Americans and Canadians after one training session and we found lots of oranges in the toilets. I remember the talk was going around that something had been injected into the oranges, otherwise why would they have consumed them in the toilets? It made sense at the time to ask that question: that's how innocent and strange it all was.

Just ten days before my first event and before I could really get into village life I became very ill with asthma. At first I stayed in the village but was later moved to the village hospital. I was miserable. I'd been so excited and now here I was lying by myself and missing all the fun. Not only was I having difficulty breathing, there was also a lot of mucus on my chest and they were hitting me with penicillin. I couldn't accept that I'd trained so hard for six months since the Nationals in Sydney and now I might not even be able to compete. But the experience did teach me something. I learned to control my asthma better and I started to plan for big races, formulating a race plan in my head beforehand. It also taught me how to calm myself before important events. I had never done that before. Harry had always done it for me but now, lying back in hospital, I found myself thinking clearly about the process of planning the race and talking myself into calmness.

While I was in hospital I missed out on being a guest on the popular TV quiz show *Bob Dyer's Pick-A-Box*. They'd wanted me to go along and try to win a car, a little Morris Minor. I really wanted that car and I hate to admit that for a brief moment I was more annoyed about missing out on the car than the possibility of missing my races. To make matters worse, Lorraine Crapp replaced me on the show and won the car.

Once I was in hospital I was strictly off limits to visitors, and even Harry had trouble getting in to see me. When eventually he was allowed in, he kept telling me that the rest would do me good.

I got back into the pool just a few days before the opening ceremony. I felt sluggish and it took me a while to get the feel of the water once more, but I soon realised that the rest in hospital *had* done me the world of good, and I'd had the chance to plan and think through my races.

Harry took Jon and me over to Ken Rainsbury's just before the swimming events started in the second week of the Games. He made us put on our swimsuits and mine was so tight I felt I could barely breathe. It had a skirt on it but the skirt was pulled tight across the costume and looked more like a cummerbund. I screamed blue murder, said I was flat chested enough, and took it straight off again. I whinged and whined so much that Jon threatened to put me into it himself, which only made me scream louder about bloody perverts. Eventually I lay down on Ken's dining room table while Harry rubbed all the hair off my arms and legs using emery paper. Jon was told to shave his legs in the bath. After that Harry took us down to the pool and talked to us about how far we'd come and how the pool was our friend. He told us we were ready to win.

From the time I arrived in the village I was in awe of everything that was going on. There was a giant totem pole outside the Melbourne Olympic Pool, which was opposite the MCG. You'd say casually to people, 'I'll see you at the totem pole,' as if you'd been meeting there all your life, but that churned-up excited feeling never left me until the Games were over. Like all the athletes, we had a badge on our uniforms to show that we were competitors and this enabled us to attend any event we liked. The swimming wasn't in the first part of the Olympic program as it is today, so I was going to all sorts of things that were within walking distance of the pool, like the boxing, some track and field events, and of course I watched Adele in the diving.

When the day of the opening ceremony finally rolled around on November 22nd the air at the village was electric, something I had never experienced before and still find hard to adequately describe. We were all keyed up for the march into the stadium. We'd been trained to turn our eyes to the right as we passed the Duke of Edinburgh who was to open the Games. That I had made it this far was almost beyond belief and to be part of the Australian team made me determined to do my best at all costs. After years of sore eyes, aching muscles, agonising earaches, battles with Harry, loneliness in Adelaide, wet hair, cold mornings, early mornings, asthma attacks, Lorraine beating my times…the moment had come.

All the athletes were taken by bus to the Melbourne Cricket Ground for the opening ceremony. We were a group of nervous, bantering teenagers all anticipating the march into the arena. As the host nation we had to go last and we could hear the noise of the 120 000-strong crowd as we waited and waited underneath the stadium. Finally we were told to get into position and out we went. A thunderous roar from the stands erupted as we marched in. It is something that has stayed with me all my life, and I can still feel it whenever I walk into the MCG. It was overwhelming and I had a hard knot in my chest all the way around the arena. We turned to the Duke with great precision just as we had practised over the previous weeks and we won the march past. Marching into an Olympic arena with your fellow countrymen is an exceptional and wonderful experience and an important step towards competition.

I competed in three events at the 1956 Olympics. The 100 metres freestyle was, of course, the main one for me. Lorraine and I were drawn in different heats and Lorraine set a new Olympic Games record of 63.4 seconds in the first heat, which I then broke in the fifth heat with 62.4 seconds. Because there were so many women competing in the event there were two semi-finals, the first of which I won in 63.0 seconds while Lorraine won the second in 63.1.

I went into the final knowing that Lorraine and I shared the world record of 62.4 seconds. Faith Leech was the third Australian in the final, having swum 65.2 in the semis. As I waited in the marshalling area before the final I found myself practising gamesmanship to ward off nerves. It wasn't something I'd been taught, I just had it in me and I have to admit it is not something I'm especially proud of. I would eye off the opposition and be fairly aggressive with my body language—stalking around and staring at my opponents. There were many times when I believe I demoralised other swimmers. It was cruel behaviour and I hate to think about it now, but it was a weapon I used time and again. And I became better and more purposeful at it as my career progressed and my reputation grew.

If you want to succeed at the highest level you have to be competitive and I was very, very competitive. I had an incredible hunger to win and, as the saying goes, I would have crawled over broken glass to win the gold medal. Come to think of it, I probably went through a great deal more pain than that, as most elite swimmers do. As I've said, I became competitive very early in my family life and that helped me when swimming. And being banned from competition as a twelve-year-old only fed that hunger. I wanted to get even.

Once I left the marshalling area I never gave other competitors a thought. After mentally preparing myself, which helped calm my nerves, I might as well have been the only one swimming. Just before a race I'd feel as if I wanted to urinate but that was definitely a mental thing because you'd dry out as much as possible beforehand. Often when I did try to go to the toilet just before leaving the marshalling area there was nothing there.

I was in lane four and Lorraine in five. Lane four is given to the fastest swimmer and then five, three and six. I was never a great lover of lane four because it became so churned up when everyone was racing. I breathed on one side when swimming, the left side, and Lorraine was a right side breather. She was in lane five so I would only be able to see her to my side for the first half of the swim. This didn't bother me. You have to block out everything else anyway or you won't swim the two laps perfectly as you have planned them, and if you don't swim perfectly you don't win.

It was a great race. The gun went off and I couldn't believe how loud it was, even though I'd swum the heat and semifinal; it sounds like a cannon when you're there on the blocks. The Melbourne Olympic Pool was fast, which means the water feels softer than usual and you can go faster in it. I had already decided where in the race I was going to swim hard and where I was going to swim a little bit slower and get a breath.

We went together on the first lap and then Lorraine got a great turn and mine was pretty ordinary. In the last 25 metres I could see Lorraine under the water and realised we were still pretty even, so for the last few strokes I didn't breathe and just managed to beat her in my best time ever of 62.0 seconds. It was a new world and Olympic record. It was bloody amazing. Lorraine came in just behind at 62.3 but it was almost enough to give Harry a heart attack. Faith was third with 65.1. The Aussie girls had beaten the American favourites one, two and three and the crowd rose as one to cheer us loudly for a very long time.

As I turned to the board and saw my name up there as number one, I felt a surge of elation. The starter, George, who I had got to know well by involving him in my practice dives, came over to me as I was climbing out of the pool and told me to look up at the stands. 'Hey Cracker, have a look over there. There are some people in the stand you know.' Following his direction I turned and saw straight above the press stand Pop and Mum, Joycie and Bill. I couldn't believe it. Of course I knew Pop and Mum would be there because the people of Balmain had raised the money for their train fares but I hadn't expected to see Joyce and Bill too. I have always been very grateful for the Balmain chook raffles and cake stalls because it was to be the only time my parents saw me swim in an Olympic Games.

After the race we all went to the marshalling area and changed for the medal ceremony before going into the press conference. To see the Australian flag raised like that in honour of the win was the most wonderful moment for me. I searched for Harry's face in the crowd immediately after the race and again when the medals were awarded. After any race I would always look for Harry first to see if he was happy. He had sneaked onto the pool deck to give me a few words of encouragement before the race but now I couldn't see him. Ricksie had won the same event the night before so Harry must have been elated that all his hard work and effort in cajoling the two of us to train for several years had paid off. In fact he had watched me swim from a distance and later wrote that he'd been silently praying, 'Let the wild one win.' Immediately after the medal ceremony I climbed over the press stand to my parents and hugged and kissed them. I asked them if they were proud of me and we talked about Donnie.

Harry wasn't allowed into the marshalling area after the medals ceremony because the official ASU coach was the only one with that privilege. But I knew who had got me there and the following night we had a celebration dinner together, along with Jon, at the famous Melbourne restaurant Florentino.

After all the excitement it was back to the village because I still had to race in the 400 metres and the relay in the coming days. Mum and Pop were staying in a caravan at a petrol station in Brunswick and I got to see them briefly the next night. They'd go to the pub across the road for their meals but they didn't have to pay for anything because the people of Brunswick knew who they were and looked after them. They really took them to their hearts and I loved seeing my parents being treated so well. My gold medal was passed around the pub for people to touch and my parents were shouted beers by everyone.

In the 400 metres heats a few nights later I set a new Olympic record which was immediately broken by Lorraine. I knew I couldn't catch Lorraine in this event and in the final she came in first with a time of 4:56.6, more than 10 metres ahead of me in second place with 5:02.5. In the 4 x 100 metres freestyle relay Lorraine, Faith, Sandra Morgan from New South Wales and I won just ahead of the Americans and set a new world and Olympic record of 4:17.1. Several journalists, including Ken Knox in his book *The Dawn of Swimming,* suggested that I loafed in the relay and that's why we only just won. This has always puzzled me as I have never taken it easy in any race, let alone an Olympic event. How anyone could loaf and still achieve a world record time is beyond me. It may have seemed that I was loafing because my swimming was frequently described as effortless but nothing could have been further from the truth.

I stayed at the village until the end of the Games, sleeping with my medals under my pillow and having a wonderful time. During those last days I was invited as one of the Australian Olympians to have lunch with Prince Philip in the village dining room. It was very exciting to meet royalty and I chatted to him about my medals and the events I had swum in. I'm never intimidated and I wasn't nervous at all. The Duke put me at ease and we spoke of things I knew a lot about.

Once I sneaked out of the village with Adele to see a surf carnival at Torquay on the Great Ocean Road, south-west of Melbourne. I met a surfer there called Michael Hall who I really fancied. He was from Bronte Beach in Sydney. I saw him again after the Games and whenever I visited Sydney, and when I was back in Adelaide we'd write to each other. He was extremely handsome and athletic and we were able to talk easily with each other about sport and competing. I gradually fell in love with him, although I don't know if he felt that way about me. I've never forgotten him and think that if I hadn't been completely dedicated to my swimming a long way from Sydney it may have gone much further. This was to become a pattern for me throughout my career, with my love affairs and social life always taking second place. My main love affair would be with the water for many years to come and I never hesitated in those early years to put my swimming first.

For the first time in my life I spoke often to the media. But when I saw myself on television and heard myself on radio I was shocked. The studio had put make-up on me and done my hair and I didn't like what I saw. In fact I didn't recognise myself at all because Pop had forbidden us to wear make-up until we were twenty-one. Listening to myself on radio, I realised I had a high squeaky voice with a pretty broad accent. From that point on I was determined to change and make sure I presented myself as I wanted to be seen. I knew I would have to learn to speak properly and I would also have to stop people from taking over and slapping make-up on me. It was already becoming clear to me that to protect my public image I would have to start asserting myself.

Having arrived in Melbourne as a virtual unknown except for a brief mention in articles mainly about Lorraine, I left as an Olympic champion known around the world. This was a sudden and radical change. I was recognised on the streets and sent sacks of fan mail. Despite all this we had to settle down again pretty quickly. We all needed to earn money and the State Championships were coming up in January, to be followed closely by the Nationals in Hobart. Before returning to Adelaide I went to Sydney to see my family and took my medals across the road to Birchy to show all the school kids. Rosie's daughter, my niece, was already a teacher by that time and she took the medals to her school for everyone to see too. The medals were passed to all the little kids to touch and they actually became quite worn. I wanted to share the medals with the people I'd grown up with. Even when I returned to Adelaide and they tried to claim me for South Australia, my heart was in Balmain.

5

YOU SAY TOMATO,
I SAY TOMAYTO

Along with many other Olympic medallists I didn't attend the February 1957 Nationals in Canberra because Harry felt there should be a bit of a rest period following the Games. After the championships Bill Berge Phillips, still the Secretary of the ASU, announced that the stars from the 1956 Olympics would be too old to compete in the 1960 Rome Olympics as we would all have lost interest and enthusiasm. Maybe that was wishful thinking on Bill Berge Phillips' part. I only wish some of the officials had lost their enthusiasm early because there are some on the pool deck today who were there when I was swimming and their attitudes towards the competitors haven't changed. Looking back, I may have retired earlier if my clashes with Bill Berge Phillips and the ASU hadn't driven me on. In 1957, though, with my worst problems with the ASU still ahead of me, I had no thoughts about retiring because I knew I hadn't reached my peak. I was young and on top of the world, and I wanted to repeat my gold medal performance in Rome.

Back in Adelaide in late February I was straight into heavy training. That meant eight miles a day over two sessions, six and a half days a week. I'd start my workout at 4.30 a.m. and finish at 8.00 a.m. before showering, grabbing breakfast on the run and reporting into work at Charles Birks by 9.00 a.m. By then Mr George had moved me to the bulk store, which made it easier to get time off for competition and extra training. Also I was paid full wages instead of part-time, even if I wasn't there much of the time. In the lead-up to any serious competitions I'd be training in the middle of the day, too. They were very good to me and whenever I came back to Sydney during the winter they'd get me a job at David Jones in the city. I always felt comfortable with Mr George and we had a strong rapport even though others were frightened of him.

My parents had quizzed me quite a bit when I was in Sydney about whether I had any boyfriends. My father didn't approve of his daughters dating boys until the age of twenty-one—as he constantly reminded me in letters. I didn't tell Mum and Pop but I had in fact been going out with Peter who played AFL for the West Torrens Football Club. Harry had been conditioning the team during the winter season and the swimmers and footballers would end up training together in the weight room two or three times a week. Peter was very tall, and as I'm five foot nine that suited me. He was also good-looking and lots of fun. I think our relationship may have been a bit frustrating for Peter because I wouldn't go all the way with sex. Overall it was really a rather innocent relationship, as many were back then. My upbringing meant I was terrified of becoming pregnant and I was still mindful of Pop's warnings about doing my best and not letting the family down. My swimming career definitely came first. We four girls who trained together at the pool—Dale, Margaret, Vicki Page and I—would go together with our partners to dinner dances or picture shows. Although it may seem hard to believe now, our relationships were more about friendship than love affairs, and I was simply too preoccupied with three jobs and too tired from training to go out very much anyway. Nevertheless Peter and I saw each other on and off over three years.

We also spent time together in sporty pursuits. Waterskiing was a big thing to do and we'd go together down to Dale Krieg's house at West Beach, where her family had a boat. Dale's father, a TAA pilot who I called Captain Krieg, was great to me and made me my first set of waterskis. I'd often stay with the Kriegs on weekends because it was a chance to get away from the pool.

My relationship with Harry had changed after the Olympics. He had managed to do what he'd said he would—make me an Olympic champion. He had brought me to a peak at exactly the right time and his tapering-off program—the training you do leading up to the very big competitions—had proved perfect not only for me but for all his swimmers. He just seemed to know what was best for each of us: how to make you hit the wall faster, how to fix the little imperfections in your turn, how to come off the blocks better. I trusted Mr G completely and came to be very dependent on him. I already knew I wanted to go to Rome and I knew he was the one to get me there.

Harry had also shown me a whole new way of life. When I played the jazz records he'd introduced me to in my flat above the pool, the moods of the music sometimes made me homesick, but I was also starting to build a life that pleased me, and I knew in even my loneliest times that this was where I wanted to be.

Harry sought out and mixed with interesting people in Adelaide and gradually I came to as well. Some of them I met through the pool and others through the various functions and special occasions in which the prominent swimmers were included. After I became better known, people began trying to help me in all sorts of ways. The parents of the other swimmers made sure I was invited along to barbecues and parties, which meant I wasn't left at the pool by myself so often. I don't believe they felt sorry for me, just that I was cheeky and made myself known to people. When you're full of fun, as I was, you do get noticed.

Anne Kidman, a descendant of the great cattle king Walter Kidman, used to come to the baths and train with Harry in water ballet and synchronised swimming. They performed duets at swimming carnivals and I suspect she had a bit of a crush on him. Anne was a few years older than me but we became good friends and I was invited to the magnificent family home, Eringa, for dinner. Meeting the Kidmans was a formative experience for me. They were part of Adelaide society and their home was full of exquisite antique furniture (my eyes almost popped out of my head when I first saw it). I learned about manners at their dinner table—I didn't hold cutlery properly until I met the Kidmans—and how to behave in other ways by observing them. Hearing their family stories also fed my interest in Australian history.

Another renowned Adelaide family, the Bonythons, also became friends. They lived next door to Dale Krieg's family at West Beach and we'd often go into their house to look at Kym Bonython's art collection. Harry had introduced me to art and now Kym Bonython continued that education. Kym owned a speedway track at Torrensville, so I learned all about hot rod racing as well. Mr Bonython would give me and my friends tickets to watch the car races on the weekends—heaven for a girl who had rarely seen a car until the age of eight.

I met the great ballet dancer Robert Helpmann at a function held by Sir Robert George, then the Governor of South Australia, and Lady George at the Adelaide Town Hall. He asked me if I liked ballet and when I told him I'd never seen any he invited me to go to the Theatre Royal to watch a rehearsal one Saturday afternoon. Helpmann was dancing with Margot Fonteyn and I watched fascinated from backstage. I had always thought ballet was for sissies and suddenly my eyes were opened to the beauty of dance and the sheer physical strength and grace of Helpmann. I went along backstage to rehearsals whenever I could after that. We became good friends and he would occasionally send me invitations to opening nights—very much the thing to go to in Adelaide.

Sir Robert George and his wife had come along to my first South Australian Championships in 1956. They asked me where I was living and I told them that I was their neighbour because the baths were across the road from Government House. They immediately invited me to come and visit them on a Sunday morning for a cup of tea. I thought it was just one of those polite but meaningless invitations, but others who overheard it urged me to go; they felt it was a genuine invitation and an honour to have been asked. Still, I was only eighteen and very rough compared to them. I didn't feel I should just turn up on their doorstep. But every morning I'd walk past the police guard at their gate on my way to work and I'd say hello, and every now and then he'd say, 'You know the Governor is expecting you to visit.' Sir Robert had obviously told them to let me know it was OK. So one day I did go over. I can remember walking into the most exquisite and plush surroundings and being pretty overawed by it all. The Governor soon put me at ease, though, and continued to be very kind to me during my years in Adelaide.

These days our athletes are systematically groomed and introduced to various aspects of society but that didn't happen in my time. If anything, I was looked down on by certain sections of the swimming community. Luckily for me, Harry and the people of Adelaide were giving me that grooming. Part of it was deliberate and part of it just happened because I was brushing up against people from all walks of life.

•

Harry bought a property outside Gawler after the Olympics. It had a typical old settlers' cottage made of mud bricks with a dirt floor and I'd often go there on weekends and help clear the land for a new house to be built. I'd drive the tractor Harry had bought, fell trees and chop up the timber for firewood. It made me strong, and the fresh air and hard work were great for my lungs. There was no electricity on the property, so we'd use hurricane lamps and cook over an open fire with an old frying pan and a billy. There were two horses on the property for me to ride and I even swam in the pond. Harry's mother and stepfather had moved out to the cottage by then and part of the property's attraction for me was to be there for them. To be honest, I felt terribly sorry for them. Although I loved being out there, the farm was extremely primitive and lacking in comfort, and here were these two elderly people living in isolation after spending most of their lives in the city. It seemed cruel. They didn't drive, so I would even have to do their shopping for them and take it up on the weekend, and Mrs Gallagher was always very pleased to see me when I borrowed Harry's car and got up to the farm on a Friday night. Harry seemed to have left them stranded out there and I didn't know why, but when I read his memoirs many, many years later it occurred to me that perhaps he was ashamed of his stepfather's drinking and the behaviour it caused. Harry might disagree with me but it was certainly my impression.

When I was at the farm or down at Dale's house I occasionally missed my perch above the pool because when I was at the baths I could get into the water at 4.30 a.m. and avoid the public. There were never any special lanes and we had to just make do. I sometimes hated my afternoon training sessions because it took so long to get the miles in with everyone jumping and splashing around me. I was still helping earn my keep by cleaning the pool. The five of us—Harry's parents, his fiancée Jill, Harry and I—would get in the pool when it had been emptied and scrub every little tile. We'd also clean the sand filters and I shudder to remember the garbage we found in them.

I was much happier doing water work for the famous horse trainer Colin Hayes.

This came about through a jockey by the name of Billy Pyers, who I met when I arrived in Adelaide. He had just won the South Australian Jockey Championship. He was a red-haired, freckle-faced guy and as cheeky as cheeky—naturally we got on very well. He would come into the Turkish Baths at the pool for a massage after his track work, and once I'd finished my Saturday morning training we'd sit together in the sauna, kidding each other and talking. He'd be there trying to lose weight for the afternoon races. Afterwards I'd hang out in Alex's office with Billy and study the form guide, and get some tips for Saturday afternoon. That helped put some money in the bank, and I started to build up a bit of a nest egg.

Billy was doing water work for Colin Hayes and he introduced me to Colin, saying I'd like to help with the horses too. Mr Hayes asked if I could swim and if I could ride and then took me on. On Sunday mornings I'd swim his horses down at Semaphore Beach, which was right near the stables, sometimes riding them bareback to the beach. It's hard to sit on a horse when it's swimming, so it was a challenge and great fun; I loved it. Decades later, when Colin Hayes was inducted into the Sport Australia Hall of Fame I went up to talk to him after the ceremony. He called some of his children over and said, 'This is my water girl. You don't know it but she used to ride beach work for me.'

I learned to jump horses in Adelaide, too, after answering an ad in the paper. Going over the jumps was very exhilarating, and it helped me thrash out some of the pent-up feelings that came from being a very fit, young and perhaps overly regimented person. Swimming all the time can make you stale, and I found I'd return to the pool fresher for having taken on these different activities.

Gradually I got to know the racing fraternity in South Australia, including Windy Hill-Smith, a horse breeder and trainer who owned a vineyard in the Adelaide Hills. I'd go out to his place on a Sunday morning after my beach work and learn about wine-making. Whenever the Australian cricket team were in town they'd go to Windy's place too and I'd give an exhibition swim in the pool (after getting permission from the South Australian Swimming Association of course). Although I couldn't be paid I'd come back with some nice wines and I enjoyed mixing with the cricketers. I loved meeting all those talented and famous people and I am glad I can mention them now: not because I want to name-drop but because they helped me so much and gave me a close-up look at how other people live their lives. I am grateful to them for including me in everything and teaching me so many things.

•

After the Games, Lorraine Crapp and I had been invited to swim in Honolulu in the Keo Nakama Swimming Invitational, named after one of Hawaii's great swimmers, with everything paid for by our hosts. It was considered a prestigious meet, with lots of excellent swimmers coming over from the mainland. That year we came up against the Americans Sylvia Ruuska and Shelley Mann, both of whom had been at the Melbourne Games, and a young newcomer, Chris von Saltza, who was only thirteen at the time but who became a world record holder years later. We were to leave in late June 1957, which meant the added bonus of swapping the cold Adelaide winter for the warmth of Hawaii.

This was to be my long-awaited, much-dreamt-about first trip overseas and I was extremely excited—a naive nineteen-year-old with stars in my eyes about the big wide world beyond Australia. I started to work more often at the petrol station on weekends to save money for shopping and then went to Melbourne to train for a few weeks leading up to our departure. The weather in Adelaide was too bitter by then for training and Melbourne had the only indoor pool. Our chaperone was Mrs Dot Quinton, a swimming official from Victoria and a truly lovely lady of about forty-five who Lorraine and I called 'Aunty Dot'. When I first met her before we boarded the plane in Sydney she said to me, 'I've been warned about you, Dawn Fraser. I believe you're hard to handle. I hope you're going to behave yourself.' Dot was a gentle woman and we ended up getting on very well during the trip, although Lorraine and I were to play some terrible pranks on her.

Jon Henricks had been to the Honolulu carnival before and had talked about how wonderful it all was, which only added to my excitement. He told me that we'd compete in a 110-yard swimming pool, something I hadn't seen before, and that it was difficult swimming in the salt-water pool because you couldn't refer to the black lines on the bottom. He explained that I should pick out spots that marked half and three-quarters of the way down the pool and how I should use them as reference points to plan my swim. My early training really helped me in Honolulu because I had grown up swimming in salt water with my eyes open—I used to like to look at the fish swimming past—and I was able to pick my spots, as Ricksie had suggested, and swim to them with my eyes open, seeing exactly where I was up to. As well, I was a very balanced swimmer, with almost even arm strokes left and right that kept me going straight up the middle of the lane rather than swimming on the ropes.

Lorraine and I didn't really know each other up to that trip. We'd been trained by rival coaches so there hadn't been many opportunities to talk, although we were always polite and warm towards each other. I have always regarded Lorraine as my best competitor during my career, along with Ilsa Konrads and Natalie Steward from Great Britain in 1960. I never really felt threatened by any other swimmer apart from those three. Maybe if my swimming career hadn't been brought to such an abrupt end I would have felt more heat later on. It was Lorraine who really pushed me on to better and better times during the years leading up to the 1956 Games and, while I reclaimed many of my records, she held many of her own in the longer distance swims. During the trip to Honolulu Lorraine and I got along brilliantly. We were like two over-excited schoolgirls taking off on that plane and we had so much fun together.

Our hotel was a little place just across the road from Waikiki Beach. Even though we were being hosted, the accommodation was nothing lavish compared to today's standards and Lorraine, Aunty Dot and I shared a single hotel room. I'd been dying to see Waikiki Beach because I remembered it from so many films at the old Balmain cinemas and when I first saw it for real I wasn't disappointed. All I wanted to do was get into that surf and over to the Outrigger Canoe Club. The pool where we would race was also a thrill. It was right on the edge of the sparkling blue ocean at Diamond Head, with only a wall separating the pool from the sea. We immediately started training morning and afternoon because we had only a week leading up to the competition, but every opportunity in between would find us down on Waikiki Beach learning to surf on a board, socialising at the Outrigger Canoe Club, shopping for mu-mus and Hawaiian shirts, and being taken on tours by our hosts. We went to all the different beaches, including the one where *From Here to Eternity* was filmed. I was very starstruck by Hollywood and had read all about the things I was now seeing. Johnny Weissmuller, the star of the Tarzan films, was a celebrity guest at the swim meet. I was a fan, and he was a brilliant swimmer who had won gold medals in successive Olympic

Games—1924 and 1928. I enjoyed getting to know him. Tarzan, as we called the poor man, was incredulous at the amount of training we did and the fact that even though we were putting in so many laps we also spent the afternoons in the surf. He commented that our training was harder than that being done by any blokes in the States at the time. Chris von Saltza's parents had accompanied her to the meet and kindly took us on trips around the island. For me, a kid from the Adelaide City Baths, it was all new and glamorous and I wanted to experience everything.

The first time I walked out onto the pool deck, saw all those lovely Polynesian people in the stands and heard the applause I was overwhelmed. I knew I would be swimming well because my training sessions had felt good. But we didn't really expect to beat world records. In fact Lorraine won the 400 metres and broke the 800 metres world record, and I broke the 100 and 200 metres records as well as that for 110 yards. The 110 yards record was at 62.0 seconds and on my way to winning the 110 I was clocked at the 100-yard mark with 56.3 seconds, breaking the US record for that distance too. However, a few months earlier the 100 yards race had been deleted from the official list of world records by FINA, so this has never been regarded as a proper record. Still, Lorraine and I had beaten the American girls and once again shown we were the best in the world at the time. Johnny Weissmuller presented me with the trophy for the Most Outstanding Swimmer of the meet as well as my medals, making it even more special.

While we were still in Honolulu we received a cable from the ASU saying that we had been invited to the US mainland to tour around for eight weeks doing some exhibition swims leading up to the US championships. We had been getting quite a bit of press attention because of our success and I think the Americans felt it would be good to race some of their swimmers against us. Naturally we jumped at the opportunity and, after some frantic cables backwards and forwards to gain permission from our parents, set off for San Francisco and our host in America, a man by the name of Jim Green who was a fundraiser for the US swim team. (Forty years later I would meet up with him again at the Sydney Games.)

Just before leaving Honolulu we were invited to a dinner dance at the Outrigger Club. Aunty Dot had been invited too and she agreed we could go as long as we all left at 10.30, no questions asked. At the curfew we had no choice but to leave with Dottie. But back at the hotel, when it came time to have a nice cup of tea before bed, I found some sleeping tablets in my sponge bag which we slipped to our unsuspecting chaperone. Then we lay on the beds quietly until Aunty Dot started to snore. I looked at Lainey, as I called Lorraine by then, and Lainey looked at me, and in no time we were dressed and back at the party.

By then everyone was ready to go and jump in the surf so we all piled into cars and took off for the other side of the island. It was a brilliant moonlit night and we ended up at a beach house with everyone racing in and out of the water. In between we were drinking fermented coconut juice. When the dawn rose we took one last swim, knowing we had to head back before Dottie woke up. One of the girls suggested that we skinny dip but while we were in the surf the boys stole our clothes off the beach. So we all had to stay in the water for ages till they finally relented and brought towels down for us. It was all pretty innocent fun back then in 1957. A couple of guys drove Lorraine and me back to our hotel and we raced into bed with our hair still wet. We were extremely lucky that Aunty Dot seemed not to notice, and many years later when I told her the story she laughed and said it had been the best night's sleep she'd ever had. I'm grateful for her humour because when I recall that particular prank now I'm horrified to think of the harm we could have caused her.

In San Francisco Jim Green loaned us his brand new Cadillac and we headed out over the Golden Gate Bridge, driving on the wrong side of the road and pressing the button to make the roof go up and down. It was an enormous car and at that point the most tangible example of glamour and financial success that I could possibly imagine. I loved that bloody car. For years my favourite car had been a Ford Thunderbird and I adored the idea of a convertible. I just kept thinking how lucky I was that swimming had brought this to me—it was my overwhelming emotion at the time. I truly felt that the movies had come to life and I was living what I had only seen on the big screen. It completely turned my head.

In San Diego we went to stay with Chris von Saltza and her family. It was fun catching up with them again and really the beginning of becoming part of an international swimming and Olympic family.

Another memorable part of the trip was staying in an oil town called Ponca City in Oklahoma where the oil company had a pool with a roof that could be opened in the summer. I swam the fastest 100 yards in history in that pool: 55.5 seconds. Although the townspeople really looked after us and took us to rodeos and parties I remember being shocked by the reprimand my host family gave me for talking with the black maid who looked after me at their house. She was a big, warm woman and reminded me of my mother, but I was told not to fraternise with the servants. Up until that point I hadn't been aware of any racial prejudice, although I must have been surrounded by it on that trip.

In Houston, Texas, where we were to participate in the American Nationals we stayed at the Hilton Hotel and could look down from the room into the pool where the competition was to be held. The pool was built to look like a grand piano, with the lanes as the black keys. The image has always stuck in my mind and at that time it was the most extraordinary thing I had ever seen.

When the trip was over, Aunty Dot said how much she had enjoyed being with me on the tour and that she would be very happy to accompany me on such a tour again. I didn't often get that sort of praise from a swimming official so it was a really lovely vote of confidence that I've always treasured. Thank you, Aunty Dot!

By the time we returned to Australia in September 1957 I had acquired an American accent and a desire for luxury. There was a big homecoming for me back in Balmain with the usual keg in the backyard and all the neighbours who'd heard there was a party on at Kenny Fraser's house. I was very excited arriving home with mu-mus and Hawaiian shirts for all my brothers and sisters and lots of stories about what I'd seen. I had new clothes too and wanted to let everyone see them; in other words I was showing off. I'd been feted in America, the place we all dreamed about, the place to go, the place we'd only seen on the screen at the Amuse-U cinema on Darling Street.

My plan was to stay home for two weeks, during which time we'd celebrate my twentieth birthday. A few days after the welcome home party I went out with Michael Hall on a date. I told Mum and Pop I was going to the cinema with my girlfriends because I still wasn't supposed to be dating boys, and secretly met Michael on the corner of the street. When he walked me home later that night we stood outside the house talking because I knew Pop was safely asleep inside. Suddenly water poured down on us from above and when we looked up Pop was standing there on the balcony with a bucket. For one horrible moment I thought it was the bucket Pop used as a chamberpot; I was almost relieved when I realised it was just a bucket of water. Then I became furious. How dare Pop tip water on me and my boyfriend. I had been living independently in Adelaide for almost two years. I'd travelled the world and now I was being treated like a child. Soaking wet and as mad as hell I apologised to Michael and stomped upstairs to my bedroom. I was still angry the next morning, a Saturday, when I had to run to the outside toilet in the rain. I complained loudly all the way about how everyone else had a toilet inside so why couldn't we? I was shouting it out as I ran downstairs: 'Shit! Why don't we have an inside toilet like all the other people in the world?' My father followed me downstairs and when I came back inside still complaining I ran bang slap into him standing at the back door. He said to me in his broadest Scottish accent—that should have alerted me to danger ahead—'What do you mean by that, Dawnie?'

I kept up my complaint, telling him that everyone else had inside toilets and I thought we should too; telling him I hated running out in the rain and thought we should be more modern. I had been staying in luxurious hotels in the US and I'd been thoroughly spoiled for almost two months. For the first time ever I found our house shabby and hated my parents renting such a dump where there was no hot water unless it was boiled, the linoleum on the floor was worn to threads and, worst of all, the dunny was out the back.

Pop sat me down and explained that he thought I had a swelled head and that I was getting too big for my boots. He thought my accent was shocking and that I was bunging it on—which up to a point I was, but we'd also been speaking with the accent to make ourselves understood in shops and restaurants in America.

Pop went on that when he'd let me go away to Adelaide this was not what he'd had in mind for me and that he was very disappointed with me. He thought the 'swimming business' had changed me for the worse and I should pull myself into line if I wanted to be a part of the Fraser family.

I don't know what got into me. I think I was just so thrilled about the wide world opening up for me and, after the luxury of America, Balmain seemed so ordinary. I was spreading my wings and trying to break free of my parents. That might be appropriate for a nineteen-year-old these days but back then it was very wrong to be rude to my father. Looking back it was a difficult situation for both of us. I had become used to my independence, yet Pop felt that while I was living under his roof I should do as he wanted me to.

I told Pop I didn't want to come back down to earth, that I liked what I was doing, and stubbornly said again that they should get an inside toilet. Finally he said very quietly and sadly that I should pack my bags and go.

Being the person I am, I packed my bags. I had never stood up to my father before—had never really had to because I usually got the things I asked for. I didn't really know what to do except to go through with it and I left the house in a taxi and went to the airport. Then just as I was about to board the plane I realised that I was walking away from my family. I immediately cancelled the trip and went back to Balmain. Pop was down at the Riverview and Mum was inside getting ready to go. She was so relieved to see me and urged me to go and meet Pop at the pub like I used to. When he saw me he just grabbed me and hugged me. Later the two of them sat me down and told me that whatever I had achieved in life, I couldn't have done it without the sacrifices and support of the family and that I should never forget or be ashamed of where I came from. I'm glad my parents had such a perspective on life because I think it has been good for me. I have never forgotten my feelings after that unpleasant episode and have never been ashamed of where I come from again.

I celebrated my birthday at home, then a week or two later returned to Adelaide to train for the State Championships and the Nationals in Melbourne the following February. Life went on as usual in Adelaide with training dominating my days but I made the momentous decision to buy a motor scooter. A man named George Bolton, who was Mayor of the Adelaide suburb of Burnside, and his wife were two very kind people who took me into their home after we'd been introduced at a swimming meet, and I sometimes visited them on weekends for lunch. Soon after we met, Mr Bolton took over a franchise for the Diana Motor

Scooter, which was manufactured in Germany. I rode a pushbike, so I was obviously a potential customer for a scooter, and Mr Bolton invited me to go and have a look at one. It was 295 pounds—an enormous amount of money—but I was very taken with the idea of having the scooter. I told him I couldn't afford it but he persisted, saying I could lay-by it and ride it while I was paying it off. Pop had always warned that I shouldn't buy something unless I could afford it: Mum had sometimes bought items on lay-by from door-to-door salesmen and when she couldn't afford to pay an instalment she'd be all upset and unable to answer the door. I went back to my flat at the baths and started to work out my finances, weighing them up against Pop's advice. It was a tough decision. Eventually Mr Bolton gave me a little book of deposit coupons and showed me what a small amount—about a guinea per coupon—I'd be paying each week. He was very good to me with the terms he offered and suddenly I was very, very mobile!

•

When the State Championships were over—I had qualified for the Nationals—I was off to Melbourne for a special carnival to swim against two Dutch swimmers, Cockie Gastelaars and Corrie Schimmel, who had come to Australia for the carnival and also to compete in the New South Wales Championships and Victorian Championships by invitation from those States' swimming associations. I had been disappointed not to catch up with Cockie before because she had twice broken my 100 metres record, the second time in the lead-up to the Games. Ilsa Konrads, who was thirteen at the time, represented New South Wales at the special carnival. Both of us had victories over the Dutch swimmers and I felt that I'd beaten Cockie over both the 110 yards and the 220 yards without feeling much competition.

Selection for the 1958 Empire and Commonwealth Games to be held in Cardiff in Wales would hinge on the National

Championships in Melbourne in February and once again the pressure began building as selection time approached. Cardiff would be my first overseas trip with the national team for major competition and I very much wanted to go.

At the South Australian Championships I had won the 440 yards and therefore would be swimming that event in the Nationals, even though it wasn't my favoured distance and it was expected to be fought out between the two New South Wales girls, Lorraine and Ilsa. So the surprise of the championships came when I won the 440 yards with a time of 4:55.7—the first time I'd broken the five-minute mark in that event. Ilsa came second at 4:56.2 and Sandra Morgan beat Lorraine to third place. This was a huge upset but Lorraine's poor form was put down to the fact that she'd been to America and later Italy that year and hadn't been training to her usual level.

It was thought that Ilsa could have beaten me in that race if only she'd taken up the challenge. There was talk in the press that Ilsa had a 'Fraser complex', but I don't agree with that assessment. After all, Ilsa went on to beat me in the same event in Cardiff. Ilsa was young and I had quite a bit of major competition experience under my belt by the time of the Nationals in Melbourne. I was considered a very old swimmer by that stage (I was later described as the 'grandmother' of the Cardiff team). I was also quite shrewd at gamesmanship by then, both before a race in planning my strategy and also in working out what I thought my opposition would do. Ilsa's 'complex' was just a press beat-up involving me which I read and dismissed, and there would be more to come.

I went on to win the 110 yards and the 220 yards during the championships and Lorraine came second in the 110 yards to secure a place on the Cardiff team. Harry and I had been talking for some time about my breaking the one minute barrier on the 100 metres, and at the Nationals I brought my previous world record of 62.0 down to 61.5: I was getting closer. And I'd taken three seconds off my world record in the 200 metres, clocking in at 2:14.7.

The Amateur Swimming Union felt that the Townsville experience leading up to the 1956 Games had been so successful that we were once again sent out of the cold of winter to the sunny climate of North Queensland to prepare. Even though I was the oldest girl on the team, had won gold medals and set world records at the championships, I wasn't appointed captain of the girls team. I was never selected as captain for any Australian team I was part of. This was really the beginning of my strange double life. On the one hand I was breaking more and more records and becoming widely recognised and appreciated by the Australian public, and on the other I seemed to become more and more alienated from the ASU. I was very disappointed that I didn't gain that position for Cardiff and I have always firmly believed that it was the usual problem of having come from the wrong side of the tracks. Added to that, swimming officials in those days wanted total control and I was a maverick. But that didn't mean I wouldn't be a good captain. There were even press reports at the time of the Nationals saying how well I had acquitted myself when speaking to the media that week despite having less formal education than most of the team. It was supposed to be praise but really it was just patronising—as if they were surprised I could do anything given my background. That hurt me too, but I clung to Pop's advice that while they were having a dig at me they were leaving some other poor bugger alone. I decided to look on the bright side and enjoy the extra time not being captain gave me to concentrate on my swimming. And though I wasn't given the position I nevertheless helped a lot of the younger swimmers who came up to ask my advice.

It was great to be back in Townsville and I went back to the Bartletts who I'd stayed with in 1956. The ASU paid them the billet allowance for me and I settled straight back in. While in Townsville I had a very close encounter with a shark. During the training camp the whole squad went to Green Island on the Barrier Reef for a recreation day. We were all out snorkelling and our manager called us in to have lunch before heading back to Townsville. A couple of administators were standing on the coral keeping watch in case a shark swam into the area. We were in deep water off the edge of a reef, and when we started swimming back Lorraine and I were behind everyone else. When we got to within about 20 yards of the shallow coral we could hear people shouting to us about a shark. We both turned and saw a fin protruding from the water just a short distance away. Underwater we could see the shark feeding off shoals of little fish. Lorraine and I both swam like mad to reach a small submerged coral island—me losing a flipper in the process. We were still about 20 yards from the main reef where everyone else was standing and our little coral outcrop was in fairly deep water. I began bashing the water with my flipper to frighten the shark away. By now our group was yelling at us to swim for it because the shark looked like it was in a feeding frenzy, moving very fast, its fin slicing through the water. It probably wasn't even interested in us but it was terrifying all the same. Eventually we just dived in and swam for it, and when we reached the main coral we just clambered out and kept running across it. My feet had cuts all over them from the coral and later that night John Devitt and Brian Wilkinson had to pick the pieces out with tweezers. Lorraine had sensibly worn some light shoes under her flippers but as usual I hadn't bothered. My feet became infected and I couldn't train for a couple of days. Even now, around July or August each year, coral grows out of the scar on the side of my foot. I've had a healthy respect for sharks ever since, and even when the famous shark expert Val Taylor asks me to go down in a cage to watch the sharks with her I just can't bring myself to do it.

Four carnivals were held in June that year in Townsville to show that we were fit enough to take off for Cardiff. In the 440 yards Ilsa, Sandra Morgan, Lorraine and I all swam the distance in under five minutes. I won the 110 yards each time I swam it but was quite disappointed with my best time of 62.7 seconds—which shows how ambitious I'd become about getting that time down, preferably to under the minute. All in all, the nine of us set out for Cardiff with great times and high hopes.

•

The journey to the village in Cardiff was arduous and took almost fifty hours. We travelled via London and then had to catch a bus to Wales. On the way we stopped at a little inn to use the toilet and I drank my first ever Babycham—a miniature champagne drink that was the rage at the time. We all had a few Babychams although our Manager, Mrs May Williams, didn't know it. It was the last taste of luxury we were to have because when we got to the village— a former RAF camp—fairly late that night, we found conditions that can only be described as primitive. I was used to roughing it but this was something else again, especially after a long, long journey. The accommodation was dormitory-style huts with the beds lined up along the wall. The nine of us were to share the same room. But the worst was yet to come. A look at our bathroom revealed two baths and three toilets to share between all the females on the Australian team. The beds were wire cots with thin mattresses on top. Talk about shades of Birchgrove Road! We had to run from the dormitory across to the shower block and we were issued with potties in case we needed to go to the toilet during the night.

We were all so very tired it was agreed that we'd have a bath and get into bed then fix things up in the morning. Next day May Williams got onto the organisers and had several showers installed. These were really only shower heads along a single pipe, with no shower curtains or screens. The English girls couldn't understand why we were insisting on the showers and making such a fuss. May also organised some temporary partitioning to go between every few beds. Swimmers are used to undressing in front of each other, so the shower situation was fine for us, but some of the other athletes found it very difficult. Even now people think living in a Games village is a great thing but mostly it's pretty basic. Sydney 2000 was an exception, and the accommodation offered was of a much higher standard than usual. Cardiff definitely took the prize for the worst!

As usual the women were confined behind a big gate. One morning Herb Elliott was training outside and we egged him on that he couldn't run into the women's quarters, past the guard, run around the compound and out the other side before they caught him. It was a challenge he couldn't resist. He ran through the gate, he saluted the guard and said good morning, then ran on, eventually making it back out the other side—and no one had done a thing. We thought it was hilarious, and this was the start of a lot of pranks on that tour. Outside our hut there was an air-raid shelter and on the second-last night of the Games my bed, my wardrobe and potty were put out on top of the shelter as a joke—I slept all night in the rain.

We found the Welsh people hard to work out and felt they were hostile towards us from the start. They would begin a slow hand-clap, which we interpreted to mean, 'Come on, get on with it.' Later we realised it was a sign of appreciation. Even so, no matter how much we turned it on, there just didn't seem to be any warmth coming back from the crowd. Being a practical joker and a bit of a ham before an audience I wanted the crowd to respond. It didn't bother all the athletes and swimmers, but I had always used the energy of the crowd to get into my race and the cold treatment really got to me as the Games went on. Eventually, just after I had broken the world record for the 110 yards and been presented with my gold medal, I leaned down to the pool to kiss Gary Chapman, who had just sprinted against John Devitt over the same distance, and Gary and John reached up and pulled me in. Emerging from the water holding my medal above my head and laughing to myself

I realised the crowd was laughing too. From then on things changed and the Aussies became much more popular.

Towards the end of the Cardiff Games I organised a mock competition in which all the Australian team had to compete against each other in something other than their own event or sport. The swimmers were doing track and field and the athletes were swimming in the little pool at the village. It was great fun and really drew the team together. On tour, different parts of a team tend not to mix with each other, so this was a chance for us to meet each other, bond and to round off the overall experience.

The night before we left Cardiff the Australians all went to a charming stone tavern where we drank beer and Babycham and sang songs like *Waltzing Matilda* with the locals. I remember it as a magical night when the team was happily together after doing so well at the Games. Eventually I ended up in the flowerbed back at the village, where I slept through the night out of harm's way while the practical jokes rolled on and on.

Back in London a reception was held for us at the Guildhall, and instantly we Australians all set about souveniring items with the Guildhall's emblem on them. Cups, saucers, champagne flutes: you name it, we lifted it. One team member had wine glasses tucked into her suspender belt and I took a cup and saucer. When it became apparent what we were doing, some guards came in and told us to return everything or strict measures would be taken to retrieve the missing items. After that announcement was made you could hear the tinkling of glasses and china and see people surreptitiously emptying their pockets of cutlery. I got a rare case of nerves and quickly put my items back but I think some people did get away with bits and pieces. There was a furore over that particular night but, right or wrong, teams to this very day do their share of souveniring.

After London we went to the French championships where I won the 100 metres in 61.7 seconds. The joke at the time was that it had taken us more than an hour in London traffic to get to Heathrow and only forty-five minutes to fly to Paris. In between swimming we went shopping and I bought a pretty blue dress to wear to my twenty-first on my return. We also went to the Folies-Bergère, which at the time seemed very risqué.

The team then separated and we girls went by bus to Schiedam in Holland where I would again compete against Cockie. The pool was freezing but we still had to get in. On the day of the race I asked Cockie what the water was like and with a completely straight face she told me it was fine, but when I dived in to get myself used to the temperature I came out blue. I was furious with her for fooling me and I probably swam my world record time of 61.2 seconds that day out of pure anger!

Next up was Vienna. I loved the Spanish Riding School and one of the highlights of the trip was being invited to ride the horses that had been used in the making of *The King and I* through the Vienna Woods. Shortly after that, while travelling through Dusseldorf, Heidelberg, Munich and Berlin we were asked to keep a close watch on Ilsa Konrads. There had been some suggestion in letters to her mother that Ilsa, whose family had come from Eastern Europe, would be snatched and taken back behind the Iron Curtain. This threat was taken very seriously, and we older girls became temporary bodyguards, never letting Ilsa do anything on her own.

On the way home we travelled through Rome and Cairo before arriving in Singapore for a holiday and a carnival at the Singapore Swimming Club. We'd come out of freezing weather and water to humidity and hot water—so much so that they had to bring ice in to cool the swimming pool down for us. It was Non-Spitting Week in Singapore when we were there—they were trying to stop the spread of disease due to people spitting in the streets—and we saw a couple of unfortunates being bundled off to jail. The club we stayed in was also very exclusive and we each had our own maid to clean and look after us—a bit different to Cardiff. My swimmers were laid out for me and my towels warmed—I had no idea why, in that hot climate—my clothes were washed and pressed almost as soon as I'd worn them, my shoes polished and my room cleaned and made orderly. I am pleased to say that this time I did not come home expecting the same at Birchgrove Road! We'd been away for just over six weeks and I returned to my twenty-first birthday party, although I'd celebrated the actual day in Singapore. On the plane coming home the girls on the swimming team gave me a ring of brown onyx surrounded by marcasites. They were all invited to my party.

My father had hired the Workers Institute Hall in Darling Street, Balmain, for the party, and Mum and Pop used the celebration as a bit of a thank you to the people of Balmain who had supported our family in the previous years, particularly during the Olympics. It was an enormous gathering which filled the hall. I had four different birthday cakes and Pop had organised five 18-gallon kegs: three at the party and two in reserve at the pub. My brothers were soon sent up for the reserves. As he finally tapped the fifth keg later that night Pop said, 'This is all that I'm bloody well paying for. I'm not putting any more beer on.' Nearly all of Balmain was there and everyone brought a plate. Any young men who hadn't been invited had to go up to Pop and introduce themselves before asking if they could come in. There'd be no party crashing in those days. If Pop had said no they wouldn't have dared try anything.

I was given the symbolic key to the door and a gold watch by my parents, both of which I still have. It was a Fraser tradition. Pop allowed me to drink beer officially for the first time with the family and we all had one together. I'd tried beer before that night, but once I drank it openly with the family I really liked the taste. I continued to drink quite a bit of beer from then on, but never to the detriment of my training—as my record will testify. The party went on into the early hours of the next day.

I had twice travelled around the world and now reached the magical age of twenty-one when many of my girlfriends had married and even started families, I returned to Adelaide still quite naive and in love with one thing only: the water.

6

THE BEST OF TIMES,
THE WORST OF TIMES

As swimmers become very fit the water begins to feel different. You start off a season feeling sluggish and low in the water, and as your fitness improves you gradually lift up on top of it. Towards the end of 1958, following the Cardiff Games, I was right up on top of the water and as I swam it seemed to peel back and open up for me. It is a glorious feeling and the best way I can explain it is to tell people to think of how the water looks in biblical films when Moses parts the Red Sea to let his people through. It feels as if that's what the water is doing.

I have never felt beautiful on land the way I do when I'm in the water. When you're at that stage of fitness and going into competition it's like a love affair. I couldn't wait to be back in the pool, and when I was away from it during the day I'd be thinking of how it felt, anticipating going back to the water in the afternoon. It is an extremely sensuous experience to swim at that level of oneness with the water, feeling a tingling sensation on the fingertips and the skin. I don't know if it's something I was born with or something that has come from years of swimming but I am very tender in the fingertips and they work with the water to give me my strong stroke.

My stroke under the water was very different to that of most swimmers. Most are taught to stroke with a bent arm, but I am a straight-arm swimmer. It felt natural to me and I think it developed when I needed the extra strength to swim in the Swifty. I had very strong forearms and always felt there was more to be gained from swimming with a straight arm. Harry never tried to change my style, which was already fully formed under Chut, perhaps because in our early days together I was swimming mainly in salt-water pools. It wasn't until we were in Adelaide that Harry got a good look at my stroke under the water. In Townsville in 1956 Forbes Carlile took lots of underwater photographs and they confirmed my straight-arm stroke. I'm sure it is what gave me my strength and speed, and I found the bent-arm method far more tiring when I tried it. My style looked very relaxed on the surface, but under the water there was a helluva lot of hard work going on.

Just when I was training at that wonderful level and building towards the 1959 Nationals I became extremely ill. I have always loved children and they like me, which is how I came to catch hepatitis in November 1958. Robert Thiess was one of the swimmers who trained at the baths, and his little brother would always kiss me when the two of them arrived at the pool. I didn't know he had hepatitis—the disease was raging in South Australia at the time—and I soon came down with it too. In the end I became so sick that Mum and Pop came down to nurse me. Captain Krieg arranged for them to fly down on a cheap flight with TAA: the first time Mum and Pop had been in an aeroplane. The three of us took a flat at Glenelg, not far from the beach, where it was thought the sea air would do me some good, and Mum and Pop would go off for walks down the beach while I was sleeping. For six weeks I could do little more than lie in a darkened room because I was so sensitive to light, while Mum cooked beetroot for me in every imaginable way. It had been prescribed as being good for the liver and it was also all I could keep down. Any other cooking smells made me violently ill. For more than two months I was jaundiced and hardly felt like eating. I lost so much weight that a few months later when I swam in the Nationals several of the journalists covering the event were quite shocked by the change in me.

When I finally got back into the pool my first training swim was three miles. Each quarter mile took 5 minutes 15 seconds and I knew then that I was on the road to recovery. It was a relief to know I still had the stamina and, as usual, the rest had done me the world of good. I started to take little walks with Mum and Pop and gradually began to feel normal again. Because I'd swum continually throughout the year and been at my peak before becoming ill I was able to come back quite strongly and quickly. I was never someone who liked to take long breaks, even after major competitions—it was simply too hard to get back into the water. My almost continual swimming through down seasons and down years certainly prolonged my career and stood me in good stead through the 1958/59 season.

Mum and Pop took me back to Sydney briefly for Christmas and then I returned to attend first the South Australian and later the Victorian Championships. By special invitation the US swimmers Chris von Saltza and Sylvia Ruuska had been brought out to swim against us. Chris was billed as my major competition.

In Melbourne I beat Chris at my favourite distance of 220 yards but this was only a build-up to the real clash at the Nationals in Hobart. Despite my recovery I was still feeling well below form and was having little relapses, which meant I had to sleep most of the day during the competition and couldn't train as much as I would normally. If the Americans hadn't been in town I wouldn't have attended the Nationals in 1959. The ASU always seemed to find ways to attract the crowds to the pool, even when there was no major competition looming. But I very much wanted to defend my titles and not be seen as avoiding Chris. I felt that a withdrawal on any grounds would automatically be seen as a backdown, and I didn't want to let the Australian public down after the build-up to these swims against Chris had been so intense. That sounds very sugary but I genuinely felt a responsibility to the public, as well as to my State. The South Australian swimmers were my firm friends by then and we were beginning to show great promise as a team. I didn't feel responsibility towards the ASU; it was more that I was still wary of them and didn't want to attract any negative attention. In truth I should have stayed at home in bed for at least three or four months to fully recuperate, and some journalists at the time suggested I was risking my long-term health by swimming.

Nevertheless, I swam in the 110 yards and 220 yards finals and won them both in just over world-record times. Chris von Saltza, for all the anticipation, came third in both behind Ilsa Konrads. I also matched my world record of 61.2 in the first leg of the medley relay for the South Australian team. It made me wonder what might have been if I'd been in top form.

It was a relief to return to Adelaide after the Nationals and take things a bit easier while I built up my strength and weight again. The so-called 'down years' between Olympic and Commonwealth Games are naturally less memorable for athletes than the big years. You have your sights set firmly eighteen months ahead but the intensity is not there and nor are the overseas trips, which have always been one of my major incentives. I continued to live at the baths, work in my three jobs, go out with Peter and generally settle down to an ordered life in what was now very much my home town. As Harry remarked to a journalist back then, 'Dawn goes to the occasional party and loves surfing and waterskiing, but she only does those things when they will not interfere with her training program.' I still felt I had a job to do for Pop, even though I had more than proved myself. Swimming still came first. I might have been the life of the party but I was also shrewd about my career. I knew what it had brought me and I had dreams and solid goals about what it would continue to bring. I think people have sometimes seen me as a one-dimensional, devil-may-care party girl who just happened to have a natural talent. What they didn't see were the hours and hours of training, the endless planning conversations with Harry and my mental preparation alone at night above the pool.

As in the previous few years, I returned to Sydney during the winter when all my training would be done outside the pool anyway. Along with two friends who trained at the baths, I rode my motor scooter all the way from Adelaide to Sydney. The journey took us two days because the scooters' top speed was only 58 miles per hour. It was a very funny and enjoyable journey, although my bum was extremely sore by the time I arrived in Balmain. We got permission from a truckie to sleep under his semi-trailer at night and we ate and showered in service stations. It gave me a wonderful sense of freedom to be doing something so spontaneous and silly after all the rigid structure of my life at the baths.

It was great to be back with Mum and Pop. I got a job in the sportswear department at David Jones in Elizabeth Street in the city and trained myself at City Tattersalls Club in Sydney, as well as taking long runs according to the program Harry had established for me before I left. Harry kept in touch by letter, suggesting that I try this and that, as we still didn't have a phone at Birchgrove Road.

While I was in Sydney I went to parties at Codocks and at the tennis club in the neighbouring suburb of Rozelle with Alick and his girlfriend. Alick was still at home then and we immediately took up our matey relationship from where we'd left off. By this time Michael Hall was off the scene. His mother had said he shouldn't go out with me because I wasn't Catholic, and Pop had never liked him anyway. Between them they'd made it too difficult for us to continue seeing each other. But it was a shame they interfered because I believe I truly loved Michael, even though I was very young at the time.

It was at one of the tennis club parties that I met Kenny Robinson. He was a quiet, good-natured bloke, and Pop approved of him more than he had approved of Michael—although he wasn't over the moon about him. Kenny, who worked at Cockatoo Island Docks with Pop, somehow plucked up the courage to ask my father if he could take me out. Pop had a talk to me about it and as was the ritual back then, told Kenny he could take me out as long as he came to the house to pick me up, which Kenny did several times during my stay in Sydney.

I flew back to Adelaide for the start of the season in September, leaving my motor scooter for Alick to use. Over the following year Alick got me back for the times I'd damaged his bike when we were kids by getting the wheels caught up in the tram lines and bending the scooter out of shape. In Adelaide that season I didn't have much need of a scooter because we were working so hard in the lead-up to the Nationals in Sydney where the team for the 1960 Rome Olympics would be selected. I'd also made good friends with the lovely Rodda family by then and they occasionally loaned me their car. Judy Rodda worked with me at Charles Birks and she also came to the baths to swim. Once a week I'd have a home-cooked meal with the family at their home in North

Adelaide. Over the years I'd take the colour slides from my over-seas trips to show them and whenever I couldn't remember what a certain building was I'd say it was the bank because Mr Rodda was a bank manager. He always called me 'the bank girl' after that. They had a house at Noarlunga Beach and I'd be invited down there with a whole bunch of the swimming girls for weekends.

During this period I also spent a couple of months with another swimming family, the Mills, at their home at Henley Beach. I became very attached to their severely mentally disabled son, Noely, and I'd borrow the family's Morris Minor to take him with me on drives into the country and to the beach. I even took him sailing in their little boat when he was about nine years old. Mr Mills was terrified but Noely loved it. Harry sometimes loaned me his car, too, as did another swimming family, the Aungers, so all in all Adelaide was not so difficult to get around in without my scooter.

One of the ways Harry kept us interested in swimming was to make us do different strokes. Medley swimming was also gaining prominence and he felt we should have a range of strokes in our repertoire—I didn't mind backstroke and butterfly but I hated breaststroke because my knees just couldn't do the correct kick. It was great training and stopped us getting bored. You can't talk to people when you are doing freestyle but I could chat to people in the next lane when I was doing backstroke training.

Although I'd only taken the two new strokes on as training for freestyle, I won races in both at the State Championships in the 1959/60 season. This wasn't especially significant because swim-ming in South Australia was still just coming of age and there weren't many swimmers of my calibre at that stage. If you could swim well in freestyle, as I clearly could, it was also possible to do a reasonable backstroke and butterfly. Harry, however, decided that I should contest the butterfly title at the Sydney Nationals in February. I always did as Harry suggested without any question whatsoever. A journalist once asked me if I would stick my head in an oven if Harry asked me to and I said 'yes'. What's more I meant it. The trust between us as coach and swimmer was absolute at that time. He was in charge and I trusted him to make me win in Rome. Without Harry I would never have been as good as I was and without me he would never have been as good as he was.

Leading up to the Nationals we were keeping an eye on Ilsa Konrads, who was being trained by Don Talbot in Sydney. She'd swum great times in the New South Wales State Championships, while I had swum only comfortable times in ours. We'd been hearing a lot about Ilsa throughout the season and I knew from watching her that she had the ability to be very, very good. I was also aware that at twenty-two I was an older swimmer. It didn't help that I was being referred to as 'Granny' both by the press and some of the other swimmers.

Ilsa had set a world record in the 440 yards earlier in the month and that was firmly fixed in my mind at the Nationals as we left the marshalling area at the North Sydney Pool for the quarter mile final. It wasn't an event I really liked because I didn't train for the longer distances—the training required is quite different from sprint training—and I found they hurt me when I swam them. Still, Harry wanted me to contest the quarter mile because I had done well in it at the Melbourne Games and we were still experimenting, both with different strokes and distances.

Harry had always said that I should leave my socks on until the last minute to keep my feet warm so that the circulation was good before a swim, and I used that advice in gamesmanship against Ilsa. I waited with my socks on until we were called to the blocks, then pretended I had forgotten to remove them. That gave me the chance to walk back and slowly take them off. I had wanted to unnerve Ilsa and perhaps I did. I trailed her throughout the race and then did the last lap in 33 seconds to Ilsa's 37.3. I'd won in 4:47.4. Of course everyone said Ilsa had a 'Fraser complex' and that I'd swum to her race, pouncing at the end. The truth is that

I swam the race I'd planned and even if Ilsa had done something completely different I would still have swum my race exactly the same way.

The next night I contested the butterfly, not really expecting to do anything remarkable, and set a world record by swimming the race in 1:10.8. The 110 yards freestyle, my favourite swim, was scheduled for an hour later, so I went and did a swim down between races. All swimmers do it now but back then it wasn't common to swim after a race. I'd always find a diving or practice pool and swim for a mile or so. It helps the muscles relax and wind down from the intensity of the race and I'd do it even if I had no more competitive swimming coming up that day.

More than four thousand people had come to watch the Nationals that night and as I came back for the second lap of the 110 yards they rose and cheered like mad as I set a new world record of 60.2 seconds, beating my own previous world record by a whole second. I had set three world records that night and John Morrison, the President of the ASU, announced over the loudspeaker: 'You have just seen the greatest performance of any woman athlete, in any sport, the world has yet known.'

On the last night, in the 220 yards championship, I did what I consider to have been one of my best swims ever. I took 3.1 seconds off my world record and touched the wall in 2:11.6. Bill Berge Phillips said to the press, 'She's proved she's outside the range of women swimmers—she's in the men's class.'

In training with Jon Henricks I had always based my swimming times on those of the men; it was an integral part of my regime. If Ricksie swam a bit faster so would I, never wanting to be more than a few seconds behind him. If I'd trained with the women I would have been the fastest and wouldn't have had anyone to chase. I don't think I would ever have achieved the same results without that mindset and training method.

In another upset at the Nationals that year Lorraine was beaten into fourth place in her favourite swim, the 440 yards, and it was only when she came third in the 110 yards that she managed to find a place on the team that was once again heading north to Townsville. We didn't have as long in Townsville as usual because of protests from overseas that our preparations were too intense and professional to suit the amateur sport. But I didn't feel, as some others did, that we left for Rome under-prepared. I knew I had done the right amount of training and had more than enough miles under my belt. By that stage I would just do it as a matter of course, which I think was true of many of the women swimmers on the team. That was often overlooked by some of the swimming officials associated with that 1960 team, who seemed to want to have such complete control over us regardless of our level of maturity and ability to prepare ourselves for what was ahead. We were, after all, the ones doing the miles at dawn each day; we knew what we had to do and how to conduct ourselves. But we were rarely given the opportunity to show that, with officials trying to have a hand in all aspects of our lives. Even then it rankled with me.

My original plan—well, Harry's plan and then the ASU's plan— had been to swim in the 100 metres butterfly in Rome. I was happy to go along with that given my performance at the Nationals but while I was in Townsville I strained my stomach muscles quite badly in butterfly training and was advised by the doctor to give away this strenuous stroke. I was relieved to be able to make the decision based on medical advice. It had never been a stroke I particularly enjoyed and it hurt quite a bit to execute it, particularly at major competition level. You don't go to an Olympics to wear the blazer, you go to win, and that means swimming as if your life depends on it. I felt there was no way I could continue with butterfly at that level. It was made clear to the swim team manager, Roger Pegram, and the chaperone, Mrs Ross, that I would not be entering the butterfly event and I immediately stopped training for it. That, unfortunately, was not to be the end of the matter.

Something else happened in Townsville that seemed innocuous at the time but was to lead to major problems for me following the Games. Joycie and all my old friends at Larco sent me a lovely white tracksuit with a map of Australia embroidered on the front of it. I was really thrilled with it. It was made of light nylon, which was very comfortable in hot weather, and I also thought it was very smart and modern. All through my career the people of my home suburb had supported me with lots of lovely gestures and gifts of this kind and I wore the tracksuit with great pride.

Ken Robinson rang me regularly while I was up north and finally asked me to marry him. I was a bit startled by that because although I thought he was very nice and I did have feelings for him, we'd only known each other for a short time. The hours we'd spent in each other's company had been few and far between given my schedule over the previous months. He was very persistent, though, and wanted me to give him an answer and preferably get engaged before I left the country. Looking back, I think Ken was a bit caught up in Dawn Fraser the name rather than Dawn Fraser the person, although not in an awful way, and I was a bit caught up in the idea of having a nice ring on my finger and the excitement of an engagement. We agreed we'd talk more about it when I arrived in Sydney en route to Rome. We would be in Sydney for about a week, during which time the women would train in the swimming pool at the City Tattersalls Club and the men at Tattersalls Club, which was, and still is, a club for men only.

I finally said I would marry Ken and just before we left he gave me a ring that his uncle had made for me, although by the time I got to Rome I'd started to have misgivings: I simply didn't feel I knew him well, however much I liked him. We announced our engagement to the press and that took some of the heat off Lorraine who had also announced her engagement to Dr Bill

Thurlow, who had been working with some of the swimmers in Townsville. Bill and Lorraine told the press they didn't know when they'd marry but then went and married in secret on the eve of our departure for Rome, while I celebrated my own engagement at a keg party in Mum and Pop's backyard.

Lorraine and I sat together on the plane and I reassured her that no one could throw her off the team for being married; there were other married people on the team, after all. But she was worried about the official reaction—another example of how we didn't feel we were or would be treated as adults, even though we were old enough to be married with families—and so decided not to make it public.

On the way to Rome the engine of the plane I was travelling in, which carried half the 188-strong Australian team, was found to have a fissure in it and we had to wait overnight in Bahrain while a new engine was flown in. This unscheduled stopover had some disastrous consequences. First of all two male members of the team stole some cameras from a duty free shop at the airport. The police were brought in, the cameras were returned and that potential crisis was averted. Then, some of the team drank soft drinks with ice cubes in them, although we had been advised not to drink the local water, and they were extremely ill by the time we finally reached Rome. Jon Henricks was so badly affected he was taken to hospital. I had my own stomach upsets, which continued through the next week, but not from drinking the water on the way.

The Olympic village in Rome was a new complex, about fifteen minutes taxi ride from the middle of the city, with the men and women segregated as usual. The public highway actually crossed the complex in the form of a bridge lined with flags. We didn't know it straightaway but some of the local men would line up with binoculars on the bridge, where they could look right into the women's quarters. There were heatwave conditions during the Rome Games so we often left the blinds up and windows open just to catch some fresh air. When we found out we were being ogled some of us would carry on and get dressed in front of them, saying things like, 'OK, it's brown eye time' or 'Let's give them something to look at' before backing up our words with the appropriate actions. Eventually the police were called to clear the road because it had become so obstructed by men with binoculars.

One of the really awful things that happened in Rome—and there were a few—was that the swimming team was forbidden to march in the opening ceremony because the ASU officials had decided it was too close to our competition days and would upset our form. We'd known this before we left for overseas but I have always regretted this sadly, sadly missed opportunity. To march for your country at the opening of an Olympic Games is an extraordinary experience that lifts you throughout the competition and fills you with such an intense pride it is indescribable. To take that away from people, many of whom wouldn't have an opportunity to march again, is unforgivable. We staged our own mock protest march in the village but the damage had been done. Now, four decades later, it seems an unthinkable act of petty officialdom.

Lorraine, the thirteen-year-old Ruth Everuss and I shared a room in the Rome village and the three of us were real soul mates. Ruth and I started to cover for Lorraine, who was sneaking out to be with her new husband. I should actually say that I was covering for Lorraine and the much younger Ruth was following my lead. To my mind it is completely understandable that a newly married, very much in love young woman would want to be with her husband but Lorraine was terrified that she'd be found out and thrown off the team. Lorraine wasn't making many appearances in the dining room and Mrs Ross had begun to ask questions.

'Where's Lorraine?'

'She's gone to the pool.'

'Why has she gone to the pool while you and Ruth are still here?'

'Oh, well, Lorraine wanted to do some extra training today and we're going to join her later.'

And so it went on.

In the end I suggested Lorraine should sleep in the village for a night because we were running out of excuses. We'd be sleeping in her bed or mucking it up to look as if she'd been there and in the end it all became too difficult. Finally Mrs Ross said, 'Tell Lorraine I want to see her in half an hour.' I couldn't do that so I said, 'I'm sorry, I don't know where she is.' That's all I said. Later Lorraine had a talk with Mrs Ross, and I have no idea what went on between them but I was relieved that her marriage was finally out in the open and I didn't have to cover for her any more. I had enough on my plate getting ready to swim.

Lorraine was, in my opinion, treated very badly after she told the authorities, and perhaps she'd been right to try to keep her marriage quiet. It was as if she was a naughty schoolgirl and there was a lot of rumour and unpleasantness surrounding her, despite her experience and all she had given Australian sport. She didn't swim well at the Games and retired soon after. She later said that her heart was no longer in it after the way she'd been treated, especially given all her achievements up to that point. It was another example of poor handling of an Australian team member in 1960.

I had a lot of fan mail to contend with when I was in Rome. I was well known this time around following the Melbourne Olympics and other major competitions in between, and in fact there was a bit of pressure on me to defend my title around the village. I'd hear people say, 'There goes Dawn Fraser; she's defending her title.' I taught Ruth how to sign my name so she could help me with my replies. I liked to get back to everyone who had written but there was no way I could do it on my own each night before lights-out. Ruthie still tells that story today and we have a good laugh.

Another interesting story from Rome was what I call 'the other flag incident'. I was training at the pool one day leading up to the start of competition and the Australian water polo players were also training there. I knew some of them very well and was enjoying mucking around with them. As usual I was more comfortable with a bit of exuberant male company than I was with the girls and decided to stay with a few of the players and go back to the village in their Kombi van. We were all in high spirits and after training decided to do a bit of sightseeing and have something to eat before returning to the village. As we came up to the bridge over the village we stopped and some of the players opened the side door of the van and held me on their shoulders while I took down one of the Olympic flags lining the bridge. We sped up again then slowed down for another flag, and then another. I think we had about four or five in the end but our haul was cut short when Herman Doerner, the Team Manager, who was driving the van, yelled to Keith Whitehead, 'Get her back in for chrissakes, we're being chased by the police.'

We all looked out the back and there were two policemen galloping towards us on horses. Hermi took off at full speed and I was still hanging out the door with flags all caught and tangled around my legs, but I was pulled back inside and we made it safely back to the village. They hadn't even been able to record our numberplate because the van was so dirty. I seem to remember there were about ten flags souvenired at the Rome Games by the Australian team. I didn't end up with any of those taken that day by the water polo team, or any others for that matter, but recently Keith Whitehead's son called and said he thought they had something of mine: a flag from the Rome Games. I told him it couldn't possibly belong to me.

When the Rome swimming team finally packed to leave the village there was so much extra luggage because of all the souveniring that had gone on that everyone had to send extra suitcases and boxes home by ship. We all had to empty our bags at the airport because we were overweight and as the Chef de Mission started walking around, one of the female swimmers sat on her overflowing suitcase and refused to budge because she had so many stolen Olympic items in her bag.

As usual the coaches had to pay for themselves and find their own accommodation if they wanted to be with their swimmers during the Games. Harry flew over with Jill and they stayed in a local hotel. He wasn't allowed on the pool deck and hadn't been able to gain any sort of accreditation to watch us swim or speak to us before our races. He missed Jon swimming in his 100 metres heat, which must have been crushing after working with him for so long. Neither had he been able to get important instructions to Henricks, who had been very unwell and, according to Harry, shouldn't have gone in too hard in the heat. Ricksie did swim hard and had nothing left for the semifinal, which saw him knocked out of the competition altogether: a great shame given his brilliant swimming times in Townsville before we left. I was really upset about it because Ricksie and I had talked about getting the gold medals again for Harry and we had worked together for so long.

When it came time for my heat I pushed Harry past the official who tried to stop him entering the pool with me. When they refused him entry I refused to swim: 'He no come in, I no swim.' I held my ground and eventually they relented. He didn't have any trouble getting into the pool after that.

I was still suffering quite badly from stomach upsets and wasn't feeling great when I stepped up onto the blocks but I won my heat. Over the next few days toast was just about the only thing I could keep down and I had to sleep for much of the time. I seemed to have formed a pattern of falling ill before major competition swims, but many people on the team had the same problems this time round. I knew going into the semifinal that my old rival Chris von Saltza had broken my Olympic record in her heat, but as her semifinal race was before mine I had the advantage of knowing she'd won it in 62.5 seconds, which meant I could plan my race to make her feel less comfortable over the days leading to the final. I touched the wall in 61.4 seconds and got my record back.

The night of the final was tense. I hadn't been well all week and we were still experiencing heatwave conditions. Harry told me not to go out too hard too early because of my health problems. As usual I listened to every word and followed his plan exactly. I turned with Chris von Saltza but pulled ahead halfway through the second lap to set another Olympic record in 61.2 seconds. I had successfully defended my title to become the first swimmer ever to win the same event at two successive Olympic Games, but that wasn't what I was thinking about during the medal ceremony. It was one of the rare times when I cried publicly, I was so completely thrilled and happy to have achieved my dream. I was thrilled for Harry, too, and so proud to be standing up there for my country. I was wearing my white tracksuit because my other one was wet, and I was holding a toy kangaroo. I felt as if I would burst with excitement as the crowd called out my name.

•

During the Rome Games I started to go out quite seriously with one of the members of the Australian men's water polo team. I'd known Keith Whitehead for a long time through training at the same pools and through the Melbourne Games, although he was quite a bit older than I was. After the swimming events were over we went out in Rome for dinner and celebratory drinks with Lorraine and Bill. It was a fantastic night and we didn't come back to the village until the early hours of the morning.

Keith and I got along very well, and although it didn't become a sexual affair there was a strong attraction and we talked about how we loved each other and wanted to be in each other's company. I'd already been having second thoughts about my engagement, and now Whitey suggested to me that if I was attracted to him perhaps I shouldn't be marrying Ken Robinson.

I had a special leave pass from Mrs Ross to go into Rome to be measured for a wedding dress from the Fontana Sisters, who had read of my engagement in the press and had written to me saying they would like to make me a gown. I asked Keith to join me afterwards. He waited outside while some press photos were taken of me wearing a dress from the rack, and we went sightseeing around Rome in a horse and carriage. By the time we'd finished it was afternoon and the shops were closing. We decided to head back to the village. That's when Keith said to me, 'You are mad. You don't love this man and you shouldn't be getting married to him. You're getting into something you'll need to get out of later.' From that point my doubts about getting married became more serious, but I still wasn't sure what to do. I realised I wasn't missing Ken and in fact I was having a pretty good time with someone else. On the other hand I was carried away with the idea of a fairytale marriage, and the fact that Lorraine was married and Ricksie was about to be married influenced me too. Basically, I didn't have the experience to know what to do.

Back at the village the dining room had almost closed and all the chef could offer us was spaghetti Napoletana. We said that would do us and we ate it hungrily, along with some bread. Just as we were finishing, at about 4.00 p.m., Roger Pegram, the Section Manager for the swimming team, came up to me in a real flap— as if he'd been looking for me and had finally found me. He said that I was required to swim the butterfly leg of a medley relay heat in an hour's time. I thought he must somehow be joking, but knew in the same instant from the look on his face that he wasn't. I explained that I'd been given permission for a day off; that I hadn't been informed I would be required for such a swim; that I'd just eaten a huge plate of spaghetti; and, apart from all that, I'd made it clear in Townsville that I wouldn't be swimming butterfly any longer and therefore hadn't been training in the stroke for weeks. I was told that I would have to step in because Jan Andrew, a butterfly swimmer, had to rest herself for the final of the 100 metres butterfly that evening, having swum the second fastest time in the heats. I still refused, for all of the reasons I've just stated.

Roger Pegram is on record as saying that I had agreed to swim butterfly if required to do so in Rome, but I disagree. Further, even if I had agreed to swim butterfly when required, which I hadn't, I would hardly have been able to swim butterfly with a stomach full of pasta. Of course I was perfectly entitled to eat pasta on my day off at whatever hour I chose, and it seemed logical to me that I would not have been given a leave pass if I'd been expected to swim.

I have since apologised to Jan Andrew for not swimming because I certainly didn't feel any ill will towards her in making my decision, but the fact is I should never have been asked to swim in that race. In 2000, at the reunion of the 1960 swimming team in Townsville, the Sydney-based journalist Tracey Holmes asked me if I had any regrets and I nominated that incident in Rome, and I meant it. I never wanted to hurt Jan, but ultimately the question must be asked: if I was required to swim, why was I given a day's leave pass? While I was pleased to clear the air with Jan with a public apology, I know the mix-up was not mine. Jan is a good mate and someone I trained with at the very beginning with Harry's Drummoyne mob, and I know she understands it was never a personal issue that I chose not to swim.

I've thought about this incident sometimes since those Games, given that it ultimately did me so much damage, but I firmly believe I had my job to do at the Games and it was not, in my opinion, up to individual team-members to make up for a lack of organisation on the part of the officials. My coach wasn't with me while Roger Pegram was speaking with me and I remember feeling cornered. Maybe, just maybe, I would have agreed to swim had I not spent the morning rushing around Rome and the afternoon feeding my face because I was very aware of the importance of representing my country. At the time I had been looking ahead to the freestyle leg of the medley relay the next day, which *was* part of my commitment. It was not a matter of being irresponsible or unprepared because I knew exactly what was expected of me. If anyone let Jan down, it was the officials.

Jan still came third in the final and to say she would have done better had I swum in the medley heat, as many people have alleged both on and off the record, is, in my opinion, drawing a long bow. These days Jan herself puts her swim down mostly to inexperience. It was still a wonderful achievement and an Olympic medal. Later, after the Games, Jan broke the world record in the same swim, so perhaps something was going on during the Games.

In the end, Alva Colquhoun stood in for her in the relay heat. The team qualified for the final but in the slowest time. In the final Jan and I both swam our legs, while Marilyn Wilson from Victoria did the backstroke and Rosemary Lassig from Queensland the breaststroke, but we still only came second to the US team.

When the girls returned to our quarters that day after Alva had stood in for Jan, they came into my room and started saying what a lousy bitch I'd been. They were really angry and vocal at first, and then they wouldn't talk to me. Basically I was frozen out. Being the person I am, I stormed into Jan's room where she was resting before her final and asked what on earth was wrong with her. I don't recall the exact details of what took place, and neither does she, except that I suggested she was being a wimp and wanted to know what she was saying to provoke such a reaction in everyone else. I was older than most of the team and tended to do my own thing—which is another reason why I'd been hanging around with the water polo players, who were more my age—so I was especially angry that the girls were all getting at me. At some stage I grabbed a pillow and threw it at her from a few feet away and told her not to be such a wimp. I guess I may have thrown it hard, and I did get her square in the face, but it was a pillow, after all. It has been reported also that Jan's eyes were red from crying when she lined up for the final but she herself says she was never a crier. This incident has been blown out of proportion so many times and was described by some after the Games, when all my misdemeanours were reported by the press, as a 'violent episode'. According to some reports I hit Jan across the face or punched her. This is absolutely not true and neither Jan nor I remember it like that. I don't know where the story came from: it wasn't from either of us. But it certainly damaged my reputation and I guess that was the intention of those who told and retold the story. I'm not proud of this particular episode and I wish it hadn't happened, but it was not entirely out of the ordinary in those close quarters in the Olympic village, where girls would be bitchy and irritated by each other on a regular basis.

My last swim at the Rome Games was the final of the 400 metres. I'd qualified in the slowest time and only managed to come fifth in the final behind Ilsa in fourth place. Chris von Saltza won the gold. I had previously swum this distance in much better times, which led to press reports that I hadn't tried or had thrown the race. Later some swimming officials said similar things. My competitive streak would never have allowed me to throw a race and even now I become impatient at having to deny these allegations. Perhaps it was the illness I'd battled since the beginning of the Games, or the emotional stress of the week, or the fact that it was never my main event, or that the other swimmers were just better over this distance. Who knows? Fifth in the world wasn't bad.

•

You would think I could have attended the FINA (Federation Internationale de Natation) carnival without getting into any more trouble. It was a relaxed event and regarded by most as more of a casual exhibition swim than major competition. It immediately followed the last swimming events in Rome, and the trip to Naples also took in Ricksie's fairytale wedding to his stunning American bride, Bonnie. The whole swim team attended and it was a wonderful occasion. Some of the other athletes had accompanied us to watch the carnival, and on the way to Naples in the train opened some Chianti in the traditional wicker-wrapped bottles. It was the end of the swimming and we were in a party mood. When we arrived in Naples I was given permission to accompany some relatives of our Italian neighbours in Balmain to their house for a birthday lunch to be held in my honour. I had turned twenty-three a few days earlier and hadn't yet had a chance to celebrate. There was a birthday cake for me, which followed a nice lunch of ravioli and a little red wine, and later in the day I returned to the pool for my race.

I swam hard up and back, touched the end and floated back in the water, very relaxed, feeling the effects of the wine but far from drunk. Then, as I looked up, I realised that all the other swimmers had turned and were halfway up the pool again. That's when the realisation sank in that I was in a 200 metres not a 100 metres race. Whoops!

I know I should be serious about this and feel slightly ashamed but I just look back on it as being very funny. It wasn't funny at the time, though, because Bill Berge Phillips was there, being the Vice President of FINA at the time, and he made it clear to me he wasn't impressed. Let's face it, it was an honest mistake in an unimportant event and not something that could ever occur in major competition. But that's not the way he saw it, and this was yet another black mark against my name for which I suffered later.

During the Rome Games I'd been given permission to travel to Scotland for four days immediately after my last swim, which was at the FINA carnival. I'd been given leave to visit Pop's relatives, as long as I rejoined the team in Paris where we were to take part in a carnival after the Games had finished completely. Mr Pegram and Mr Grange, the Chef de Mission and General Manager of the

Australian team, had agreed I could go, and I made and paid for all my own travel bookings at the village travel agency. Unfortunately this little trip was to become yet another problem for me in the future. Harry and Jill were also leaving the Games after the swimming events and taking a short holiday, so they suggested I join them for a day or two before flying on to Scotland. The three of us took the train to Switzerland and spent a day in Zurich, where Harry had some friends. It was nice to be in their company after the pressure and unpleasantness of the previous weeks.

You always have to train after a major competition to help ease the muscles; it's like swimming down after a fast race. When we got to Zurich Harry rang a college he knew of that had an indoor swimming pool and asked if I could go there for a two-hour training session. They agreed and Harry took me to the pool. We arrived during school hours and the headmaster happened to bring a few classes of school children in while I was training in the pool—some of the kids tried to keep up with me in the water. By the time I climbed out the mayor had arrived and lots of people had gathered and they gave me a bunch of flowers. They were excited that an Olympic champion was in their city while the Games were still going and uppermost in people's minds. It was really lovely and some of those who had gathered at the pool even came to wave goodbye at the train station when I left Harry to head to London. That happy occasion was eventually marred by the ASU's charge that I'd given an exhibition swim without permission. That was all ahead of me, though, as I set out for Scotland oblivious to the storm that was brewing among the ASU officials.

The journey to Scotland to see Pop's sister, Aunty Mary, and her family who lived in Dumbarton was the first time I'd had to manage myself and my luggage in a foreign city. For all the travelling I'd done and all the things I'd seen I distinctly remember being quite excited to be negotiating my own way. It was so lovely for me when I finally arrived because the living quarters at Aunty Mary's house were so cramped, it was as if I were walking into a replica of home. There was oatmeal porridge for breakfast and haggis for dinner. The whole family came over to meet me, including my cousin Barbara and her children. It was difficult to understand them and I had to ask them to speak more slowly, even though I had grown used to the Gaelic spoken by Pop's brothers and cousins who visited us in Australia when I was a child. I only stayed for a few days because of my commitment to rejoin the team in Paris, but seeing where Pop had come from was a special experience that I'm glad I had. Altogether, though, Rome 1960 had been a tough trip and I was happy to be heading home.

When I arrived back in Sydney my family threw a party as usual. Kenny wanted me to go out but I just wanted to stay home and tell everyone all that had happened and about the things I'd seen. Alick took me upstairs on the balcony and told me I should think carefully about marrying Kenny and what I was getting myself into. He said that Kenny had been at the tennis club dating other girls a few times while I was away. It was just one of those caring brother and sister talks. I couldn't really be cross with Ken, given what I'd been up to, but it did make me think more about what I was doing. Nevertheless, Ken and I went out a few times before I went back to Adelaide and still I didn't break up the relationship.

•

During my preparation for the Nationals towards the end of 1960 I received an invitation from the Japanese swimming union to attend a special carnival in Tokyo the following April. I hadn't been to Japan, but some of the male swimmers had toured there after the Cardiff Games when the women's team was in Paris and Holland, and because of their stories I was pretty excited by the idea of it. I advised the South Australian Swimming Union of the invitation, said I'd love to go if everything went well in the

Nationals, and the Japanese were advised to deal with the ASU for all arrangements. I really began to look forward to the trip and was working very hard leading up to the Nationals because unless I did well there I wouldn't be going anywhere. It was clear to me that I was getting on in age, and that after I'd successfully defended my title in Rome most people thought it was fairly unlikely I'd get to Tokyo and do it again. I thought otherwise, though. I already had my sights set on Tokyo, so continued with my usual training schedule despite having just come back from the Games. A week or two before the Nationals the ASU announced a team to travel to South Africa and New Zealand later that year. My name wasn't on the list, despite the inclusion of others who had not even qualified for the Olympics. It really surprised me after my achievements in Rome but I figured that I was being sent to Japan and couldn't do both. Eventually, just before the Nationals in Brisbane, a newspaper journalist called and told me that when pressed for an answer a spokesman for the ASU had explained I had been excluded because I wasn't available. It was then that I first suspected all wasn't going well for me at the ASU, but as no one from the organisation had made any official contact with me and nothing had been said for almost four months since the Rome Games, I was a bit confused by the mixed messages and decided just to get on with my job.

On the night before the Nationals started, with no warning and no opportunity to defend myself to the ASU before it became public, Roger Pegram's official report on the Rome Games was released to the media. The ASU's annual conference would begin the next day and after that the press were free to write about the contents of the Annual Report. Pegram criticised me in no uncertain terms for refusing to swim the butterfly leg of the medley relay, saying I had kept someone else out of the Australian team by having agreed to swim butterfly before I left for Rome, and further that I hadn't even swum in the 100 metres butterfly event. He said

I had embarrassed the team by refusing to swim. At the time I wondered who they were all embarrassed in front of, and still do as I recall these events. It was hardly an international incident and why was it embarrassing? More embarrassing was the fact that we had no one to swim in the event that day due to poor planning by the ASU. I wanted to ask: why was I given the leave pass for the day if I was expected to swim the butterfly leg of the medley? It was no secret that the medley heat was being held that day. What if I hadn't been found in the dining room? What if I hadn't returned in time? What would the story have been under those circumstances? But I wasn't given an opportunity to ask those or any other questions.

Mrs Ross also reported unfavourably about my behaviour in Rome, which disappointed me because I liked Mrs Ross and thought her an excellent manager. I had thought she liked me too. She stated that my refusal to swim had so upset Jan Andrew it may well have denied her the silver medal. It appeared Jan had been upset enough to miss silver but not quite so upset that she missed bronze. Far from addressing any embarrassment I was supposed to have caused the team in Rome, the release of the report whipped up the whole story again with considerable embellishments, including that so-called 'violent row' with Jan, and it started to appear in papers around the world.

Tom Herraman, the President of the South Australian Swimming Association, had asked Bill Berge Phillips at the annual meeting if ability had been the only criterion on which the selection of the team to visit South Africa had been based. Berge Phillips replied it was not but Herraman did not pursue the issue as perhaps he might have done given he was my representative in this matter. Now I knew I had been excluded from the touring team due to my behaviour in Rome. It was a terrible way to find out, at the beginning of the Nationals, and deeply frustrating because I never had an opportunity to respond before my name and reputation were widely discussed in the media and basically dragged through the mud.

Although not part of any official report, various other stories about my behaviour were brought up during the Nationals and somehow found their way into press reports and general conversations around the pool. I was attacked for wearing my lovely white tracksuit from Joycie and Larco when I received my gold medal for the 100 metres. My supposed lack of effort in the 400 metres was talked about, as was my so-called 'exhibition swim' in Switzerland and my 'drinking' and botched race in the FINA carnival in Naples. These incidents were all dragged up in one form or another to support the case for Dawn Fraser's basic bad character and inability to adequately represent her country. Looking back, the white tracksuit wasn't the smartest move I've ever made, but certainly not a defiant or intentionally rebellious act. Not a single official said anything about the tracksuit during the Games but now, a good six months later, it appeared that they were all very upset about it. As I have said, I liked the tracksuit and my official one was wet.

The worst aspect of that week in Brisbane, however, was Bill Berge Phillips' comment to reporters that there was something 'much bigger' that I had apparently done. He couldn't go into it, he said, but suggested the reporters try to find out. The same comment was repeated to the media later that week. To this day rumours circulate about what that 'bigger thing' was but no one has ever been able to explain his comment and I have long since given up trying to work out what he meant. Naturally one would hope that something 'much bigger' had happened to explain my ban from participating in all Australian teams at the height of my swimming success, but there is simply nothing that I can think of to explain the extreme actions of the ASU, and none of the officials have ever stated what that 'bigger thing' was. One of the rumours is that I was sexually aggressive towards female members of the 1960 team, and this story still reaches my ears from time to time. There are even stories about who I was sexually aggressive towards and what effect my actions had on them. I have since approached that person to check out the story and they thought it was as funny and ridiculous as I did last time I heard it. Over time the pain that such stories caused me has eased and the whole thing has become silly. I am fairly sure I know who keeps it going but I don't know how to make it go away. Basically I have to ignore it and put it down to petty jealousy. I have always tried to live up to the saying that living well is the best revenge.

I was twenty-three years old at the Brisbane Nationals and I felt the full weight of the ASU's disapproval with no one I could particularly turn to. Even Harry encouraged me to write a letter of apology to the ASU, which also ended up being misconstrued and rejected. Later I felt very angry with Harry for not putting up his hand to take the blame for the swim in Zurich and for not giving me more support. I was used to relying on him in all things and I felt deserted in my hour of greatest need. I believe Harry left the Nationals early after a fight we had about the whole episode. I don't know if that's why he left but I know we had a row due to the strain of the situation and he disappeared early. To be fair, Harry wasn't the most popular person with the ASU either. Like many of the coaches who still lacked official recognition and support he'd had his own brushes with officialdom.

In the letter Harry urged me to write I had asked if I was to be banned from all Australian teams in the future. It was never made completely clear whether I was or wasn't banned forever; it was just left hanging there for me to wonder about. The response to my letter was not sent to me; instead it came in the form of a press release issued by the side of the pool on the last night of the championships when I was about to swim in my favourite event, the 200 metres. I had made a statement the day before this public response to my letter was handed out to reporters on the pool deck.

I had said that if my letter wasn't accepted I would retire. Was that a mistake I wonder now? Is that what they wanted? In any case I learned the ASU's response from a particularly vindictive reporter who told me about the ban just before I went to the marshalling area to get ready to swim. The reporter even followed me into the women's changerooms where I'd fled to try to compose myself. I wondered what on earth the ASU was trying to do to me. I cried, I hit a wall, I tried to get myself together, and all the while this journalist pretended to comfort and support me.

Just a few moments later I was back on the blocks and went on to win the 200 metres championship, creating a Queensland record. There was no way I was going to let anyone see that they'd got to me. I may have been unsure about how to handle the matter away from the pool but in the water I knew exactly what to do. The crowd was right behind me that night, which once again shows that I had public support, in contrast to ongoing official disapproval. When I first appeared on the blocks I was given a long ovation by the crowd and one of the timekeepers came up and kissed me. That night I accepted my medal and a trophy from the President of the ASU, Mr Ive Hicks. I can't believe I even congratulated him on becoming President in an acceptance speech. Looking back I'd say that I was showing the courtesy I'd been trained to show, that I didn't want to reveal my hurt even though I was fighting back tears, and I was also a bit confused about what had gone on. Later I went to a journalists party attended by all those who had written about me and my troubles that week. I turned the other cheek, purposely greeted everyone cheerily and showed that I was fine.

I wasn't fine, though. I had won the 100 metres freestyle, the 200 metres freestyle and the 400 metres freestyle at the National Championships but I returned to Adelaide crushed by what felt like a witch-hunt. By the end of the Nationals the team for Japan had been announced, and even though they'd asked for me specifically and sent me a personal invitation, I couldn't go. My future was uncertain. I wondered if I would swim for Australia again. An unnamed 'senior official' from the ASU was quoted in several papers, including the *Sydney Morning Herald* on February 28th, 1961, as saying, 'Dawn will never make another overseas trip.' No one had told me that officially but of course I took notice of the comment. Mr Herraman from the South Australian Swimming Association, on the other hand, was reported as saying he didn't think the ban really applied to any trips other than the immediate ones and, further, he queried why the ban had been imposed then, six months after the incident it related to. The SASA also called for a report from the ASU about the issue. I wondered if I should make good on my promise and retire. When I returned to Adelaide a crowd had gathered to greet me and when I walked out into the airport lounge they sang 'For She's a Jolly Good Fellow'. That really touched me and even made me teary: a hero to the public and a pariah to the ASU.

Meanwhile the debate continued about whether I had been treated fairly or unfairly. Much of the press was in support of me, describing the ASU and Roger Pegram's report in particular as 'vindictive'. A Labor senator in South Australia asked the Federal Treasurer in Parliament if an Olympic swimmer with the fastest times had been excluded from a team that was touring internationally on government grants due to a 'petty official protest'. The Federal Treasurer responded through another minister that the government would not intervene.

Gradually I got myself back into training and that felt good. The water came to my rescue again and I thought I'd probably keep training for my State and enter the Nationals for South Australia. I didn't know what else to do at the time but I didn't really want to give in and give the ASU the satisfaction of my retirement. I still felt I could win again in Tokyo if only I was given the chance.

7

GOODBYE POP,
HELLO ME

At the beginning of 1961 I found myself unexpectedly back at square one, watching while my swimming friends toured overseas and wondering if I would ever be part of an Australian team again. By the end of 1961 I was just glad to see the end of what would have to be one of my worst years ever. The Queen used the phrase *annus horribilis* many years later but I desperately needed it at that time.

I was deeply frustrated and hurt but uppermost in my mind was proving myself by being the best swimmer they had ever seen. I kept thinking that if I could just be so, so, so good they could never leave me out again. I had realised there was no point in pursuing the ASU officials for answers about my future because they were untouchable and there was no way of breaking into their inner sanctum. It felt then, as it has often felt through my career, that many of the officials were in it for themselves and not for the swimmers. Not a single person from the ASU spoke to me directly from the end of the Rome Games to the end of the following year, even though I was going through a major crisis, so I reached the stage where I could no longer be bothered with any of them.

I resumed all of my usual activities in Adelaide but with little enthusiasm. It was a grind to keep training but I did it because I just wasn't prepared to let go. This wasn't a very positive approach but it kept the fire and the hunger alive. I could even see the funny side of drawing incentive from the ASU's disapproval and apparent desire to rub me out altogether. If only they'd known. Harry and I discussed whether I'd give it up or keep going, and he quizzed me about what I was doing with my life as far as marriage and Ken were concerned. It was a rare time of self-reflection for me. Up until then I'd really lived day to day, with major swim meets and the next Olympic Games the only goals.

I still had my very good friends around me and in late April we went to a ball at the Adelaide Town Hall. My partner for the evening was the South Australian swimmer Kim Aunger. After the ball all sixteen of us who had gone together agreed to meet at the coffee lounge where I sometimes worked in Norwood, just a short drive away. Kim drove an MG sports car and when we pulled up across the road from the coffee shop we had to wait for a parking spot to come up. When a car finally pulled out, Kim did a U-turn and parked. The next thing we knew, a police car had pulled alongside. The police officer asked to see Kim's licence and then told him he'd been clocked driving over the speed limit at 80 miles per hour up another street, travelling in a different direction to the coffee shop in Norwood. When he tried to explain where we'd been and that we hadn't been anywhere near Burnside Avenue, the street in question, he was told to keep quiet. I then got out of the car wearing my ballgown and asked if I could help but was also told to keep quiet and to get back in the car. I knew very well that we hadn't been anywhere near where they'd clocked the speeding car, so I continued to stand my ground.

The young policeman, who was fast losing control of the situation, said that if I didn't get back in the car and keep quiet he'd take me in and charge me. By then Kim was also out of the car, so I took his arm and started to move towards the coffee shop. Once again I was told by the young policeman that if I didn't obey his instructions I would be charged. I was still explaining that he'd mixed us up with somebody else when he lost his patience and grabbed my arm, telling me I was being arrested for 'loitering', an antiquated charge that is no longer used. Kim protested but it was too late. I told him to contact his parents and explain what had happened and was then escorted to the patrol car. Down at the City Watchhouse I was formally charged, fingerprinted and photographed before being shown to a cell containing a number of homeless women and working girls. It was absolutely terrifying, dirty and cold. One old love kept asking me what I was in for. I had surrendered my jewellery and shoes but was still wearing my strapless gown, its wide petticoat underneath making it look even more ridiculous in a prison cell. When I contemplated how all of this would be reported in the press and what my poor parents would make of it I became very distressed, although I was also still fuming at the injustice of it. I hated being locked up and can still remember the awful feeling of having no escape. Eventually after two hours I was allowed to see Kim. He hadn't been able to contact his parents but he told me that bail was being arranged. I was finally released in the early hours of the morning, by which time the police were backpedalling and saying a mistake had been made.

Kim and I drove to join his parents, who were away waterskiing for the weekend on the Murray, and they were very supportive and pretty concerned about what had happened to us. I appeared in court the next day, Monday, represented by a Queen's Council, some security officers from the old Charles Birks store, which was by then David Jones, and some officials from the South Australian Swimming Association. Just walking into court knowing what people must be thinking and saying was a terrible ordeal in itself. The case was immediately dismissed and apologies flowed. Don Dunstan, then the MP for Norwood, called for a full investigation into the incident in Parliament and the Premier, Sir Thomas Playford, also spoke in support of me, pointing out that I had already suffered enough criticism elsewhere. Still, the damage had been done. Mum and Pop were very upset and I had to call and explain the whole episode. Once again I was defending myself against rumours and gossip over which I had no control and found myself wishing for a more private life. Fortunately I was able to escape the next day to a swimming carnival in Alice Springs for the National Heart Foundation and so kept out of the way till the fuss died down.

By the middle of the year Pop had become very sick with lung cancer, although I don't recall anyone saying the actual words until later. I figured if I wasn't needed to swim for my country I was certainly needed at home, so I packed my bags and flew to Sydney in May, planning on a long down season so I could spend as much time as possible with Pop. During that time Kenny and I agreed to end our engagement. There had been phone calls in the intervening months but no really close contact. I hadn't felt I could turn to Ken when I'd been banned, so there didn't really seem to be any point in continuing with the engagement. My heart at that time was with Pop, as well as with Mum who was nursing him around the clock. Pop wouldn't consent to being put in the lounge room because he saw it as a sign of weakness, so Mum had to walk up and down the narrow stairs whenever he needed anything. I really wanted to be there to share some of that load.

Pop was in nappies by the time I arrived back in Sydney because he'd lost control of his bowels and he needed changing quite often. It was very demeaning for such a tough, proud man, as well as very sad for us. The first time I went to change his nappy we had a big fight and he kept saying, 'You're not bloody well seeing me.' I'd never seen my father in less than his quite substantial underwear. I said, 'Don't worry, Dad, I'm a swimmer and I've seen these before.' He looked at me and started laughing and I promised I wouldn't look. After a month or so he became used to me nursing him and changing him and it really helped Mum get some sleep.

As Alick was still at home he'd do all the heavy work around the house, and once a week Nurse Walker came up from the hospital to give Mum a break. Although I didn't know it at the time, because she kept it from me, Mum had had a mild heart attack in the back garden a few years earlier, and Mrs Baker next door was always telling me that I should look after her because she was very tired. We were all doing it tough and the atmosphere in the house was very different from how it had been just a year earlier as we celebrated on the night before I left for Rome.

Pop and I chatted often during those months. I told him how I was thinking of giving the swimming away. We talked about the terrible rumours that were swirling around me and how the ASU seemed to have it in for me. Pop didn't think I should quit swimming because, like me, he saw it as giving in. He told me that if I gave up now I'd be playing into their hands instead of making my own decisions about my life. He said I'd been raised to be strong and tough, and he repeated his earlier advice that while they were talking about me they were leaving some other poor bugger alone and that I was someone who could handle it. I hoped I could handle it.

Pop also told me he was pleased Ken and I had separated and confided that he'd never thought Ken was really right for me, although he'd wanted me to be happy. I found those chats very comforting. It had been a long time since I'd spoken with Pop daily about my life and the decisions I was making.

I think I changed a little bit deep inside in 1961 and certainly I started to grow up. Pop said they'd always try to knock the champions off their pedestals but I couldn't see any other champions being knocked down. I became distrustful and a bit angry. I was angry with Harry for not protecting me, angry that Pop was unwell, angry that I wasn't with the Australian swim team after all my records. And I was lonely, too. My engagement had broken up partly because I'd been out pursuing my career, and now my career appeared to be finished and here I was back at home. As much as I loved my parents, I wondered where I was going with my life.

In August the Victorian Winter Championships were held in Melbourne and someone from my club in Adelaide had entered me to swim. Unfortunately they hadn't checked with Harry or me first and didn't know I'd taken time off to be with my family. I was widely criticised by the media for not showing up when so many members of the public had come to see me swim. Once again no one called me to hear my side of the story. I let it slide because I was too concerned about Pop and my family to worry about such a silly incident but I was beginning to feel my life was being invented by the media and I had no say in what was being reported.

At the beginning of the new season I went back to Adelaide and resumed training with Harry. I'd been ready to throw in the towel but my parents were so persuasive during my stay in Balmain that by September I was feeling extremely determined. And what I didn't have going for me in my head, Harry made up for by tricking me and coaxing me along. He was a great one for psychological games.

Amazingly, the South Australian Swimming Association managed to organise a trip to New Zealand for me later in the year. The ASU were not happy but agreed to allow me to accept the invitation from the New Zealand officials as long as it was clear to everyone that I was representing the State and not my country. I was to make the trip with Nola Shepherd, a South Australian breaststroke swimmer, with her mother as chaperone.

I went to Melbourne in October to train at the Olympic Pool and at the Richmond Baths because it was still so cold in Adelaide. I was craving the company of people I knew well, so I stayed with my dear friend Adele and her husband Brian. I went to a party one night while I was there and drank quite a bit of wine. It was something I hardly ever did because I was a beer drinker, and I soon became quite drunk. A guy I met at the party took me back to a hotel room, and I don't remember much at all except that when I woke up he was gone. These days it would be called date rape but back then it was my fault for having put myself in such a vulnerable position. I was very scared and pretty disgusted with myself because I'd always been so very careful and had never gone all the way sexually before. I worried myself stupid about the incident and also felt terribly used and angry. I had been completely out of control and I didn't like the feeling at all.

When I returned to Adelaide before the New Zealand trip I was very low and Harry immediately sensed something was wrong. My training was poor, whereas I'd been doing well before I left. I didn't even want to go to New Zealand any more. Then I missed a period. I finally went to see a doctor and he suggested we wait another week before rushing to conclusions but he told me I should tell my parents. Of course I couldn't tell Mum and Pop after all their warnings and my strict upbringing, so I told Harry. He was very supportive, as I'd thought he would be, and didn't lecture me, knowing that I was already going through enough grief. We went back to the doctor and a test was done just before I flew off to New Zealand.

The trip to New Zealand was very busy and that kept my mind off my problems. We were feted by the Maoris and I was made an honorary princess of a tribe in Rotorua. I remained friends with one of their real princesses, Princess Raui, and we played golf together in later years. Nola and I then went to Auckland and Dunedin and I set a New Zealand 110 yards record at 61.9 seconds. We swam, gave talks and posed for photographs everywhere we went. Then just before the end of the trip Harry sent me a cable to say the pregnancy test was positive and I should return home immediately. I used Pop's illness as an excuse and left. On the way back to Adelaide I stopped in Sydney for a day to give Mum and Pop an enormous Christmas ham I'd been given just before leaving New Zealand. Then it was straight back on the plane to meet Harry. He already had a doctor organised so I took off once again for Melbourne to have an abortion. It went against every instinct I had and I did seriously think about going ahead with the pregnancy. I'd always wanted children and I had a bit of a fantasy that I could keep this baby. But deep down I knew it would be impossible, and the public attention unbearable. Coming from my background, good girls went quietly away and put their babies up for adoption without anyone knowing. How could I have done that quietly even if I'd wanted to?

I can still see the terrace house in Little Collins Street where I'd been told to go. I was all alone and quite scared. I had to be there early in the morning and I remember the humiliation of having my feet in stirrups and knowing I was doing this terrible, wicked thing. I would have loved to talk to Mum about it but that was simply out of the question. The procedure was completely clinical. There was no counselling or cups of tea and sympathy. I was in and out. There were no instructions for after care, either. I had to get straight back on a plane, because Harry was picking me up at the airport and taking me back to his place, and I had an enormous rush of blood at the airport just before boarding. I was very ill on the plane and felt appalling back in Adelaide. The whole episode had been horrific but I tried not to dwell on it afterwards. I felt I'd made the right decision, and tried to comfort myself with the thought that one day I would marry and have children.

I was to face something far worse when I returned to Sydney for Christmas. I knew that Pop was dying and there wasn't long to go. I sat upstairs on his bed all Christmas Day and talked to him. My brothers and sisters had all spent time with him while I had been away in Adelaide and now they were giving me my turn. Pop was drifting in and out of consciousness that day. I knew I had to go back to Adelaide that night but I didn't want to leave a minute earlier than I had to. We talked over the events of our lives, and I thanked him for being a good father and told him I was proud of him for hanging in there. As always, he encouraged me to keep swimming and never to let them know they'd hurt me.

By the time I got back to the baths Harry was on the phone telling me Dad had died, and so on Boxing Day I caught the next flight out to Sydney. I was immediately grateful that I'd spent the previous day with him, and I wasn't angry he'd been taken away from me because he'd been so very, very sick and it was a release for him and for Mum. He'd been going downhill for thirteen years and I said to Mum it was a blessing that he wasn't suffering any more. But to this day my heart lurches every time I see a photo of my father and I try to make sure I'm travelling somewhere or at least very busy on Boxing Day.

•

Even though years don't get much worse than 1961, I did get a nice surprise towards the end when I received an award from the Helms Foundation in the US. Each year it presents awards to the six most outstanding athletes on each of the six continents around the world. I was the 1961 Australasian winner in recognition of my world records that year in the 100 and 200 metres freestyle, and my second fastest time over 400 metres. I joined Lorraine Crapp and Fanny Durack as one of only three Australian women to win the award.

With all that had gone on during the year I wasn't up to much at the State Championships in January. I did my job and won each of my swims without breaking any records. Mum had come back with me to Adelaide for a holiday and we went on together to Melbourne for the Nationals. She stayed with our good friends the Rainsburys in Richmond—my hotel room was too small, too hot, and I was getting up at 4.00 every morning—but each night I would join her there for dinner.

During the Nationals I broke the Australian record for the number of championships won by a woman. By the end of the meet I had twenty in my bag, beating the previous record of eighteen. I also returned to butterfly. This probably seems odd, given my earlier refusal to swim it, but Harry was encouraging me to include it in my training repertoire again and I found I was able to cope with the stroke at national level, although I was never going to contest it on an international stage. I won the butterfly and also my sixth 110 yards freestyle sprint at a National Championship. What I didn't manage, despite my serious attempt to do so, was to swim the 110 yards in under a minute. Harry and I had asked permission to contest it in the 4 x 110 yards relay on the last night of the championships, because by swimming first with the starter's gun my swim could be officially timed. Leading up to that swim I had a typical piece of bad luck when I fell getting out of the pool during a training session and severely strained my back. I kept my injury quiet so people wouldn't think I was using it as an excuse and still swam on the last night but once again I didn't manage to come in under the elusive minute.

The first time I remember talking seriously about being the first woman to break the minute was with Ricksie during our preparation for Rome in Townsville, although Harry and I had thought about it for longer. It started out as banter after training, gradually developed into a more serious philosophical talk about how it could be done, and then it became part of my training, with Harry's ever-helpful advice along the way. After a while it became a quiet obsession for me and was one of the things that kept me interested in swimming during 1961 when I couldn't travel overseas. At one stage Chrysler South Australia even loaned me a car with the numberplate 59.999. But no matter what car I drove, how hard I tried or what advice Harry gave me, breaking the minute continued to elude me.

Early in 1962 I decided I wanted a change in my life. So much had happened in the previous year and I finally decided that a move from Adelaide to Melbourne would do me the world of good. My enthusiasm was fading again and I thought a new start would freshen things up for me. In some ways I didn't feel as close to Harry any more. I felt I didn't need his advice as much and that he was preoccupied with his own life and his marriage. I suppose some part of me was jealous, and I was still hurting from the ban and the business about the swim in Switzerland. I'd been tied to Harry for many years and had alternately worshipped him, been disappointed in him, loved him, had a crush on him, been frustrated to the point of fury with him, and finally I was ready to break away and get on with my life. I had grown up a lot since those days at Drummoyne. It has always been reported that I followed Harry to Melbourne when he took up the coaching rights at a new pool, part of a sports complex owned by a man called Bill Appleton, but in fact I was planning to move on anyway. I intended to train at the Olympic Pool, which had been opened to the public, and at the heated Richmond Baths. That Harry took up coaching at Appletons Pool was a bonus but I'd already made

The Australian team entering the MCG for the opening of the Melbourne Olympic Games, 1956.
I am in the second row.

Taking a photograph of the Duke of Edinburgh on Harry's camera as he arrives for lunch during the Melbourne Games. Faith Leech is behind the chef.

With Betty Cuthbert in the Olympic village.

Dale Krieg, Adele Price and myself showing the Italian cyclists around the Olympic village, 1956.

Me and Harry after winning my first gold medal in 1956.

Serving in
Charles Birks,
Adelaide.

Perfecting my dive at the Adelaide Baths.

Doing our winter workout at the Adelaide City Baths.

At Tobruk Memorial Pool, Townsville, 1956

Adelaide City Baths.

Adelaide picnic, 1956.

Being a bridesmaid for girlfriend Dawn Hart, Sydney, late 1950s.

Ilsa Konrads, myself and Lorraine Crapp in Holland during our European trip following the Cardiff Games, 1958.

With Harry Gallagher, Adelaide, 1958.

With Harry and Ricksie, Townsville, 1960.

Cutting the cake at my 21st birthday at the Balmain Institute, 1958, surrounded by (L-R) Ilsa Konrads, Sandra Morgan and Beverley Bainbridge.

The Australian Swimming Team, Tobruk Memorial Pool, Townsville, August 1964.
I'm on the lowest step in sunglasses.

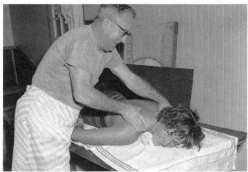

With Stumpy Lawrence, 1964.

odelling swimwear, Townsville Beach, 1960. Arch
aley wanted 'different' shots of the swimmers!

Time trials, Tobruk Pool, 1964.

With my gold medal and white tracksuit at the Rome Olympics, 1960. The medal was presented by John Morrison (centre), an Australian swimming official.

Modelling my new white tracksuit in Townsville.

With Harry Gallagher (right) and some of Harry's friends in Holland after the Rome Games.

the move to be among good friends. It worked out well because while I continued to train under Harry I also had a new, more independent life.

By officially contesting my record in the 110 yards freestyle at the Nationals I had again come into contact with the ASU, and somehow it gradually became evident that I would have a chance to be part of the Australian squad going to the Commonwealth Games in Perth later in 1962. In retrospect it seems strange that nothing was ever said, but at the time that's how it was all done. I'd found out about the ban through the media and now the lifting of the ban had happened in an almost haphazard way: no official announcement or letter, just a general feeling that everything was once again all right.

I wrote to the ASU to see if I could work while I was training in Townsville for the Games but was told I couldn't and that in any case I was already being paid two pounds fifty shillings per week by them and that should be enough. After that I decided not to head north to train with the rest of the squad. I didn't have enough money to afford any level of comfort because I had bills to pay, such as my rent, plus Harry had decided not to go that year either. He objected to the way the boys and girls were going to be segregated up there and he also had his pool to run. Harry believed we could do just as well in the heated pool in Melbourne so we stayed behind and trained towards the October trials for the Commonwealth Games on our own. My sights were just as much set on breaking the minute as they were on getting to Perth and doing well. In the end, though, it was Tokyo that I really had in mind.

I began working at the new Myer store in Chadstone as a saleswoman when I arrived in Melbourne. As this had been my training at Charles Birks (later David Jones) in Adelaide, I continued with this sort of work when I arrived in my new home town. In 1963, when the Queen and Prince Philip docked in Melbourne on the

Royal Yacht *Britannia*, I was one of those lucky enough to be invited to lunch onboard, and I shopped at Myer with Mum for a nice two-piece linen suit to wear for the occasion. The After 5 buyer helped me choose it and, if I remember rightly, the suit was given to me by Myer. It was exciting not only for me but for everyone around me.

My most vivid memory of that day is of standing a little anxiously in the library cum drawing room on the royal yacht, talking to various people who had also been invited along. In one corner lined with wonderful history books there was also a baby grand piano, which really impressed me. While I was looking at the books, the Queen came into the room, and after greeting a few people she came up to me and we talked for about fifteen minutes. We talked about her history books, and she told me about her experiences during the war when she was driving trucks, and how once she'd got a flat tyre and had to change it in heavy rain in waist-deep mud. She mentioned that all the trucks were run on methane gas and I told her about the mine in Birchgrove and the methane gas supplied from there. I thought she was tremendous. After we'd finished chatting and just before we were called in to lunch, Dame Patti Menzies, the wife of the then Prime Minister, came up to me and began telling me loudly not to forget my manners. She asked if I knew how to use a knife and fork and said she hoped I'd be all right. I felt like giving her a piece of my mind but assured her I had been trained very nicely by my mother and father, thank you, although sometimes we just used our fingers. There it was again, the double life: invited to dine with the Queen in a select group and then looked down upon by petty people who felt they were better than I was. I didn't let her spoil my day, though. At lunch I was seated next to Prince Philip, who was aware of what Dame Patti had said to me in the library, and he gently sent her up by laboriously explaining in a mock-serious teaching voice that I should start from the outside and work my way in, and if we skipped a course I should also skip the cutlery. I had never cared for Menzies himself either after I'd learned about him selling our iron ore to the Japanese during World War II.

•

Back in training through the winter of 1962 it was sometimes bitterly cold, despite the heated pool. In the early mornings as I set out for Appletons I had to wash the ice off the windscreen with hot water before being able to drive. But I was gradually moving up on top of the water and feeling that I was getting into very good form. Harry had a new squad that year, mostly drawn from Melbourne, although there was one South African long-distance swimmer, Warwick Webster, who I paced myself against. It was never the same as with Ricksie because he wasn't a sprinter for a start and not as much fun, but, to be brutal, he served his purpose in training. He was less than 1 second faster than me on every lap, and less than 14 seconds faster over a quarter of a mile, so it worked out well. We continued with our weights and pulleys all through winter and when the squad was given a five-mile swim I would adjust mine to, say, seven miles, and so on.

When I first moved to Melbourne I lived with my good friends Adele and Brian at Mount Eliza before finding myself a one-bedroom flat at the back of a house in Clayton. It was very small but it was private and I had my own bathroom and my independence. There wasn't much social life because 4.00 a.m. starts don't allow for it, and though I'd go to the movies or have a barbecue occasionally with Adele, Brian and a few others, I was leading a fairly solitary life and certainly didn't have a boyfriend. The events of the previous year were still fresh in my mind and I was content to run along at my own pace.

When the other swimmers returned to Melbourne for the Commonwealth Games trials in October they were no fitter than we were. They were certainly browner but that was about the only edge they had over us, which showed that Harry had been right about us getting on better by staying where we were. During the week of the trials I was determined to break the minute in one of a series of 110s we'd be swimming at the Melbourne Olympic Pool. I went out hard and fast on the first night and came in dead on the minute, breaking the records for yards and metres. Harry hadn't timed me because he was so excited but I was just left feeling flat because I'd been sure I would be under.

I didn't break the minute on the next trial night either, and had more or less decided I would never break it. But Harry kept urging me to hang on because I was so close, truly believing I would break it soon. He told me to concentrate on my starts and turns and advised me to go out with my friends, have a few drinks and relax. So I did.

Then, towards the end of the week, I arrived at the pool and told Harry I felt dejected; that although I was at a physical peak I wasn't mentally right. Harry said, 'Well in that case, just have a swim and enjoy it. Forget about the minute tonight.' Then he chatted to me, preparing me for the race, and I got in the pool and warmed up. He asked me again how I was feeling and I said, 'Pretty sick, actually. I'm not going to swim well tonight.' I felt agitated, so I got out and put on a dry pair of bathers and sat around until the event was called. Once again Harry urged me just to enjoy myself, reassuring me that he really didn't expect a fast time from me. He knew I'd be in the team with the times I was doing anyway so there wasn't any pressure.

I got a very good start, which is what we'd been working on, and I was swimming down the first 55 yards thinking how great I felt. I was enjoying the race and then I just did an ordinary turn and pushed off thinking, 'Oh, I might swim a little bit faster now.' I didn't think I was really going for it and then about 25 yards out I could hear the roar of the crowd. I could hear whistling and I could see everyone standing up, going a bit crazy. Then I wondered if I could go a little bit faster and I put on a sprint for the last 25 yards. When I put my head up I couldn't believe the noise. I looked over at the timekeepers but I wasn't supposed to be told until it was announced, so I looked for Harry as usual and he was at the other end of the pool mouthing, 'You've done it! You've done it!' and tapping his watch. Then a timekeeper kindly came over and said, 'You've broken the minute.' It felt like the easiest swim I had done in my life. Relaxing and enjoying the moment had paid off.

The announcement was: 'It's official, Dawn. You've done it.' I'd swum it in 59.9, breaking my previous world records over yards and metres and becoming the first woman in the world to break the minute over the 100 metres distance. I was unofficially timed even faster but the recognised time was 59.9. I was in shock really. The goal had eluded me for so long and when I'd finally done it, it had felt so simple, so easy, so perfect. When the reality sank in I felt elated and proud that the years of training had paid off in that way. The press asked me what I was going to do that night and I made some flippant comments about having a few beers, something for which I was later chastised by the ASU, who didn't think it was quite the thing to say. As it happened I did have a couple of beers back at the Rainsburys' place with Mum. I celebrated quietly with friends and went to bed to prepare for the rest of the trials the next day. It has often been intimated that I was a wild party animal who would go out carousing after every swimming triumph, but anyone who knows the effort that goes into swimming at that level will know that it doesn't go hand in hand with Olympic-style drinking.

Later that night I broke the minute again in the relay in an even faster time, and from then on I never looked back and my swimming began to improve more and more. I decided that night that I would go on with my career; I would be the best and I would go to Tokyo. I think what happens is that when you try very hard for something you throw your timing out, and then when you relax, as I did on that last swim, your timing falls beautifully into place. You're no longer worried about your start and your tumble-turn as you pull through the water so easily. The water opened up for me that night.

I now knew I would be in the Australian team for the Perth Commonwealth Games, and even back then I was cynical about the ban being lifted just in time for a major international competition. I felt then, and I certainly do now, that the ASU had their eye on gold medals and saw me as one of the people who could go out and get them for Australia. So with no official statement about the ban being lifted I was brought back from the fringe and placed on the team. I'd served my time, I'd missed out on my overseas trips, I'd paid the penalty for disobeying Roger Pegram's instructions, and I was back. I'd also started a new life and I was feeling happy both with myself and my world as I headed to Perth.

•

In early 1963 I was teaching swimming to blind children from a local school on a voluntary basis and I began taking them to a new sports complex called Squashways. I had asked Bill, the Manager of the complex, if we could have a little bit of space a few times a week and he allowed me to rope off a bit of the pool for the lessons. The nuns who ran the school would sit on the side and keep an eye on the kids while I taught them to swim. Eventually Bill asked me if I'd like to organise the schedules for all the sports facilities in the complex. It was a job that suited me well and offered quite good money. My name and success was important to them and in turn the job would give me the flexibility to train through the day. It meant leaving Myer but I was excited by the idea of a new direction in work. Unfortunately the spectre of professionalism raised its head again when I was warned by the Victorian Amateur Swimming Association, to which I now belonged, that my name could not be linked with commercial ventures. My name was removed from my office door and I was very careful not to let my amateur status be threatened by anything Squashways did.

The complex included the pool, squash courts, trampolines, ten-pin bowling and table tennis. One of my roles was to encourage local schools to use the facilities, and for the first time I began to use my name and profile to promote something for commercial gain; not my gain, mind you, but that of the centre. I built the business up quite quickly and had many classes running on Saturday mornings.

Ever since seeing and hearing myself on TV and radio after the 1956 Games I had cringed at my speaking voice and the way I presented myself to the media. To be accurate, I didn't present or control myself at all; I just said whatever was on the tip of my tongue. I didn't like my delivery—my voice seemed rough and a little bit squeaky—but I'd never had a chance to do anything about it. Now that I was going around to schools speaking to groups of teachers about Squashways, Bill suggested I take some elocution lessons. He said that if in the future I wanted to make the most of being a prominent athlete I should learn to speak properly—in this he was ahead of his time.

Mrs May Hoben, a wonderful lady in her early eighties, gave lessons in a studio in the city. I was terribly nervous the first day I climbed that flight of stairs to her door because this was so out of the ordinary for me. All my life I had been a physical person who felt at home around the pool, football grounds and gymnasiums. I had absorbed many things about manners, mixing in society and the arts but I hadn't consciously worked on changing something about myself before. The idea of setting myself apart from my upbringing and shaping myself by changing my voice and my manner was still a rather uncomfortable notion.

I liked May Hoben almost immediately. I had always enjoyed the company of old people, ever since my days running for Lenny in Balmain, and May was very kind to me. I was fascinated by her poise. You could feel her presence as soon as she walked into a room, and that's what I wanted to learn from her. As soon as I heard her velvety voice I knew she had something to teach me that could be very valuable in the future. And I knew that if I were to continue to be successful and walk on the world stage, I had to learn to present myself appropriately.

May Hoben was a significant person in my life, even though I didn't take lessons for very long. Even now it is difficult to put my finger on exactly what she did for me. Certainly she taught me how to speak into a microphone, how to project my voice and how to be calm when speaking; but more than that, it was with May Hoben that I first realised there was an inner life. Until then I had been all on the surface, rushing about, being a lair, trying not to show my emotions or my pain and trying not to cry. May encouraged me to look inside and use my emotions to read Shakespeare and poetry. She told me I was a person of quality with presence when I didn't really believe I was either of those things, and she told me I could learn how to harness these aspects of myself.

May would sit at the back of a darkened room and I would sit under a single spotlight and read and speak. She could open the black curtains and let in the daylight or she could close them so tightly you truly felt you were entirely alone in the room until you heard her commanding voice from the back. For the first time, at the ripe old age of twenty-five, I was facing a part of myself that I had covered over and ignored all my life. It was just me and May calmly talking about what I had inside. It was quite different from swimming training, where it was important to get tougher and ignore the pain by swimming faster. The only pain I had acknowledged until that point was the pain that I felt in the last 25 metres of a race. To deal with that I just trained harder. Now I was being encouraged to be softer and seek out inner emotions and pain to express myself. It was a complete revelation about who I was as a human being. It was also the first time I had found solitude, and I liked it. At times May Hoben may as well have been absent, because I was having a brand new conversation with a voice inside that I had never listened to up until that point. These emotions I was allowing to flow were entirely different to the emotions I felt on a swimming block or a winner's podium. They were about me the person, not the swimmer.

May taught me why feelings would well up inside me when I was speaking in public and how I needed to be in touch with my emotions if I wanted to be able to control them. She explained why I didn't have to be boisterous or a lair to cover shyness and why I didn't always have to be the life of the party in order to be liked. Perhaps all this sounds very wishy-washy, but those weeks with May Hoben were electrifying and they seemed to wake me from a very, very long sleep.

On the practical side, I was given exercise books to follow and each week I was taped doing my lessons, so that by week ten I was able to read various pieces of literature and drama onto the tape and hear the changes that had taken place since the first week. By the end of my time with May it all came out very easily and I was amazed at the difference. She told me I had been one of her best pupils, and I remember being thrilled that such an important lady had given me so much time. She assured me that from then on people would notice me when I walked into a room or spoke, and while I don't think that has actually happened I do know that since then I have had more confidence in public and in speaking.

•

It has been reported that I underwent an operation in early 1963 that prevented me from attending the Nationals in Perth, but in fact I didn't swim that year for completely different reasons. The first was that I couldn't take the time off work, and besides that I had only just returned from the Commonwealth Games in Perth a couple of months earlier. My life was very settled in Melbourne by then and I was reluctant to interrupt it for a national meet in a non-Olympic year. On the face of it this may seem selfish, but I had devoted years to attending such competitions. My priorities at the time were to continue steady training, earn enough money to pay my bills, and aim for Tokyo in 1964. As much as it is important to be part of a team and work within an organised framework, it is also important in swimming at an elite level to be focused and self-contained; to set your own goals and program to succeed. I had also developed a bit of an attitude that if the ASU could drop me at will I too would make up my own mind about where and when I would swim.

Around that time in my life I was awarded a trophy that meant an enormous amount to me, and still does. It was the Babe Zaharias Trophy, which is given annually to a woman athlete. I had just finished reading a book about the remarkable Babe Didrikson Zaharias, so the award was especially timely. For those who don't know of her, Babe Didrikson Zaharias was an amazing American athlete who was a brilliant golfer but also excelled at many other sports, including basketball, tennis, swimming, boxing and volleyball. When asked if there was anything she didn't play, she famously responded, 'Yeah, dolls.' Associated Press of America selects the recipient of the trophy and I was the first Australian ever to receive it. Babe's husband, George, sent me a very nice letter at the time, explaining that his wife had been voted Athlete of the Year many times by Associated Press but had never received an award, so just before she died from cancer in 1956 she founded her own. Like me, she'd had all sorts of accusations levelled at her for being too muscular and masculine, but she kept going because she loved to win at sport. She was also gritty and got people offside because she was so single-minded. I love having her award and it was a great encouragement back then because I could relate to Babe, who had always been regarded as a tomboy and had a lot of trouble finding a place to belong during her glory years. This, along with the Helms Award, was the beginning of my excellent relationship with the sporting world in the US; a better relationship, it must be said, than I enjoyed overall with Australia's sporting bodies and press at the time.

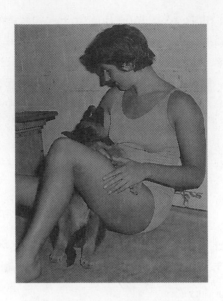

8

TWO SIMPLE
DECISIONS

How I loved to kick up and down the pool as the sun came up in the mornings during that wonderful summer of 1963. It was a golden time, my best season ever, with all my troubles seemingly behind me. At the Commonwealth Games in Perth I had won four gold medals. I was heading into another Olympic year and the prospect of my third Olympic Games, in Tokyo, was exhilarating. Maybe I would be the first swimmer ever to win a gold medal at three consecutive Olympics.

The bitter cold at the start of the season was subsiding. It had been tough, as usual. Green water, no goggles, no cap and long, slogging sessions that consisted of a slow warm-up mile, followed by a fast mile, followed by another slow one and so on. By the end of the year it was four miles per session three times a day, as well as full-time work at Squashways. It didn't feel like an effort, though, and I embraced the workload with relish. At least now wet hair after lunch wasn't a problem with my boss.

I knew that I was in for the hardest and most consistent training I had ever done. At twenty-seven I would be older than my competitors, and by any standard too old to be contesting sprints at an Olympic Games. The Victorian State Championships in December 1963 would help me gauge what sort of work I would need to do before the Nationals in Sydney the following February. I was confident of gaining a spot on the Olympic team but didn't want to become complacent.

Getting back to Sydney for the Nationals was a major incentive in itself, as I couldn't wait to be with Mum. We'd become much closer since Pop died and Mum was now following my career with an even greater interest, but I didn't return as often as I used to from Adelaide because my life away from home had begun to take more shape. So leading up to the State Championships it was up at 4.00 a.m. for a couple of slices of toast and a cup of black tea, then out the door for the first of the day's sessions. The pool was my friend all summer and a refuge from the customers at Squashways. I hadn't felt so joyful in the water for a very long time.

I cleaned up at the Victorian Championships, winning all titles from the 110 yards through to the 880 yards, which was not a swim I ever enjoyed. I would be in Sydney in eight weeks time and I even got on the old Al Capone and told Mum we were off to Tokyo. We'd agreed that if I made the team Mum would come to Tokyo with me on her first overseas holiday. It was a little early to be sure of a place, but my times had been so good at the State Championships that I couldn't wait to include Mum in the anticipation of the trip. I had saved some money and the whole family had agreed to pitch in and help too. Mum was ecstatic about the idea but, as usual, wanted to wait till she saw me to really talk about the trip—she always worried about the phone bill. Little did she know that lovely Doris at the exchange was still helping out with phone connections and making a three-minute charge for hour-long calls. I never knew your surname, but Doris, wherever you are, I thank you from the bottom of my heart for helping me keep in touch with my mum.

I flew to Sydney from Melbourne with the rest of the Victorian team for the Sydney Nationals. My best friend, Wendy, who I'd met while working at Myer in Chadstone, came with me for a holiday and to attend the Nationals. The team stayed at a hotel in Sydney called the Continental, although I would really have preferred to be with the family in Birchgrove.

At North Sydney Pool I again won the 110 yards sprint—my seventh national title in this event—in under a minute. My 58.9 was a world record at the time but I mostly remember the race for how nervous I felt before it and because I caught my fingernail in a small crack in the wall as I touched to turn for the second lap. I had seen the crack from the blocks and had been very conscious of needing to avoid it. It seemed to take an eternity for me to pull my finger free of the wall, and when I got to the end I couldn't believe the time that I'd done.

I also won the 440 yards swim in Olympic record time. I was definitely off to Tokyo and absolutely over the moon about the direction my life was taking.

Staying in Sydney after the Nationals I spent a few days catching up with family and friends. One night the Balmain Leagues Club put some dinner on for us and later we all went down to the Riverview for drinks. I went out sailing on the harbour on Sunday and then it was back to the Leagues Club that night for dinner. Most of my brothers and sisters and their partners came, as well as some of my football friends, Wendy and a couple of other girl friends I hadn't seen in quite a while. We'd had a big weekend and around 10.30 p.m. we were playing the poker machines when Mum asked me if I'd drive my sister Rose home to Kyeemagh, just south of Sydney Airport, because she hadn't been able to get a taxi. I had the use of a very long Plymouth sedan for the weekend, courtesy of an old family friend, Johnny Leach, who was a car salesman and always loaned me cars when I visited Sydney. Of course I agreed to drive Rose home, and Mum and Wendy came along to keep me company. It proved to be the worst decision of my life and one I will regret till the day I die.

We were travelling along General Holmes Drive, a main road that heads to the airport, when I suddenly saw a shape on the outside lane next to the kerb. I swerved to avoid whatever it was and just as I did Wendy yelled, 'Watch out, Dawn!' All I remember is the sound of metal on metal, screeching brakes and swirling lights. When I woke up I was in St George Hospital.

I was lying on a bed in Emergency when I heard someone saying, 'She was DOA.' I asked what that meant, and when they told me it meant 'dead on arrival' I asked who had died. A nurse said 'the older one.' I then told them that was my mum. They were shocked, because they hadn't been supposed to tell me and hadn't meant to break such terrible news like that, but they also hadn't realised it was my mother. It was all very confusing, but what I did understand before I was given a needle for the pain and to make me sleep was that my eldest sister, Rose, had been rushed into surgery, Mum was dead and my best friend was injured and undergoing an examination, all because of an accident in which I had been the driver.

When I awoke the next day I was in a state of shock. By then my brother Ken had arrived and was able to fill in some of the terrible details. In the bed next to me was Rose with severe facial injuries and concussion. There were lots of cuts and abrasions on her face and glass all through her hair. My friend Wendy was in the next bed with facial injuries, including a fractured nose. I had seriously damaged my spine at the neck. And Mum was gone forever. Poor Mum. Her life was over because of me.

On the second day in hospital I was moved to a room on my own because there were too many disturbances and the staff were concerned about Rose and Wendy. Flowers and cards kept arriving, messages were continually being relayed to me by nursing staff and various journalists were trying to make contact. Of course being in a room all alone made me even more miserable.

I was able to remember after a few days that we'd come around a sweeping curve and I had swerved to miss a table-top utility parked on the nearside kerb. Its owner said later he'd gone down the bank to fish at the nearby beach and that his parking lights had been left on. I hadn't seen the ute until the last second, and even then it had just looked like a shape in the darkness and I didn't register that it was a car. I definitely didn't see any rear or tail lights and believe to this day they weren't illuminated. But in the end it was the owner's word against mine because the Coronial Report concluded that it was impossible to tell whether or not his parking lights had been on. The back passenger side of my car had hit the ute and the tray had sliced into the car where my mother had been asleep and my sister Rose just dozing in the seat behind me. Wendy had been in front with me. Mum died from massive head injuries sustained in the accident.

Some of these things I remember, others I know from being told at the time, and the rest I've discovered from the Coronial Report on the inquest into my mother's death, which I read only recently, more than thirty years after the accident. It was the first time I could bring myself to do so.

What I do and don't know about the accident remains hazy, partly because of the concussion and shock I went into afterwards and partly, I believe, because the truth is sometimes too difficult to bear and becomes distorted over time. Immediately after the whole horrible tragedy things seemed surreal. I clung for years to the idea that Mum had died of a heart attack prior to the accident, which was something my family told me to help me through my grief, although it seems so unlikely when I really think about it. Until I decided to write this book and really examine the details of my life I had thought it was pouring with rain on the night of the accident because this is how I remember it more than three decades later. I now know from the report that it was a fine night. I know too that the lighting on the road where I hit the truck was completely inadequate, and that I had been doing no more than 40 miles per hour, which was well within the speed limit. My mother was a nervous passenger so I was in the habit of driving extra slowly and carefully when she was on board.

Back then people whispered quite loudly that I had been drinking, and I'm sure there will be those reading this now who will nod wisely and say the same. I had not in fact been drinking that night because I was planning to return to heavy training the next day. I did drink at times over that weekend of celebration, but as it drew to a close on Sunday night my thoughts had turned again to getting ready for the Olympic Games. There is no mention of reckless driving in the Coroner's report, and all the witness statements, including those of the police who attended the scene, concur that I had been driving carefully. On that night I had clung to the kerb lane because I was familiar with the extreme speed of much of the oncoming traffic on that road. My solicitor, Ted France, cast some doubt at the inquest over the condition of the truck I hit and suggested the lights and numberplate had possibly been obscured by dirt. Later I was told it was a truck for collecting scraps and garbage from restaurants to sell to pig farmers and that the truck was in a very dirty condition, although this is not mentioned in the report.

The inquest, which was held at the beginning of April, found that my mother's death had been due entirely to a very sad and unfortunate accident, and in an unusual but very comforting gesture the Coroner, Mr John Loomes, extended the sympathy of the court, which is recorded in the Coronial Report:

> Mr France, may I through you extend to the party you represent, Miss Fraser, the sympathy of all associated with this Court on this tragic accident, so very tragic when the victim is one's mother.
>
> Your client has earned respect and admiration for her deeds as an Olympic representative of the Commonwealth of Australia, and I'm sure she will find comfort and solace in the thought that she has the sincerest sympathies of a host of people throughout the Commonwealth she has so worthily represented.

Wendy had been my very close friend since we'd met at Myer. In fact, I was as close to Wendy at that time as I was to anyone. She was a few years younger than me and came from a very wealthy family who had kindly taken me into their lives. I often stayed with them at their city home and their beach house, and ate at their house just about every week. I loved being with them and especially liked Wendy's younger sister, Zelda, who was a really fiery little redheaded kid. A whole bunch of us used to hang around together, including Adele, Brian, and some of the other girls from Myer and their partners, and we had some great times as a group.

Two days after the accident Wendy's father stormed into the ward Wendy was sharing with Rose and demanded that Wendy be moved. He was extremely angry and wouldn't talk to Rose or me. He completely blamed me for what had happened to Wendy and wouldn't let me give him my account of the accident, and he didn't even express sympathy for Rose and me, though we'd lost our mother and also had serious injuries. Wendy was moved, and I never saw her or heard from anyone in her family again, except for her younger sister who said she hated what had happened and was very sorry about my mother. To this day I have no idea what Wendy has done with her life or what happened after the accident, except that it hurt like hell to lose her from my life. I do understand her father's reaction, though. It must have been a terrible shock to find his daughter lying there covered in cuts and bruises and with her nose in plaster. Wendy's statement made immediately after the accident and tendered at the inquest into my mother's death makes it clear she felt I was driving at a normal speed at the time of the accident and concurs that she too saw the ute only suddenly.

I didn't become bitter about Wendy and her family, although I'm sad our friendship finished like that. I knew that if I did I would be harming myself even more. I also had my brothers and sisters around me insisting I get on with my life and my own recovery. It was terrible for them to have lost their mother but they never showed me anything but support and love. They knew what I was going through with my own grief and my guilt. It took several weeks for me to recover enough to leave the hospital, but I find it difficult to list my own injuries because they were absolutely nothing compared to the loss of my mother. Even now I feel selfish talking about what happened to me, but it's necessary to do so in order to explain the recovery that followed. Basically, three vertebrae in my neck were severely damaged and it was thought at the time that the only reason my neck wasn't broken was because of my strong neck muscles. I couldn't turn my head without searing pain. As well, my knees had been forced up under the dashboard in the accident and their ligaments were torn and strained. They still trouble me and sometimes cause me a lot of pain. Swimming was the furthest thing from my mind while I lay in hospital, and half the newspapers had me written off anyway. On the other hand a great many people were exceptionally kind and concerned as the steady stream of cards and flowers showed. There were literally hundreds of bunches of flowers and thousands of cards from all over the world. The only visitors allowed in were family.

I was told I would have to wear a neck brace for some time, maybe up to six months, and I thought, 'So what? My mother is dead, my sister is injured and I've lost my best friend.' I would have gladly worn a neck brace for life if it would change the fortune of these other people I cared so much about. I was the lucky one. Rosie and Wendy were to have more surgery for their facial injuries.

The news about the neck brace combined with my deep sadness led me to believe that I would not swim again and I couldn't have cared less. I did not, however, suffer a nervous breakdown or depression at that time, as suggested in a recent article. I was sad, shocked and grieving yes, but didn't suffer any kind of mental breakdown.

What particularly upset me about the article was that it also made me into a hero for coming through adversity. I cannot bear the thought of gaining admiration out of my mother's death. For some time after the accident I wished it had been me who had died and not my mother. She was buried alongside Pop and Donnie. I didn't go to the funeral because I hadn't recovered enough and was still in hospital flat on my back.

The hospital staff were kept on their toes holding the media off. It got so bad that at one point I looked out the window to see a press photographer sitting in a tree outside my room. I felt sorry for him after a few days and I thought that I'd never want to be a photographer earning my living out of other people's grief. In the end we let the press in to hear a statement from the head doctor, although I wasn't present when it was read.

When I left hospital Ken came to pick me up and after saying goodbye to the staff, who had been amazing to me, we sneaked out the back way to avoid the media. When we approached his car Ken tossed the keys to me and said, 'Get in and drive.' You can imagine the look on my face. I said I couldn't possibly do it at that time: I didn't have my licence, I wasn't feeling well, and so on. Ken just calmly got into the passenger side and waited. When I finally got in he said, 'You're driving us to my place and I've got plenty of time to wait.' He went on, 'You'll stay with us until you're ready to go back to swimming.' I had never heard my eldest brother speak that way to me before and, in typical style, I thought, 'I'll show you. I'll drive to kingdom come and I won't let on how scared I am behind the wheel.' If Ken hadn't made me drive that day I may never have faced it again. As it was, I was very nervous for a long time after the accident. But I did it, and it's a good example of the sort of strength and sensible advice my family gave me.

The press camped outside Ken's house twenty-four hours a day trying to get a shot of me in the steel neck brace, and they ended up becoming so frustrated by not being able to photograph me that they went to Rose's place to get some photos of her. Heather was tracked down too but they never discovered Joyce's married name. All the while I longed for privacy and quiet. If I wanted to leave the house when I was staying with Ken and his wife, Thelma, I had to go through the next-door neighbour's backyard, then a hidden gate into the back lane, from where I could get to the garage. I'd hide on the floor of the car while someone else drove it out and away. Eventually I stayed with a series of good friends, moving house as I was tracked down each time. That went on for weeks. Finally the press lost the trail and I was able to try and collect my thoughts.

One day during my stay with Uncle Dick, from my mother's side of the family, Ken rang to say Sir Leslie Herron had called and wanted to talk to me urgently. Sir Leslie was the New South Wales Chief Justice at the time and the President of the New South Wales Swimming Association. I assumed it was a sympathy call. He had been so kind to Mum and Pop with tickets for the National Championships in 1956 that I didn't hesitate to call him. When I got through to his office I started to explain who I was when the receptionist said Sir Leslie had been waiting for my call. That really gave me a boost. I had been feeling I wasn't a very worthy person and this recognition from someone so important really cheered me up. A very kind, warm voice then came on the phone. 'How are you, Dawn? I've been meaning to call. I'm sorry it has taken me so long. I did have a little trouble finding you, but being Chief Justice does have its advantages.' He invited me to morning tea in his office but I told him I hadn't been out in public yet and that I still had my neck brace on. It wasn't that I was feeling guilty, it was just that I didn't want everyone staring at me. It was different being stared at in the pool, my domain, as I moved through the water with ease; in the neck brace I felt terribly vulnerable and a bit clumsy. And I couldn't stand sympathy and morbid curiosity. He wouldn't take no for an answer, though, and I agreed to see him in his office at ten the following morning.

I ended up being quite excited about going in to meet this kind, wonderful man who had known my parents. I wanted the contact and the conversation with someone who seemed genuinely concerned about my situation. When I arrived, the receptionist said Sir Leslie was waiting for me. As soon as he was told I was there, Sir Leslie came out and said, 'Come on, Dawn, the cuppa's getting cold,' and that immediately put me at ease. He went on to ask if I'd started to train for the Olympics and I just stared at him with a stupid look on my face. Couldn't he see the neck brace? Hadn't he heard about the accident? Then he said, 'Dawn, I want you to be my guest for an official lunch at the Royal Easter Show where we will appear before the public.' Once again he wouldn't take no for an answer. And it was no use protesting because he wasn't listening to me: we were going and that was that.

When the day arrived he sent a car for me and in spite of everything I couldn't wait. Sir Leslie just made everything seem all right and safe again. That outing broke the ice. The crowd at the Easter Show cheered for me and it really brought me back from the worst despair. The feeling was very much one of 'Good on you, Dawn, for coming back. We don't blame you for what happened. We just want to see you back out there swimming. Please go out and try.' By then everyone was encouraging me and insisting, but I still wasn't sure. Nevertheless, I felt much better after the Easter Show and I assured Sir Leslie and others I'd think about it. Quite apart from my mental state I had severe physical problems to overcome before I could contemplate returning to the water.

For weeks I didn't think seriously about swimming. I was quite relieved by the thought of not going to Tokyo because I knew Mum wouldn't be there with me and I didn't think I could stand that after all our excitement and planning. Anyone and everyone I came into contact with during this period said how sorry they were about Mum, then immediately asked if I would swim again, which was sometimes upsetting because I was still trying to sort out my feelings about it. I couldn't discuss it with anyone. My brothers and sisters kept telling me that Mum would have wanted me to go on with my career, and urged me to do all the things I had promised her I would. They were doing what they thought was right but they didn't know what I was going through. I didn't have the heart to get back in the water.

Eventually I had to go back to Balmain to collect my clothes and the other things I'd left there when I arrived from Melbourne for the National Championships so very, very long ago. Seeing the house without Mum in it was a very low point. I remembered how I'd said I would buy the house for them on the day I'd been rude to Pop and criticised where we lived. Now they were both gone before I could fulfil my promise. In the following months I did the next best thing and used the money I'd saved for Mum's trip to Tokyo as a deposit on the old house. I made an offer to the owner and he agreed to sell. Finally the Frasers would own the little terrace in Balmain where so many family dramas and celebrations had been played out.

Just before I went back to Melbourne, Rosie and her husband, Bill, gave me my first German Shepherd dog, Rajah, and I haven't been without one since. I loved that beautiful little puppy and he kept me company through many dark hours. I was also given Mum's wedding band. It was the one thing of hers I really wanted, and as the other women in my family all had wedding bands of their own, my brothers and sisters kindly agreed that I could have it. That too was a comfort.

I wasn't able to discuss the accident with my brothers and sisters. Even when I wanted to I thought, 'Why put them through it again?' So I kept quiet and so did they. Perhaps they talked between themselves and perhaps they didn't want to put me through it again. In any case we handled it the way Frasers handle things: quietly and without sentiment.

Going back to my flat and my job in Melbourne was the best thing I could have done at that point, even though I didn't want to leave my family. My great friends Joan and Alan Stoller stepped in and supported me in a most remarkable way. I had met Joan at Squashways, where she used to come in and swim and then ended up teaching trampolining. Alan was an official with the World Federation for Mental Health and an officer with the World Health Organisation. He was also the Chief Clinical Officer of Victoria's Mental Hygiene Department. Joan took on a lot of Mum's role, nurturing me and caring for me in a very maternal way. Alan started to counsel me and got me talking about my grief and feelings of guilt. He also helped arrange physical checks to see how my injuries were healing. Between them they brought me back from a very dark place and helped me cope with what had happened. Dr Stoller also helped me deal with a new wave of nasty rumours. These included the ludicrous idea that I hadn't been able to attend my mother's funeral because I'd been partying that day, and further stories that I had been drink driving when the accident happened. He not only helped me arrange legal letters that headed off the worst of these, but was able to explain to me why people would say these things and how their minds worked.

Finally I was convinced by these remarkable people, and my family and friends, that I should get back in the water. I also clung to the thought that Mum wanted me to win the third gold medal in Tokyo. There were no sentimental walks around Balmain Baths or a sudden glorious rekindling of my association with that place, as has often been reported. How poetic that would have been, and of course it was a scene created in a film later made about my life. What really happened was much more mundane. I went for a swim at Squashways at a time when I knew no one else would be using the pool. It wasn't miraculous and it hurt like hell. My neck was stiff and sore and I couldn't turn it to breathe. All I could manage was a pathetic breaststroke, the one stroke I had always hated. I felt sure after that first swim that I would never swim at an elite level again, despite my doctors' assurances that there was nothing stopping me from returning to form.

That's when Harry came into the picture. We talked as we had always talked and worked it out between us. I was going to swim again and Harry was going to get me there. I would somehow get to Townsville with the Australian squad. I had been told by the doctors that I should persevere with the training, and they'd given me a whole range of exercises which I'd been doing religiously. I had also been told I shouldn't dive into the water except when I absolutely had to; the diving, they said, would put too much pressure on my head and neck. I could lower myself into the pool to train, and when we had time trials for those few months in Melbourne I'd push off from the wall, so the lack of diving wasn't a major problem at that stage. Time trials took place at the end of a week's training. I would swim as hard as I could over 50 metres and 100 metres so Harry could see where I was going. At best I was doing about 63.3 seconds for the 100 metres, a big change from the sub-minute swims I'd achieved before the accident. I had lost a lot of weight, too, and generally things didn't look very promising early on. I started to train a fair bit on my own, feeling more comfortable testing myself without everyone watching. My heart still wasn't in it, though, and each day was a major struggle in contrast to my enthusiasm of just a few months earlier. I was allowed to take Rajah to the pool and he was my constant companion. One day I had him tied to a stack of chairs beside the pool and when I jumped in so did he. He managed to free himself of the chairs but by the time I saw him on my return lap he was dog paddling pretty hard.

I found that I could no longer do tumble-turns. It was too painful to get my head down onto my neck to execute the turn properly. Fortunately I had practised both the tumble-turn and the touch-turn all through my swimming career and had perfected both. Many of my best swims had been done with touch-turns, and over the years I'd come to find them easier. This worked very much to my advantage after the accident.

Gradually I started to improve through a steady program of swimming and weights, until eventually I was ready to join the squad in Townsville to prepare for the Olympic trials. I hadn't spoken to anyone from the ASU throughout my entire recovery. Harry was contacted about my going to Townsville and through him the dates for the training squad were conveyed to me. I had to be there in August for a seven-week period. I was reluctant to leave Harry, who had opted to remain behind in Melbourne after Appletons Pool had been ruined by a fire. We'd trained a little bit at Appletons after the fire, but it was dark and quite smoky. The Olympic Pool was closed at the time too, so we mostly went over to Richmond. Harry had no financial resources to go to Townsville with me, and was still of the opinion that we could prepare equally well in Melbourne. Terry Gathercole, a recently retired swimmer, had been put in charge of coaching the girls in Townsville but I knew he'd have nothing to offer me—I knew far more about preparing myself than he did. So before I headed north Harry and I worked out a program for me to follow.

It seems ironic that for years Harry had to scrape together fares and was never given any recognition by the ASU, and now they had officially appointed a professional coach to look after the team and it was Terry, someone who'd only retired from swimming a few years earlier. To be fair, Terry had said to my face that he couldn't coach me, that he didn't know how, so at least we were in agreement and I wouldn't be required to do things that were of no benefit. It seemed silly to me to place a swimmer who was virtually our peer in charge of the squad. While it was all right for me, I believe some of the other girls who didn't have a Harry or enough experience suffered.

I planned to keep out of the team's way and fit in with their schedules in the pool. I was only too happy to avoid contact with people. But I really needed Ricksie or at least a male sprinter to pace myself against. I knew before I headed to Townsville that I was coming from a long way behind, having been out of the pool for such a long time during the crucial lead-up period and still only swimming at about 63 seconds. I would have to swim under the minute to win the gold medal.

Just before flying north I attended an Olympic fundraising carnival in the outback town of Woomera. The Defence Force workers stationed at Woomera's rocket range had just built a swimming pool, but it was empty when I arrived and the water was being trucked in. Looking around the rocket range fascinated me, and I had a wonderful time with the five-thousand-strong population, pulling beers at the local pub to raise money and later selling the men kisses for a pound each. Flying out to Alice Springs was a bit hairy, though, because the whole area was enveloped in a dust storm and our Fokker Friendship seemed to stand still in midair, with dust coming in through the air vents and getting over everything in sight. In the end the pilot had to put down in Oodnadatta to wait the storm out. The experience didn't do much for my fear of flying.

I arrived in Townsville in August having just removed my neck brace for good but still feeling very low. I felt isolated from the others, not only by age but also by grief. Harry was there for me as he had nearly always been, only this time in spirit and via the written word. His letters would contain swimming schedules, which I'd send back to him with the times filled in so he could write again with a revised schedule, but he'd also ask me how I was going, how my neck was, and write encouraging things about dealing with my grief. I had been cranky with him on and off over the years but he was mostly there when I needed him and I still followed his every instruction. I had never prepared myself for anything major before without his physical presence. He'd always watched me swim and corrected this little flaw or that little problem as I went along. The letters were great but it wasn't the same. I had to think so much more about what I was doing and try to identify and correct my own mistakes—which is not easy when you can't actually see yourself swimming. I knew that Sharon Stouder in the US had done the sprint in 60.8 seconds during their summer. As always, I was watching my competitors.

In Townsville I went to stay with the wonderful Bartletts again. Sometimes during those weeks leading up to Tokyo I would find myself staring out at the ocean for hours and I would receive a call from the Bartletts asking if I was coming home for lunch or dinner and that would bring me back to reality. They drew me out of my misery and into their family warmth. Stumpy Lawrence, the Pool Manager, was another great support for me. I had always loved him and now he took me under his wing even more. He'd let me spend time off over at his house on Magnetic Island where he kept birds and dogs. I'd just muck around and enjoy his company and play with the animals. It was a little bit like having a father again.

He was one of the only people I ever spoke to about the accident and I knew it wouldn't go further. I owed him a lot.

I realised around that time that I no longer had anyone to swim for. First there'd been Donnie, then Pop, then Mum, and of course there'd always been Harry. Now I was on my own, swimming for the memory of people, and that seemed hollow. So in the end I decided I would swim for myself. I wanted that gold medal for me.

The girls on the team for Tokyo were a great bunch of people. They included Linda McGill, Jan Turner, Marguerite Ruygrok, Lynette Bell and Robyn Thorn, Nanette Duncan and Marlene Dayman. There were only fourteen of us and we got along well. Soon after we arrived in Townsville Linda McGill and Jan Turner took pity on me and asked me to go out with them to the Allan Hotel on a Saturday night. I wasn't interested in going out at all, let alone with younger girls, as nice as they all were. But they kept insisting and in the end I quite liked the idea of getting out again. We were only given a few social days while we were training so this would be one of my few opportunities. I was, after all, a social creature and still only twenty-six. My decision to go out that night changed the course of my life forever and—in one special way that did not become apparent until much later—for the better.

We were going to the pub to see a band and have a bit of a dance. I guess there was an idea between the other girls that we might meet some blokes but it was the furthest thing from my mind. By then I was on a mission to win that gold medal and I'd also lost interest in meeting anyone since Mum died. One of the guys who worked at the pub told a group of three local blokes that we were with the Olympic team and on our own, so they came up and asked if we'd like a glass of champagne, which we happily accepted. The others got up to dance and I was left at the table with a bloke called Gary Ware. I think he'd been hoping he'd be paired off with one of the others but he ended up with me and we got talking. I don't think he had a strong idea of who I was, or at least he didn't care, and that suited me just fine. He was shy but also dressed quite sharply in a suit and hat, which appealed to me. He'd apparently been at the races that day and had a big win, and as I liked the horses we started to get along quite well.

Gary ended up driving me home to the Bartletts that night and asked if he could take me out. I explained that my schedule was pretty tight and he accepted that, but over the next few weeks he began to pick me up after training and take me for a milkshake and scones at the Ozone Cafe, known to us all as Aunty Nell's. She was making fantastic pumpkin scones before Flo Bjelke-Petersen was even heard of. After that he started coming to any social events the swimmers had after training, and that included my birthday barbecue, at which he gave me a marcasite watch. On another occasion I was asked to present the Townsville Cup and the owner of the horse happened to be Gary, so it was quite lovely and romantic. I enjoyed being with Gary because he was fun and I loved his flamboyance and cheekiness, which matched my own. But there was also a shy side to Gary and I liked that too. I was able to show him my soft side and vulnerability, which I had rarely shown anyone outside my immediate family, except perhaps May Hoben, the Stollers, Stumpy and Harry. For some reason I felt I could do that with Gary. Although I was wary of sex and still shy of going too far very often, we were physically very attracted to each other as well. Gary was a horse owner and trainer and also a licensed bookmaker. We shared all those interests and found we talked easily.

I had some great times in Townsville during that training period and not all of it with Gary. One day I took the girls to watch a football match because Stumpy was the club's masseur. Afterwards we all went down to Townsville Railway Station because Col Joye, Little Patti, Judy Stone and quite a few other well-known singers were touring Australia on their own train and had arrived in town to perform some concerts. When they found out the Olympic training squad was in town we all started to spend a bit of time together. It was very hot and they came back to the pool for a swim. Judy Stone was terrified of the water and she made a pact with me that if I could teach her to swim she'd teach me to sing. I don't think either of us got too far.

I still put swimming first and I knew I had to put the relationship with Gary on hold if I was to succeed. I also knew that if it was meant to be it would last. On the other hand, realising how deeply I felt about Gary made me start to look beyond swimming. I started to think I would like more time to socialise without worrying about getting up the next day, and to be able to give myself completely to someone without swimming interfering. At the time it seemed quite a breakthrough for me to feel like this, but looking back it was also completely natural given that my life had been on hold for swimming for over ten years.

Gary asked me to marry him just before we were due to leave Townsville for Tokyo. I thought it might be a bit soon but I was sure I loved him and was terribly thrilled that he thought so much of me. I asked the Bartletts for their advice and they suggested I wait till I returned from Tokyo and see if we still felt the same. They knew Gary and liked him but felt it was all very sudden. Gary still insisted we at least become engaged and I agreed we would. The Bartletts were very happy for us when we made our decision and the two of us spent a bit of time with them in between training. Gary gave me a diamond solitaire ring and I called my family in Sydney to tell them the news. They were no doubt a little surprised, but I was twenty-seven and it was very much my decision. I was also given Gary's most promising horse, Booberana, as an engagement gift and I basked in this romantic gesture.

Gary's family lived in Townsville in a typical Queenslander-style house, and I had previously met his parents, Don and Olive, and his sister, Sally. His father wasn't terribly well but they had welcomed me in and seemed to be pretty well accepting of the

situation. Gary's mother, Ol, was the sharp one and was very forth-
right in pointing out that I was a very well known and worldly
person while Gary was just a country boy. I reassured her that I
loved him just the same, and when we became engaged she said
that she was pleased for us. She'd just been looking out for her son
and I don't blame her.

As usual the ASU kept us all thinking that not all the swimmers
in the squad would go to Tokyo, but in the end we did. I hadn't
swum under the minute since arriving at Townsville but felt sure
I would be able to when it mattered. I was timing myself secretly
when no one else was at the pool, and even my recorded times
were good, with a 60.6 just before we left.

The plan was to pack up and fly to Brisbane where we'd connect
with a planeload of Olympians on their way from Sydney then fly
on to Tokyo. The flight to Brisbane was delayed due to some
mechanical problem, or possibly due to the Dawn Fraser flying
jinx, and when we finally got there we discovered the flight from
Sydney was also delayed. Gary had driven down to Brisbane to see
me off, and as our engagement had more or less leaked out anyway
we announced it to the press who had crowded around to get the
story of the team leaving for Japan. Gary wouldn't be photographed
or interviewed, which was probably the first indication I had that
it was all rather overwhelming and awkward for him. I didn't pay
any attention, though. I was too excited about going off to defend
my title knowing my wonderful fiancé would be there for me when
I returned.

9

DAWN FRASER-SAN
AND THE FLAG

When I flew off to Tokyo with the rest of the Australian squad it was with the knowledge that no other woman in the world had swum the 100 metres in under a minute. That included the fifteen-year-old American Sharon Stouder, who I regarded as my biggest rival at that time. I wasn't concerned about not having done it myself since the accident, because I knew I would be able to when the time came and I knew that if anyone were to beat me they would have to do it too. Not having swum that fast for several months, it was a bit of a psychological trick: I had done the training and I just needed to believe I could do it, and I did believe it as I sat on the plane on my way to my third Olympic Games. I hadn't been training with the squad in Townsville but I'd been doing my own secret time trials with Stumpy Lawrence and knew where I was at. In front of the others I'd only come in a little way ahead but I knew what I was really capable of doing. I also hadn't dived off the blocks since the accident, as per my doctors' warnings, and though I feared it would be very painful I knew that I would dive when I needed to. If I was going to be in pain, I told myself, I would do it when it really mattered.

I was deeply in love with Gary Ware by the time I went to Tokyo, and very proud and happy to be engaged. Though I was a little bit troubled by Gary's reaction to all the attention at the airport, I knew I had to put that part of my life on hold again if I was going to win in Tokyo. I wanted to be completely focused on the challenge ahead, and told myself that this was only three weeks out of my life, I'd worked long and hard for it and it wouldn't come round again.

The Yoyogi Olympic Village was about half an hour's drive from the inner city of Tokyo. It was comfortable enough and I roomed with Lyn Bell, Robyn Thorn, and Marguerite Ruygrok, who I called Sly Grog or Grog for short. All of them had been brilliant to me through our training in Townsville, never leaving me on my own when I was clearly sad about Mum. Being so much older than the other girls in the squad—everyone was calling me 'Granny' by then—I became an adviser to several of them on how they should approach their swims. I would never have volunteered that help, but girls asked for advice, as they had in Rome, and I always tried to give them something useful to work with. Although it sounds mercenary, I have to admit that I would never have given advice to anyone I considered a serious rival, and I was only prepared to help some of the girls because they showed a lot of potential but didn't really present a threat at that stage.

Sometimes we had to ride pushbikes to the dining room in the Tokyo village because it was such a long way from our rooms, and as usual the women's section was fenced off to keep us out of the clutches of the marauding men. It was also about forty-five minutes bus ride to the swimming pool.

Despite all that had happened to me that year it was still as exciting to be there as it had been for my first Olympic Games in Melbourne in 1956. It was then, and still is, the biggest and best sporting competition in the world. If you become blasé at that level you're never going to do well. By this stage, even though I was still terribly sad, I had allowed myself to have a life and move beyond the guilt and self-blame for what had happened to Mum. From the minute I arrived in Tokyo I was feted by the Japanese and also by a large part of the international press, in part because I was there to defend my title for the third time, a highly unusual circumstance in swimming, and also because of the publicity surrounding my banning after Rome and the accident. I guess I was a good human interest story.

I liked the Japanese people. They showed me great kindness and hospitality while I was in their country and I returned in the following years to find the same welcome and warmth. I particularly liked their attitude to fitness and cleanliness, two things I've always valued throughout my life. Many Japanese people at the Tokyo games told me they liked my fighting spirit.

During the week leading into the Games I was able to confirm to myself that I would swim under the minute in the 100 metres: not because I had actually done so in training but because I knew how I felt in the water. I was at that wonderful point in my tapering-off program where I was right on course for my best swims to happen at the time when it counted. Even though Harry wasn't with me his letters had helped, and I was old enough and experienced enough to get myself to exactly the right level at the right time.

The other major factor in getting yourself in the right frame of mind to win is absorbing the village atmosphere and excitement.

Getting the adrenaline flowing via the anticipation and energy that abounds in an Olympic village is something I would never under-estimate. Which is why I fought so hard for the swimming squad, and particularly the girls, to march in the opening ceremony.

Soon after arriving in Tokyo we were told by Bill Slade, the Section Manager of Swimming, that we could not march in the opening ceremony if we were to compete within forty-eight hours of the event. This ruling was often reported later as being within three days of the event. I said to Slade, 'Look, if I'm not fit enough to walk around an arena in an opening ceremony and survive it to swim a few days later, then I'm not fit enough to compete and you should send me home now.' My complaint fell on deaf ears and he reiterated the directive, which was, of course, handed down by the ASU. I'd known the issue was going to come up and it was an open secret that I planned to march no matter what. I had missed out on marching in the opening ceremony at the Rome Games four years earlier over a similar stupid rule.

As the swimming was the first part of the Games program the ruling involved most of our team; I nevertheless went and said my piece to the Chef de Mission, Len Curnow. I not only told him what I thought of the decision but that I intended to march because my first swim was just over twenty-four hours from the opening ceremony. It was never Len's decision to stop us from marching, as he made clear in several press interviews at the time, and he said to me, 'Dawn, go and get yourself a pair of gloves.' Mrs Hatton, the team chaperone, took me into town to buy white gloves like those issued to the rest of the team and I also bought some for Linda McGill, Marlene Dayman and Nan Duncan, who also intended to defy the order and march.

I have never ceased to be appalled by the pettiness, the abuse of power, the stupidity, the cruelty and the sheer overbearing nature of this command issued by the ASU. Exactly what scientific

evidence were they operating under to make such an arbitrary decision? Surely cycling to the dining room was more taxing than
walking around an arena? I am glad I marched, even though it
caused me immense difficulty and heartache later on, but sadly it
was something taken away from many of us in Rome and now in
Tokyo. The buses that took us to the arena before the afternoon
opening ceremony left the village from about 10.00 a.m. onwards.
I didn't even hide myself on the bus. I simply hopped on an early
one with other athletes, and when one of the officials came onboard
and said, 'Is there anyone on this bus who shouldn't be?' everyone
said 'No.' I don't know whether the official turned a blind eye or
mistook me for Helen Frith, the high jumper, who I was often
confused with. In our uniforms and those funny little hats we
looked even more alike. I was not smuggled onto the bus the way
it has been reported, although possibly the others on the bus
covered for me. I would like to think they did. To this day I don't
know how I made it. Nan Duncan and Linda McGill were
removed from another bus, but Marlene Dayman made it through
and marched too. Linda later left the village again and was able to
watch the ceremony from the grandstand.

When I arrived at the marshalling area, several officials who
knew I shouldn't have been marching nodded and winked at me.
Len Curnow, when he saw me, said, 'Good on you, Dawnie.' And
when the press questioned him about my presence he humorously
replied, 'You must be mistaken. I don't see Dawn Fraser.' Good
old Len! Unfortunately, being so tall, I was put in the front row,
and was therefore leading off and terribly conspicuous. I just
wanted to be there, I didn't want to rub the ASU's nose in it, but
there I was stepping out right at the front of the team. I was the
only individual athlete to be given special mention by the march
commentators, which is something I relate not to show off but to
explain the extent to which I'd been adopted by the Japanese
people.

Naturally I was immediately reported after the march by Bill Slade for disobedience towards him and towards the ASU. I couldn't have cared less as I'd heard the roar of the crowd and felt the surge of pride in wearing the Australian blazer. I returned to the village elated and ready to take on the world.

•

Leading up to the heats I would try to get to the pool to train when Stouder was training or just finishing. I had always checked out my opposition meticulously and now I sat and counted how many strokes she did to a lap and tried to work out what she was doing in her tapering off. Was she going out hard in her first 25 metres? What was her turn like? Would she come out ahead of me, and how was she coming into the wall? Was she just gliding in or finishing off? All these things would give me clues about the performance I could expect from her.

I won my heat in 60.6 seconds and didn't feel that I'd extended myself. In the semifinals later that day I pushed myself harder and won again in 59.9 seconds, coming in under the minute officially for the first time since the Sydney Nationals in March. My diving was under control and, surprisingly, my neck had not hurt me at all. For both races I wore non-regulation swimsuits, as I had in my relay heats. When the official swimsuits had been issued in Townsville I found they were too short and tight in the body for me and I'd had to send them back to be remade. Length was added to the shoulder straps, but this didn't work because the costumes were still too tight across the body and cut me up the middle. The costume was also now filling with water around the chest because there was too much fabric around the neck area. Given that we shaved down just to save a fraction of a second when swimming, it seemed rather pointless dragging along an extra weight of water. When this problem was worked on I felt constricted in the chest because it had become too tight across the front, which was a real hindrance to an asthmatic. Even with the extra length I was still falling out at the bottom whenever I bent over. With five officials behind me each time I took to the blocks, not to mention the crowd, I wasn't happy about my bum being on display. The official swimsuit company made several attempts to fix the costumes for me but in the end they were still hopeless and I started wearing swimsuits I already had. Some of those had been made for me by a friend who had a small swimwear company, Sterling Swimwear, and some I had made myself. I had actually given a swimsuit I'd made to Sterling Swimwear a year or so earlier to use as a model for other costumes because the one I'd sewn fitted me perfectly and had taken a while to devise. I always carried well-fitting swimwear in the Australian colours because experience had shown that the official ones were rarely adequate for my build. We did of course make the costumes to look just like the official ones, with green and gold stripes and the map of Australia on the front. At no time did I attempt to promote the swimwear company that made them for me and nor was I paid to wear them. In fact, for all I knew I may have been wearing the one I had made myself for at least one of those swims in Tokyo. It wasn't a big deal except that I was completely comfortable in mine and very uncomfortable in the official suits. The lengths to which the ASU went in insisting I wear the official costume before the finals makes me wonder about the so-called amateurism that was always being preached. Sponsorship appeared to be alive and well as far as some of the officials and the team equipment went.

After the heat I had received a message from Bill Slade via Anne Hatton, which had undoubtedly come from Bill Berge Phillips in the first place, that I was to wear the official swimsuit. I told Anne that I had trouble swimming in them and felt it was more important to be comfortable. She didn't press the point. Again after the semifinal came a more insistent message that I wear the official swimsuit and again I refused. I had heard I'd been officially reported for not wearing it on the day before the final and I went to see Len Curnow about it. He wasn't there but I saw Julius 'Judy' Patching, the Assistant Manager, instead. He argued with me for a long time before the final and ended up asking me to wear the official costume for Len Curnow's sake. I finally agreed but regretted it immediately, finding when I went to do a warm-up swim that all the old problems were there with the costume and it made me nervous. It was an extra worry I could have done without.

Going into the final, Sharon Stouder still hadn't broken the minute, but she'd stayed quite close to me in the semifinal and I was very conscious of the fact that the winner can come from any lane. I was still mindful of the terrible scare Natalie Steward had given me in Rome in lane eight as she produced a time no one expected of her. I knew the trap long before Kieren Perkins had his amazing win from lane eight in Atlanta, and I was aware that a challenge could be there from any one of those swimmers, but would most likely come from Stouder. I was anything but relaxed before the final at Tokyo.

I had made these Olympics at the age of twenty-seven because my times were still improving. My career had started comparatively late and I was still making great advances at this older age. Really twenty-seven was just a number to me and didn't indicate what I was or wasn't capable of doing. Nevertheless I was very aware that Sharon Stouder was so much younger, as was another American in the race, Kathy Ellis. I was also aware that they had possibly held something back in heats and were young enough to be making enormous advances on the day. That's one of the reasons I played particularly hard gamesmanship before the race. I had my race worked out already. I'd done all my preparation and so I was able to go into that marshalling area and spend the time doing something other than thinking about the swim. While others were gathering their thoughts quietly I became very boisterous and started having a very noisy rubdown from one of the Japanese masseurs. I kept calling out in mock horror, 'Oh you've hurt me, you've hurt me, you've given me cramp, I won't be able to swim.' Then I'd get up and hobble about a bit and I had all the Japanese attendants and masseurs giggling. Others wanted to be quiet and think about the race but I just wouldn't let them do it. I was stalking around showing I was totally confident and in control. I owned the marshalling area. I owned the race. If any of those competitors had been able to see inside my head or my heart they would have been able to get an edge. No doubt about it, I was frightened. I wanted to vomit and run to the toilet. It was just the most crushing pressure. This race was so important to me and I felt an immense desire to win it for Mum. I had to have struggled back for something. At the same time I knew I was going to beat my record time. I knew, and perhaps Stumpy did too, that my push-off times had sometimes been faster than my diving times from previous years.

The main problem in a sprint like the one I was about to face is that you become so tired by the second 50 metres that it feels like your flesh is falling off your bones, and the last five metres is like swimming in a bowl of spaghetti. I had planned this race so precisely. I knew I was going to do a touch-turn and that Stouder would do a tumble-turn. She came out a bit ahead of me on the turn but I got myself settled again and we were pretty even. Then I swam a little faster and she came with me. Next I eased back and she did too, so I felt I was controlling the pace. I went fast for another four or five strokes and she came with me again, but this time I kept the speed up for a little bit longer, and when we got to the halfway mark on the way back, I was ready to go much faster. I was always known as a good 25-metre sprinter and now I employed that speed. As I took off I knew Stouder couldn't stay with me and I just had her there at my shoulder all the time. If I kept the speed up she wouldn't beat me. For the last five strokes I didn't take a breath and it was clear she'd have to really swim much harder than me to have a chance. It is a completely technical race over that distance. Harry and I had tried a hundred different strategies in training, and I'd analysed, planned and swum the 100 metres so many times that I had, I believe, perfected it. When a competitor went with me, as Stouder did, I was in control because of my planning—as long as I could find the stamina and speed, which on this occasion I did.

I touched the wall and knew immediately I'd won it. Still, you wait for the official announcement and the light next to your name on the board. Then you look to see what time you've swum. It was 59.5, four-tenths of a second off my previous swim. In those days we were allowed to float on our backs a little way to recover, so I lay back on the water while it started to sink in that I'd done it. I couldn't look for Harry in the crowd because for the first time he wasn't there. Afterwards at the medal ceremony I let all the emotions surge through me—pride, great pride; sadness for Mum but pleasure that I'd won the medal she'd wanted me to win; relief that it was over; and about a million other feelings all racing around inside—and I actually cried a bit on the victory dais. I'd done it. I was the first swimmer ever to win three Olympic gold medals in a row. Then it was off to a press conference and a TV interview for Australia before I went back to the pool with Mrs Hatton and my Japanese pen pal, Tomoko, who I'd kept in touch with since the Melbourne Games.

When we finally arrived back at the village later that night it was pretty quiet. Mrs Hatton and I went to see Len Curnow, and Len and I had a beer and he congratulated me. Then I called Gary and we had an emotional talk before I had to hang up. It has been reported that I drank some more beer with the hockey players and then went and had cake with the basketballers, who gave me a bugle. I did none of those things. The bugle was given to me by the water polo players after the Olympics, although I used it a couple of times during the Games, as did several other people when we were cheering the team on. After my beer with Len I went back to my room, which was in darkness, and I slipped quietly into bed because we all still had swims coming up in the next few days. As I sank into the sheets I felt a squishy, crunchy, slimy mess. The lights suddenly came on and everyone was yelling and jumping around me. My corner of the room had been decorated and my bed was full of Activite, honey, cereal, baby powder and lots more unidentifiable substances. We all carried on for ages and when I'd finally made my bed sleepable again I was almost too excited to settle down.

I still had to swim in the 4 x 100 metres freestyle relay in the following days and had to prepare for that, so the celebrations over the 100 metres victory stopped as abruptly as they'd begun. There was quite a rivalry between the Australian and American women's relay teams, as we'd been neck and neck in the two previous Olympic Games. The Americans cleverly placed Sharon Stouder to swim first, and later we were criticised for not responding by putting me in against her, but we had our race planned the way we wanted to swim it. That's the way it is: you plan your race and take your chance. Stouder went all out and gained such a strong lead that we slipped further and further behind. I took off for the last two laps and did the swim of my life, covering the distance in 58.6 seconds, the fastest 100 metres ever but not an official record because I hadn't gone off with the starter's gun. The crowd went crazy because of my swim and even though we came second it was perhaps the Olympic swim of which I'm most proud.

At the end of the swimming events I was supposed to join the team going to the FINA carnival in Osaka, the equivalent of the one I'd attended in Naples on my birthday in 1960. However the team's Medical Officer, Dr Howard Toyne, decided that my asthma wouldn't allow me to participate and I was given the week off, which was strangely convenient given my other commitments.

During the Tokyo Games a film producer by the name of Lee Robinson was making a documentary about me and my swimming career. It was sponsored by Bonds. Much of it had already been shot in Sydney and the officials in Tokyo knew that filming would continue over there. I was given permission to leave the village about a week before the end of the Games to join the filmmakers at the Imperial Palace Hotel, which was about half a mile down the road from the Emperor's Palace and about an hour from the Olympic village. After the somewhat Spartan village I was looking forward to a week in a luxurious hotel. The job I'd come to do was complete and I was in high spirits.

We spent a fantastic few days touring around the city to private homes of prominent Tokyo citizens, and to the Ginza District and the Queen Bee nightclub where the geishas performed for us. Usually they don't either perform for or serve women but they looked after me, I think because I was drinking beer, which usually only the men drank, and because they knew I'd won a gold medal. Funnily enough we ran into Bill Slade at one of the nightclubs and he was very shocked to see us. I don't think he was supposed to have been there but I couldn't have cared less. I certainly didn't report him.

The Australian men's hockey team won a bronze medal on the last day of the Games and they all came back to the hotel to celebrate. There was a big bunch of us, including the film crew; the hockey players and their Manager, Charles Morley; Dr Howard Toyne, who had attended the last hockey match in an official capacity; the film crew's Japanese interpreter and me. Before the hockey players had arrived we'd been brought beer in little glass boots by the hotel management and had great fun working out how to drink from them without spilling the beer. We'd mastered the art by the time the hockey players arrived and got a laugh out of watching them trying to do the same. The group was too big to remain in the foyer bar, so we all went back to my room, which was a suite and big enough to contain everyone. The party continued and we all had a great time into the early hours of the morning. At one stage our interpreter gave her kimono to Lee Robinson while she wore my bathrobe, which was several sizes too big for her, and they danced about in their ridiculous outfits. If it sounds raucous, it was in fact an innocent gathering of some very happy people at the end of a long, hard road. Press reports in Australia throughout the Tokyo Games were very critical of the Olympic team, with suggestions of a lot of wild partying and pretty poor behaviour, but on returning to Sydney most of the team were genuinely perplexed when the press put these claims to them. It was almost as if some of the officials were determined to find fault as well as to exercise a ridiculous level of control over the athletes.

I had certainly joined in that party with the hockey players and had drunk a few beers but was pretty clear-headed when Dr Toyne suggested to me that we go and souvenir some Olympic flags— the classic white flags with the coloured rings on them. I can't blame the alcohol for what followed. Being spirited and unable to resist a challenge I went along with Howard and one of the hockey players, Des Piper, who had overheard us plotting. We took off anything that could distinguish us as Australian, such as our ID cards, blazers and badges, and sneaked away from the party.

Howard Toyne took us to an avenue leading towards the Emperor's Palace, filled with flagpoles about fifty feet apart. We decided we wanted a flag each, and Howard and I held Des up on our shoulders because Des was the smallest. They were quite easy to get loose and we had two down and were going for the third when whistles started sounding. Des had actually thrown the third flag to the ground at that point. One of us yelled out, 'Run! Here come the police,' but I gamely picked up the flag and folded it up under my tracksuit top before we separated and ran up a fairly steep rise towards some bushes. It was dark and quite close to the palace. I could see the police coming towards the bushes and they started beating them with batons. We were hit a couple of times and then Howard called out, 'We'd better run, Fraser!' I replied, still having great fun, 'It's all right for you; I can't run, I'm a swimmer.' Howard and Des raced away but I decided to stay put; I figured that if the police followed the others I might be able to get away myself. There were police running everywhere by then and after a few minutes of hiding alone in the bushes I began to feel a bit frightened. It was pretty dark further into the park and away from streetlights, and it was cold. I was aware the Japanese police carried guns. After about ten minutes I decided I'd make a break for it and jumped down from the wall that ran across the top of the rise where I'd been hiding. My ankle twisted under me as I landed, but I ignored the pain and ran on towards a low hedge, about three feet tall. I went to jump over the hedge, not realising it had barbed wire on top, and for a few moments I was spread-eagled on the wire as I desperately tried to untangle myself and jump down on the other side. Unfortunately this time I landed in a pond and found myself waist-deep in cold, murky water. At least now I was more in my element. I stayed very quietly in the pond for about another fifteen minutes. It began to get very cold and the pond was a bit smelly.

After a while I felt pretty safe to come out. The noise of the whistles had subsided and I was sure the police had headed off in a different direction after the others. With my flag still tucked in my top I clambered out of the pond, trying to see in the darkness. I decided to climb back over the hedge, making sure not to get tangled in the wire again, and when I saw a park bench, sat down to get my bearings and think about what to do next. Just when I was working out where I was in the park two policemen came along, and one of them put his hand on my shoulder and spoke to me in Japanese. The only word I recognised was *konichiwa* and I replied 'Gidday', which didn't seem to get me very far. They were trying to interrogate me and I kept trying to tell them that I didn't speak Japanese. They then tried to speak a bit of broken English, all the while pushing and tapping me with their batons, which actually hurt quite a bit.

'What you do here?'

'I'm waiting for friend.'

'No you pinch flag.'

'No I didn't.'

Then I got up to go and the rope on the end of the flag fell down from underneath my tracksuit top. One of the police started pulling it and the flag came out.

'You come.'

With that they started to walk me out of the park. All through the park there were little police or security huts that had been erected for the Games, and next to one of them I saw a bicycle. I had some idea of where I was by then and could see a pathway that seemed to be leading out of the park. I thought that if I could get on the bike I could probably beat them—I was a pretty good bike rider from my time in Balmain and my days getting around Adelaide without a car. I shouted really loudly, 'There are my friends, over there!' And when they looked I ran forward, grabbed the bike and started pedalling like crazy. All of sudden police came from every direction blowing their whistles again and I was forced to get off the bike and go with the police down past the Imperial Palace Hotel to Maranouchi Police Station on the corner.

They took me upstairs at the station and put me in a room on my own. They somehow got it across to me that an interpreter was on the way. I sat on my own in a room for about twenty-five minutes while the reality sank in that I'd once again landed myself in quite a bit of trouble. I was very scared. It was about 3.00 a.m., I had to march in the closing ceremony later that day and I'd been arrested in a foreign country where I couldn't understand the language or what was going on around me. I thought, 'Hell, I'm really in big trouble now.' Eventually a middle-aged man came in and introduced himself in English as Police Superintendent Kamira. He told me he would be interviewing me and then asked me for my name. He was walking up and down past my chair with his hands behind his back, looking pretty stern. I said I was Dawn Fraser and again he asked me my name.

'Dawn Fraser.'

And again: 'What is your name?'

'Dawn Fraser, swimmer from Australia.'

'Where is your ID?'

Of course I had left this at the hotel in case we got into trouble.

'I don't have ID.'

'What is your name?'

'Dawn Fraser.'

'No, no, no.'

'Yes, yes, yes.'

'Dawn Fraser-san, she not do something like this.'

'Oh, yes she would,' I said, looking him in the eye with a bit of a twinkle. 'Oh yes she would.'

With that he smiled very slightly and I think he then thought I probably was Dawn Fraser.

He went on, 'You win gold medal,' and I said, 'Yes, I win gold medal for 100 metres freestyle.'

Now he seemed more convinced. I explained as best I could that I had no ID on me but that if I could ring the hotel someone would bring my passport down. He then allowed me to make a phone call and I called Lee Robinson, the documentary producer, who was hilarious, giving me a real blast over the phone and asking where the hell I was. When I told him I was at a police station he let loose with a whole string of expletives. 'Where the *!@# are you and what's going on? It's 3.00 a.m.!' I tried to tell him calmly that I'd been arrested for souveniring flags and that he should go to my room and get my ID from the drawer. I also told him where he

Standing on the victory dais after breaking the minute in Melbourne, 1962.

Chrysler South Australia lent me a car to encourage me to break the minute. Note the numberplate.

With backstroke swimmer Tony Fingleton, performing in the concert held at the Commonwealth Games village, 1962, to raise funds for the Children's Christmas Appeal.

Dressed in my new linen suit at photographer Ken Rainsbury's house before going on board the *Britannia* for lunch with the Queen, 1963.

My favourite picture with Mum, when we attended a special awards ceremony
for the Babe Zaharias Trophy.

The Royal Easter Show, 1964, wearing the steel neck brace after the accident.

With Rajah (my first German shepherd) at Appleton's Pool in Melbourne, 1964.

My controversial march in the opening ceremony, Tokyo Olympics, 1964 (I am in the middle).

My three Olympic golds.

Making the headlines after winning my third gold medal for the 100 metres freestyle. Sharon Stouder (L) and Kathy Ellis (R).

Being introduced at the 100 metres freestyle final, Tokyo, 1964.

Dancing in Tokyo's Queen Bee nightclub after the Games.

Speaking at the Balmain Council reception given in my honour after Tokyo.

Being driven down the straight at Flemington in front of 85 000 people at the 1964 Melbourne Cup. One of the most exciting things that has ever happened to me. (Inset) Watching the Cup with Gary.

January 1965, my wedding reception at the Balmain Town Hall.

With Gary and his mother, Olive, at our wedding.

The attention paid to our wedding by the media was overwhelming for Gary.

Our honeymoon in Tahiti as reported in *Woman's Day*.

could find my gold medal and to bring that too. I told him the police station was just around the corner, then added quite firmly, 'Don't be long!' When he arrived, Lee was made to sit in a separate room while the Superintendent looked at my ID and my medal, and came to the conclusion that I was telling the truth. I then wrote a note of apology to the Japanese police, saying that I'd just wanted to souvenir the flag as a memento to take back to Australia and that I was terribly sorry I'd caused so much fuss. All the while the Superintendent was saying things like, 'Oooh, you very naughty girl,' and I was saying, 'Yes, I very naughty girl,' which I guess was fairly accurate.

I was extremely embarrassed at the time and felt like an idiot for causing so much trouble. The police were being extremely nice and the Superintendent in particular was a very lovely man. I felt that I'd been a bit disrespectful, although that had never been my intention. I signed my letter of apology, and just as I did Des Piper's voice rang out from the next room: 'Don't sign anything, Fraser.'

I called back, 'I just did.'

Piper and Toyne had been picked up just before I had but they didn't have any flags on them. They had heard my voice in the room next door and realised I'd been arrested too, although none of us saw each other at the station.

The police then folded the flag and put it on the edge of the desk, and the Superintendent went and got his camera. I put the gold medal round his neck. By now the whole atmosphere was very chummy and quite excited. He had his photo taken with me and with the medal and he told me he was going to let me off. He nevertheless explained that in Japan what I had done was not souveniring but rather stealing and it carried a jail term of up to four years. That gave me a fright and I realised how lucky I'd been.

Finally the Superintendent arranged to get some policemen to carry me back down the stairs because by then my ankle was swollen and sore from when I'd sprained it jumping down from the wall. Unfortunately they dropped me on the way down because they were quite small and I was quite tall. That made my ankle much worse.

When I was finally downstairs and hobbling out to the police car they'd provided I said, 'You keep the gold medal and I'll take the flag.'

'Oh, no, no, no, I could not do that.'

With that the Superintendent put the gold medal around my neck and wished us well. Back at the hotel I told Lee the whole story while we waited for Des and Dr Toyne in my room, which is where we'd agreed to meet if anything went wrong. When they didn't come back after a while, Lee went off to bed to get a much-needed rest and I took a shower. I'd begun to pong of dirty pond water. Then I snatched a few precious hours sleep before the others finally showed up at about 7.00 a.m. Dr Toyne examined my ankle, which was pretty sore by then, and told me it was badly sprained and possibly even broken. He strapped it using bandages he had in his bag from when he'd attended the hockey match the night before.

Neither Des nor Howard signed anything or confessed to anything at the police station, and no one even knew they'd been involved until many years later. For twenty-eight years after that night my lips remained sealed about their involvement because Frasers never dob. Lee Robinson was in no fit state to remember much about the whole event and I doubt he would even have known who Des Piper was. So it really was my secret. And it was in the best interests of Piper and Toyne not to tell the story themselves. I could understand Howard Toyne keeping quiet—he was an official—but I believe Piper should have come forward to help me shoulder the blame after the story leaked out in the newspapers. Des Piper eventually told the story himself, in 1988, because he had been appointed Manager of an Olympic team and said he thought I might have brought it up at that time. I would never,

ever have named him, as I think so many years of silence more than proved, and I wonder if he finally came clean to try to get some publicity. If that was the plan it backfired because so many people said he'd let me down and should have owned up when the whole episode first came to light.

While we were chatting about the events of the previous night, there was a knock at my door and in walked Superintendent Kamira and four other police. As you can imagine, I was getting pretty tired of the whole incident by this stage and just wanted to get to the village for the closing ceremony. The Superintendent carried a large box and he kept saying, 'Open, open, open,' which I did, and it was full of beautiful flowers. I thanked them very much, and then he kept saying, 'No, open, open.' I looked in the box again and opened another flat parcel on the bottom, and it was the flag. My flag. The bloody flag that has haunted me for the rest of my life. These days I tell the story to kids at school, the moral being: if you want something ask for it but don't steal it. I still have the flag in a very safe place, despite the many other theories and claims as to its whereabouts that people have made over the years. At the Sydney Games the IOC official Dick Pound suggested to me that I return it, just as 1920s American bronze medallist Hal Haig Prieste did in 2000. I told him I would never part with my flag because it is worth so much more than others, having cost me my career.

One of the great misconceptions about my life, however, is that I was eventually banned from competing again because of the flag incident. In fact officially I was banned for entirely different reasons. When I took the flag I was not even with the team, although I still had to wear the uniform, and consequently the episode was never raised officially when I was back in Australia. Nevertheless, it was somehow reported in the press, although I never told anyone, and I think the flag incident was taken into account off the record when I ran into trouble again with the ASU after I came back from Tokyo.

Over the years the story of that night has been retold a thousand different ways by many people who don't know the truth. It has been told with me being the one up the pole, with me swimming in the Emperor's moat, with me stealing it from the actual palace, and so on. Can I please just put to rest the story of the moat here and now. If I had swum in that filfthy, dirty moat I wouldn't have lived to tell the tale. There was certainly no way I could have got into the palace grounds, either. The walls were far too high. The flag has become part of many more interesting episodes in my life, and has also been a bedspread and horse blanket for a photo opportunity, among other uses over the years.

A few days before the closing ceremony, Len Curnow had asked if I would carry the Australian flag. He said that many of the other athletes had suggested I be the one and he agreed I was the right choice. It was such a great thrill to be asked, and I would have done it no matter what, despite my now extremely painful ankle. Now, arriving at the village on the big day, I told Len about my part in the events of the previous night in case it leaked out and he heard it from someone else first. I thought he was an excellent Chef de Mission who'd given me lots of support over the period of the Games and felt I owed him the confidence of the flag incident. He wasn't overly concerned and actually thought it was very funny. He certainly didn't take the flag carrying honour away from me, which was such a contrast to the opening ceremony when I had to go against the instructions of the swimming officials. To me it is a contrast in management styles. One lot was there for their own self-aggrandisement and the other was there to help the athletes perform at their best and enjoy a unique experience.

I had my ankle strapped even tighter by Dr Toyne before I put my stockings on. It was quite difficult to get a shoe on because it was so swollen. Toyne had diagnosed sprained tendons but said I'd have to leave it like that till I flew home. He was concerned about me marching in that state carrying a heavy flag but I took a couple of painkillers and kept quiet in case they took the role of carrying the flag away from me. I set out to walk to the arena and then twice around. It was a two and a half mile walk in all and I just floated around. You don't think about pain at a time like that. I was deeply honoured. Just before I stepped out into the arena Bill Northam, who had won a gold medal in yachting and was the oldest Australian ever to win an Olympic medal, said, 'Here Fraser, have my hat,' and with that he snatched my hat and gave me his sailing cap. I couldn't do anything about it because he ran away with my hat. I have always felt it was a lovely sort of gesture. The photos and film of the closing ceremony show me smiling in a larrikin sort of way with his cap perched rakishly on my head while I give the Emperor a bit of a thumbs-up. It was a joyful experience that I will never forget.

•

I had received so many letters of congratulations and good wishes while I was in Tokyo that I asked the Japanese businessman Mr Shoriki, who ran the respected *Yomiuri* newspaper, to print my letter in response on the front page of the paper. He did this for me and I was very grateful as there was no way I could have acknowledged so much correspondence individually. I also received a special request to appear on NHK TV, the national network that broadcast through more than two hundred television stations around Japan. The interviewer asked if I wanted to say something to the Japanese people and I said, 'Thank you for your support and kindness and may God be with you.'

•

When I returned to Sydney the next day my ankle was so swollen that I had to remove the strapping before being taken from the plane in a wheelchair to meet the press. Gary was there, along with Rose and Bill, and it was wonderful to see them all again. When the media asked what had happened to my ankle I just said it was sprained and I'd been advised to keep off it.

One of the most wonderful things that happened when I returned to Australia was that the Victorian Racing Club arranged to have Gary and me driven down the straight at Flemington on Melbourne Cup Day. It was an honour that had only ever been given to the Queen before that day, and even as I write this now I feel embarrassed by the comparison. There were over 85 000 people watching as we waved from an open-topped car. Gary was overwhelmed and totally mortified. I, on the other hand, was overwhelmed and completely thrilled. So at least we had one thing in common. I wore a pink duster coat and skirt suit with matching hat and shoes loaned to me by Maggie Tabberer. For someone as athletic and svelte as I was at the time, I certainly did a good job of hiding myself under the coat. It made me seem very wide and Maggie later described me as looking like a big pink sofa. Back then, though, it was very fashionable and much admired. All I can add is that Maggie chose it!

There were many civic receptions and other functions held in my honour following my return home, including a welcome parade through the city streets of Melbourne. At one reception, in the Victorian country town of Sale during a tour of the regional areas, Gary and I had hundreds of rose petals thrown all over us, which left Gary not knowing where to look or what to do, but I adored it. I went to lots of schools and children's wards in hospitals, which was something I loved. In keeping with my other near misses in planes, Gary and I were flying into Melbourne Airport in a light four-seater aircraft when we were put in a holding pattern (yes, it even happened back then). Eventually the plane's engine started to splutter because we were running out of fuel and we made an emergency landing just in time.

I was also given a civic reception at Balmain Town Hall, which was attended by all the area's dignitaries and my neighbourhood friends and family. Balmain Council had to borrow the red carpet they rolled out for me from Ashfield Council. I thanked all the people who had helped from the early days and made special mention of my cousin Ray Miranda and also Harry Gallagher.

Gary was seriously struggling with the level of attention we were receiving, but I kept reassuring him that it wouldn't last and eventually things would settle down. We agreed we'd get married in January and perhaps move to the countryside or back to Townsville. I was reluctant to give up the idea of living in Balmain but sort of went along with our plans at that stage. I toyed with the idea of giving up swimming, too, although a part of me had already set my sights on the Mexico Olympics. I guess I was torn. To give it all up just like that wasn't a possibility, but I also loved Gary and wanted to be his wife and have a family. In those heady months after the Games I found it easiest to push the dilemma to the back of my mind.

Over Christmas, which we spent in Sydney, I was also busy planning a wedding for January 30th. Adele helped me plan it and I asked her to be my bridesmaid, along with Janette Simpson, the fiancée of my nephew, Billy Quantrill, Joyce's son. Janette's mother made the bridesmaids' dresses, which were teal blue, full-length silk, in her shop at Leichhardt. I wore the wedding gown I'd had made by the Fontana Sisters in Rome in 1960. It was a very elegant, white full-length lace dress over a pale pink underskirt. The neckline was scalloped and deep and it also had three-quarter-length sleeves. The veil was held in place by a pearl coronet. All the flowers were done at Cooper's in neighbouring Rozelle. The men, including Gary, his best friend Eric Barnett, who'd played football with him, and my brother Alick, wore black tails, as it was an evening wedding which started at 6.00 p.m. We married in St Stephens, a grand old church in Macquarie Street in the middle of Sydney, which I'd always liked, with a reception to follow at Balmain Town Hall. The Codocks Women's Auxiliary arranged the catering for the three hundred guests, who included all Mum's old friends; the Balmain neighbourhood; my swimming friends, including Harry; and Gary's racing friends and his family, except for his father who wasn't well enough. We paid for the food but those fantastic women did everything else: the cooking, the serving and the cleaning up. Being a part of the fabric of Balmain never felt so wonderful.

It completely astonished me that on the day of the wedding so many people lined the streets around the terrace in Balmain that the police had to come down and make a path for the wedding cars to depart for the church. My brother Ken took me in one car, as he'd be the one to give me away in place of Pop. The cars were all supplied by our family friend Johnny Leach and included a white Plymouth.

When we arrived at St Stephens the crowd outside the church was at least five hundred strong and once again it was a bit of a struggle to get through. The whole service was recorded and televised by an exclusive crew inside the church—the first time filming had been allowed inside—but by every news station outside. To this day people tell me that Gary and I talked through the whole service. Basically he was nervous and I was reassuring him. We were driven back to the Balmain Town Hall and the scene was the same. Gary and I had to go out onto the balcony to wave to the crowd that had gathered below and started chanting, 'We want Dawn! We want Dawn!' It was great fun and very touching. Adele came home with me between the wedding and the reception because I'd forgotten something. Neither of us now has a clue what that important thing was, but to avoid the media still waiting outside we climbed over the back fence in hysterics. All Adele can remember of the incident is me hoisting my wedding gown up and her shoving my bum over the fence. The reception went into the early hours of the morning and Gary and I had a bit of an argument over a singer he had brought down from Townsville to perform with the Maori Band, who were friends of my brothers. I felt he was showing her a little too much attention.

That night we went to what was then a very fashionable hotel, the Chevron in Kings Cross, and the next day visited my mother's grave. I placed my wedding bouquet on her headstone and spoke privately to her, Pop and Donnie. How I wished they had been at my wedding to see me so happy. The many bouquets of flowers I'd received, along with those I'd ordered for the reception, were sent to the Balmain Hospital.

After all the excitement and public scrutiny, Gary and I were looking forward to being alone when we flew out to Tahiti on the following Wednesday. Unfortunately there was a barrage of cameramen at the airport to see us off and Gary was very cranky, saying to the press, 'We just want to be alone but it looks like we haven't got off to a very good start.' Then, just as we began to relax on the plane, I saw a photographer I knew sitting quite near us. That's when Gary told me he'd done a deal for our honeymoon with *Woman's Day*. We had given the magazine an exclusive on the wedding, but I didn't realise it was extended to the honeymoon. I was shocked beyond belief and dismayed that someone who had objected so much to the media attention had now gone and organised exactly that for what was supposed to be our most private and intimate time together. What I didn't really know about Gary then, but eventually came to realise, was that he did indeed hate media attention, but he was a gambler and desired the money more then he loathed the limelight.

I felt very cross with Gary for making this arrangement with *Woman's Day*. We still didn't know each other that well, with me having been away in Tokyo and then on the road since returning. Now, when we had a chance to get to know each other better, we would be followed by a photographer. I can remember one incident early on when we were lying on the sand kissing and the photographer literally came up behind us and asked us to smile.

Everything we did was photographed. We dressed up in traditional Tahitian gear one night and there was the photographer; we had dinner together and there was the photographer; and so on. One particular night we came back from dinner and Gary, who'd had a few too many drinks, started to accuse me of having an affair with the big Tahitian man who was looking after our hospitality. He'd noticed that the man laid out my nightgown on the bed each night when it was turned down. As I was with Gary twenty-four hours a day, with our every move being photographed, I'm not sure when I was supposed to be having the affair. Fortunately Gary shied away from actually picking a fight with my suspected Tahitian lover when he saw the size of him close-up one day.

Lighter moments aside, it was on our honeymoon that I found out how jealous Gary could be and how much he wanted to control me. Gary was very sweet and I liked the fact that he was a bit of a lad, but he had some deep insecurities that drove the free spirit in me to distraction. Like many other people in my life up till then, and some still in my life now, Gary wanted to control and change me, and I cannot bear to be controlled for the sake of it. Harry Gallagher is a great example of someone in my life who didn't try to change me but instead worked with who I am. That's why that relationship developed so well over so many years.

I'm not suggesting that everyone should bend to my rules while I go about doing whatever I please, because I have always been easy to get along with when people aren't trying to control me for the sheer sake of exerting their power. I'm the first to muck in and get along with the next person and help the underdog, or just enjoy the easy company of those around me. It may surprise you to know that I like my life to be peaceful. If someone can point out a logical way of doing something I'm more than happy to adopt their method, but I have a very short fuse for pettiness, jealousy and trumped-up people who don't really know what they're talking about. Gary definitely fell into the 'jealous' category, as much as I loved him for his other qualities.

While our domestic squabbles punctuated the bliss of our honeymoon, a storm was brewing back in Sydney. A letter dated February 16th, 1965 had been sent to me care of my brother Alick at the caretaker's cottage at Leichhardt Swimming Pool, where Alick now worked. I had never lived at the pool caretaker's cottage in Leichhardt, a suburb near Balmain, and nor had Alick, so why the letter was sent there remains a mystery to this day. And just as mysterious is why the sporting body of which I'd been a prominent member for so long didn't know where I lived. Alick didn't open the letter at the time, understandably assuming, given the amount of fan mail I received, that it probably wasn't anything that couldn't wait till we came home.

The letter had been written by none other than Mr Bill Berge Phillips, then the Secretary of the ASU. When I read it I already knew the gist of its contents from newspaper posters and billboards that had greeted Gary and I as we drove along King Street on the afternoon we got back from our honeymoon: 'Dawn Fraser Banned for 10 Years'. Gary was the first to notice them, and he turned to me and said, 'What did you do in Tokyo?'

'What do you mean?' I said. He pointed to a billboard and I said, 'We'd better stop and get a paper.'

We pulled up on the corner of King and Castlereagh streets and the newspaper vendor put his head through the window and said, 'Dawnie, what have you done?' The *Sun* newspaper had broken the story a day before everyone else and Gary got the shits and said, 'I think we'd better go home and discuss this.' I just laughed. I hadn't done anything.

The ban was announced to the whole press the next day at the Hobart Nationals, where the ASU were holding their annual meeting to discuss the year's events, including the tabling of reports from Tokyo. Gary immediately assumed the worst and the calm that had descended on us over the last few days of our honeymoon flew out the window in a barrage of accusations and anxious questions. Later, when he read the scurrilous newspaper report in the *Sun*, penned by E. E. Christensen, who seemed to have a direct line to the ASU throughout my career, Gary asked if I had been attending wild parties in Tokyo. It appeared I had been sentenced once again without a hearing, and once again there was a lot of speculation that something 'much worse' must have happened for the sentence to be so tough. Although I didn't want to derive any comfort from the misfortune of my fellow swimmers, at least this time I was not alone. Linda McGill had also been banned for four years, and Nan Duncan and Marlene Dayman for three years each. The ASU had once again neglected to actually explain the reasons for the bans, suggesting that it would be better for us if our terrible deeds were not divulged to the public. In any case, that was how married life began for Gary and me, and the ban was to cast a long shadow over the rest of our time together.

The Australian Swimming Union yesterday expelled four Olympic girl swimmers for periods ranging [up to] 10 years.

10

FALLING

The letter from Bill Berge Phillips on behalf of the ASU said I was being charged with two offences, and that if I had anything to say in my defence I should send a written statement to the Board. But by the time I read the letter it was too late for me to answer the charges; in fact, I would have to have been standing at the Leichhardt Pool caretaker's house when the postman arrived in order to take up that particular opportunity.

The first charge was (A) disobeying the Team Manager for wearing an unofficial swimsuit, and (B) disobeying the ASU for wearing an unofficial swimsuit. The second charge was

(A) disobeying the Team Manager and marching in the opening ceremony, and (B) disobeying the ASU and marching in the opening ceremony.

The letters, one to each of us who'd been suspended, were sent about two weeks prior to the ASU conference in Hobart, where the official reports of Bill Slade and our chaperone, Anne Hatton, would be tabled. Of course by the time I became aware of all of this the ten-year ban was firmly in place. The same applies for the other girls, although I seem to remember one of them received and read her letter in time but didn't front the conference. I was quoted in the Sydney *Daily Mirror* the day after the ban became public knowledge as saying, 'We weren't given the rights of any normal Australian—that's a fair trial. We should have been allowed to appear before the committee to answer the charges and been given the opportunity of reply. Even the worst criminals—rapists and murderers—have the right to appeal, and if I can find a way to do it I will certainly do it.'

Anne Hatton weighed in a day later: 'I named the four girls in my report, but the most I expected would happen was that they would be reprimanded, or at worst suspended for a year. It's appalling. And the sentences were imposed in such an undemocratic manner, allowing the girls no right to appeal.'

The charges against me, as simple as they were, never became clear in the papers in those days immediately following the ban but were instead muddied by a whole range of additional comments and much innuendo. It began with the Sydney *Sun*'s exclusive by Ernie Christensen, which had been fed to them by someone at the ASU. This article later became the subject of a legal action in which it was revealed that the story of us misbehaving by attending drinks parties and sneaking out to the men's quarters had been given to the newspaper by the ASU. That newspaper report, for all the grief it caused me, was one of the only glimpses I've had of what may have been contained in the official report.

Sometimes I felt the two groups, the officials and the press, were one and the same. Mr Edgar Tanner, then the Secretary of the Australian Olympic Federation, was quoted in an *Age* story about the bans as saying it had taken him two weeks to recover from the shock of reading the ASU's official report about the activities of the swimmers at the Games. Subsequently, and understandably, everyone thought we four must have done something far worse than march in the opening ceremony against instructions.

Newspaper reports from the time remind me now that I immediately sought legal advice and decided to take the ASU to court. Just two days after the story appeared in the *Sun*, my solicitor, Ted France, told the *Daily Mirror* that he had briefed the QC Clive Evatt and his junior counsel, Andrew Leary, and that we were considering taking action against the ASU for 'denying me natural justice'. He also said that if it could be shown that I had been held up to public ridicule, we would consider taking action for defamation. Ultimately, we also sued the *Sun* for defamation over Ernie Christensen's article which had broken the story.

Despite the general smear campaign run by the *Sun* in Sydney, whose breaking story on March 1st, 1965 carried the headline '4 GIRLS PUNISHED; Drink, parties in Tokyo report', there were many, many people who came out on our side. The New South Wales Premier at the time, Mr Renshaw, described the expulsion as having 'all the elements of hate rather than a reasonable approach'. He continued, 'I don't know what the facts are, but the penalties in their scope and extent seem savage in the extreme.'

The Victorian Premier, Mr Bolte, attacked the Amateur Swimming Union in Parliament for not explaining their extreme actions. He said, 'No government could get away with this arbitrary action without sufficient explanation.' He went on to cast doubt over whether funds would be so easily granted to the ASU next time round unless a more detailed explanation was given for their actions. 'When governments and people are asked to subscribe to funds to send our teams away to the Olympic and Commonwealth Games, surely they are entitled to know why this action has been taken,' he added. In a rare show of unity, the Victorian State Opposition Leader, Mr Stoneham, joined the general roar of disapproval. He described the expulsions as 'outrageous' and also said, 'The penalties inflicted on these girls are out of all reason.' Anne Hatton said the bans were 'savage in the extreme' and intimated that if she'd had any inkling of what the punishment would be she may not have reported us at all.

The story of the bans made the press around the world, and ran on the front pages of London newspapers, which unanimously decried the actions of the ASU and described them variously as 'lunatic', 'shamefully humiliating', and 'high handed and autocratic'. Pat Beresford, one of Britain's leading swimming commentators, said, 'What a dreadful thing to have done to Dawn after all she has done for Australian swimming.' Judy Grinham, a women's backstroke gold medallist from 1956, said she was 'flabbergasted' by the ASU, and continued, 'We English swimmers regarded Dawn as not only the greatest woman swimmer in the world but as a grand person.' Thank you, Judy. Even Avery Brundage, the President of the International Olympic Committee, said he was 'surprised by the ban' and other US officials said the ASU were 'cutting off their nose to spite their face'.

More important to me at the time was the response of the Chairman of the Olympic Organising Committee in Tokyo. Mr Yasukawa said the ban was 'drastic action' and that 'We in Japan don't recall any incident involving Australian swimmers which would warrant such action.' He also added, which I thought was pretty pertinent at the time, that he could not understand why they had waited so long after the Games to place the bans.

So much for all the support from overseas. Back in Australia the President of the ASU, Dr Dowling, said the reasons for the expulsions would never be made public. So there it was again: secrets, innuendo and hidden reasons. I wasn't going to stand for it this time, having suffered one round of whispering and finger pointing following the publication of Roger Pegram's report from Rome.

Support for the bans came from unexpected quarters, with both Harry Gallagher and Jan Andrew saying they felt it was time some action was taken. Jan was quoted in the *Daily Mirror* on March 2nd as saying, 'The penalties were a bit harsh but it is high time something was done to stamp out some of the behaviour in Games teams... She [Dawn] is a law unto herself and always goes a little too far.' And from Harry, my mentor, in the *Daily Mirror* on March 3rd: 'I am sorry that Dawn and Marlene were involved but I firmly believe the Amateur Swimming Union of Australia had to take a stand against the misbehaviour of swimmers on tours. The suspensions could be the first step in putting Australia back on top in world swim-ming...we want to break records not rules.' I was then quoted in response: 'I don't know or care what Harry Gallagher or anyone else thinks.'

At the time of writing this book I approached the ASU in its current incarnation, Australian Swimming Incorporated, to obtain access to Bill Slade's official report on the swimming team in Tokyo because I have never seen it. The well-known sports writer Harry Gordon, my biographer from the 1960s, has also tried to get hold of it on various occasions without success, and on his last attempt said that the only version he'd seen had all references to the so-called misconduct cut out with scissors. I found the same thing this time round, and I don't know if an uncensored version of the report still exists. All that was sent to me after repeated requests was a single page from the minutes of the conference, which is dated February 28th, 1965. In reference to me it reads as follows:

The Conference continued in Committee.
It was unanimously resolved that, in the opinion of the Union:

Mrs G.Ware, nee Dawn Fraser, had been guilty of misconduct and it was further unanimously resolved that Mrs G.Ware, nee Dawn Fraser, be expelled. If, after a period of ten years from 1st March, 1965, she so desires, she may make application to seek to have the expulsion lifted.

The page then goes on to outline, in similar terms, the bans imposed on the other three girls. Presumably much discussion preceded this point in the conference, and presumably the report in full had also been tabled. The judgment from my defamation action against the *Sun*, the only other glimpse I've had of the actual proceedings and report, states that our behaviour was discussed for two hours on one day of the conference and a further four hours the following day. What was in the report and the discussion that followed its tabling continues to elude me and others who have gone looking. The judgment does say that Mr Slade had made drinking charges against two of us and a further charge that one of us had been sneaking out after lights-out to party in the New Zealand men's quarters. None of the latter charges appeared in my letter, and the judgment doesn't say which of the four girls was guilty of what. As I received the longest ban, it was assumed by most that I was the one who'd done all these things. I have been told I cannot use the Freedom of Information Act to gain access to the report because the ASU was not a government body. According to other advice, there is possibly another legal avenue I could use—if indeed an intact copy of the report still exists—but I have not attempted this, and part of me, at my stage in life, doesn't want to spend time and money fighting old enemies.

Some newspaper stories from around the time of the bans suggest there was general nervousness about revealing what was in the reports because of possible problems with defamation. One such story, in May 1965, suggests that the Australian Olympic Federation was very worried about the reports becoming public. It says in part:

Today's AOF meeting was expected to be the most fiery in its history but it fizzled out like a damp squib when it ousted the press after Mr McKenzie's warning. Mr McKenzie, a Sydney solicitor, suggested secrecy when discussing confidential reports from sectional managers on the behaviour of athletes in Tokyo. He told me that if the contents of the reports were published at the meeting while non-delegates were present 'we would lose our defence in defamation'.

Coincidentally, David McKenzie, who was then the fencing delegate at the AOF, later became a very dear friend of mine.

Another report, in the *Sydney Morning Herald* of March 29th, entitled 'Officials Cut Report on Swimmers', says that certain pages of the official report by Bill Slade, which was released to the media in Melbourne on that day, had been deleted or cut out under the direction—according to a note attached to the front of the report— of the ASU. The charges listed in the ASU's letter to me still appeared in the report, so there were clearly other allegations made by Mr Slade which had been deleted. I'll never know for sure whether these missing allegations had anything to do with the flag incident. A version of the flag story appeared later in the year when my autobiography, *Gold Medal Girl*, ghosted by Harry Gordon, was published. Harry and I had been working on the book since the year before, and as far as I knew, this was the first time the flag story was widely known. Len Curnow had of course known about the incident since the Games, but I don't believe he would have told anyone, and anyway, he wasn't one of those who voted on the bans. There was, however, one newspaper report, in the *Daily Mirror* of March 2nd, that mysteriously said the following: 'A spokesman for the Maranouchi Police Station said Dawn Fraser and three other Australian girls were brought to the station about two days after the close of the Games because they had taken a flag at a fountain in the Palace Hotel in front of the Imperial

Palace. The girls probably did it for fun and they were released after they were questioned.'

The spokesman went on, 'The girls never entered the Imperial Palace and they did not swim in the Imperial moat.'

That report is clearly false, but it does suggest the flag story was known to some at the time. Perhaps someone can produce the elusive official report and prove me wrong?

In 1965, straight after the announcement of the bans, I spoke to the media and said, 'I want to have the whole matter out in the open. I want to see how big these people are who have slandered my name.' I felt that what has been left unsaid was worse than what was being said, and practically begged Dr Dowling to give 'the real reasons' for the bans. I wanted to know what the hell I was supposed to have done, and so did the other three girls. Nan Duncan's mother was quoted at the time as saying, 'I am greatly distressed. I can't believe it. I can't understand the whole thing. Poor Nan can't make it out; she's in a daze. Why she's never been to a school dance.' It went on and on and it was distressing and still no one would reveal the real reasons for the bans.

These days, with the media reporting humorously on how many condoms are delivered to Olympic villages, it is difficult to comprehend the level of rumour and gossip surrounding the bans back in 1965. What is worrying is that some of the officials from back then are still around the sport today.

Even before Tokyo, Gary and I used to talk in general terms about my going to the Commonwealth Games in Jamaica in 1966 and maybe even getting as far as the Mexico Olympic Games in 1968. When I got back I felt I was still improving, as my relay swim had shown, and told the press at the time that I'd take the season off and then see how I felt in the summer of 1965/66. The ban unfortunately intervened and I needed to think about trying to get that lifted before I concentrated on my next career move. It was clear to me, however, that I didn't want to give swimming away. As much as I was foxing around the issue and wanted a season off, I had it in the back of my mind to go to Mexico and win again. The ban served the purpose of making me more determined to continue, just as the previous bans had done.

Almost from the beginning, marriage to Gary was not an easy thing. We loved each other very much and were very suited physically, but those elements don't always make for a stable, enduring marriage, which is what I was hoping for. The traits that had attracted us most to each other were almost straightaway the things that started to grate on our nerves. He had been proud of my achievements when we first met and now he felt they overshadowed everything else. Naturally the persistent innuendo in newspaper stories and the constant media attention, good and bad, interfered as we tried to get to know each other as husband and wife. I used to remind Gary that he'd known exactly what the deal was before we got married. It wasn't as if I had hidden the fact that I was an Olympic swimmer, and he'd seen, almost from day one, that I was followed everywhere by the media. To be fair, though, neither of us could have been prepared for the level of attention I received after Tokyo and again following the ban.

The fact that I'd liked Gary's flamboyance, easy charm and involvement in the racing world did not make up for the fact that I now found him more than irresponsible with money and with his commitment to our marriage. At one time his many distractions at the track and his devil-may-care personality had made him exciting and interesting, but now when he came home late, without a word of where he'd been, I was just plain annoyed. I started to notice what I felt were large sums of money being taken after a big win in one hand and given straight back in bets on the next race with the other. Coming from my working-class background where money was scarce, and having had an entirely amateur career in which earning money to pay bills had not always been easy, I couldn't come to terms with such terrible waste. Perhaps I made the very mistake with him that people had often made with me. I tried to change him. But I did have very good reasons for wanting to do so.

I became pregnant almost as soon as we were married. I know for a fact that we conceived on March 8th, 1965 just a few days after we returned from Tahiti. I was absolutely head over heels about being pregnant. It was what I wanted more than anything. Even though I hadn't really focused on what I was going to do about the ban, for the time being I was telling myself that the pregnancy was more than enough because I was with the man I loved and we were going to start a family together. And it may have been enough in the long term if my marriage hadn't started to split at the seams. In those early months I was able to push the ban issue aside and concentrate on the wonderful idea of becoming a mother, something I had wanted almost all my life. I would have my children, love my husband and the ASU could go and get stuffed.

If only it had been that simple.

From the beginning we heard rumours that I'd conceived before the wedding and people started to do their nasty little calculations to try and catch us out. I was used to that sort of gossip by that stage but Gary wasn't and it annoyed him. We returned from our honeymoon to live in Balmain in the old terrace house. Alick had moved out when he married and I was thrilled to be back in my neighbourhood where I knew everyone and they knew me. Gary, on the other hand, was a fish out of water. As his mother Ol had gently warned me, he was a country boy and just couldn't fit into the inner-city environment. Things soon went from bad to worse, and I couldn't even be sure in those early months that Gary would come home at all. I was desperate about the situation but also desperately in love and too proud to admit we had any problems. Most of our fights were over money being spent on gambling when we had precious little to spare, or because he'd been out half the night and had worried me senseless. But whatever we argued about, it would often conclude with Gary hurling accusations at me about my so-called 'behaviour' in Tokyo, all based on stupid speculation he'd read in the papers. He'd also nag me about spending too much time up the road in the Riverview with Mum's old friends, and especially with Red, her best friend. I was mostly at the pub for the company. I'd been away a long time and I was basking in the security of being among the people I'd grown up with. Besides, it was something my family had always done. But Gary couldn't understand it, even though he was rarely at home himself.

Around May that year it seemed that the best thing to do would be to try going back to Townsville. At least that's what Gary wanted. I was reluctant to leave the neighbourhood that I knew so well, especially when I was pregnant, but I wanted to make the marriage work and there wasn't much holding me in Sydney. I was only working at cleaning houses to try to make ends meet, as I didn't want to work at anything that might threaten my amateur status because I was sure I could successfully fight the ban. Gary and I used to talk quite a lot about overcoming the ban and seeing me go to the Mexico Games. We'd even discuss how we could arrange the training around the baby and who would do what to make it happen. It was still a bit of a vague plan at that stage and I was more preoccupied with holding my fragile family life together. Looking back, it was laughable to think Gary would have made the sacrifices necessary for me to return to swimming, but when we were first married, the lovely side of this man was still shining through often enough for me to have my dreams about the future.

In Townsville we first moved in with Gary's parents and then to a small flat off The Strand, a main street in Townsville. Even though I knew a few people there I was lonely and anxious about the pregnancy so far from my family. Gary wasn't much help in this because he'd leave early in the morning for the racetrack and more often than not go straight from there to a pub, leaving me completely alone for the entire day and evening. I knew he was heavily into gambling, although he denied it whenever I brought it up. I suffered from night sickness during my pregnancy, rather than the more common morning sickness, and felt unwell much of the time because I was missing out on so much sleep. Gary began to bring home some of the jockeys and other people he'd meet around the track quite late at night and I was expected to cook them a meal, which I did because I wanted to please him and make the relationship last. I was very scared of losing him because I wanted my child to have two parents and I was also still very much in love.

Eventually, in about October, when it became too much being stuck in the flat by myself all day, I said firmly that I wanted to go back to Sydney to have the baby. I wanted to be with my sisters and friends and live in my own home again. Gary was very agreeable to this idea because he had accumulated gambling debts in Townsville that he couldn't service and his horse training hadn't been going so well. I had said I would introduce him to some of my contacts in Sydney so he could find new work as an SP. So we set out quite optimistically for a new life in Sydney two months before the baby was due to be born. I felt it was important to take Gary out of the environment he had become used to up there in Townsville, but as it turned out I took him out of the frying pan and into the fire. He was to become a worse gambler almost overnight in Sydney and by then I had less strength to fight him. I felt weighed down as my pregnancy progressed, sad at what was happening to my marriage and angry about the ban, as well as suffering withdrawal symptoms from my previously all-consuming swimming career. I had gone from the limelight in Tokyo to sitting at home wondering where the next pay cheque would come from. I had bills to pay and no idea from one day to the next if the money would be there. Even at that advanced stage of pregnancy I took up cleaning a few houses and doing some filing work at a local office.

Gary was by now involved in blackjack games and many other forms of illegal gambling that were easily found in and around Forbes Street in the inner-city at that time. Soon he wasn't coming home much at all, and rarely before the early hours of the morning. I knew in my heart of hearts that it was wrong and not the way the marriage should be going but I kept pretending otherwise because the baby was due and I really couldn't face what was happening at that time. There wasn't a lot I could do anyway because it was an addiction for him. As I sat at home alone and heavily pregnant I began to wonder if there were other women on the scene and what exactly he was up to for so long every night.

During the daytime Gary was either at Canterbury Racetrack, or Warwick Farm, or Kembla Grange or Randwick. It had become apparent that Sydney was the last place I should have brought him. I'd gone from living a fairly straight life of training day in and day out to being married to someone who smoked several packets of cigarettes a day, often had alcohol on his breath in the afternoon, studied the form when he was home, and usually had no money to give me for food. On the other hand, I had all the support in the world from my sisters and my doctor, which was quite comforting as I didn't have a clue about giving birth or taking care of my baby. I also began to work as a swimming coach at a girl-friend's private pool to help make ends meet. Under the charter of the ASU it was not permissible to use your swimming skills, or your name in swimming, to earn a living, so I knew this job might affect my amateur status, but I had no choice. I had to put food on the table and pay my mortgage.

I was swimming for my own health right up until the birth. It was reminiscent of Mum swimming while she was pregnant with me. I was still overjoyed about the pregnancy, and when our little girl was born just a few weeks before Christmas in 1965 Gary and I were both so happy. Little Dawn-Lorraine, as we named her—I added the 'Lorraine' after Lorraine Crapp—was a beautiful child weighing in at seven pounds six ounces. I had a very easy labour, perhaps due to my extreme fitness, and ended up with so much breast milk that I began to express some for the premature babies on the ward at Canterbury Hospital where Dawn-Lorraine was born. I actually kept expressing for around six months after I left hospital and they would send a courier to collect the milk. It was a bit embarrassing actually, because the milk was just so plentiful I was teased by my friends and the nurses, who called me 'Dawnie the dairy cow'. From the minute I held my baby in my arms I loved her desperately and was quoted at the time as saying, 'It was a lot of trouble but worth it all. When I held my baby in my arms I knew it was the most wonderful moment of my life.'

In the meantime I'd had a long talk with Gary and said I felt our marriage wouldn't last unless some changes were made now we had a daughter. He did pull himself together in some ways and started trying to transfer his bookmaker's licence from Queensland to New South Wales. He had to go through a trial period for a while, when he worked on a different part of the course from the main enclosure at Randwick with a provisional licence of some kind. I'm not completely clear on the details of this arrangement, partly because Gary was secretive about his activities.

It seemed to me that Gary did try for those few months after Dawn-Lorraine was born, but there were plenty of bad days among the good ones and soon he began to break the cardinal rule. He was bookmaking but he was also punting—the sign of a very bad gambler as far as I was concerned. We began to fight again soon after I came home from hospital and this time I was very tired because I was up through the night breastfeeding Dawn-Lorraine. Gary would bring up Tokyo as a response to lots of the arguments and he'd yell, 'Tell me the truth, what did go on?' That hurt because I had always told him the truth, and I could never satisfy him with answers because nothing *had* gone on for him to be upset about.

As the months went by we had our good times out at dinner or at the races together while someone minded Dawn-Lorraine. Going out, however, brought its own set of difficulties because people would constantly come up to me and want to talk or shake my hand or get an autograph, and Gary would become impatient and jealous. I have always felt, but especially back then, that I owed the public some time and response after what they had given me, particularly the people of Balmain, who had helped my family and my career so much. What's more I liked many of the media, despite my loathing for a few particular journalists. They had generally been pretty good to me, so I would stop for an interview or agree to do a story from time to time. And I did shake people's hands and listen while they told me where they were when I swam a particular race, or that their grandmother had met me at a particular event and did I remember her? I'd respond to some letters and sign photos and autograph books, and Gary couldn't bear the fact that I would participate. But what irritated him more was that he couldn't stop me doing it. He wanted to be able to direct my every move, and I would not be directed.

Something else that worried him greatly was my large group of male friends. He couldn't grasp that they were just friends who I'd known most of my life and with whom I enjoyed talking about sport. I tried to explain that I'd always had male friends because I enjoyed male company, but this idea was ahead of its time and Gary immediately concluded there was something more sinister about these simple friendships.

For all my frustration with Gary and all the hurt he caused me, I understand that it was an awkward situation for him. He was unable to deal with the media, the attention, the idea of being a small fish in a big pond married to a big fish in a big pond and I tried—how I tried—to make him feel more at ease and more confident in himself. I used to look back years ago and wonder if I'd considered him enough at that time and whether I could have done more to help him through, to make that giant leap from anonymity in a country town to seeing his face on the front page of Sydney newspapers. He had been thrust into something that I'd gradually grown used to. It must have been horrible for him.

Despite the rows, our lives ran reasonably smoothly for about four months after Dawn-Lorraine was born. It is such a fleeting period but I remember it as being happy and the closest I would come to that dream of a settled marriage. Being the sort of person who had always worked, I now leaped at the opportunity to be a consultant at Sterling Swimwear, who had made some of my controversial swimming costumes for the Tokyo Games. They wanted me to help design a swimsuit, which would be known as the 'Dawn' and would be sold complete with swing tags bearing my image and a little biography of my achievements. They were planning to launch it in Osaka at a trade fair and invited me to travel to Japan to help them promote it. It was an opportunity to make a bit of money, which I was grateful for. Part of me felt I deserved to make some money out of my name after all these years, and another part of me was terrified that my husband was gambling away everything we had and I knew that I had better make some money where I could. My solicitor had advised me earlier to keep the house in my name, and I still felt I might have to bail Gary out of his problems at any moment.

Taking up the offer to go on the promotional tour would be outside the guidelines set down for amateur swimmers, and I still hadn't completely given up the idea of swimming again for my country. I knew that when the ban was lifted—and I was deter-mined that it would be—I would have to apply to regain my amateur status. But I kidded to myself that Mexico was still a long way off and I would have time to make all these arrangements. In the meantime I had a daughter to feed.

The trip to Japan was just a small taste of what it would be like to use my name to promote commercial products. This was a new idea at the time and seems especially small bananas in light of what goes on today. We went to Osaka, Tokyo and Yokohama, and while we were there I had a chance to catch up with my pen pal Tomoko and meet her family. The horrible and distressing postscript to this was that soon after I returned to Australia I learned that Tomoko and her family had all committed suicide because Tomoko's marks at university hadn't lived up to the expectation of her academic father. They had lost face.

Dawn-Lorraine was only four months old when I took her on the promotional tour and I had a special little carrying frame for her that could be used on the plane, in a car, in a restaurant or anywhere I went. She was a very placid, happy little baby, which made it possible for me to take her along. I was accompanied by some of the staff from Sterling Swimwear and we were all very well looked after in nice hotels. We went to lots of swimming pools, which were all sponsored by different swimwear companies, and showed them our range, including the 'Dawn' costume. I spoke to salespeople, attended trade fairs and 'meet and greet' dinners. The whole trip took about six weeks. Some of the autograph-signing sessions that were supposed to last an hour ended up lasting three or four because the queues were so long. I enjoyed the experience because of the warm welcome from the Japanese people and I also found it financially rewarding.

Gary had stayed behind, and as far as I could see on my return he had not changed. Still, I had missed him and he seemed to have missed me, and we were briefly happily reunited. Then we took Dawn-Lorraine to Townsville to meet her grandmother, Olive, and her other Queensland relatives. Olive adored Dawn-Lorraine, and it was also lovely taking my baby to see the Bartletts.

While we were in Townsville Gary decided he wanted to live there again but I refused point blank. By now I was fully aware that I was going to be the breadwinner in the family, and I could only do that in Sydney where my family would help mind Dawn-Lorraine and where I would be close to all my contacts, who could help me find work. So we returned to Sydney and the terrace in Balmain, where our marriage really began to crumble.

Gary began to drink a lot, something he hadn't particularly done before. I think his gambling debts had probably got to him. He went back to staying out night after night playing cards and pursuing other forms of gambling. When he was drunk he became aggressive towards me, something else I hadn't seen before or even suspected he was capable of. I had been brought up never to let anyone make me feel inferior and I was completely unable to tolerate Gary's physical abuse. A few people I confided in at the time told me that I could look after myself, but in fact I was very intimidated by his behaviour, both because I hadn't experienced it before and because I had a little baby in the house.

It came to a head round about May 1966. Gary had been out all night, and when he rolled in drunk at 4.00 a.m. I told him to go and sleep downstairs. With that he hit me so hard that out of shock and sheer blind anger I grabbed one of Dawn-Lorraine's baby bottles, which were of course made of glass, and followed him downstairs, breaking the bottle over the banister ready to attack him. In that instant I was so fired up I wanted to kill him and the strength of my feelings frightened me. Fortunately I was able to stop myself in time and at that point I said to Gary, 'That's it. I want you out. It's over.' He knew I meant it and maybe he even welcomed it. I'm sure he was as sick as I was of fighting and we could both see it was escalating. I still loved him but I knew that if he could get me so worked up and aggressive that I wanted to kill him, it had to be over. It had only been a momentary thought, but it had happened, and it told me the relationship was past the point of no return.

The next morning Gary got up from where he'd been sleeping on the lounge, had a shower and went out as if nothing had happened. While he was gone I packed his bags and put them out on the verandah. It broke my heart but I clung to the thought that I couldn't live with a person with the potential to drive me to commit murder. I'd spent those few hours in prison in Adelaide when I was arrested for loitering and I had no intention of ever going back for anything ever again.

When Gary arrived home that night to find his bags packed on the front verandah he knocked on the door and said that he loved me. I said, 'Yes, I love you too but we have to stop this. We need time away from each other and I have a baby to look after.' I used to worry that he'd turn on the baby the way he'd turned on me, or that Dawn-Lorraine would get a bit older and see what was going on, and I knew I couldn't allow that to happen. It broke my heart but I had no choice.

Later I discovered that my suspicions about him taking out other women had been true. I'm not naive. I know this goes on when men go off to nightclubs by themselves and have a few drinks. Gary certainly wasn't a strong person and I don't think he would have found that sort of female attention easy to resist. He was a good-looking man and I wasn't surprised to find out he'd been having affairs, but I was aware that affairs like that could easily be reported in the press, and I could well do without that sort of publicity after what I was already going through over the ban. Most of all I was just exhausted from the sixteen months of marriage and wanted to jump off the roller-coaster and get my life in order.

Gary went back to Townsville and I didn't see him again for a very long time. I used to write to his mother once a month to let her know how the baby was and I'd send photographs up too, but I didn't hear from Gary much more at all, and a few years later I decided it was time to file for divorce. I never regretted the marriage because I truly loved Gary and he was the father of our beautiful daughter. Even after he walked away that day, I was sorry that it didn't work out, but I did regret the extensive gambling debts he left behind, which I now had to pay off. Some of these had been run up with people I'd introduced him to from the old Balmain neighbourhood. That was difficult, although when I eventually paid them off I found people in that part of my life respected me for it.

Eventually Gary moved to England to work in a betting shop and he married again. Even after everything that had happened it hurt terribly when I first heard about his second marriage. I saw him only once after he returned to Australia, and the Bartletts arranged for Dawn-Lorraine to meet with him at a hotel they owned on the Gold Coast. She was only a little girl and it was confusing for her but I felt it was fair that she should have some contact with her father. I feel very strongly that problems between adults should not, as far as possible, be inflicted on their children. Gary returned to Townsville, where I believe he worked for the rest of his life for Wormald Security, and I let him know that we were, and always would be, living in the house in Birchgrove Road if he wanted to make contact with Dawn-Lorraine. Over the years Dawn-Lorraine saw her paternal grandmother once or twice, and when she was in high school we heard that Gary had died of a heart attack in Papua New Guinea, where he'd been working for Wormald. It was very sad for both of us for different reasons, but mostly I felt for my daughter.

•

After Gary left I had to face up to life as a single mother with virtually no income other than what I was picking up from bits and pieces at my girlfriend's pool. I had lost the man I loved and I was banned from doing what I loved most. I became very bitter: bitter that my marriage was over; bitter that swimming was no good to me any more and wouldn't come to my rescue this time; bitter that the court case hadn't been scheduled and my chances for Mexico were slipping away. Within the space of two years I had gone from feeling I was at the centre of the universe to living in almost complete obscurity and relative poverty. Losing swimming was the most painful part of it all; it had given me everything in life and now I didn't have it any more.

Although it was far from ideal, because it meant my amateur status would be well and truly wiped out, I started coaching at Prince Alfred Park Pool in inner Sydney. The classes went from early morning through the day and then after school, which meant leaving Dawn-Lorraine for long periods with her Aunt Joyce. I did, however, enjoy the work because I loved children and had missed the water. Down at the Balmain Baths I also started to do some training sessions with the women's water polo team, until it was made clear to them that if I continued to coach them they too would possibly face a ban.

While I was still being punished by the ASU, I was informed that I was to be made a Member of the British Empire for 'services in sporting and international spheres'. I wanted to go to England and receive the honour from the Queen at Buckingham Palace but I couldn't afford it, so I went to receive it from Sir Roden Cutler at Government House, along with the other seventy-three men and women nominated. I was thrilled, and once again the stark contrast between what the ASU thought of me and what others thought of me was there for all to see.

One night towards the end of 1967 I went out to the Motor Club in Sydney with a couple of my girlfriends, who were trying to get me back on my feet. The Motor Club was one of *the* places to go in those days. As we came to the top of the stairs we could see three prominent footballers from the legendary St George Rugby League Club first-grade side, John Raper, Graeme Langlands and Billy Smith, being prevented from going in because they didn't have partners. As we approached, John Raper said, 'Look, here comes Dawnie Fraser. These are our partners,' and with that we all went into the club together. From that night on I started going out with Graeme 'Changa' Langlands and, much to my surprise, it developed into a close, fun and loving relationship. Although we didn't move in together we spent most of our time at Balmain and we may as well have lived together. Unlike today, when the media pounces on any relationship between two well-known people, it all remained quiet. It just wasn't part of sports reporting in those days, and nor were sports people written about in society and gossip columns. We stayed together for the next few years and had what I still regard as one of the most significant relationships in my life. He always included Dawn-Lorraine, and when he went off as Captain of the Australian Rugby League representative side, the Kangaroos, at the end of 1967 he brought her back a beautiful white coat with a hood. He always treated me very nicely and I enjoyed his company immensely. We'd spend time going to clubs and pubs, and of course we both loved talking about football. His mother, however, was very unhappy that we were going out together. For a start he was a bit younger than I was, and she knew I was not yet divorced. The relationship endured, though, in spite of her disapproval.

All through these troubled years I was waiting for a hearing in my action against Associated Newspapers Limited, publishers of the *Sun* newspaper, for the article written by Ernie Christensen. I was also suing the ASU, and specifically Bill Berge Phillips, for defamation. The case against the ASU took an interesting turn one day when my friend, Joan Gandy, who was the host at the Jet Bar in the city and the wife of one of the Balmain detectives, Jack Gandy, said there was a woman I should meet who had come into the bar looking for my solicitor, Ted France. Amazingly, just when it looked as if the case against the ASU might get away from us, the woman looking for Teddy turned out to be none other than the ex-secretary to Bill Berge Phillips. She was disgusted with the letters Bill Berge Phillips had dictated to her to send off to other swimming officials, both in Australia and around the world, following the ban, and had read in the newspapers about Ted representing me. She eventually met up with us and handed over her shorthand notebooks from that time.

Finally in February 1968 the defamation case against Bill Berge Phillips went to court, with Clive Evatt, QC, representing me: 'This young lady comes into the Supreme Court to vindicate her reputation. This is of the utmost importance.' One of Bill Berge Phillips' letters, which Mr Evatt read out in court, had been sent to a FINA official overseas and said in part: 'It is a pity that the world's greatest woman swimmer should be a person such as she is.' In another he had written, 'if the full facts were publicly made known the girls' reputations would be ruined for life.'

In all, we knew of five letters defaming me, which had been sent to people in London, Sweden, Japan, Brisbane and the US. William Berge Phillips, by then the President of the ASU, eventually made a public apology to me in the Supreme Court, but it was a bitter-sweet victory. I turned to him to shake his hand afterwards but he turned away. The financial settlement was made out of court, and it was stipulated by the court as part of the settlement that I could apply to have the ban lifted—and that it should be lifted quickly after the official request was made. Teddy wrote requesting this and newspaper reports show that it was lifted within about eight weeks of the end of the trial. On March 28th, 1968 the *Sydney Morning Herald* reported, 'The 10-year suspension of former champion Dawn Fraser may be removed within a fortnight.' I can't be exactly sure now when it was lifted, except that it was too late for the Mexico Olympics. To swim for my country again I would also have had to apply to regain my amateur status and attend the national trials in February 1968, and there was no way I could turn back the clock. The financial settlement must remain confidential, and although it was a very welcome financial relief it wasn't a staggering amount given what I had lost. Nothing could have made up for what had happened in the past years.

With the court case against Bill Berge Phillips and the ASU
down and the defamation case against the *Sun* still to go, I was
invited by the organising committee in Mexico to attend the 1968
Olympic Games as a special guest. I accepted immediately because
I still very much wanted to be a part of the Olympic family, and
I was honoured to be asked after all that had happened.

While I was in Mexico, at the pool one day a journalist from
Melbourne bet me that I couldn't break 62 seconds for the 100
metres. Harry was in Mexico as a coach and he acted as timekeeper.
With minimal training or preparation I swam it in 60.2 seconds
and won a hundred bucks from the journalist. The gold medal for
that event in Mexico was won by the American Jan Henne in 60
seconds flat. At the very least I would have won the silver medal
but many have said, with all due respect to Jan, that I would have
won a fourth gold, and I'm afraid I have to agree. I know I could
have won it.

I was unfortunately called back from Mexico early because, after
years of waiting, my defamation case against Associated Newspapers
finally came up for hearing in the Supreme Court. I hung around
waiting to watch the final of the women's 100 metres freestyle and
in doing so almost missed the plane. Back in Sydney in October
1968 we won damages of ten thousand dollars against the newspaper. We won on one count and lost on two and the newspaper
appealed the award the following year. However the judge in the
Supreme Court of appeal upheld the original finding and the award
of ten thousand dollars remained in place.

After I came back from Mexico I went back to work and the
excitement from that trip and the success in the defamation case
carried me through on a pretty even keel till the middle of 1969.
Then Changa's mother, who I had never spoken to, called me and
told me that I shouldn't see Graeme any more because he had a
girlfriend who he was going to marry and that she was pregnant.
It was like a bolt from the blue. I was shocked and deeply

saddened. I'd loved him dearly and felt we were very well suited. We understood each other, had great fun together, had a wonderful physical relationship, and I'd believed we had a future together. I took the break-up very hard and cried a lot more over it than I had over Gary. We did go out for dinner after that and talked about the situation but I didn't really show him how hurt I was—my usual Fraser pride wouldn't let me—and I certainly didn't let anyone know that I cried each night for weeks. At the time I wasn't divorced so I didn't really feel I was in a position to make any demands.

That's when I fell into a very black hole. Once again I'd lost a man I loved but much more than that, I was devastated when it really sank in that I could have won that fourth gold medal in Mexico. The winning time in Mexico had been slower than my winning time in Tokyo, and I believe to this day that had I not had to go through several nasty court cases over the ban and the defamation issues, I would have been standing there on the victory dais in Mexico. Instead I sat at home in Balmain, began to drink heavily and sank into a very deep depression. I'd had a great time in Mexico, but now I was back I couldn't stop thinking about what might have been if the ban had been lighter or more in proportion with my so-called offences. What if the ASU had spoken to me about Tokyo and discussed the reasons for their extreme concerns? What if I'd had a chance to defend myself? What if I'd been suspended from participating in Jamaica but been free to go to Mexico? What if the ban had been lifted sooner? What if, what if, what if...?

I began to binge drink in mid-1969. Dawn-Lorraine had been staying with my sister Joyce while I was in Mexico and also during the week at various times when I was training kids early in the morning. Now she was back with me and soon I was only doing the most basic things to care for her like feeding her, washing her and putting her to bed, in between which she played in the back-yard or watched television while I lay on the couch and drank sherry. I'd start in the morning around breakfast time and didn't stop until I collapsed asleep at night, still on the couch. I wasn't a very nice person to know at all. I was hurt and I wanted to hurt people in return. I mostly wanted to hurt Bill Berge Phillips but he was out of reach as he had always been. I felt so completely cheated out of that fourth gold medal, and felt that my career had been ended for me by people who had no idea what it had taken to swim as well as I did. They had made decisions without hearing my side of the story. It seemed unthinkable in a democratic country like Australia, but that is what had happened and I had to deal with it on my own. At no time in the four years since the issuing of the ban had I heard from anyone at the ASU. It was as if I had never existed. I was a nothing to them, but worse than that I was a complete nothing to myself.

I was still coaching at Prince Alfred Park at the time but I had to give that away because I knew I couldn't be in charge of children while I was drinking. I knew I wasn't doing my job properly so I quit and went onto a supporting mothers pension.

My divorce was about to go through and I was feeling so rejected by Changa and depressed about the ban that my drinking got even worse and I contemplated suicide. It had been at the back of my mind that Changa and I would marry after the divorce, even though we'd never talked about it.

At one point during this period I managed to get myself together enough to go to a party at a house a few doors down from mine while Red minded Dawn-Lorraine. Everyone was smoking marijuana and they were passing it around but I said I would never touch it. Given the amount of alcohol I was consuming it probably sounds stupid to say this, but I have always been violently opposed to drugs of any kind. Eventually, though, I'd had enough drinks for someone to talk me into having a drag of the marijuana. It was to be my first and last. I had to go home, where I was so sick for the next twenty-four hours that I completely hit rock bottom. I will never forget my little daughter watching me vomiting and then dry retching as if I would die. I wanted to die.

I felt I had no friends, which was wrong, but I pushed away anyone who tried to help me and I lay on the couch with the door half closed and the curtains drawn. I had a video camera and one day I taped a message for people to hear after I'd died. It was going to be my video suicide note. That may sound melodramatic, but I'd gone way past self-pity to a point of real clinical depression, and I couldn't see any way out.

Added to this, I hated myself for not being a good mother. Eventually I had to call my sister Joyce to come and get Dawn-Lorraine because I just couldn't get up and look after her. I dressed Dawn-Lorraine and handed her over to Joyce at the door. I didn't say anything and Joyce didn't ask. She remained with Joyce for a few days, and during that time, at the end of another day on the couch, I got myself up to look in the bathroom mirror. I remember being shocked and thinking, 'Wow, this is really bad. If I don't do something about it now it will get the best of me.' I began to lecture myself about pulling myself together and not letting the bastards ruin my life, and slowly began to drag myself back from the brink. This time it wasn't just about a swimming career; it was about my life and my child's life, and I knew I had to do something right then. I went through all the pros and cons and I just kept coming back to the fact that I had a three-year-old daughter who needed me. How would I have felt at three seeing my mother like that? The thought shocked me deeply and made me very sad, but it meant I could feel something for someone else, instead of being completely turned in on myself. That was a turning point, and though I didn't stop drinking I never got as bad as that again.

I started to look for work but nothing was available immediately so I remained on the pension, which allowed me to feed Dawn-Lorraine and myself but not much more. People would try to cheer me up by reminding me of what I'd achieved, to which I'd say,

'You can't eat gold medals.' Being out of work left me with a lot of free time during the day to go to the Riverview. I thought about selling the house but I still felt it was Mum's house so I couldn't do that either. We muddled along somehow and I'd progressed from the sherry to beer and a bit of scotch, which had to be a step in the right direction. I also wasn't consuming quite as much on my own, although it was the only way I could get to sleep at night. I lost an enormous amount of weight because I wasn't eating properly.

Dawn-Lorraine started across the road at preschool and during the day I'd head up to the Riverview and have a few beers with Mum's old friends and others from the neighbourhood. I was so bored and lonely that sometimes I'd spend the better part of the day there just chatting, before collecting Dawn-Lorraine from the school. Sometimes I'd take Dawn-Lorraine back with me and everyone would make a fuss of her and buy her lemonade the way Pop had bought me a juice at almost the same age.

One particular day—I remember it because the pub was tele-vising the first moon landing—I ran into Red up there and she asked me how was I really getting along. She obviously sensed things were beginning to deteriorate again. I told her I was depressed and drinking too much and she gave me some motherly advice, saying it was not only about me but also my daughter. She added that Mum wouldn't have approved, and would have wanted me to go on and be a good mother. That sort of care from someone I'd known all my life and who had known my mum really jolted me, and after that my life started to improve again because I felt rather ashamed of myself.

When I look back on that stage of my life I think I sank so low because I had been robbed of the chance to make the choice and say, 'All right, I am ready to finish swimming and now I'm going to start a new part of my life.' I hadn't had a chance to make the necessary adjustments to start an entirely new life. There were no great jobs offered to me and I didn't have a nest egg put aside from my swimming years. These days prominent athletes who make the decision to retire often still have enormous difficulty adjusting, despite job opportunities, support networks, counselling and excellent financial resources. But they are usually part of a community that continues to honour them and their achievements, and so they gradually adjust to the idea of a quieter life away from the limelight. Perhaps I would never have been given those things anyway, but in my era none of them were available, and it was also an era when people didn't accept depression. You were told to just get on with it and stop being lazy; or worse, if you did go to a psychiatrist you were considered to be barking mad and dangerous. So I did get on with my life at that point. I tried to put all the events of the last few years behind me.

•

I was working at Botany Pool and felt I had really begun to find myself again, when something very shocking happened to me. I can barely bring myself to think about it, let alone write about. It was 1971, and I was still going up to the Riverview regularly, where everyone knew me and I felt safe among friends I'd mixed with all my life. I knew the Hicks family, who ran the pub at that time, and would even help them out on occasions. It was Saturday afternoon, and a few of us were playing euchre and listening to the races, as we always did. Among us was Ray, who we all knew as Fat Face. Dawn-Lorraine was upstairs playing in the Hicks's private quarters. At about 3.00 p.m. we were watching the football and still playing cards when a Polish sailor from a Swedish ship docked at Howard Smith's wharf off Birchgrove came into the pub. As the afternoon wore on he got talking with a few of the regular drinkers. He introduced himself as the captain of the ship and, although a bit drunk, he was pleasant enough and buying some of the boys drinks. Eventually I was asked to call him a cab because he was a bit under the weather. When the cab arrived, he decided not to leave but handed the cabbie a twenty-dollar note for his trouble. I told him that was too big a tip in Australia and got most of it back for him. He went on to buy the local boys a few more drinks before buying a couple of bottles of whisky to take back to the ship with him. Fat Face ended up leaving with him, along with someone else, although I don't recall exactly who went back or how they got there. The record of the court proceedings for some reason suggests I drove them down to the ship, but that isn't what happened. I didn't actually arrive at the ship until sometime later, after the boys had called from the ship to request a carton of beer be delivered. We often delivered alcohol around the neighbour-hood, and Fat Face had been a close friend all my life so the request didn't seem that extraordinary.

When I drove the beer down for them I carried it to the top of the gangplank and tried to leave it but was ushered down to the cabin where Fat Face was having a drink with the man I'd been led to believe was the captain. I was offered a drink, which I accepted but didn't consume, and after a bit of chat Fat Face decided he would come back with me to the Riverview, where I had to collect Dawn-Lorraine and take her home for dinner. Fat Face added that before we left he wanted to go to the toilet. The sailor got up to show Ray where to go and as he came back into the cabin he shut the door behind him and locked it. I was instantly terrified and started to plead with him, saying my daughter was waiting for me, but he pushed me up into the corner of the cabin and told me to get undressed. I managed to reach for a bottle opener and started to fight back but then he produced a knife. He held it straight to my throat, so I wasn't sure how big the knife was, and he told me to take my clothes off. I started to undress slowly, hoping that Fat Face would miraculously reappear, then my bracelet caught on my sleeve and he became very agitated. In the next forty minutes he ripped my clothes off and raped me.

When I screamed and struggled he became even more aggressive, and I began to think he would possibly kill me and throw me overboard. It's amazing what goes through your mind in those desperate circumstances.

The door of the cabin was so thick that I don't know if anyone would have heard me screaming early on, although I could hear knocking on the door and noises outside. In the meantime Fat Face had fallen over in the corridor and when he eventually came back to the door of the cabin he couldn't get in. He went back to the Riverview, and when I wasn't there he called the police. He knew something was wrong and that I wouldn't just leave my daughter like that.

After a while my attacker was sitting on the bed swilling scotch, getting drunker and drunker, while I cowered in the corner thinking I would probably be killed. Then there was loud knocking at the door and someone called out, 'Dawn Fraser, are you in there?' I screamed as loudly as I could. Two detectives on duty at Balmain Police Station had come down to the ship and finally, with assistance from another sailor from the ship, forced open the door. It was humiliating to be found in that state but I'd had a chance to get dressed before the door was opened, and I still had the presence of mind to ask the detectives to charge the man who had raped me. By that stage I'd been in the cabin for nearly four terrifying hours.

The detectives took me to another cabin and interviewed me before enlisting the help of other personnel on the ship to arrest and charge the sailor. All I wanted to do was to go home and have a shower and make sure my daughter was safe, but after being interviewed I was taken to Balmain Police Station and put in the care of some policewomen who'd been brought into work especially to look after me. I was taken to Royal Prince Alfred Hospital and examined by a doctor who recorded the details of the bruises all over my body and my badly cut and swollen lip. I felt dirty and embarrassed, as if I should have been more careful. At first I thought it was all my fault. Many years later when I talked about the incident to Jack Gandy, who was by then retired, he understood that it was in my nature to be open and friendly towards people rather than suspicious and careful. Of course I'd felt safe. I'd gone to the ship at the request of a close friend I'd known all my life and who always looked after me. In the end that friend also saved me. Unlike Jack, though, there were many others who said things like, 'What was she doing there?' or 'She was asking for it' or 'She put herself in a stupid position.' Jack even recalled meeting a judge at a cocktail party—although not the judge on my case—who asked him, 'What was she doing on the ship anyway?' Apparently Jack left him in no two minds about my open nature. Other people felt I should have forgotten about the whole episode because of my high public profile. I didn't forget about it, though. I was very angry.

It never occurred to me to go quietly on the whole thing. I was outraged by what my attacker had done to me and I wanted to see him rot in hell. As it turned out he wasn't the captain but a stoker mechanic on the ship, and he was charged and then held for a few weeks until granted bail after the court had established he had no contacts in Australia. Amazingly, he remained on the ship for another two months until the final committal proceedings. I had to be a witness, of course, which meant reliving the entire hideous ordeal in front of strangers, describing personal and horrible details for the court. At least one saving grace was that the judge allowed my name to be suppressed. That didn't completely work, though, and some details leaked out, with the scummiest newspapers reporting the rape in detail. It was extremely traumatic to find the story in the papers and it compounded my anxiety and desperation over the whole incident.

Eventually the judge ruled that there was insufficient evidence for my case to go to trial. Although I was able to describe the knife that had been held to my throat, because I'd seen it after he finished attacking me, the judge cited the fact that the knife hadn't been produced (a knife had been seized from the cabin and exhibited in court but I testified that it wasn't the one used in my attack). He also noted that my clothes weren't ripped; I was a healthy, strong woman and yet the cabin wasn't wrecked (basically I wasn't sufficiently beaten up); and that I hadn't replied instantly to the detectives knocking on my door (because I'd been getting dressed). One piece of evidence the judge took seriously was a card with my name on it and the number for the Riverview. It was suggested I'd been a willing participant in the whole thing because I'd given him my name. What wasn't made clear was that I had given him this before he'd left the pub. The man was subsequently freed and I can remember the feelings I had of utter rage and fury. The only concession the judge made to me was that I hadn't been intoxicated at the time of the attack, which was true.

After this the locals who drank regularly at the Riverview became much more protective of me, especially later when I took over the running of the pub, and remain so today. I have never fully recovered from that incident. Until then I just didn't think anything like that could happen to me, particularly in my local area. I think what had made me so vulnerable was my lack of understanding of my vulnerability. These days I always lock my door when I get in the car and I'm very security conscious altogether.

I lay awake at night for many years thinking about the rape and playing over in my mind alternative scenarios where I left the beer at the top of the gangplank. For months afterwards I felt very dirty and didn't want to be touched by anyone. To this day I find physical contact difficult, and I believe the anxiety can be traced back to the rape. I still can't stand anyone grabbing me by my arm, and when I'm being guided around by strangers at public events, as I often am, I shrink away from being touched. And because people often want to touch me and make contact, this can be very awkward. I also hate being in cabins on boats or in confined spaces generally, although I've had to be a few times over the years. Each time I get very claustrophobic and panicky.

Even after everything that had happened to me up to that point, being raped had a very profound effect on my attitude towards life. I became harder, and put up barriers where there hadn't been any before. I felt let down by the legal system, that a man could do that to me and walk free. No woman should have to put up with that sort of physical violence and then walk quietly away so as not to draw attention to herself. My anger over what had happened didn't subside for a long time, and when I did finally stop thinking about the rape itself I was determined that I would never allow myself to be so vulnerable again.

11
SEA
CHANGE

The main thing that lifted me out of my depression and got my life right back on track after those horror years was the very challenge that drives many people crazy: golf. My brother Ken and his wife, Thelma, played, but I had always avoided it, thinking it was for old people. Ken kept insisting I give it a try because he felt I was wasting my life away, and to an extent he was right. I was still teaching at Botany Pool and going to the Riverview in my spare time, but there were no challenges, apart from the very obvious one of raising my daughter as a single mum. Ken, along with many of my friends, was concerned about my physical state, as I had lost an enormous amount of weight and at 54 kilograms could even be described as scrawny. For someone with my height this was not a good look.

Eventually I agreed to go and play a few rounds of golf with Ken and Thelma and it became clear that I had an aptitude for it. I liked the fact that while you got your exercise you could meet people, walk, talk and enjoy the fresh air. As well as that, Babe Zaharias had played it and she was my hero.

Around the time I took up golf I received a letter from the International Swimming Hall of Fame, located in Fort Lauderdale, Florida, inviting me to a ceremony in my honour at the Hall, which I'd been inducted into in 1965. While it was a great thrill to be asked, I knew I couldn't afford the airfare and would probably have to resign myself to being honoured in absentia. My old training partner and great mate Ricksie was to be inducted at the same time, so I really wanted to be there too. I had a friend in Balmain by the name of Jack Stanistreet, who was the Secretary of the Railways Union, and he lobbied the Whitlam Government for my airfare to the US. Jack was very kind to me over the years. I first met him when he approached me in the late 1960s to enter into politics for the Labor Party, which I tried to do but was told by the local branch to come back when I was less well known. Figure that one out! Jack, who was a widower, was very much a father figure to me back then. He had two lovely neighbours, Catherine and Louise, and the four of us would meet at the Riverview for lunch on Saturdays after shopping. It was a great circle of friends and we all became quite close.

The Whitlam Government did pay for my airfare to the US, and Jack and the girls minded Dawn-Lorraine while I was away. I left at the end of 1972 and was over there for New Year celebrations. It was a very exciting trip and Ricksie and I were made much of all the way. My weird luck with flying continued on this trip.

My flight landed in New York too late for me to connect with the plane to Florida. I later heard on the news that the plane I'd missed had crashed into marshland around Fort Lauderdale and everyone onboard was killed.

In New York I met up with Sir Robert George, who'd been the Governor of South Australia and my neighbour when I was living above the City Baths all those years ago, and who now had an official posting in the US. He and Lady George drove down to Fort Lauderdale with me and stayed for the ceremony. As always, they were very kind.

At the ceremony Ricksie and I had to put our signatures and handprints into cement outside the Sports Hall of Fame—just like the stars on Sunset Boulevard. It was all very exciting, especially as I had been one of the first Australians to be inducted. This was the biggest acknowledgment I'd received overseas and it helped me a great deal in coming to terms with the loss of my career and my treatment in Australia. I'm invited back every year, and though I've never been I intend to go soon because I am so impressed with what they have done there.

After the ceremony I flew back to New York and stayed with old swimming friends over New Year's Eve. It was snowing so hard I had to rush out and buy a coat I couldn't afford. It was suede lined in faux fur. I loved it and kept it for years, until I loaned it to a friend to take overseas and never laid eyes on it again.

•

A few months after my US trip Dawn-Lorraine began school at St Vincent's College in Potts Point, Sydney. Jack helped me choose the school, and even came to the interview with the Principal. I trusted his judgment, and I also had friends who had sent their daughters to St Vincent's and were very happy with it. It was a big wrench sending Dawn-Lorraine to boarding school but it was clear to me that I had to get out and work, and the best way to do this was to use my profile as a swimmer. It would involve travelling around a fair bit, as well as keeping the odd hours that are a part of coaching, and I knew that would be no good for her. I wanted her to have a stable environment and a good education, because I knew by then what education could bring. She hated it to begin with, especially when she was only allowed home once a month, but I used to visit her regularly, and as she got older she came home every Friday for the weekend. The other big factor in my decision to send Dawn-Lorraine off to boarding school was that I was still trying to regain my sanity. Although I was getting on top of things I was still pretty fragile, and I felt that Dawn-Lorraine would be better off in a strict daily routine that the school could provide.

Socially I began to spread my wings a bit by going to a few parties thrown by the filmmakers I'd worked with on the documentary in Tokyo. I found myself with a whole new crowd of people, most of whom worked in the Arts and had very different backgrounds to mine. It was quite exciting and led to other invitations to go to film sets, meet talented actors and actresses, and go to the theatre. I was seeing a whole different side to life. Apart from meeting Robert Helpmann in Adelaide and my lessons with May Hoben, as a swimmer I'd had little contact with this glamorous and creative world where people not only shared their emotions but made a living out of them.

One of the people I met frequently at these parties was a woman named Joy Cavill, the scriptwriter on the Tokyo documentary. I didn't really know her when the film was being made but I was introduced to her at one of the parties and we got chatting. Gradually I got to know her better and we'd meet for coffee or have dinner at her flat, or I'd go along to parties with her friends. She was working on various TV series at the time, including *Skippy*, and I'd meet her on the set and behind the scenes. She was very kind to me, drawing me into this new world, and I enjoyed her company tremendously. It was especially good to be around people who weren't part of the swimming world, and who knew of my achievements but didn't gossip about me.

Joy was about fifteen years older than me and very motherly, something I was particularly receptive to at the time. I'd missed my mother desperately through those difficult years after Tokyo and I hadn't experienced the sort of kindness Joy showed me, except with Mum's friend Red, who had many of her own family problems to deal with at the time.

Joy told me that she'd like to make a feature film about my life and we both became quite enthused about it. After finishing at Botany Pool in the morning I'd go straight to Joy's house in Paddington, where Joy would record my stories on tape to be gradually turned into a script. The whole process fascinated me and it was great to be collaborating on something so different.

I became very comfortable with Joy and after a few months the relationship also became physical. I was very surprised at this turn of events, and also very embarrassed about it. From the beginning I felt a terrible awkwardness and also a certain amount of shame. I couldn't reconcile what was happening with other parts of my life, such as being a mother, being a public person and being part of a closeknit traditional family. But the comfort of the relationship and the safeness I felt in Joy's company for a time outweighed the guilt and confusion I felt about having a love affair with a woman. There had been so many rumours about my sexuality circulating during my Olympic career, even though I had never been involved with a woman, or a man for that matter, that I now started to think perhaps I could be gay. After all, that's what people had always said about me and now I was actually sleeping with a woman.

On the other hand, I never felt I wanted to apply that label to myself, and I still don't, because it doesn't explain who I was then and it's not who I am now. Nor is it anyone's business to know about the sexual side of my life, whatever it embraces, unless they are my partner at the time. In numerous media interviews I have denied the suggestion that I am gay because I truly don't regard myself as 'gay'. The reason for revealing this part of my life now, with great trepidation, is that I am sick and tired of the gossip and know that if I don't at least address this aspect of my life there will be many detractors saying that the book isn't the 'real' story. So now you all know and hopefully I can continue my life without the constant speculation that I hear about through friends. I also trust, as much as I respect the right of people to be who they are, that I will not be approached to become some sort of symbol for gay people. I see myself as a woman who had a couple of relationships with other women and then found it wasn't for her. I want privacy for that part of my life because I am, after all, a sportswoman and ambassador, not a sex symbol.

There are a few reasons why I've been reluctant to relate this part of my life. First, my high public profile makes it tougher for me than for others who manage to remain anonymous regardless of what they do in their lives. I also had a daughter to raise, and I didn't want her to grow up seeing the details of her mother's sexuality paraded in the public arena. And lastly, I didn't want to offend my more traditional and conservative friends, who I value in my life. On the other hand, I believe I am entitled to lead my life as I choose to, as long as I'm not hurting anyone else, and that is something I would also support others for doing.

Joy helped build my self-esteem and reintroduced me to a side of my life I'd let slide. I hadn't listened to music or read books for years. I hadn't thought about meeting new people and broadening my horizons. If anything, I'd shut down many parts of my life after the ban, my marriage break-up and the end of the affair with Changa. The attack on the ship had left deep emotional scars and I think I had closed myself off so I wouldn't be hurt any more. Joy was able to lead me back to who I really was, and I started to regain

a bit of the old confidence. Our relationship was always more intel-
lectual and emotional than it was physical. That side was there too
but it wasn't strong, unlike my relationships with Gary and
Changa. I didn't crave Joy's company in the way you do when an
affair is exciting and all-consuming. We'd see each other once a
week for dinner or the movies and that would be enough. My close
friends and family must have known what was going on, because
I'd often turn up with Joy to family gatherings, but no one ever
commented. I was the one who never really came to terms with
what was happening between us. I hated the idea that I was in a
relationship that had to be secretive. Even if my family and friends
didn't seem to notice or mind, I couldn't take Joy to an official
function as my partner, or go to the pub and hold hands or touch.
It was too hard, too hurtful and not something I wanted in my
life. I'd think, 'Can I still go out in public and be Dawn Fraser
and her girlfriend?' and I decided I couldn't. Having experienced
the venom of rumours about my sexuality when I wasn't involved
with anyone, I was very wary of what would happen now if people
discovered I was.

The relationship failed quite quickly, I think partly because Joy
lived with her sister, who didn't know about us, and I lived with
my daughter who I didn't want to know about us. It was still the
early '70s and a far more conservative society than the one we live
in now. Anyway, which parents even these days discuss their sex
lives with their children? These hurdles aside, Joy and I were both
set in our ways and in the end couldn't find enough common
ground. Quite soon we went our separate ways and I really threw
myself back into the golf scene, feeling yet again that I just couldn't
get personal relationships right, but also relieved to return to being
open about my life and to be back in my neighbourhood social
circle.

Ken and Thelma had great golfing friends—I called them Aunty
Dot and Uncle Peter—who used to play at the New Brighton Golf

Club just south of Sydney. I began to caddy for Aunty Dot and Thelma when they played in grade games on Fridays and I started to learn a lot about the game. Uncle Peter then put up a net in his backyard after he'd seen how I was hitting the ball. I was strong and could hit a great drive. He said, 'All right Dawn, you're coming up to practise,' and he started to coach me as a bit of an interest. Having read about Babe Zaharias hitting a thousand balls in a session I decided I would do that too. I'd be in the backyard belting away and when my hands became sore I'd think about how Zaharias used to hit balls till her hands bled. So there I was; I'd transferred the intensity of swimming training over to golf training and it was doing me the world of good.

By this time I'd joined the New Brighton Golf Club too and was winning some tournaments at golf days. I really got interested in it to the extent that I couldn't wait to get out there again and play. I started off with a handicap of thirty-six and gradually got it down to seventeen in one year. A lot of the club's members were young women, which was great because I'd always thought of golf as a retirement sport and now I was seeing a very different side of it. I began to travel around, and I went up to Kempsey and played in the Northern Rivers Golf Championship. I did well in that and the next thing I knew I was involved in the 'Proette' competition, which was the name for lady golfers on a State handicap of four or less. Proette was the equivalent of the men's Pro circuit, 'pro' not being considered a very suitable title for a women's comp.

I made myself available as a caddy so that I could learn from all the top players. I was caddying for great golfers like Jackie Pung, Penny Pulz, Betty Dalgleish, Jan Stevenson and others, and found myself travelling fairly constantly. Unfortunately the Proette only lasted for a couple of years because it was impossible to get sponsors for women's golf. But at least it was a start and I've always felt these women were the pioneers of an international-standard competition for women in Australia. I am glad I was part of it.

I continued to be involved with women's golf for the next few years and in the third year managed to get down to a handicap of nine. It could never replace swimming, of course, but golf gave me the outlet I needed to get over my forced retirement from the sport I loved. I enjoyed the competition element because I'd grown up in competition and I missed the intensity of it.

In 1974 the coaching rights for Botany Pool came up for tender but I wasn't successful in winning them again. The council had given me the coaching/teaching rights for nothing when I started but by now I'd built up a nice little business and it was understandable that they'd want to put the rights up for tender. I wasn't prepared to pay what they were looking for and, frankly, that wasn't really a problem because I'd had enough after so many years of getting up early and staying back late. I had even spent some nights every week sleeping on a portable bed in my office at the pool when the hours were especially long. The job had saved me when I most needed the work but it was time for me to move on. I'd had some great times there and loved coaching the kids, but it was also hard work. After the training in the mornings I'd sit in my office and plan my lessons for the afternoon. I took the responsibility very seriously and really my life revolved around it. There was also a lot of extra child-minding when parents left their kids at the pool unattended and I had to take up the slack. Quite a few times one particular family of six accidentally left one kid behind when they went home after my classes, and I had to drive the child home so they'd get to school on time. It was a bit like the *Home Alone* movies.

I wanted to make a fresh start in a completely new area, so I took a job with Driclad. The company was best known for its above-ground swimming pools, but I worked in a different side of the business, selling their wet weather gear, lifejackets and life rafts. Driclad had the agency for the British company Beaufort and they sent me over to England for three weeks to be trained in selling

Beaufort's product range. I had spent all my training years working in sales, and although that had been in retail rather than wholesale I knew how to sell and I wasn't too bad at it. My customers were airlines—Qantas was one—shipping companies, fishing outlets, marinas and golf clubs. I enjoyed the challenge of it and remained at Driclad for the next couple of years.

•

When I'd travelled to Kempsey for the Northern Rivers Golf Championship I had met a very nice older woman who was an official at one of the Northern Rivers clubs and we got along very well. She told me her daughter, who was about my age, was coming back to Sydney after living in England and that she thought the two of us would get along well. I agreed her daughter should look me up and then forgot about the conversation—as far as I was concerned we were exchanging pleasantries.

Eventually, however, her daughter did call me and we did get along well. We both loved golf and she was lively and very humorous. She was several years younger than I was but we found we had a great deal in common and began to mix together within a social group of women golfers. She was to become the second and last woman with whom I had a sexual relationship. It was, however, much more than that. I was very much in love with her, and we had some wonderful times socialising and playing competition golf together. Then in early 1976, following an overseas trip with a couple of friends after I left Driclad, we went into business together. The Dawn Fraser Cheese Shop in Balmain was admittedly an unusual idea, and probably ahead of its time, but we did quite well. My friend came up with the idea and she introduced me to two mates of hers, Peter and Don, who agreed to come onboard as silent partners. They were part of my friend's social circle but they left the running of the shop to us and worked at other jobs during the week. Sometimes they helped on weekends and gave us some time off, but really we women did the day-to-day work and I loved it. I'd spend quite a bit of time sourcing and buying unusual cheeses, and we made patés at home and prepared gift baskets of biscuits, cheese and fruit for the local hospital, as well as platters for parties and office lunches. Unfortunately, we were all too close socially for it to work properly. It could have been a very profitable business for one person but the income was split four ways, and, as in so many businesses owned between friends, we became sick of doing all the work while the boys continued to take a share of the profits. We wanted to upgrade the business by altering the shop and increasing our range of products but after a couple of years our partners wanted to get out. Towards the end we'd work at the shop all day, cook for the shop at night, open the doors again the next day, clean the premises, go home and do the books the next night, and so on. While it was great fun and wonderful to be reasonably independent, we had no life away from the shop. We didn't have enough money at the time both to buy the men out and invest further so that we wouldn't be doing absolutely everything, and in the end we agreed to sell.

During these years when I was working for Driclad and then running the cheese shop, Joy and I continued to work together on the film. Joy had finished writing the script and in the intervening years she was raising funds to get it made. I didn't see much of her until we actually started filming in 1977, although we'd kept in touch and she'd often invite me to parties at her apartment or out for coffee. We were still friends, although looking back I believe what other people were saying at the time, that Joy was still trying to hold on to me and draw me back into her life. I didn't pay much attention to that, and was probably a bit naive about the whole situation.

While the film was in production I was busy with the shop and happy in my relationship. I had to take several months off work to play my part in the making of the film and my partner ran the shop on her own during that time. I was to be paid as a technical consultant on the film and to receive a percentage of the gross profit after it was released, but I didn't get all the right documents signed and so ran into trouble later trying to extract my payment. My main input over several months was working with Bronwyn Mackay-Payne who was to play me. Because she was a water polo player, Bronwyn swam too high in the water to portray me and didn't like putting her head under. We trained together for many weeks at Sydney University pool, working on her fitness and style so that she could do the swimming scenes with a degree of authenticity, and I improved my fitness into the bargain. The time spent together also enabled Bronwyn to get my mannerisms right. We ended up becoming good mates, but this simple friendship between Bronwyn and me was to cause some jealousy on Joy's part and some tension during the shoot. I have always loathed jealousy and it makes me run in the opposite direction, and now Joy would call me in to watch the rushes and make me sit next to her. She'd accuse me privately of spending too much time with Bronwyn and the make-up artist on the film, Peggy, and generally try to control my every move. As always, I wouldn't be controlled, and then would go out of my way to stir her up, which was probably pretty childish but my natural reaction to her behaviour.

The whole crew plus Dawn-Lorraine and I went over to Japan for about two weeks to do the scenes set in Tokyo. Dawn-Lorraine, who was eleven at the time, had a Japanese tutor while we were there. Bronwyn fell in love with the film's director when we were away and that really set Joy off. She'd lecture us for not concentrating on the film, and we'd all roll our eyes and say, 'There she goes again.'

In the end I never received the percentage of gross profit I had been promised. I had signed a contract but the filmmakers never signed and returned a copy. I had trusted that I would be paid and never pressed anyone for a copy of the contract before I did all my work on the film. When I chased payment after a few months, everyone denied that a contract had ever been signed or that a percentage had ever been offered. I fell out with Joy and everyone else on the film over that. Going to court wasn't an option for me. I'd spent so long fighting people in court that I just let it fade away. The broken trust hurt me more than it made me angry, but these days I am a lot more vigilant about making sure things are in writing.

Apart from not being paid, I have always been very disappointed with the film. I had been promised it would be completely honest and show my life as it was. In the end, though, it showed people in my life as composite characters and therefore some of them were barely recognisable. And because they were all rolled into one I don't think the film showed the richness of my life and the neighbourhood I lived in. It also skimmed over some significant aspects of my life and weighted others more heavily than they should have been. I know that liberties are taken in filmmaking and that it's necessary to condense parts of a person's life to fit everything in, but the film didn't, in my opinion, capture the spirit and some of the important facts of my life as it was back then. Certain aspects were way off beam, and the film actually helped perpetuate some of the myths about my life that linger to this day. Watching the rushes after filming each day I started to suspect things were not quite right, and when it was all together I could see large bits had been cut and edited, to the point where sometimes I could hardly recognise the part of my life it was supposed to depict. The Harry Gallagher character, for example, didn't go close to showing what Harry was like or what he was doing at various times.

I attended the premiere of the film at Hoyts in Sydney and helped promote the film by doing interviews with the press and on radio. The film drew me back into the limelight for a while but it was at a point when I actually wanted to go a bit quietly. To be perfectly honest, I was feeling guilty about having another affair with a woman and the last thing I really wanted was public attention. If I'd go out to a gay nightclub with a whole bunch of friends, for example, I could hear people saying, 'Oh look, there's Dawn Fraser,' and that would upset me, making me feel everyone knew my personal business and that it would leak into the press and hurt my family. It was a very happy time in my life, but I was torn between my public and private lives and I couldn't reconcile them.

Most people's public and private lives are much closer together than mine ever were. In public I was recognised instantly as a swimming star and an admired Australian and in private I was having a relationship with a woman, which a large part of the public would have found quite shocking. This was at a time when the Gay Mardi Gras in Sydney, rather than being a fun night out and broadcast on mainstream television, was a protest march at which people were being arrested. My main circle of friends was gay but they knew I was reluctant to go out with them in public, and most of them understood my dilemma. Some of them had their own difficulties about being gay, and I understood that because I still didn't know if I was or wasn't, but I was also the only one who was recognised everywhere I went.

Another worry was that I was often in contact with children either as a coach or a guest speaker at schools and so on. I'd read in the paper about parent outrage over a gay teacher coming out and I'd think, 'Wow, I'm teaching kids and having a relationship with a woman.' That was very difficult. There was no one that I could really talk to about it and I didn't think many people would have understood anyway. My relationship continued for several years but I was never comfortable about it being out in the open for all the reasons I've just mentioned.

I haven't had much privacy in my life and I do try to hang on to bits and pieces. Some people will no doubt suggest this is a hypocritical statement given that I'm now writing the story of my life. However, I acknowledge that parts of my life are very public and in a way belong to the public, and so many other people have had a go at writing those aspects of my life that I wanted a chance to do that too. I have represented my country and chosen to be a public person on several levels, and in choosing that path I have also had to reveal and defend parts of my life that I would have preferred remain private. You don't necessarily realise the price you might have to pay when you set out on that path. I certainly didn't as a young swimmer, although if I had I doubt it would have changed anything, because swimming was my passion.

It's a very tricky balancing act for many people in the public eye, and one you're never going to get right to the satisfaction of everyone. But I've realised that in the end I'm the one who has to be happy with my choices and my life, and even then I allow myself some mistakes, some misgivings and some grey areas.

12

THE RIVERVIEW
YEARS

Towards the end of our time in the cheese shop I became
aware that the lease for the Riverview would soon become
available. My business partners in the shop thought it
would be good to take up the lease together, but by then I'd had
enough of the arrangement at the cheese shop and thought I'd like
to take on the pub myself. The idea of running the Riverview really
appealed to me, since I knew all the locals who drank there and
had been in and out of the pub since I was old enough to walk.
Over the years when the Hicks family owned the lease I'd worked

in the snack bar, the bottle shop and the front bar and really enjoyed it. Mrs Hicks had even taught me the books.

So in 1978 I became the new licensee at the Riverview, just up the road from where I lived. The licence was expensive, and I had to mortgage my house, use all the money I had saved and borrow some from friends in order to secure it. It looked great on paper and I felt sure I could build it up. I let the house, moved into the rooms above the pub and set to work cleaning the place up. The terms of my licence specified that I had to live on the premises, and of course I thought it would be great living above the pub. My original plan had been to do up some of the upstairs rooms and let them, but eventually I realised we'd never escape from the customers if they could live at the pub as well, so all the rooms became ours—all fourteen of them.

For me it was a business opportunity I really needed because I had to put Dawn-Lorraine through school. She was twelve at the time, and when I told her we were buying the lease of a pub she was pretty unimpressed, but I tried to explain that I needed the money and it was going to be a great thing for us.

When we moved in we took all our furniture from the house and stored most of it in two of the rooms at the pub. Then we put the furniture that came with the pub into another room because we didn't like the idea of using it. My partner moved in with us at the pub and each of us had our own bedroom, bathroom and toilet. There was also a formal dining room, a casual eating room, a large lounge room and a room for Dawn-Lorraine to use as a recreation room where she could bring friends over to watch TV and so on. We scrubbed out the upstairs to within an inch of itself and painted it all because we knew the hours would be long and we wanted a comfortable environment to come back to. We had plenty of room up there, but as it turned out we rarely used it because the hours in the pub were so demanding. I guess I had only seen pub life through the eyes of someone who could walk in occasionally and leave at the end of the day, and I was soon to discover that running a pub twenty-four hours a day, seven days a week was a whole different kettle of fish.

We did everything ourselves. My friend worked in a managerial role and, although she didn't have a financial commitment, was to all intents and purposes a partner. When she was working front of house I was behind the scenes, and vice versa. This unfortunately meant that when one of us had a day off—we'd invariably play golf—the other one was back at the pub. We hardly ever had time off together, except on Sundays when the pub was closed, and this definitely put a strain on the relationship, although for our first few years together I was probably happier than I had ever been.

Dawn-Lorraine was a weekly boarder by the time we took over the Riverview, which meant she came home every Friday night. She'd help me put the food together from the snack bar, and when she wasn't working she'd go into the ladies bar where Nana Fraser had sat with her friends shelling peas when I was a child. All the older women were still there and they'd spoil Dawn-Lorraine rotten. She'd play video games while I worked in the front bar, and we also had a pool table, so both of us became pretty good at it.

The hours were the longest I had ever worked, rivalling, and often overtaking, the amount of time I used to put into training. I have never in my life worked as hard as I did at the Riverview and I hope I never have to work that hard again. We couldn't afford cleaners, so we'd clean the bars and the toilets ourselves. On weekends Dawn-Lorraine and I would scrub out the toilets after the pub had closed and we always commented on how much cleaner the men's urinals were than the women's toilets.

We moved in and opened again just before Christmas 1978. At the changeover we closed the pub for the weekend to clean it and get ourselves organised. The walls were a creamy yellow colour when we took over but we started scrubbing them down and found they were in fact white. It was the years of built-up nicotine and grime that had made them the colour they were. All the locals came and worked that weekend. Peter, Fat Face, Johnny, Dickie Hunt, Chalky and little Frankie all mucked in. It was very exciting and everyone had a great time. People seemed to think it was pretty good that one of their drinking buddies was going to take over the local.

Then we opened and I quickly realised it was very different being a local drinker to being the licensee. As a customer, when you see a glass broken you just watch while it is kicked into the corner, but when it costs you a dollar every time a glass is broken it makes you stop and think. You see your profits dwindling in broken glass. Then you start picking up glasses constantly and find that you are, in fact, obsessed with the glasses because they are costing you so much money. Then you hire people to pick them up because you can't pick them up as well as do everything else. Then you start thinking the person you've hired is not picking them up fast enough and you see your profits dwindling in wages, and you're still picking the glasses up yourself anyway. Soon you're picking up glasses in your dreams.

The routine that we would pretty well maintain for the next five years was bedded in early. Up at 6.00 a.m. to clean. Clean the toilets, clean the bar, clean the floors, clean the windows, hose the pavement, stack the fridges, stack the bottle shop, do the stock-take. If there wasn't enough stock in the bar or the shop we'd haul it in from the back. Sometimes I worked a twenty-hour day, with a couple of hours off and then two hours sleep. Once a week we'd clean the pipes and all the lines from the barrels. The outside of the pub was cleaned twice a day. It was always said that I ran a clean pub, and I have to admit I am a bit fanatical about cleanliness. My mum passed that on to me and I passed it on to my daughter.

As if we didn't have enough to do at the pub, we had nightmare tenants in the house. The first lot were students, all making noise and having so many people sleeping over that our neighbours complained. They were followed by someone who worked for Telecom and had about a thousand phone lines running into the place. Later we wondered what on earth he'd been up to and thought it might have been an SP shop.

As Dawn-Lorraine grew older she began working in the front bar and really loved it, but I was concerned that it wasn't the best place for a young girl. Looking back on it though, the locals and funny characters who used to come in were really just beautiful and in many ways it was a great education for her. Everyone looked out for her because they knew if they didn't they'd have to answer to me.

One of the great old ladies was Mary Sullivan, our resident SP, and she'd sit in the alcove seat at the front and have all her paper-work spread out on a little round table. She'd be one of the first to arrive and even in the morning she'd have Tia Maria and milk. People would come up and place their bets with her. Eventually she'd get up to make a phone call or go to the toilet and most of the time when she came back she'd go off at me: 'Dawn, some bastard's come and drunk me drink again.' The pub was usually quite empty that early and I'd say, 'Mary, no one's been here.' I always assumed she'd drunk it and forgotten. Then one day we heard her from the women's lounge: 'You bloody black bastard!' Next second she appeared at the bar and said, 'Dawn you owe me a Tia Maria.' It turned out that our beautiful dog, Benson, a black shepherd–labrador cross, would wait till Mary had left the room then go and slurp down her Tia Maria. I'd never seen him do it and it had taken months to work out what was going on. That morning when he was finally discovered I looked at Benson over the top of the bar and he looked at me and slunk away, knowing full well he'd been caught out. I had often been able to smell alcohol upstairs when he was around, and he'd burp and hiccup just like an old man, but we'd never put two and two together until Mary finally caught him at her glass.

Benson was a present from Dawn-Lorraine. She'd arranged for him to be delivered to the Riverview for Christmas, and we were cleaning the pub when he arrived. There was a knock on the door, and when I asked Dawn-Lorraine to answer it she refused, even though she was standing right beside the door. Exasperated, I yanked the door open and looked out, but there was no one there and I shut it again. Then there was another knock and Dawn-Lorraine insisted I look again. This time I looked down and saw Benson sitting on the pavement with a big red bow around his neck. Dawn-Lorraine said, 'Happy Christmas, Mum,' and I said, 'Well you'd better come in,' and with that he walked straight in and followed me over to the window seat and tried to jump up beside me. Dawn-Lorraine said, 'He's a black shepherd, just what you wanted,' and I said, as tactfully as I could, 'I don't think he's a shepherd, darling.' With that, Dawn-Lorraine burst into tears and sobbed that she didn't think I was going to keep him. She rang the breeder, who confirmed he was a cross, and I told her firmly that I didn't want a labrador, which she regretfully accepted. The problem was the dog wouldn't leave my bloody side. I picked him up and said, 'Well you're a bit of a shepherd cross but what else are you? Heinz 57 varieties by the look of things!'

'But do you like him, Mum?' Dawn-Lorraine pleaded.

The dog and my daughter kept looking at me mournfully and eventually I said, 'I think he's lovely but he's not a shepherd.'

'He mostly is,' said Dawn-Lorraine.

'No, sorry darling, he's not. He doesn't have the right ears and his nose is too short. There's a bit of shepherd there but he's definitely more labrador.'

In the end we kept him. We were going to call him Kamahl, but Kamahl is a friend of mine and we thought if he came over he'd be offended, so we settled on Benson after the butler in the TV series, for obvious reasons.

Benson became a familiar sight in the pub and everyone loved him—most of the time. On Saturdays workmen would come to the pub after their shift and they'd buy pies from the snack bar to have with a beer. They'd be talking and drinking as they ate and Benson would come up and nibble on the pies, so gently they wouldn't see him at first, then suddenly they'd discover half their pie had gone. If they left one on the table while they got a beer Benson would take the whole thing, no matter how hot it was. I'd look the other way when I saw him doing it and keep serving. What could you say? He was a real Balmain boy that dog, always into mischief. Sometimes he'd disappear for days and then come home when he was hungry, or courtesy of the local dog catcher who knew where he lived.

Another of the great pub characters was Dickie Hunt, still a good friend, who would go to the snowfields every year and come back with a hugh trailer-load of snow. He'd call the pub an hour before getting to Sydney to warn me he was on his way. I'd say, 'Dawn-Lorraine, start picking up glasses please,' and she'd instantly know what was happening. I'd start quietly taking bottles down from around the bar and clearing away everything that I could. The boys in the bar would gradually catch on, and by the time Dickie arrived with the snow there'd be a pub full of adults acting like little kids on Christmas Eve, waiting for Santa to arrive. When he got there it was on. Dickie would shovel the snow onto the pavement and we'd have these massive snow ball fights in and around the pub. We'd build a snowman on the corner outside, and there'd almost be car accidents when people saw it and then saw us running in and out of doors like maniacs with snowballs in our hands. Once the police arrived because Dawn-Lorraine had been carried and dumped into the snow and was screaming so hard they'd received complaints that someone was being attacked. Afterwards all the boys would pitch in and help clean up, mopping up the sludge and water before all the bottles were put back in order.

Another time a bloke called Johnny brought a wild pig into the pub and Dickie Hunt shut all the doors. The pig tried to jump the bar and attack me, and then it ran around the bar, butting people in the backside. It had enormous tusks and everyone in the place was terrified. Another of Dickie's tricks was to let off flares in the hotel every now and then for no particular reason, and the bar would be so full of smoke no one could see what was happening. He was really just one of the local larrikins but sometimes things did get a bit out of hand.

Christmas at the Riverview was special. Dickie Hunt and my good friend Chalky would go and get an enormous tree for the pub. It was usually as tall as the roofline and we'd tie it to the outside of the building, sticking the trunk in the sewer pipe to keep it stable. We'd decorate it and then have carols by candlelight with all the local kids. The first year was a bit of a disaster because although the kids sat outside their parents came inside the hotel carrying the candles, and wax dripped everywhere and little fires were started accidentally. After that we had the carols outside and put the candles through coasters so the kids didn't burn themselves. Santa arrived one year on the back of a ute, the next on a motorbike, then the garbage truck, a fire engine and so on. We'd put on a band for the parents, and one year it was Col Joye and the Joy Boys. We'd print up the words to the carols, and the local footballers, water polo players and rowers would all join in the singing with the kids. It was a tremendous evening and a great atmosphere.

During my Riverview days I had very little time to visit friends so they'd come to me instead. It was a constant passing parade of interesting and colourful characters, and I could probably write a book on the Riverview years alone. John Singleton, the advertising and media guru, has been one of my best friends since the 1960s, when we'd meet up at the races, and now that I was at the Riverview he'd come by with his wife of that time, Maggie Eckhardt. One particular night he brought his dog, Thug, as well.

I'd told Singo to call by because I'd made steak and kidney pie and, though I say so myself, I do that dish well. Anyway, Singo being Singo, he ordered three serves—one for him, one for Maggie and one for Thug—and the three of them sat in a row at the bar and tucked in. I wish I'd taken a photograph.

The tourist buses carrying Japanese tourists started to roll past the pub in those narrow streets on such a regular basis that we started to wonder what was going on, until we found out we were part of the itinerary for some tour companies. Even as late as the 1980s, I was told Dawn Fraser was still well known to the Japanese. Other Japanese people would seek us out on their own, and I was always expected to have a drink with them. Drinking was a bit of a problem in the pub because everyone wanted you to have a drink. Naturally I didn't want to drink my profits, and nor could I allow myself to drink with the long hours I was working, so occasionally I had to fake it, and I learned to sit on a drink. After getting up at six and working through till one, when I'd do the lines and put water through the pipes and get rid of the dead beer after measuring it up to see how much I'd lost, I didn't really need to be drinking too. To solve the problem I kept J&B scotch bottles full of cold tea and soda behind the bar, which I'd get one of our barmaids, Patty or Mona, or Dawn-Lorraine to pour me when I wanted to be friendly but not get drunk.

Halfway through my time at the Riverview I was surprised by the crew of Channel 7's *This Is Your Life*, who came to do an episode of the program about me. My partner had set it all up, but hadn't thought about the implications of me playing an illegal card game in the pub when the camera crew came through the door that Friday night. I kept thinking, 'Why am I playing cards when we're so busy?' The pub was absolutely chock-a-block but the guys had conned me into playing cards by challenging me as the prevailing champion in the pub tournament at the time. I protested but they kept insisting. They even made me sit in the chair I hated by reassuring me it would allow me to keep an eye on the pub. When I saw the camera lights beaming in through the door and windows I thought, 'Shit, I'm being raided,' and took off out the door and down the street, where I was intercepted by Roger Climpson, the host at the time, who handed me the famous red book. When I look at the footage of the show now I can see I was a very reluctant participant. I loathe surprises, and I'd warned everyone in my family not to let them do the show on me when I heard they were making approaches. Before I agreed to go on the show I extracted various promises, including one that I would be given the master tape of the show, which I still have today. Just before this book was due to be published I was caught yet again by *This Is Your Life*, but this time it was Mike Munro with the red book. I was on the beach supposedly filming a commercial for Kellogg when Mike appeared carrying a surfboard. At least this time I was gainfully employed when the crew arrived.

I'd never wanted to be part of the show, but it was quite good fun on both occasions. The first time, we went out to the Channel 7 studios in Epping to film it and the biggest surprise was that they'd brought Superintendent Kamira, who'd given me the Olympic flag, out from Tokyo. He gave me another souvenir that night, a set of medals that had been struck in Japan during the 1964 Games. It was also fun to see Ricksie again, who'd been flown over from the US, as well as all my brothers and sisters, Dawn-Lorraine and my two coaches, Chut and Harry. My old roommate from 1960, Ruth Everuss, even demonstrated her ability to sign my name for the cameras. And I had a chance to wish our Olympians well on national television before we all headed back to the Riverview where the party went on for some time.

Our neighbours at the Riverview were very tolerant of us when we had all-night private parties, and on occasions we'd even have the whole street blocked off, just like when I was a kid, for cricket

matches on the road. Sometimes on a Saturday afternoon the pavement outside the pub was so full of people that no one could pass
in a car or on foot. All in all, our neighbours had to put up with
quite a bit, but never more than when I campaigned against Prime
Minister Malcolm Fraser's stand on the Moscow Olympics.

After the Soviet Union invaded Afghanistan, President Carter of
the US tried to persuade other world leaders that the best form of
protest against the invasion would be to boycott the 1980
Olympics. At that time I was adamant that politics should not
impinge on sport, apart from the obvious need for funding, which
I believe should be given without strings attached. The Fraser
Government made it clear that any funds they had given to the
AOC should not be used to send athletes to Moscow, and so I set
about some independent fundraising for the Olympians. I helped
form a group called Australians for the Olympics, and I was the
main spokesperson. We numbered in the hundreds, although I was
the only Olympian in the group. Our campaign was launched at
the Riverview and we organised a big fair in Birchgrove Road
around the pub. The street was blocked off and there were all sorts
of stalls from which I took a percentage for the Olympic fund. The
pub sold cans from the cellar and beer from the bar and I gave the
same percentage from my sales. We also put on a jumping castle
and a barbeque. The neighbours were sympathetic and even joined
in by allowing the visitors to the fair to use their bathrooms. It was
a wonderful day and we raised about $35 000.

My stance on the Olympics became very well known because I
was so outspoken over it. The media covered the fair and I talked
about how important I felt it was that the athletes should not get
tangled up in Fraser's politics. Bill Hayden, then the Leader of the
Opposition Labor Party, decided to make an official visit to the
Riverview to talk to me about my stand. I had written several
strongly worded letters to the Prime Minister at the time as well
as to various newspapers. We knew Mr Hayden was coming and

we cleaned the pub for days beforehand. Federal Police came and checked the place out, and the whole street was cordoned off on the day. Mr Hayden arrived with his entourage of police and other minders and officials, as well as the press, and we took him to our upstairs lounge for a private chat. We spoke about the fundraising day and why the athletes should go to Moscow. He stayed for quite a while and had a cold beer before leaving. He wished us all the best and promised to help our cause.

Herb Elliott was one athlete who spoke out in favour of the boycott, and several other countries joined with the US, including Japan, Canada, China and West Germany. I was bitterly disappointed when the government paid cash to some athletes and associations to stay away and boycott the games. I also felt that Malcolm Fraser had placed such strong demands on athletes that many were intimidated. What's more, during the crisis, wool from Malcolm Fraser's property, Nareen, was still being exported to the Soviet Union. We were tipped off about it by wharfies who actually saw it being loaded onto ships. It seemed that only the athletes were suffering. I was quoted at the time in the *Sydney Morning Herald* as saying, 'The Prime Minister is totally hypocritical. He sold his wool to the Russians yet he wants young Australian athletes not to compete with the vast majority of international sportsmen who will be going to the Olympics to do their best for their countries.' The press cartoonists had a field day. Many played on the idea of Fraser versus Fraser, with the two of us diving into swimming pools, or Malcolm Fraser lugging wool bales in an imaginary Olympic event.

The debate raged on until our AOF Board voted six to five for the athletes to go. The Murdoch Press had been very much against sending a team and strongly supported the Prime Minister's stand; that is, until we won our first gold medal, and suddenly all was forgiven and it was 'Go Aussie go!'

The issue became very nasty for many people, and along with several others I received death threats by phone and other threats were made against my daughter. We were advised by the police to take these seriously, and Dawn-Lorraine had to be escorted home from boarding school on Fridays, usually by my friend Chalky. We even had bodyguards for a few months. I felt sorrow for Afghanistan but I strongly believed that politics should not have had such a big impact on sport.

Because of my stand I was invited by the Moscow Organising Committee to attend the Games as their guest. My partner agreed to look after the pub and I took off for three of the most fascinating weeks of my life. I had been issued with a special visa allowing me all sorts of access, but it disappeared mysteriously when we stopped over in Singapore. I didn't know it had been removed from my papers until I landed in Moscow. I was taken off to a little room by KGB officers and told to get undressed for a search, which I refused to do and asked for an interpreter. Eventually my bags were brought in and I was allowed to open my case and show the official letters, all written in Russian, that I'd received. After that there was a great deal of embarrassment and lots of apologies, and I was put in a car and taken to the hotel. A new visa was issued almost immediately.

It was especially fascinating to be visiting Russia in those days because it was behind the Iron Curtain, and I was keen to find out more about the place. My invitation included the use of an interpreter, a security guard and a driver. I had the right to go almost anywhere in the USSR and it didn't cost me anything. We would go to the best restaurants and my interpreter or guard would mention something to the people at the head of the queue and suddenly I would find myself at the front of the line. I also went to visit ordinary people in government flats and on farms. I know my room was bugged, and halfway through my stay the first interpreter and security guard were replaced, I suspect because we became too friendly. I was taken to many places which I believe were usually out of bounds to ordinary visitors, including defence installations, and underground cities built in case of nuclear attacks, and I got around quite a bit to other places, including Kiev, Georgia, Leningrad and Stalingrad. Every time I caught a plane I would find myself on the best seats available and was given everything I could possibly need. I loved the Russian people and I enjoyed the architecture and deep sense of history.

•

It wasn't all fun and laughs during the Riverview years. People would often be knocking on my door at midnight looking for a bottle of this or that because they knew I was there, and I loaned a lot of money during that period that I never saw again. I figured that if I wasn't kind to these people they'd go and drink elsewhere, so in the end it was no different to lending them some money. At least if they stuck with my pub I had half a chance of getting some of it back. Besides, these were my people, my neighbourhood and my friends. I often didn't want the money back, but at times I really needed it.

One sad time at the pub was when our neighbour across the road, who'd had all sorts of problems in his marriage, walked out of the pub one day, through his house and into the yard and hanged himself from a tree. Old Ted was always saying he was going to neck himself but no one had believed him. Snowy, another local, who was staying with Ted at the time, came over to the pub and asked me to come and help him cut Ted down. His daughter, who was down at the baths with Dawn-Lorraine, came back to the house and watched from the bathroom window. I'll never forget that image.

I tell this story not to sensationalise but to show that the neighbourhood was not always happy and full of fun. Balmain was still a working-class area where people had their problems and struggles to deal with.

While I was at the Riverview I became quite close to David McKenzie, who was the Australian Olympic Federation Vice

President and a member of the IOC. I'd first met him in 1956 when he was a member of the Australian fencing team at the Melbourne Olympics and then kept in touch in 1960 and 1964. He'd become a member of the IOC after he retired and he was the Assistant Chef de Mission for the Australian team in 1968. We were already friends by the time I took over the Riverview, and then he came to drink at the pub almost every Thursday and Friday night and we became pretty close. We'd talk about sport and the IOC but we also used to talk about the role he saw for me on the AOF Board. He knew what I could do to help prepare athletes for elite competition and he also knew how powerful I could be in fundraising for them. Understandably, I was also interested in helping retired Olympians adjust to their lives after competition. I very much wanted to be the first woman on the AOF Executive Board. Well, I wanted to see a woman on the Board at least, and at the time David and I were of the opinion that it should be me. I began to go to dinner at David's house and I became very fond of his wife, Sue, who I still regard as a dear friend. And there'd be others at dinner, such as Phil Coles, John Coates, and Peter Montgomery. There was always political intrigue but overall we had good times and lively discussions about the future of sport in Australia. I found David inspirational, as well as a very good and decent man.

The common thread between us, other than love of sport, was our advocacy for athletes ahead of officials. We'd both had our clashes with officialdom during Olympic Games and we well understood some of the problems that existed. During my campaigning for the athletes in 1980 I kept in close contact with David, who shared my views completely. We were both disheartened by the government's interference in the decision about going to Moscow and both agreed that the Olympics should be above politics. I still sincerely believe that. To think that some Australian athletes who withdrew from Moscow actually took government money to compensate for their loss of involvement in international competition is beyond comprehension. How can a few thousand dollars compensate for what has been lost? I caught up with David and Sue for dinner while I was in Moscow for the 1980 Games, and just being there and knowing the Australian team was there made us feel quite elated because it had been a hard-fought battle.

Like me, David had come from a fairly ordinary background and I believe that's another reason why we had such a great rapport. I felt confident when we talked that my role with the athletes would eventually become formalised and that one day I would become part of the AOF Board. As far as he could, David had promised me a place on the Board and I saw myself in that role in the future. By then I was ready to move back into sport, and I wanted to use my experiences to help shape the future of sport in Australia—to give something back. I felt that many of my problems as an Olympian had been because I was a female in a man's world, and it seemed important that a woman should be part of the AOF Executive Board.

Tragically, as has been openly reported, David was found dead in a bathhouse in Hawaii in mid-1981 while on a business trip. It is widely accepted that he met with foul play, although no conclusion about the exact nature of how or why he died has ever been determined. David's death sparked all sorts of speculation and some rather unpleasant innuendo. As an athlete, I wasn't surprised about the bathhouse side of things. Lots of athletes use steam rooms and massage rooms, and the reports of his death didn't strike me the way they struck other people at the time. I was just very sad. His life was too short and I felt I'd lost a great friend and that Australian sport had lost a brilliant ambassador. We've never seen the likes of him since. I was also very sad for his wife Sue and their children. Later that year I was invited to an IOC Congress at Baden Baden in Germany where I was honoured for my contributions as a swimmer. I was given an IOC Silver Order, and I'm sure David was the one who had organised this honour for me.

After David's death I had lunch with John Coates and Peter Montgomery and they said they hadn't known David had promised me a role on the AOF Board, but they suggested I stand back for now and they would be supportive in the future in helping that come about. The President of the IOC, Juan Antonio Samaranch, urged that Australia think about appointing a woman to the Board to replace David, although not at his level of course, but despite that, neither I nor any other woman was appointed for quite some time.

•

By the end of 1982 I was having a difficult time in my relationship. Cracks had started to appear and I once again began to think that I just wasn't any good at the personal side of my life. My partner began to mix with people I didn't particularly want at the pub and we argued over that. At the time, I was worried about maintaining the relationship as my daughter grew older and became more aware of what was going on. I didn't want to hurt her and I was scared of how she would react.

My partner and I kept on running the pub together but the strain was fairly obvious to both of us and the relationship gradually became more of a business one than a personal one. Finally it deteriorated to such an extent, mostly through arguments over money, that we decided to call it quits altogether and I found myself on my own again. I was feeling a mixture of anger, sadness and plain exhaustion over what had gone on between us, but just a few weeks later I was to face a bigger challenge than mending a broken heart.

In April 1983 I agreed to judge a talent quest at another pub in Balmain, the Town Hall Hotel, and a neighbour and friend of mine named John John, a chief petty officer in the Navy, was coming to walk up to the pub with me. I had just finished hosing down inside and generally cleaning up, and had left the cellar door open behind the bar so the air would circulate and dry out the floor. John was late, so I thought I'd duck behind the bar and grab a coin to phone him and check he was coming. As I stepped towards the cash register I slipped on the wet floor and fell down into the cellar, which was about a three-metre drop. I grabbed the cellar door as I went down but couldn't hang on, and I landed very heavily on my knees. Amazingly, I got straight back up and climbed up the ladder into the bar, but when I reached the top I was dizzy and didn't really know where I was because the pain up my legs and back was so intense. Just then there was a knock at the door and when I answered it John was standing there. He said, 'God, are you all right? You look awful.' I told him I'd just had a fall but I was OK, so we locked up and went to the Town Hall pub. By the time I arrived I was very stiff and could barely walk enough to make my way to the disc jockey's stand to announce the winner. I kept thinking, 'I must see about that when I get a moment.' I decided not to stay on after I'd announced the winner, and someone dropped me back home, where I got into bed and slept soundly.

The next day I had to go to Melbourne to a meeting with the Confederation of Australian Sport, an organisation established as a forum for all of the different sporting bodies around Australia. I had become involved with their program for adjusting adult sports to suit children. I managed to get on the 9.00 a.m. plane, but as we started to gain altitude I had the oddest sensation in my neck. I was a bit frightened and kept thinking, 'Oh dear, what have I done?' I had pins and needles down one arm and I took a pillow and slumped in my seat as the pain grew worse and worse. Eventually I had to ask the flight attendant for a painkiller. I explained what had happened and she was very anxious that I go straight to a doctor at the other end. I was supposed to go to Jolimont for the meeting, but as I was to stay with the athlete Raelene Boyle, I went straight to her place, called up and made my apologies, and lay on the couch for the rest of the day. When Boyley arrived home she was alarmed by how I looked and asked, 'Are you OK, Frase?'

'No, I feel really dreadful,' I said miserably.

With that she called her doctor, who told her to bring me over immediately. Somehow we managed to get in the car and drive to the surgery. Initially the doctor thought I was having a heart attack because of the pins and needles down my arm, but when I explained what had happened she decided it wasn't my heart, gave me an injection of painkillers, and said I should have an X-ray the next day.

I did have the X-ray, but they wanted to do all sorts of other tests using dye, and I told them I didn't want to do anything more till I got back to Sydney and my own doctor. They did talk me into wearing a brace—I figured I'd been there, done that and it couldn't hurt. After that I went back to Raelene's and spent the week lying on her lounge room floor in a great deal of pain. One of our friends, Sue Mogg, came over and helped me during that time because I was pretty well incapacitated. I desperately wanted to be back in Sydney but I also knew I was in a lot of trouble.

After a week I managed to fly to Sydney loaded up with painkillers and I was met at the airport by another great friend, Peggy Carter, and her husband, Graeme, who were going to look after me. They were having guests to lunch at their place the day I arrived, one of whom was a neurosurgeon. Peggy had taken one look at me at the airport and insisted I go straight to bed the minute we walked in the door. When their neurosurgeon friend arrived for lunch, they asked him to have a look at me and he immediately ordered an ambulance and sent me to St Vincent's Hospital. I stayed for a week, during which time they worked out that I had some cracked vertebrae, a pinched spinal cord and bone particles floating in my spinal fluid. I'd broken the horn off vertebrae numbers six and seven, and had also fractured number five. Technically, it was a broken neck.

No one could believe I'd survived the week in that state with very few painkillers and no professional treatment. I think the swimming years must have taught me to put up with a lot. I was told I would have been killed if the muscles in my neck hadn't been so strong. Those good old neck muscles from swimming were still standing by me. There was a bit of talk that I could be a paraplegic. They packed me in sand and I lay there for two weeks in traction. It was another two weeks before they released me, saying they wouldn't do anything more unless I gave up smoking. I'd become a heavy smoker since taking on the pub. The doctor needed to do a milogram, which involved running dye through my veins, and it wouldn't work as well if I had nicotine in my system. They allowed me to go home for the Mother's Day weekend, and the following week back in hospital I wasn't allowed to do anything but lie there. It was agony. I had been smoking up to sixty cigarettes a day and giving them up for that week was hard. I thought that if I could just get through that week I'd have the milogram and then go back onto the cigarettes again.

I went back to hospital at the beginning of the week and didn't take any cigarettes with me. I had half thought by the end of that weekend at home that I might actually give up. I had the milogram and the doctor decided they'd have to operate on my neck. When Peggy came to visit me I asked her to go and buy me a packet of cigarettes. Peggy was a non-smoker and I have never asked anyone who is a non-smoker to buy me cigarettes before or since. She said to me, 'Do you realise what you're asking me to do?'

'I'm just asking you to go and buy me a packet of cigarettes. I'm giving up but I need them for security reasons.'

Peggy went and bought the cigarettes and when she came back she only had a packet of Peter Stuyvesants and no matches or lighter. She threw them at me and said, 'If you smoke a single one of these cigarettes I will never talk to you again. It will be the end of our friendship.' I knew she meant it, the way you just know sometimes. Then she walked out without another word; not a 'goodbye' or 'good luck', nothing. Another friend, Sue, came in about an hour later and said she was dying for a smoke. I told her she couldn't smoke here and she asked if I'd given up. 'I have,' I said, and handed her the packet of cigarettes Peggy had bought me. 'Here, take these. I'm never smoking again.' And to this day I haven't. Ever since I'd met her, on the film set of *Dawn!*, Peggy and I had been firm friends, and the friendship was worth so much more than a cigarette.

Back at the pub, Dawn-Lorraine and Patty had pretty well taken over. My partner had of course moved out a few weeks before the accident and I never saw her again. Dawn-Lorraine had started business college by then, so while I lay in hospital she'd stack the fridges before leaving for the day. She'd go to college and then visit me in hospital. When she arrived she usually found me asleep, and she'd eat my lunch that I'd leave for her before pushing together two big armchairs and sleeping until I woke. She'd spend the rest of the afternoon and evening keeping my spirits up, and then go back to the pub at about 10.00 p.m., clean the fridges, clean the pub, do the wages and the cash register money, and set it all up for Patty for the next day. That's how it went on for almost two months.

After the operation I had to lie face down on a bed that was like a massage table, with my face through a hole in the mattress. Dawn-Lorraine used to lie underneath and talk to me. She had promised not to come in the day after the operation because I didn't want her to see all the tubes, so she obeyed me for once and came the day after. I was very out of it for the first week and I lay there and let things run through my mind. I thought a lot about my broken relationship and how disappointed I was it hadn't worked, and how I felt let down. Then I found out that my accountant hadn't kept my medical insurance up to date, which had been part of his job. I was now in St Vincent's Private Hospital with weeks and weeks of bills to pay and no cover, so I started to worry about the business and where I'd get enough money to cover everything. What's more, my doctor had known I wasn't covered before he operated but he went ahead because he'd been concerned that the bone particles could sever my spinal cord. Sister Bernadette, one of the head nuns at the hospital, came and broke the news to me about the health fund and I told her not to worry, that the hospital would be paid, and she said, 'Yes Dawn, we know you will pay us.'

Then I started to wonder about my accounts, because other bills I'd written cheques for started to pop up unpaid. Cheques were bouncing right, left and centre and gradually, as I got my faculties back, I started to realise something was terribly wrong. Soon we realised I might lose my beloved house, which had been mortgaged to buy the business, and everything I had. The final straw was that I owed the breweries a lot of money, and cheques that I'd written had bounced and money I'd put aside for them was gone. Tooheys was fantastic at the time and let me pay the debt off gradually but others weren't so kind and started to put an enormous amount of pressure on me. My bank, which was Westpac at the time, did not show an ounce of concern or consideration though I'd been with them for years.

When I finally left hospital I was in a shocking state, both mentally and physically. My left side was paralysed and I couldn't even use a knife and fork properly. Fortunately I am ambidextrous and could do some things with my right hand, but Dawn-Lorraine had to cut up all my food and take a glass to my lips if I needed to drink.

I was still moving slowly when I ended up back at the pub working in the snack bar, and I couldn't lift anything. It was frustrating having to get other people to do so much for me as I was used to being very independent. Then Dawn-Lorraine collapsed. She was so thin from not eating during the time I'd been in hospital that I thought she had anorexia. She was taken to hospital and finally diagnosed with a ruptured appendix about half an hour before being operated on, and I remember anxiously waiting at the hospital wearing my steel brace and hardly being able to get around. Apart from the appendicitis, Dawn-Lorraine was simply exhausted, and we looked a pretty forlorn couple in Balmain Hospital that day of her operation.

It was a bitter blow that all our hard work over five years seemed to have been for nothing. Just before I'd had my accident I'd been trying to buy the lease from Tooth & Company, the brewery who owned it at the time, because I had an idea to put a restaurant upstairs. Council had opposed me, first because of the lack of parking and then because I didn't hold the lease. Eventually I'd secured the parking spaces at a petrol station up the road, which I could use after hours, and it seemed there was enough money in the business for me to take over the lease. Over the years I'd increased the turnover of the pub from twenty-two kegs a week to thirty-six, and I'd been the only pub in Balmain with beer during trucking strikes. I had a friend who carted beer interstate and he'd ring up and see how much I wanted. Other friends were truckies, who'd warn me about strikes so that I could order extra in advance. I also had a great relationship with Balmain RSL, who would store beer for me because I had a limited cellar and could only take about thirty kegs at a time. If it was hot we could take even fewer because the afternoon sun used to beat down on that little corner pub and we'd have to keep the kegs cool under sugar bags with hoses dripping cold water over them.

Tooths stood firm, though, and said that I couldn't buy the lease as they had other plans for the pub. Next I discovered that the money intended for our lease fees to the brewery had disappeared. One day one of the brewery's salesmen who used to come into the pub mentioned that I was behind in payments. It wasn't his department, but obviously something had been said to him or he'd heard something. I wrote him a cheque on the spot but by then, although I didn't realise it, we were way behind.

After being back at the pub awhile it was clear to me that the financial problems had now gone too far for me to recover. Eventually I was issued with a bankruptcy notice. My accountant couldn't produce my books to show what had actually happened, saying he'd had a fire in which they'd all been burned. There was no paper trail whatsoever. Boy, was that a hard lesson!

Tooheys were prepared to keep supplying beer to me but Tooths, who owned the lease, wanted me out immediately and wouldn't negotiate. So finally, almost five years to the day since I'd begun running the Riverview, I was given a week to get out. I would be leaving with far less than I'd had in the first place and I thought I would also lose my home. We removed just about every last drop of alcohol from the place, because I didn't want to give the brewery anything, and then on the last Sunday we put the final three kegs on tap and invited everyone in for free beer. It was a wonderful party and we reminisced and laughed together about all the great times we'd had at the pub. I was completely devastated to be leaving and all the more so because I was leaving with huge financial debts after working harder than I would ever have believed possible. On the Monday I left the keys on the counter and walked out.

That very day Dawn-Lorraine and I found ourselves back in our house, and I had to work out a way of hanging on to it, getting myself better and paying off my debts. First of all I went on an invalid pension while I rehabilitated myself, and I had a bit of personal money I'd saved while I was at the pub because in those five years I'd never gone anywhere to spend it. It wasn't much but it helped. I also had a close circle of friends who I used to listen to jazz with at different venues around Balmain and they organised a huge fundraiser for me at the Sydney Entertainment Centre. My friend Bottles, who owned the Dry Dock Hotel in Balmain, organised most of it and the event was pretty spectacular; even The

Supremes played because they were on tour in Australia at the time. In the end there was a little bit of money left over after the hire of the Centre was paid for and that went towards my medical bills.

Rehabilitation was long and slow. It took me over eighteen months to be able to use cutlery properly because there was a lot of muscle wastage in my left arm. I can remember the moment when I finally picked up a fork and was able to use it. I was having lunch with friends in East Sydney and began using the fork without thinking about it. Then I stopped and said, 'Hey, look at me!'

Immediately after coming out of hospital I started to swim at the Sydney University pool to try to get my muscle tone and control back again. I was told I wouldn't be able to play golf again, and at the time I couldn't even hold a club. After six months I was able to take off the steel brace, which was a relief because it used to embarrass me. Then Roy Pearson, the Secretary of the university's Sports Union, offered me a casual job at the pool. I had to instruct children in lifesaving and also coach swimmers from the Women's College. Other people would come in and ask me to teach them to swim, and so I began to earn a bit of money again. Around that time a permanent position for coaching came up at the pool, and I applied and got the job. I had enormous debts, though, and I was still feeling that I would lose my home because Tooths didn't let up. Tooheys very kindly allowed me to pay them off over three years, but the debt was for thousands and thousands of dollars and the constant worry and pressure was deeply upsetting.

One of the people I started to teach to swim turned out to be a manager of one of the branches of the United Permanent Building Society. He'd just had heart surgery and I was helping him rehabilitate through swimming. We got talking and I told him what had happened to me, and he arranged for me to take out a long-term loan so I could pay off Tooths immediately and then gradually pay my other debts. He got me back on track, which was a great relief, and even though I still had very little it made me happy and secure to know the debts were under control and that I would keep the house and pay off the mortgage with United Permanent gradually.

After the heady years at the Riverview this time in my life was much quieter but I welcomed the peace and steady work pattern after all the drama, and it was what I needed to be able to get myself well again. I've always prided myself on being able to live on the smell of an oily rag, so it was fine for me to live on the coaching money and start to pay off the house again. I spent a lot of time with my friends Peggy and Graeme, who had me over and talked to me and fed me before I could even move about, and as I gradually loosened up through the training I'd accompany Peggy when she'd do make-up for fashion parades and shows.

Dawn-Lorraine joined me after a while in coaching at the Sydney University Pool and we stayed there for the next five years building up a good little business. From being almost crippled I gradually found myself growing fitter and fitter through all the swimming I was doing, both for myself and through the teaching. Strangely enough, swimming had come to my rescue again, along with some good friends.

One of those friends was Singo, who I'd kept up with for many years but became much closer to during the years after I left the Riverview. It was Singo who started to organise speaking engagements for me to make some extra money. I was quite nervous about public speaking at first but found that once I'd worked out a few standard speeches about my years as an Olympic swimmer I could hold an audience, and I enjoyed the work. It was also reasonably lucrative. I practised on various branches of the Country Women's Association for no payment before graduating to Rotary and View Clubs and later still to corporations and sports functions. It is something I still do to this day and find is a steady source of income and enjoyment. It enables me to meet people and travel, two of my favourite pastimes.

In 1984 Singo arranged to take me to Los Angeles for the Games. I was still on the outer as far as the AOF went. I hadn't been given a place on the Executive Board and quite rightly suspected I would never be given one. Nor had I been invited in any official capacity, and didn't have accreditation or tickets to events.

Together Singo and I were to report on the Games for Radio 2KY in Sydney. I stayed at the Ambassador Hotel which had been opened up just for the Games because everything was full and Singo stayed with a friend, Rod McKuen, in Beverly Hills. There was a large Australian contingent at the hotel, including Norman May and Jan Thornett (formerly Jan Andrew) and her husband, Dick. We all went to the opening ceremony together to try to get in, and when Dick Thornett said to the security guard, 'This is Dawn Fraser,' they let us in and I shared half a seat at the back to watch the ceremony.

I didn't have any other tickets at the time but as the days went on Singo organised entrance to various events, including the closing ceremony. The ceremony was fantastic, but when we got back to the car park after it was all over, some of the Australian contingent were surprised to find that my car was the only one left with tyres. The others' cars were all up on bricks. The trick was, I'd chatted to the black kids hanging around and paid them to keep an eye out. Good old Balmain know-how pays off again!

Singo had rigged up a makeshift studio in Rod's house where he was staying in Los Angeles, and we broadcast our commentary from there. We had a television set just outside the studio and I'd sit there and report as if I were watching it live. Singo would sit behind the desk and I'd sit on the couch and chat to him as if we were at the Games. Once I even reported over the phone from my car in a traffic jam, pretending I was at a hockey game. It was hilarious and I'm sure we gave the listeners great value.

Singo and I are two of a kind and quite a bad influence on each other. We understand each other very well, though, and appreciate each other's humour. Whenever one of Singo's wives—and there have been quite a few of them—cried on my shoulder about something he'd done I would say, 'You can't change him.' And I know I'm exactly the same.

13

THE
COMEBACK KID

While we were staying in Los Angeles, and after we came back, Singo and I trained together to get fit. This was especially important for me because I was still strengthening my back after the accident. We'd train every day and Singo even brought in a personal trainer for us, so you can see we were very serious.

Around this time a man named Les Martins, President of the Australian Weightlifting Federation, got me involved in the Masters Games swimming. In fact Les and I went a bit further back than that. Our association began when Garry Daly, who had been the Executive Director of the Lawn Tennis Association, set up the Sport Australia Awards. Garry began to get in touch with people he described as 'sporting heroes' to present the awards. In the first year, 1980, I presented Yvonne Goolagong-Cawley with an award. It was an honour I particularly enjoyed because I'd been out of the sporting mainstream for a long time, and to be thought of in this way again was a big boost for me.

Garry Daly and Les Martins both had senior roles in the Confederation of Australian Sport, Garry as Executive Director and Les as Chairman of the Development Committee, and it was Les who rang to ask for my involvement in their Children in Sport program—the reason for the trip to Melbourne that terrible day after my fall. The program, originally set up in Denmark, involved looking at all the sports played by adults and tailoring the rules and equipment to suit children. For instance, if a cricket pitch is 22 metres long, the children's pitch might be half that. T-Ball was the modified version of baseball, and so on. I became very involved in the program and started to run it under Les's over-all direction. That was really the beginning, along with Garry's invitation to present the award, of my move back into the world of sport.

The children's sport project took me to Melbourne often, and I got to know Les better and better. He had also come from a big, poor family and we understood each other well. Eventually, in his role as President of the World Masters Games, he encouraged me to become part of Masters swimming for the inaugural Games, to be held in Toronto in 1985. I took up his suggestion and started to train pretty hard, and hadn't felt so good in a long time. I was swimming 5000 metres a day, which I thought was pretty good for a 47-year-old.

The Masters Games, which was an important international competition for veteran athletes, took me back into my swimming on a very serious basis. My attitude at the time was very much that it would bring me back into the sport I loved the most, as well as give me a focus and keep me fit. The problem was that every time I got into the water to swim people expected me to break world records, and because of that I felt too much pressure. I didn't want swimming to take over my life again because I had so many other plans. I still love swimming, and I would love to get up every morning and train and be fit, but I don't ever want the pressure to win swimming races back in my life.

While I was in training for the Games, Singo organised something for me which was to be pivotal in my recovery and my return to financial stability. He organised my first proper sponsorship, which would allow me to attend the Masters Games on an ongoing basis and to continue to train for them. The deal was arranged with what was then the quite radical luxury housing and resort development Sanctuary Cove, between Brisbane and the Gold Coast. The developer at the time was an original Balmain boy, Mike Gore, and quite soon after the sponsorship was established and signed off, Mike sold Sanctuary Cove to a Japanese company and they inherited my sponsorship along with the deal. Thank you, Mike. Thank you, Singo. In return for a quite substantial sponsorship I was to give coaching clinics at Sanctuary Cove and attend celebrity golf days, among other things. I think my new sponsors were a bit surprised to get me in the deal, but I took my role at Sanctuary Cove seriously and ended up taking classes there a couple of times every year. I also tried very hard for my sponsors at the various Masters Games and tried to get them mentions whenever I could. Part of the job was just putting in an appearance and having your face seen around the place by resort guests and that was just fine with me as I enjoyed a little luxury in the sunshine. I also wore their logo on all my clothing and other items, like sports bags.

One other sponsorship I entered into was for Zoggs, who made swimming goggles. Having grown up swimming without goggles, the Zoggs were especially welcome.

A wonderful connection I made around this time by being down in Melbourne so often was with the Power Points Swimming Club. It was really just an informal group of swimmers based at a pool in Prahran, who I met through Marge McQuade, the former Olympian and rival of mine from my early swimming days. We would all go out to dinner together and travel together often. There were about ten others besides Marge, including a lovely man called John Marriott who has become a very dear friend. John and I have a wonderful relationship that is platonic but very close—perhaps as close as any relationship I have had in my life. John is my partner for many official dinners and functions. In the early days of Masters swimming John and I went to all the Games together, and these days we always meet up when we're in each other's cities.

At the Masters Games in Toronto in 1985 I was swamped by media wanting to do stories on my comeback, until in the end I had to ban media a day out from my first race because I just wasn't able to concentrate. I'd lost an enormous amount of weight in the weeks leading up to the Games and I felt especially fit once more. I was competing in the 45- to 49-year-old age group and unfortunately in my 50 metres heat I came up against the world record holder, who had been training consistently for years. Juanita Correa touched the wall first at 31.47 seconds and I just missed out, touching at 31.51. I found I still had the hunger to win, though, and when we met again in the final of the 100 metres, a swim I still considered to be mine, I won in 69.8 seconds. I climbed out of the pool to a standing ovation and a frenzied media pack and said something like, 'This is the start for me.' I had been so happy to find that I still had it and could go for it in the end when it really counted. Back in the days when I was an Olympic swimmer

I had always felt I was swimming for Australia, but now I was doing it for me and that felt pretty good too. I knew I would probably never swim under that time again, but I wasn't really out to make a full-time career of it. I was just happy with my performance. I'd had to learn to dive again in 1985, just as I had in 1964 with my first neck injury, so I was especially pleased and relieved when that part of my swim went well.

I went on to attend many Masters Games. In Tokyo the following year I picked up five silver medals and a gold in the relay and had the time of my life, just as I'd had in 1964. It was the first time I had failed to win the 100 metres in international competition and to my surprise I felt all right about it. I had definitely moved on from the time when I had to win at any cost, and I realised that I really was in it for my health and enjoyment. In 1986 I went to the American Long Course Masters Swimming Championships in Indianapolis and the following year to the same competition in Houston, Texas. The 1988 North Queensland Games took me to Cairns and a reunion with my old friend Stumpy Lawrence, and two years previously the Centralian Masters Games started in Alice Springs in the Northern Territory. They've been held every second year since then, and I continued to compete until the mid-1990s, when I started getting heart and asthma problems. I still go along as a supporter and ambassador. At the same time an Australian Masters, as distinct from the Games in the Northern Territory, started up and I attended the first Games in Devonport, Tasmania.

I also started to travel to the US a couple of times a year with the Power Points Club to attend the short- and long-course swimming championships—the short course being 25 metres and the long, 50 metres—and our relay team did pretty well over the years. And when I wasn't travelling, I was dividing my time between Melbourne and my Confederation commitments and Sydney, where I'd still help out at Sydney University Pool, although by then Dawn-Lorraine was pretty well running the business.

•

Another sporting institution begun in 1985 was the Sport Australia Hall of Fame. Since the early 1970s Garry Daly had had it in mind that Australia should have a hall of fame museum like the other successful halls around the world. He did a lot of research about who should be inducted and, with the assistance of a few others, came up with a list of more than five hundred people. He then appointed Sir Hubert Opperman, the Olympic cyclist, Chairman of the Hall of Fame in Australia and set about organising inductions of the first members. Finally, with the assistance of businessman Peter Bartels, a special luncheon was held in 1985 at which Sir Donald Bradman gave the keynote address. Sir Donald was then made number one member and I was made number one female member. I automatically became a member of the Executive Board as well. From that point on no one was actually given a number upon being inducted, and all other inductees were made equal within the Hall. In 1985 there were 120 sportsmen and sportswomen inducted, the following year another sixty, and then another twenty in 1987—two hundred in all. In 1988, the Bicentennial year, a Hall of Fame Celebration was held, with 1844 attendees in Melbourne and another 920 in Sydney, and the two functions connected by a television link-up. At that function awards were given for the greatest male performance ever, the greatest female performance and the greatest team performance. Bradman's 309 in one day in 1930 and my third gold medal for the 100 metres in Tokyo received awards, along with the America's Cup win in 1983. Later in 1988, the Hall was expanded to induct as associate members administrators, coaches and sports scientists who had achieved international recognition and standing.

I had loved the idea of the Sport Australia Hall of Fame and had long thought we should have one because I'd been so impressed by the halls of fame I'd seen elsewhere in the world. I had, however, always thought of it as a physical place, a museum to which people could donate their memorabilia and where tourists and school children could come to learn about Australia's sporting history and heroes. When I was nominated to become President of the Hall of Fame in 1995, after Sir Hubert Opperman retired, I was thrilled. It was exactly the sort of position I had dreamed about, and I worked hard for the Hall of Fame all through my association with it. But at the end of 2000 I had become extremely disillusioned by so many aspects of its administration that I was beginning to think I couldn't possibly continue. My main concern was that after fifteen years we still didn't have an actual museum or even a plan for a museum.

Over the years various funding proposals had been put forward and different building plans and sites considered but every time we got close it all seemed to dissolve. It was slightly unlucky that a certain Mr Skase was at one time someone we were relying on to help fund the Hall, and that he'd been unable to attend a crucial meeting due to his being caught up overseas.

As the years went by the dream of an actual museum was slipping further away rather than gradually coming closer to fruition. Garry Daly was no longer involved and other original Board members had gone too. To my mind the organisation seemed to be sinking all its funds into administration rather than trying to do something practical to preserve the memory of the athletes of Australia. The annual dinners are certainly part of what the Hall should do and I have enjoyed my fair share of those, but in the end an annual dinner is hardly justification for the existence of such an organisation. Finally, after what I considered to be a series of unforgivable administrative bungles and mishaps as well as a gradually disintegrating relationship between myself and the administrators, in December 2000 I made the difficult decision to

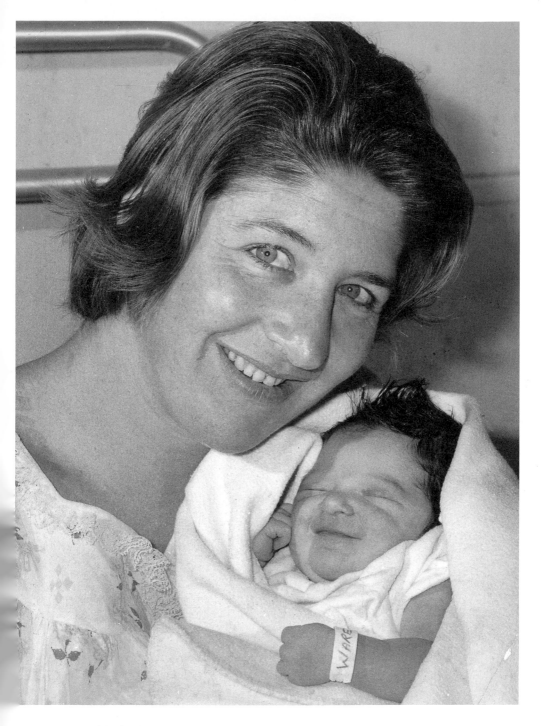

Just after the birth of Dawn-Lorraine, December 15th, 1965. She came out smiling.

With Dawn-Lorraine at Booralee Park Pool, Botany, 1971.

(Top) A tea ceremony in Osaka during a tour of Japan promoting Sterling Swimwear in 1966. (L-R) Me, Betty (sa swimwear designer) and Mrs Davidson (Betty's mother) holding Dawn-Lorraine.

(Bottom) Dawn-Lorraine surrounded by geishas.

Giving a coaching clinic in Melbourne, 1970. Dawn-Lorraine is next to me.

Dawn-Lorraine's fifth birthday.

Dawn-Lorraine's fifth birthday party at Rhonda's house with her family and our friends. (Foreground at left is Ruthie Everuss. Rhonda is behind Dawn-Lorraine.)

Being surprised by
Roger Climpson for
This Is Your Life
in 1979.

With Dawn-Lorraine in the Riverview,
1980.

Working in the
Cheese Shop,
1977.

On the deck of the
Dawn Fraser Baths,
1984.

Balmain
Girl and
Balmain Boy,
Neville Wran.

On the lawn of Kirribilli House with Prime Minister Bob Hawke, prior to leaving for the Masters Games in Toronto in 1985.

At Sydney University Pool after the first Australian Masters Games in 1987.

At my desk in
Parliament
House with my
assistant,
Roseanne
Robinson,
1988.

Speaking
out at a rally
to clean up
the local
area, 1988.

Making a point, 1988.

The Fraser family line-up. Up the stairs: Dawn, Heather, Joyce, Rose.
Foreground: Alick, Chookie, Ken.

resign. Sadly, I even took my name from the list of inductees and forbade any further use of it in connection with the Hall. I didn't want my name to be used in any way to enhance what I felt had become a mockery of all our original hopes and plans.

I have been castigated by many of those who remain in the Hall for being so public about my decision, although in official letters to me and to the media everyone is being terribly nice. I saw one letter in which I'd almost been defamed for taking my stand and resigning, and the following week the same person at the Hall of Fame wrote to thank me for all my hard work and expressed the wish that I might consider returning to the Hall at some point in the future.

I don't regret my decision but I do regret that we still don't have a Hall of Fame museum after all the hard work that Garry Daly and I and people like us put in during the early years.

•

By 1987 John Singleton was getting so many requests for me to be guest speaker or appear at different events that he referred me to a well-known Sydney-based management agency run by Max Markson, called Markson Sparks! Max took over all my speaking and advertising deals from 1987 till we parted company at the beginning of 2000. During my time with the agency, public speaking became like walking out onto the blocks at a swimming meet. Once I knew the pool it was possible to manage my fears; and likewise, if I had been briefed properly for an appearance I was comfortable in the knowledge that I could do it.

Max was very good for me, but in the end I felt like I was being wheeled out for everything that was going. I'd done so many years of charity lunches that I just couldn't face another one. By the turn of the century, what I felt I needed was consolidation and a new approach to my management. I knew it was time for me to start working with just a few clients and that's what has eventually happened.

Meanwhile, around the time I began working with Markson Sparks, my life took a turn in another very different direction.

Back in the 1960s Jack Stanistreet had wanted me to go into politics with the Labor Party, and I was interested at the time but had been told I should come back when I was less famous. Well, by 1988 I was less famous but that wasn't my reason for deciding to go into politics. I'd been thinking about it for a few years, ever since my clashes and alliances with politicians during the Moscow Olympics debate.

In 1987 one of my Balmain neighbours, Jim Gilchrist, had approached me and suggested I might like to run as an independent candidate in Balmain. I had always been inclined to be a Labor voter up until then. The area had been a Labor stronghold for years, but we'd had, in my opinion, a string of poor representatives. I felt that perhaps Labor had become complacent about their dominance in Balmain and lazy about pursuing issues for their electorate. Peter Crawford was the sitting member when the New South Wales election came up in March 1988. I wanted a new job at the time, and the fact that I would be paid a good salary in Parliament and that I would have the position for four years appealed to me. I know I'm not meant to say things like that because it's all supposed to be selfless, but the truth is, it was a job I wanted both because I felt I could make a difference and because I needed to find work. I was no longer happy at the pool. I'd been there since leaving the pub and had built the business up, but Dawn-Lorraine was really running it now and I was definitely ready for something more challenging. The New South Wales election was on March 19th and, because it had taken me a while to make my decision, it was already February when we announced that I would stand as an independent. I had about six weeks to make a go of it. Jim Gilchrist became my campaign manager and we swung into action quick smart. It meant getting a campaign together overnight, and door-knocking and pamphlet dropping day and night for the next three weeks, and boy did I cover some ground.

Singo came up with our campaign jingle and people said he'd sunk lots of money into the campaign, but in fact he hadn't. He did devise the advertising slogan, and he organised the printing and the authorising of the printing, but apart from that he offered friendly support and nothing else, and definitely not scads of money. The amusing thing was that Labor had barely campaigned in the area because they felt so safe, and when I arrived on the scene they had to step up to the plate too, so in reality I wasn't that far behind, even though I didn't have a party machine behind me. I spent a lot of time wandering around the shopping centre saying hello, and I had my family and friends out day and night armed with pamphlets too.

We needed a swing of about 12 per cent to oust Peter Crawford from the seat and with only three weeks that did seem a big ask. On the other hand, the people of Balmain were worried about issues like new housing developments and planning for the area; the lack of attention and funding for schools, roads, services and hospitals; the future of Callan Park; and the future of pensioners in an area that was changing rapidly. Balmain had become much more heavily populated over the previous decade, yet neither public funding nor planning seemed to be keeping up with our rate of growth and development, including the huge influx of cars into an area with very narrow streets and very little public parking.

I became an independent candidate at a time when the polls were showing an extraordinary amount of support for independents from all over New South Wales, although there was some pre-election scaremongering that independents would hold the balance of power after the election. I particularly benefited from being known and trusted by the Balmain people, so that even if they did vote Labor first they put me second, and I actually ended up getting over the line on preferences. I also swapped preferences with the other independent running in the area, Larry Hand.

It took until early April for all the votes to be properly counted and my victory by 846 votes wasn't announced until then. It was a 15 per cent swing and the ALP was swept from power in New South Wales. I was one of seven independents across the State to be voted in—a record number. The others were Robyn Read on the North Shore, Clover Moore in Bligh, Frank Arkell in Wollongong, John Hatton of the South Coast, who came in as an anti-corruption campaigner, George Keegan in Newcastle and Ivan Welsh in Swansea. All of the independents except me were experienced either at State or local government level. The Coalition certainly didn't need our support to govern, particularly as most of us had taken Labor seats. I was thrilled to be elected, I mean really, really thrilled, but I was actually away in Adelaide performing a public duty when the result came through so I had to put my excitement on hold. The family of Jack Lang, New South Wales Premier in the 1920s and a great old Labor character, gave me a special wooden suitcase that he used to use in Parliament. I had always admired Jack as a politician, along with Gough Whitlam and Bill Hayden.

I loved being in Parliament from the day I walked in there. I had been nervous during the campaign but ultimately I went in with a great deal of confidence in myself. It was the same old story: I'd made up my mind to do it and I intended to do it well. Naively I had thought it would be my first regular Monday to Friday job— which just goes to show how wrong you can be. Being an MP means being on call seven days a week, twenty-four hours a day. There was a minor kerfuffle over my refusal to wear a dress for my swearing in as an MP. Naturally I respected the dignity of the position but I'm just not a dress person; in fact I hate wearing dresses. When I discussed the issue with some of the others who'd been elected it was one of the few occasions that I'd actually talked about clothes with other women. They agreed that as long as we were well dressed a trouser suit was fine. And that's how I presented myself in Parliament from then on.

I think my big advantage in going into Parliament was that I knew the area I was representing like the back of my hand. But there were disadvantages too. I had no political experience and a lot of people assumed I was with the ALP. They couldn't grasp that I didn't have a big party behind me and therefore could only do so much. And because I was high-profile everyone thought I could act for them. They recognised me and wrote to me from all over the State about things that someone in my position wouldn't normally have to consider. Sue Hogan, who became my personal assistant in Parliament after her predecessor, Roseanne Robinson, went to study law, reminded me recently that this constant clamouring for my attention from people I didn't represent really sapped my energy.

Another problem I had was that I had really, really annoyed the ALP by taking one of their hitherto safe seats and they decided to get back at me in very vindictive and petty ways. I was subjected to a barrage of letters in the local papers about my performance, and there were rumour campaigns and people sent along to heckle at public meetings that I addressed. The neighbouring ALP member at the time, Sandra Nori, was relentless in her niggling, so much so that I wondered when she had time to concentrate on her own performance. Looking back at the press clippings now I see that she constantly said that while I was a nice person and a great sports ambassador, those things hardly made me a politician. In other words, she presented herself as a nice and reasonable person who recognised my good qualities—and then she stuck the knife in. In many ways she was right: I was not your regular politician. I wasn't especially cunning or tough about how I performed and I more or less performed from the heart. I did care about helping people and was genuinely upset when I wasn't able to do so. I found that it distressed me, and I started to cough and wheeze with asthma when Parliament was sitting. I sounded just like Pop by the middle of the term.

I approached politics the way I approached the rest of my life, which was, I guess, dumb in political terms. I wouldn't be bribed. I wouldn't cross the floor and vote with the other guys if I didn't agree with an issue, even if longevity in Parliament or some other favour were promised. In keeping with that approach I also took on causes close to my heart which were of no political value to me. They were difficult issues to handle or to succeed with. Cleaning up the pollution on our beaches was one such issue that I desperately believed in because I'd had so much pleasure from beach life and I wanted to preserve it for future generations to enjoy.

I became involved with environmental issues on a practical level by starting a competition between our council area of Leichhardt and that of Clean Up Australia boss Ian Kiernan, to see who could get their area the cleanest. Singo came up with a memorable campaign song for the cause that went something like, 'Yucky, yucky, yucky pooh, this is something I can do.' Having swum in harbour water as a girl I had a special desire to see the harbour being cleaned up, and I later became involved in the Beachwatch program as well. I think most Sydneysiders would agree that the beaches are much cleaner now than they were in the 1980s and I believe the Beachwatch campaign helped kick-start the clean up.

In my maiden speech to Parliament on August 23rd, 1988, I started out observing all the usual courtesies and thanking those who had helped me find my way round and get to know the ropes in my first weeks in Parliament. I slipped in a comment, however, about the recent pay rise for politicians being at odds with the new government's continual statements that in the past the State had been living beyond its means. I also noted that I was the first independent MP representing Balmain and pointed out that independents at all levels of government were disillusioned with the two-party system. The parties, I said, had failed to address specific issues in an independent manner, and I cited the lack of action on the Chelmsford case as an example. (In later months I continued to ask questions about Chelmsford because I'd been approached about the whole tragedy by a Balmain resident. In particular, I kept questioning the terms of reference that the new government had set up for the Royal Commission.)

I made reference to the fact that I was Balmain's first female member in thirty years, and proceeded to give the Parliament a potted history of my upbringing, to show how the area was changing before our eyes—so Mum and Pop got a mention! Then I curtly referred to the fact that Mr Crawford, my predecessor, had nodded to Balmain's changing character and gone on to talk about rainforests. I suggested he wasn't as in touch with his electorate as he might have been. By now I was enjoying myself. I said Balmain's problems had changed but there was still considerable poverty, something I had become particularly aware of while running the pub.

My speech ranged across a lot of issues, from the overcrowding in new housing developments in Balmain—particularly that at Mort Bay—the spectre of land subsidence at the old coal mine site on Birchgrove Road next to the school, the problem of aircraft noise, and the possibility of a helipad being built in the area.

I also talked about other matters close to my heart, such as the lack of physical education in schools which had created a glut of PE teachers, and my belief that safe, affordable abortions should be available for women in New South Wales. I acknowledged my old ally Bill Hayden by saying I understood why he felt so proud, as a boy from South Brisbane, to become Governor-General. Here I was, a Balmain girl with little formal education, standing up in Parliament making her maiden speech. I said I would do my best and that I knew what it took to achieve difficult goals, and then sat down.

I'd known that State Parliament would test me out, but I was surprised by the amount of muckraking and stirring that went on. When I attended the Seoul Olympics, for example, someone raised my absence in Parliament, asking why I wasn't sitting when I should have been. In fact this attack on me backfired because I'd been granted special leave of the Parliament to go, and I was there as an ambassador for the Australian Bicentennial Authority, not as a guest of the AOC. I actually worked very, very hard while I was an MP. Quite often, like many others I'm sure, I would sleep in my office on a day/night lounge. Dawn-Lorraine would come in and have dinner with me and then she'd leave and I'd work until late, sleep a few hours and get up early to organise myself for the morning's session. I became matey with some of the other independents. Robyn Read and I were close, and Clover and I got along well too. I made friends from both sides of the house. Bruce Baird and I hit it off and he helped me quite a bit. John Fahey and Bob Carr were both great to me, along with the Speaker of the House at the time, Kevin Rozzoli. I also found the Parliamentary clerks terrific and very helpful, and I'm sure my sporting pedigree took me a long way. I never felt embarrassed asking questions, and was happy to ask for help from the librarian, the orderlies and the clerks. I didn't have anything to prove other than that I could genuinely help my electorate, so if I needed help to do that I asked.

An accusation often levelled at me was that I was too caught up in issues that didn't truly represent my electorate, but actually I asked many questions in Parliament relating to specific aspects of my local community because I knew it so well. I was concerned about threatened closures of schools and hospitals in the area, specifically Rozelle Psychiatric Hospital and Riverside Girls High— which I accidentally called Riverside Girls Home Science School when I asked a question in Parliament. Oops! (I just know how that would have annoyed the principal in my day, who always thought her school was a cut above the old home science schools.)

I pursued developers who were building apartments and town-houses along Balmain's foreshores, changing the character of the area, and I even raised the issue of a brothel being opened in a tiny residential street in Rozelle, the neighbouring suburb to Balmain.

But it's true that I was also interested in wider issues, and I don't think that's a bad thing. While I was in Parliament I vehemently opposed tobacco advertising at sporting events and for sports bodies. I was also very outspoken about gun law reform and tried to draw attention to the sale of some particularly offensive weapons to young people. Some country people had sent me photos of someone selling semi-automatic SKS and SKK rifles, together with hundreds of rounds of ammunition, to teenagers off the back of a truck. I pushed for new legislation against such sales, and I received some very ugly mail and my office was ransacked for the photos.

I enjoyed everything about my three and a half years in Parliament, from the research I had to undertake, to the cut and thrust of question time. Sometimes I would get frightened when the Speaker would have a real go at a representative for reading at length from their notes. I worried that when it was my turn to speak on a bill I wouldn't be able to do it without my notes, but I soon became adept at making bullet points and expanding from there. Roseanne Robinson helped me write my speeches and I'd practise them before I stood up the next day. I had wonderful support from my personal assistants, first Roseanne and then Sue Hogan, who I called 'Shogun'. They both really stood by me and would spend hours researching whatever I asked for. It's women like them who really keep things going behind the scenes in politics.

I was always looking into swimming and sporting issues, which sometimes left Shogun a bit perplexed. Sport wasn't really her thing. One day when she was looking especially confused and uninter-ested I turned to her, exasperated, and said, 'Shogun, you can swim, can't you?' She, on the other hand, would get exasperated with me if I wasn't on time, and say things like, 'Well, you'd think a National Living Treasure could at least try to be more punctual!' I had enough work for a staff of two or three, and we could have achieved so much more with extra people onboard, but I only had funding for one. I did, however, have a lot of great volunteers working for me in my electoral office in Balmain.

The only thing I really hated about political life was that it was so hard to work out who was sincere and who wasn't, and that was something I'd always prided myself on being able to do. There were such clever manipulators in the Parliament with so many years of deception under their belts that it was sometimes difficult to know who to trust. I was also embarrassed when there were school children in the gallery and the politicians were behaving worse than children fighting in the schoolyard.

I did, of course, make my mistakes when I was in Parliament, and one that drew quite a lot of comment was when I backed the Greiner Government in taking planning powers away from the Leichhardt Council and giving them to an administrator. Later I changed my mind and campaigned with the residents against the government on the issue of redeveloping the Balmain Peninsula and the residents won. I never really heard the end of that issue but at least I eventually saw the light. What I should have done in political terms was deny, deny, deny and sidestep!

By the time the next election rolled around in 1991 the ALP were determined to oust me. They were still furious about losing their safe seat and they used every dirty trick in the book during the election campaign. The boundaries for my seat had been moved, making the electorate much larger, and therefore there was a lot more work to be done in areas where I didn't necessarily have ready support. Against me was the ALP candidate Sandra Nori, whose former seat of McKell had become part of the larger electorate of Port Jackson. In Parliament Sandra had gone to great lengths to question my intellect and capability as a politician, and she continued to assert that while I'd made people 'feel good' in the 1950s, that didn't necessarily entitle me to a seat in Parliament. Presumably she was more entitled than someone who'd been a sportsperson, although why she was she never made clear.

On the eve of the election a story was circulated and appeared in the media that said I had been taking bribes from Kerry Packer, who was trying to make the former Monsanto chemical factory site in Balmain into a residential development. Apparently the evidence for this claim was that I had attended a fundraising lunch at the home of the campaign manager for my second run, Cathy Harris, and that Kerry Packer's developer had also attended the lunch. In fact I had only met Kerry Packer once at that time in my life, at another large lunch gathering, and I certainly wasn't involved with him or his business. The ALP spread general stories that I had enormous financial backing from developers for my campaign and that I had advisers like Singo pulling the strings. It was also suggested I had great access to the Premier, Nick Greiner, because he liked having me around at various occasions because of the sporting connection. Overall it got pretty dirty and upsetting, and in the end the ALP regained the seat.

I don't regret for a minute my time in Parliament; in fact I feel they were three of the most interesting years of my life. The problem was, of course, that just as I started to get into it and knew what was going on, it was over.

14

DOWN ON
THE FARM

When I attended the Seoul Olympic Games in South Korea in 1988, I went not at the invitation of the Australian Olympic Committee, but as an ambassador for the Australian Bicentennial Authority. Jim Kirk, the Chairman of the Authority, had appointed me to the position. I had known Jim for a while, and he thought I had potential in an ambassadorial role. All I had been asked to do was be a representative and speak when the occasion arose about the forthcoming celebrations in Australia. At my disposal I had a chauffeur, Mr Kim, who was a wonderful driver but had the unfortunate habit of mixing his words up. Occasionally when I had some important people in the car he'd say something like, 'I'm farking par over here.' It broke everyone up, but Mr Kim never caught on and just thought we were having fun.

My accreditation hadn't turned up by the time I arrived, so I watched early events in my hotel room. However, John Coates, who was Chef de Mission for the Australian team, had invited me to march in the opening ceremony for the first time since 1964 in Tokyo because I was the Bicentennial Authority's representative in Seoul. I'd been issued with an official blazer by the AOC before I left. I was very proud and pleased to have been invited to march again. I don't believe in officials marching if they are taking the place of an athlete, but since I wasn't doing that in Seoul I was happy to step out with the team.

John Purnell, who was Director of Athlete Services at the Australian Institute of Sport in Canberra, was over in Seoul watching some of the Institute's athletes, and he arranged some tickets for me when he realised my plight. I had been working with John on the Elite Sports Program organised by the Institute to help teach Australian athletes how to deal with media, and how to present themselves and generally cope with public situations. We'd get in touch with athletes through their various sporting associations and offer the course, which partly involved videotaping mock media interviews and then watching the tape to pick up faults and weaknesses. Once we'd established where they needed to improve, they'd be given further exercises to help work on these areas.

By this stage of my life I had been drawn back into the circle of sport in Australia. People had started to see that my experience, along with that of other ex–Olympic athletes, might be useful in teaching the new generation about the world they were entering. And I was still fundraising for various sporting teams and individual athletes. My motivation for this was that I didn't want young athletes having to go through what I'd gone through, scraping a living in between training and trying to raise extra dollars here and there for tours. I could vividly recall the times during my swimming career when I'd go around the Sydney Cricket Ground, the Showground and various football stadiums at half-time with Marlene Matthews, Betty Cuthbert and others, asking the crowd to throw coins into the blanket we were carrying. We'd be hit on the head and in the eye with pennies, and it was pretty demeaning, not to mention dangerous!

Coaches had also started to seek me out to come and talk to their athletes individually about getting ready for major competition. It is a serious job and has become increasingly important as international competitions are played out under the media spotlight. People sometimes ask me what I say to athletes but I never divulge the exact details of what I say because it is private and intense. Athletes share with me deep feelings and inner thoughts that I am trusted to keep in confidence and I always will. I believe retired athletes such as myself are the best people to speak to the current crop because we understand what they are going through. I always feel that you have to work with an athlete to bring out their natural spirit and harness it in a positive way, whereas many officials who have never participated themselves are more concerned with making them conform—which is a bit like whipping a racehorse into submission and losing what makes it great in the first place. It is far better to try to understand the individual you are working with and show them how to use their natural talents and emotions. That's what Harry did for me and that's what I try to impart when I'm talking with athletes before major competitions. Athletes who reach the level of elite competition have managed themselves well to get to where they are. They don't need constant supervision and direction from people with clipboards and badges; they need understanding, inspiration, reassurance, confidence building and practical advice from people who've been there before them.

At the Seoul Games I was quite unexpectedly called upon to work with athletes in that role when Robbie Cadee, who was the coach of the women's basketball team, asked if I would come and speak to the players. They were having trouble settling down. Some of them were missing their partners, some were newly married and missing their husbands, and all in all they weren't playing well as a team even though they had all the skills and necessary training behind them. I did go and speak to them and explained that they would only be away from their homes and partners for sixteen days, and that it was the ultimate opportunity they were going to have and it might not come around again. I urged them to focus on playing for their country, and to take the sixteen days out of their lives and put them in a different category and get on with it. I was able to recall my time in Townsville when I'd met Gary but had to put that part of my life to one side for a few weeks. I explained that otherwise when they got home they would be sorry they hadn't grabbed this wonderful opportunity to do something remarkable out there on the court and play to the best of their ability.

It worked. The girls started playing well as a team and they started winning. They were unlucky not to win a gold medal and in the end came fourth because of the fall of the draw, but they definitely improved and I wasn't the only one to think so.

Because of my success with the women's basketballers in Seoul, I went to the 1992 Barcelona Games in an official capacity as an Athlete Liaison Officer, along with Herb Elliott. The role has come to be regarded as an important one. At the Sydney Games, for instance, we had ten Athlete Liaison Officers, including Robyn Maher, one of the basketballers from 1988. My invitation for the position at Barcelona came from John Coates, and I think both Herb and I did a magnificent job with the athletes, if I say so myself.

I was mostly working with the swimmers and the equestrian team, and it was a very busy time. As well as talking to the riders,

I became involved in looking after the horses in a very hands-on way, at times even holding cold towels round their hoofs on competition days because it was so hot in Barcelona. The whole thing was a great experience, but I found that because I took my role so seriously my time was stretched to the limit between various athletes and teams. I'd fall into bed at the end of the day and sleep like the dead. When I wasn't dealing with the athletes I was at events, so by the end of the Games I was more than ready to get away.

Dawn-Lorraine had come along to Barcelona with me and had an official role helping 'dress' the athletes at a stopover point in Frankfurt. It had been decided the whole Australian team would meet up there, as many of them had been training in different parts of the world prior to the Games. Dressing the athletes means making sure they are kitted out with the right equipment and uniforms in the right sizes, and it's a big job that requires many people. I lived in the village but Dawn-Lorraine stayed with quite a large contingent of Australian officials in a converted monastery about three hours train ride away. Naturally my high-spirited daughter (I wonder where she gets that from?) was less than pleased to be away from the action and she asked if she could borrow a car for the afternoon to drive down the coast to see some friends of ours. Two days later she returned, but not before I'd been driven to distraction by questions about where she was. On the last weekend of the Games she was determined not to be sent to the monastery again and somehow got herself into the high-security village. After that she was sheltered by members of the Australian team, despite not having any proper accreditation round her neck. I was completely unaware she was there, and if I'd known, she wouldn't have been there for long.

One of the officials she met in the village decided not to march in the closing ceremony and offered her uniform to Dawn-Lorraine, who took up the offer even though she was a size six and the uniform a size twelve. Now she had accreditation and, fortunately, a very large hat that came down over her face. In the marshalling area before getting on buses to the stadium Dawn-Lorraine found herself standing next to Perry Crosswhite, one of the team administrators, but he didn't notice her under the hat and she managed to get on the bus undetected. Talk about history repeating itself. I had no idea this was going on until I was sitting in the stands with Lyn Bates, the Assistant Swimming Manager, just a few rows up from the Australian athletes waiting to take part in the closing ceremony. All of a sudden Lyn turned to me and said, 'That's Dawn-Lorraine. I just heard Dawn-Lorraine.'

'Don't be crazy,' I said. 'She's not here, she's over on the other side of the stadium.' Then I heard her too. 'That *is* Dawn-Lorraine.' With that I jumped up and started walking up and down the stairs beside the seats trying to see my daughter. When I finally found her I whispered as ferociously as I could, 'What are you doing here?'

With that she looked very shaken. 'I don't know. They made me,' and she nearly dissolved into tears.

My whisper must have been even more ferocious than I'd hoped. I was utterly furious at first and whispered again, 'Don't make any kind of scene.' So she sat there and when the athletes were called onto the arena she still sat there frozen because she could see how cross I was. With that I went back down and whispered frantically, 'Get up and get out there. You're going to make it obvious.' She was now sitting all alone in a uniform three sizes too big for her in a large bank of empty seats.

So that's how my daughter came to march in a closing ceremony. I couldn't believe she had managed to get through all the security checks, and when I'd gotten over the shock I actually found it rather funny. But then I am a bit of a sucker for a prank. To make it even worse, an image of Dawn-Lorraine on the shoulders of another athlete came up on the big screen during the closing ceremony. I was just incredulous and couldn't help reflecting that the apple hadn't fallen too far from the tree in our family.

I always like to get away from high-powered, political events and all the more so this time after Dawn-Lorraine's hair-raising performance at the closing ceremony. I can't stand the bull that goes on and I just want to escape to everyday life again. There is nothing I like more than the competition but I have no stomach for the accompanying politics played out by the inevitable scrum of officials all trying to put their stamp on this or that. At Barcelona I was very concerned with what one of my particular charges was going through. Kathy Watt's experience at those Games was terrible and this really upset me because I had been her mentor over a number of years. As far as I could see it was the same old story with officials making the life of a very focused and strong-willed female athlete unbearable because they thought they had to control her rather than encourage her.

I took off down the coast of Spain to stay with friends who had nothing to do with sport. I crave normal daily life after the carry-on of an Olympic Games, and all my life, ever since my father's warning after I came back from Hawaii in 1957, I have been conscious of trying to keep myself as grounded as possible. Coming to the end of a Games is always something of a letdown, which is why I try to travel afterwards, but it is important to me to gradually ease back into everyday life. After Barcelona I spent a fortnight reading books, listening to music, sleeping, swimming, eating, playing cards and taking small day trips before finally flying back to Australia.

•

One part of my life in Australia that has kept my feet on the ground for the last fifteen years is my connection with the country. Out of the blue in 1988 I received a letter, not unlike many letters I receive, asking if I would go to a country town in the Riverina District in New South Wales and give a coaching clinic for the local kids. I certainly didn't need the money and had a pretty busy schedule but the Riverina was a part of the country I'd never seen and, more importantly, I had a strong conviction that country children were not getting enough attention from professional city coaches. My time with the Confederation of Australian Sport had shown me that a very large number of talented country children were being lost in the system. Great swimmers would come to city competitions from the country but then they'd disappear and we wouldn't see them the next season. When I talked to some of these kids I found they'd only be swimming a few months of the year because they didn't have access to heated pools, or they'd have to work on the family property when city kids would have spent the time training. So I decided to do what I could to change that and took up the offer to do the coaching clinic and see how far we could take some of the children. I didn't know a single person in the district but that first year I stayed with the White family of Barellan and I had about fifty-five children in a 25-metre swimming pool. The next year I stayed with another family, the Bandys, on their property and they gave me my own little flat to live in. I kept going back to Barellan each year and gradually got to know a lot of the locals, and I really enjoyed being among such a down-to-earth bunch of people.

In the early 1990s a property came up for sale just across the road from the Bandys' place. My asthma was quite bad at the time and I had noticed that when I left Sydney for Barellan it would clear up and I wouldn't have the tightness in my chest that I usually suffered. I loved the area by then and I had wanted to get back into riding and have my own horse, and I also had a yen to raise cattle. So after checking it out I bought the property, which covered about 130 hectares. My initial aim was to build up the property as a getaway for disabled athletes, and that's still a dream although I haven't been able to realise it yet. I'd like to put in a 25-metre heated swimming pool, too, where swimmers can train. I have done a few things with the property over the years. I've grown barley and made malt barley, which I sold for a top price. I found that walking through the barley in the breeze is one of the most glorious experiences and it sounds just like beautiful music. I've also put some wheat in and had good results from that, but it's the cattle I've really enjoyed and I've made top price on them, which is a great feeling. I also have some horses and have had two foals. Sadly, the first one died but we have a beautiful little foal at present with a white sock. The horses are bred to be stockhorses for working on the property.

I didn't know a lot about farming before I started visiting the Riverina but I love hard physical work in the outdoors and I find that once I'm shown something I learn it quickly. My neighbours and friends in the country worry about me working on the tractor by myself but I still do it and I enjoy the freedom it brings. I have a wonderful manager, Paul, who looks after the property. He's one of the local guys and, together with his brothers, Allan and Robert, he works the property for me.

While I was at the farm in early 1996 I had a mild heart attack while I was doing my fire breaks, which basically involves clearing the land to help prevent bushfires spreading. Colin Bandy, Paul's dad, taught me how to make a fire break and when I am at the property I tend to do them myself, with Paul's help. It was very dusty and windy at that particular time in 1996 and one morning, after a hard day's work the previous day, I woke up in my little flat feeling as though I was having a very serious asthma attack. I put it down to the dusty work we'd been doing and the heat of the season, but the pain in my chest was extremely bad and I couldn't lie down. I sat on the edge of the bed trying to breathe steadily and then I had a cold shower to keep myself cool. As soon as I saw signs of life in the main house I went across and asked them to drive me to the hospital in Griffith, where I stayed for a week and was treated for asthma. I never suspected a heart attack and nor did they. Then later in the same year, when I was being tested after a more serious heart attack, it was found that I'd done some major damage to my heart at some point about six months earlier. That's when I twigged that at Barellan I'd actually had a mild heart attack and not an asthma attack at all.

One of the reasons I had been so sure it was asthma at Barellan was that I'd been getting very bad asthma back in Sydney through the previous year, 1995. In fact it had become so debilitating that year that I began to seriously consider getting out of Sydney for good. I'd had three or four very close calls over the previous three years, when either I'd been rushed to hospital or a doctor had been summoned very quickly, and yet, as I've said, I could drive a tractor on the property all day without feeling any tightness in my chest. Although I'd told them I could breathe much easier at the farm, my neighbours would still worry about me being out there all day on the tractor by myself, because of my asthma and because they'd seen me arrive from Sydney feeling quite poorly. And even though I'd been convinced that my asthma disappeared when I was at the farm, when I did get chest pains in early 1996 I sort of accepted that my neighbours had been right, and that I couldn't escape asthma after all.

I was thinking a lot about the house I would build and what it would be like to have a life spent predominantly in the country with the occasional trip to Sydney, where I'd have my Balmain house as a base. My doctor felt it would be a good idea and was encouraging me to go. The move also promised a quieter life. It had got to the point where my phone in Sydney never stopped ringing with requests and invitations, which was wonderful given that I'd not been invited to anything much just over a decade earlier, but it also had its downside.

I didn't really have enough money to build a house on the property at the time, but a very welcome gesture came along in early 1995. A number of leading businessmen, including John Singleton, Kevin Weldon and Alan Jones, had got together to set up a series of testimonials for sportspeople who had been very successful in their sport at a time when it was either completely amateur or not very lucrative. The League star John Raper had been the first person to be honoured, and I would be the third, at a lunch to be held at the Regent Hotel in Sydney in September that year. It wasn't only to raise money, although that was central to the idea; it was also to say thank you to the person being honoured. I sat down with my manager at the time and organiser of the testimonials, Max Markson, to draw up a list of items I would donate for the fundraising auction to be conducted at the lunch, and to nominate a charity or cause that would receive 10 per cent of the proceeds. I chose the Australian Paralympic Federation with the specific goal of raising the money to send them to the 1996 Atlanta Games the following year.

I was also allowed to invite a special guest from anywhere in the world, and I chose Esther Williams, the great swimmer and Hollywood actress who starred in the water ballet extravaganzas in the 1950s. Esther and I met in 1985 when I was the first Australian woman to be inducted into the American Women's Sports Foundation Hall of Fame. She sought me out during the induction to remind me she was the foundation inductee, the first of all of us. I had replied, 'Yes, but I'm the first Australian.' Esther had been a US champion swimmer before becoming a movie star, so we understood each other, despite coming from very different worlds. She was so beautiful she'd been whisked out of competition swimming into the water follies and then the movies. Esther had been an idol of mine for a very long time, so it was a great thrill when she accepted our invitation to come to Australia. We had a few days together before the lunch and we took her and partner Bill to Taronga Zoo to see koalas and other Australian native animals, then out on Sydney Harbour for the day. After the lunch we went to the Hunter Valley for a week and swam together in the indoor pool at our hotel: Esther in her bathing cap and still looking glamorous; me with wet hair and no make-up!

The items of memorabilia Singo suggested I put up for the auction included my flag from Tokyo. Although it was very precious to me, I wasn't sure anyone else would be interested. Dawn-Lorraine was very sure, though, and didn't want the flag to be auctioned under any circumstances. She felt it was very much a part of our family's heritage and something we should always keep to hand on down through the generations. She was extremely upset when I decided to go ahead and let me know exactly how she felt.

During the lunch I was sitting at a table with Kerry Packer, Singo, Esther, Bill, Graeme Richardson, Dawn-Lorraine and Kevin Weldon. When the flag came up for auction the bidding was quite brisk. When it got to around forty thousand dollars Dawn-Lorraine burst into tears. 'I knew you shouldn't have put the flag up, Mum, it really is valuable.' In between sobs she kept telling me it had historical as well as personal significance. During the bidding Mr Packer asked what the flag meant to me. I think I remarked on its symbolism, in that everyone thought it was what I'd been banned for and how in many ways it was seen as having cost me my career.

It was around that time that the sports commentator Ray Hadley, who was conducting the auction, started to take some phone bids. The bidding kept going up and up and eventually reached fifty-two thousand dollars before being knocked down to a mystery buyer, after which the flag was returned to Dawn-Lorraine at the table. With that Mr Packer said, 'Now will you stop crying?' And she did.

So the flag remains in our personal collection of memorabilia and I very much doubt that a time will come again when I'm prepared to let it go out of the family. I am deeply grateful to that mystery bidder and will be forever in their debt. The auction helped me focus my thoughts about what the flag really meant to me and afterwards I knew that it meant an awful lot.

The testimonial lunch was a wonderful, wonderful day and will remain a very beautiful memory that I treasure. So many businesses from Sydney bought tables for the lunch that it was a huge success, and there were more than five hundred people there, many of whom I'd known all my life. All afternoon people said lovely things about me and I was thrilled to raise money for the Paralympians. I was also extremely grateful for the cheque handed to me some-time later. So much has gone on in my life since that lunch, that as I write this book I still haven't built a house on my property, but I have finally located an existing place that is just what I want, and it will be moved onto the farm later in 2001.

•

In mid-1993 another challenge arose for me when I became involved in a different type of swimming which I found really fascinating. Tammy van Wisse, the well-known Australian long-distance swimmer, wrote to me to see if I would help her on a brother and sister attempt to swim the English Channel. I'd had a little bit of experience in helping another long-distance swimmer, Shelley Taylor-Smith, and Tammy, who I had met previously, thought it would be good to enlist my help for her attempt.

We first did a preparation swim from Portarlington to Frankston in Port Phillip Bay, Victoria. I visited the van Wisse family in Melbourne so I could get to know them well before we undertook this enormous challenge. The swimmer has to really trust their support person, so it was important that we were well acquainted.

When it came time to take on the Channel, I was asked to help Tammy's brother John on his support boat, while a friend of Tammy's in England, Freda Stretton, would be on Tammy's support boat. Freda's daughter, Alison, holds the records for the greatest number of successful Channel swims and the greatest number of successful double crossings.

I found the whole process quite a challenge. We went over to Dover and I stayed with the Strettons, who have a summerhouse there. We were there for about three weeks leading up to the swim and during that time I got to know the local people and the beach quite well. I gained a lot of local knowledge about swimming the Channel, which, by the way, is 35 kilometres across—quite a far cry from my 100-metre sprints!

Unfortunately we didn't quite get John across the Channel. He didn't really have enough fat on him for that particular swim and in my view his coach should have intervened earlier when it was clear John was in great difficulty. I was very angry because John nearly died and there's certainly no glory in sport worth that.

I could see that John was taking in a lot of water, he was desperately cold, the water was very rough, and I kept doing the checks you do with long distance swimmers, like asking them certain questions. When he was no longer able to repeat his name three times in a row I knew it was over. The swim usually takes about nine and a half hours and we'd been out there for seven and a half by then. In a matter of thirty seconds John went from floating on his front to standing up in the water because hypothermia had set in that quickly. He went under the dinghy we were trailing at the back and I thought, 'Shit, we're in trouble.'

I had broken three ribs earlier in the swim by being pushed up onto the rail of the boat in the rough seas and I was pretty unbalanced as I went to get John out of the water. I slipped again and wasn't able to pull myself up. I called out to his coach: 'John's in trouble, you'd better get down to the dinghy right now and grab him.' John was looking like he'd float away from us because the currents were so strong. For a minute he was caught under the dinghy and I called to one of the other young guys on the boat to come and help his coach pull him out from underneath. I stopped the boat and they tried to pull him up but he was covered in the protective grease and was too slippery. You're supposed to pull the swimmer out using a towel under the arms but it was too late for that, so they started to pull him up and his head fell forward and stopped him breathing altogether. For thirty seconds he didn't get any air and he was in big strife. We eventually got him up onto the boat and breathing but he was very blue. We got a thermal blanket out and took his bathers off and wrapped him up but he wasn't getting any circulation through his body even then. I then got them to put socks on him and wrap the two of us together so he could get my body heat. It took about three hours to get him stable, and in that time I was giving him mouth-to-mouth, and lying on top of him and slapping his face and yelling his name— anything to stop him going to sleep and just drifting away. We eventually got him back to Dover where we could properly warm him up.

Remarkably, later that night he said he felt well enough to go to dinner, but he had a couple of drinks and then completely lost it. The alcohol went straight to his brain. We rushed him to hospital and they pumped his stomach to get the alcohol out of his system. He was released after a few hours.

Tammy made the swim that time and then two years later the two of them attempted it again and both made it: the first brother and sister to swim across the Channel. John had put on much more weight by then and I think it made all the difference.

In later years I helped Tammy do several more swims, including another attempt on the Channel in 1994 and the Manhattan Island Marathon Swim in New York. In 1996 she did the Bass Strait swim from King Island to Apollo Bay. That one was the toughest, except perhaps for the Murray River swim that she's just completed. We did Loch Ness together in 1999, having been there the previous year when we found it was too late in the season and too cold. It was still pretty cold the year she did it, the water temperature never getting above eight degrees Celsius. The water was like pitch from all the run-off from the mountains and all the moss, and I couldn't see Tammy's hands once they went under the water. It was very eerie on the loch and it was a very long swim. She broke the record but under terrible conditions. I sat out in the middle of Loch Ness for over nine hours in an open boat and was really cold myself.

I didn't accompany Tammy on the Murray River swim because I was in the middle of writing this book, but if she does the Mississippi next year I'd like to go along, as it's a swim we've often discussed.

It's very interesting to be a support person on a long-distance swim because it's a great psychological game. The swimmer relies on you for jokes and morale boosting, for the right amount of feeding, to get their timing right, for the ratio of fast to slow swims, and so on. I'm there telling the swimmer to swim fast for half a kilometre and then slow for two and then to pick up for a while. My job is to make it interesting in order to take their mind off the pain and what they're trying to do, but at the same time to make sure the swim is well run and goes according to plan. Bass Strait was especially difficult from my point of view. There were so many sharks, and at one point Tammy hallucinated and left the cage, thinking she was swimming with dolphins. At another point a seal got in her cage and we had to get that out while making sure it didn't bite her. The weather was truly awful and just planning when to start swimming was difficult, but the people of King Island were wonderful and gave us great advice about whether or not to wait for the next full moon, and so on. When planning these swims you budget for so many days and for all the staff, so timing is a crucial factor.

Tammy and I have always gone out on reconnaissance before a swim to familiarise ourselves with all aspects of where it will take place, then we come home to plan it all out. I just love the challenge of getting all those things right and then helping get the swimmer to wherever they're going. Even choosing the skipper of the boat is very important because they have to have a feel for when to slow and when to stop. I work closely with the skipper because when the current is strong I need to judge how far the swimmer can go in that water compared to normal smooth conditions. I never get seasick, so being on the boat isn't a problem for me, but plenty of others do. The whole process is very complicated but it's a tremendous feeling to be part of the team when the swimmer makes it. I'm very proud of Tammy because she's finished all the swims we've done together and broken records in many of them. She won the Manhattan swim ahead of the men as well as the women. She calls me Godmother for looking after her, but really it's been a privilege.

•

I was brought up with a jolt in 1995 when Dawn-Lorraine was involved in a bad car accident while I was down at the farm. I was actually at a rodeo when I was told to take a phone call. I was told she'd been rushed to hospital but couldn't find out any more clear details. My friend Rhonda Gardiner's husband, Terry, is a surgeon, so I called him and asked would he check out what was going on. It was quite tricky not knowing whether to begin the long drive back, get on a plane or sit tight for more news. Terry eventually reassured me that her injuries weren't life threatening and to wait for further information. In the end she was released later that night.

At the time of the accident Dawn-Lorraine was diagnosed as suffering from severe whiplash, but her injuries have changed her life from that of a carefree young woman to one in which she will always have to manage her pain.

All in all, 1995 had been a tumultuous year, with highs such as my wonderful testimonial and lows like Dawn-Lorraine's accident and the asthma attacks I'd been suffering. It also marked the end of four and a half turbulent years on the Board of the NRMA. I'd been elected to the Board in 1991, having been part of the Motorists Action Group. Together with Richard Talbot and others, I mounted a legal challenge to the proposed demutualisation of the NRMA. Although we were eventually successful, it was a long and bitter battle, and extremely stressful. Six years later, on August 8th, 2000, the NRMA became a public company.

•

Although I had all sorts of interesting things going on in my life during the 1990s and was busier than I ever wanted to be I was also aware that I was quite alone. I didn't have a relationship and while I didn't especially want one there were many times when I would come home from something like a gruelling NRMA meeting and find that I didn't have anyone to talk to about what was going on. It was often late at night and you can't exactly ring a friend after midnight. It can be lonely leading a very big public life and a very singular private life. There are more times when I am thrilled to get home after a big dinner or cocktail party, kick off my shoes, and watch a video without having to worry about anyone else than there are times that I wish I was coming home to talk through the issues with a partner, but sometimes it can be very lonely. Sometimes I think it would be nice to have a partner to talk to about the day's events.

For a long time now I haven't had any relationships that are more than serious friendships. I have never been able to sustain a close personal relationship that is also physical and I have been so hurt by people in the past that it has seemed safer not to go down that path again. Nevertheless, you can't help thinking about what might have been or what could still be under the right circumstances. Having moved away from the gay scene and not having met any men that could fill that special role in my life, I have remained a single woman since the early 1980s. I have my special but platonic friendship with John Marriott, who I regard as a close confidant and a lovely man to turn to in times of crisis. He is also a great travel companion and someone to call on when a dinner partner is required (thank you, John!). And of course I've always been able to turn to Singo for advice. But I have done without a relationship that has a sexual side for a very long time and I know that's how my life will be from now on. I also know I am not unique in this regard. It is, after all, the common complaint of middle-aged women that they can't find a partner, and by the time my last relationship broke up I was well into my forties. I don't dwell on this aspect of my life very often but every now and then I do think it would be nice to have someone really close.

15

SOUTHERN COMFORT

About four years after Benson our labrador–shepherd walked across the threshold at the Riverview, Zac, a pure shepherd, also came into our lives. I went to Townsville in 1984 for the first North Queensland Masters Games and while I was there Zac, an eight-week-old pup, was given to me by a long-time fan. I took him on the return flight to Sydney in a bag full of newspaper in case of you know what. When he started to get a bit restless I put him inside my blouse to keep him warm, but after a little while I felt a warm spot on my stomach and knew it was time he went back into the bag. The flight attendant came over, and when she discovered I had a beautiful little puppy in the bag she brought some warm milk for him.

Although I originally gave Zac to Dawn-Lorraine, he became my dog because I spent more time with him and I grew to love him more than any dog I had ever owned. He was a sickly pup and had to have a hip operation when he was only six months old. Having always been hopelessly concerned about animals and children who have some sort of disability, I took to Zac in a way I never had with my other dogs, even though I loved them all.

When he was about three and a half months old I began to notice that when he ran, his back legs crossed each other. The vet told me his hips were no good and suggested we try a new operation that involved removing his hip bones and plaiting his ligaments to give him better forward movement. It was a very successful operation and the only thing he couldn't do was jump. I took him swimming every day to make him stronger, but it took him a long time to learn because as a long-haired shepherd he'd get so heavy when wet that he'd sink.

Leading up to the Atlanta Olympic Games in 1996, Zac, now a twelve-year-old, had become quite frail and sick. He was becoming listless and was losing his movement and had little control over his bowels. Our wonderful vet, Janet, told me I should think about putting him down. At that point, quite uncharacteristically, everything seemed to get on top of me. At the time, I was coaching a group of Masters and triathlete swimmers at the Sydney International Aquatic Centre and was also preparing to leave for Atlanta. Dawn-Lorraine was working in Perth and I was feeling quite stressed and unable to make any decisions on my own, so I called her and asked her to hurry back to Sydney. I just didn't feel up to dealing with Zac by myself. It was unlike me to be so helpless, but Zac's illness added to my busy schedule was too much. Then, not long after, I had a very upsetting altercation with the AOC.

I wasn't especially fit at the time. Following the mild heart attack I'd had at the farm I had slowed down a fair bit on my training and had put on quite a bit of weight. I had been scared of over-doing it and now I found myself less than healthy and less able to cope with things than usual. Even recalling these events now I can see they are all tumbling out together, which is how it felt at the time. There was too much going on and I couldn't get it all in order in my mind. So, first things first...

I had been asked to be an Athlete Liaison Officer in Atlanta by the AOC. It was a role that I had enjoyed very much in Barcelona and, in an unofficial capacity, in Seoul when I'd helped the women's basketballers. I was looking forward to the involvement with the athletes and was very happy to have been included by the AOC.

Shortly before we were all due to leave for Atlanta I had to report to a hotel near Mascot, along with athletes and other Australian Olympic Committee officials, to get my uniform. It was very exciting, as it always is, to be part of an Olympic team and I was given the enormous amount of gear that people seem to get these days. If you compare it to what we used to be given when I was swimming it's like night and day. And because there is so much gear handed out I just put it all together without looking at it, drove home again and began to pack it into my suitcase, which was already out. That's when I discovered that my blazer didn't have the Australian coat of arms on the pocket. I rang the hotel, spoke to the woman who had been in charge of handing out the uniforms and told her my blazer hadn't been finished off properly. She apologised, said she'd work out what had happened and call me straight back. When she called I was told she'd spoken to 'the boys', who had said I wasn't to have the Australian coat of arms on my pocket because I wasn't really part of the team.

The absolute humiliation and distress I felt at that point gave way to sheer anger. Why did this keep happening to me? Why couldn't I wear the Australian coat of arms like everyone else? I had, after all, won four Olympic gold medals for my country and I'd worn the coat of arms in Seoul and Barcelona. I just couldn't understand what had gone on. It felt as if I were being punished all over again.

After thinking the situation through for two and a half seconds I rang the hotel again and found out who the particular 'boys' were who had made this ruling, and then I said something like, 'You tell "the boys" that I'm coming straight back to return the whole uniform and they can keep it and they can keep their job too.'

I flung the entire kit together, drove straight back to the hotel and handed everything to the woman who'd given it to me. I wanted to yell and scream at her but I knew it wasn't her fault. While I had been driving back to the hotel my fiery daughter, who had arrived from Perth a few days earlier, had rung 'the boys' and given them a piece of her mind, which I wish she hadn't done but I did appreciate her support and outrage on my behalf. I'd been so obviously distressed and sobbing, which was unusual for me, that Dawn-Lorraine had just flown off the handle.

By the time I got back home one of 'the boys' was actually on the line apologising, and I could hear my daughter telling him that they were in for a nice surprise and they'd end up with egg all over their faces. I rushed into the room and started pleading with her not to say any more, and eventually got the phone off her. Then I listened to the flow of apologies and promises to fix it all up, but by then I was drained and didn't really care what they had to say. I had been hurt once too often.

What the AOC didn't know—in fact no one in Australia knew other than Dawn-Lorraine, Singo and me—was that I had received a confidential invitation to attend the Games from the Atlanta Organising Committee. It had arrived a few months earlier but I had been instructed not to tell anyone. I knew I was to take part in the opening ceremony and that I could stay for the whole Games as their special guest. I could also take a guest who would be fully accredited to attend all of the events. In addition, I was to have a car and driver for the entire period of the Games and had been encouraged to ask for anything else I might need. It was very humbling to be honoured in this way and to be treated with such respect and consideration by another country. I had decided to take Dawn-Lorraine with me and the Organising Committee generously offered to fly her over too. At the time I had thought I would be attending as an ALO anyway and that the invitation from Atlanta was the icing on the cake.

After I'd hung up the phone Dawn-Lorraine began hopping about saying we should go to the press and tell them what sort of people were running our sporting organisations; how past champions were treated; that she'd give them a piece of her mind; and so on. I let her blow off some steam for a while and then I called Singo for advice. I have often turned to him in a crisis and he always gives me sensible guidance and tends to be very calming. He advised me not to say anything about my invitation from the US, and definitely not to go to the press. I think he felt I'd have my special moment up there onstage at the opening ceremony and that was the best thing to do—remain dignified and really enjoy the thought of all that egg over certain faces when they saw me onstage.

By the next day I was being offered all sorts of compromise positions by the AOC, such as being a VIP host, which would involve chatting to dignitaries, athletes' parents and others. To keep the peace and to have a cover for my role in the opening ceremony, I agreed to take the host's job, although it definitely wasn't the job that I wanted. I wanted to be with the athletes.

In hindsight, a lot of the athletes and their coaches asked me for help anyway, regardless of what my official role was, so if I'd refused to be involved at all I would have let the athletes down and would also have to have said why. I didn't go and get my uniform again, though. It was offered with the coat of arms, and for all I can remember it may even have been delivered, but by then I had no intention of wearing it anywhere. I'd had enough of the petty power games and had just decided to go along with the flow.

But now I'm getting ahead of myself...

By the time Dawn-Lorraine had arrived back from Perth earlier that week it was pretty clear to me that Zac would have to be put down but I just couldn't bring myself to do it. Dawn-Lorraine took over and arranged that we'd take him to the vet on Monday morning to be euthanised. That way we'd have him at home for the weekend to say goodbye. He wasn't able to walk any longer, and though he wasn't in any pain he did have to be carried to the toilet and anywhere else he wanted to go. I'd been sleeping in the bathroom with him for the past few nights and now Dawn-Lorraine took over. By Monday we knew we had reached the final point and we carried him out to the car together. Our vet, Janet, was waiting for us at the surgery and gave us a little time to say our separate goodbyes. I couldn't stay in the room while she administered the needle, and left Dawn-Lorraine to stay with dear old Zac till the last.

That night we had to go to a dinner with the swimmers I'd been training at SIAC. It was the last thing I felt like but I knew it was a birthday party for one of my swimmers and a farewell for me before I left for Atlanta. On this of all occasions I felt like a good stiff drink, but I couldn't because I'd made a pact with some of the athletes that I wouldn't drink for six months leading up to the Games if they wouldn't either. I kept my word but it was a very sad and solemn night.

When I boarded the plane the next day I wasn't especially excited to be going to Atlanta. I'd lost my dear old Zac and hadn't had time to grieve, I felt unhappy with my role for the AOC and wasn't sure what I was supposed to be doing, and I wasn't in the best state of health. Still, the invitation from Atlanta was intriguing and I looked forward to finding out more. And though I still have a slight fear of flying, one of the things I enjoy about long plane journeys is escaping the phone for so many hours—that's very relaxing when you get as many calls as I do.

Coincidentally, I sat on the plane next to an American woman I'd met in the Riverview a few nights earlier. It was lovely having someone to talk to and I have to admit I broke my pact and had two Bloody Marys with my travelling companion in an attempt to relax, which I finally did. I did feel a bit guilty but the circumstances seemed to call for one and at least it wasn't beer, which is what I'd really wanted and had sworn to keep off.

At the other end I was whisked away into a different area and driven off in my designated car almost straightaway, which caused a bit of a stir among the other Australian officials travelling on my flight. I still hadn't told anyone about the invitation from the US, but over the next few days it became clear that I was getting rather special privileges.

Almost as soon as I checked into the hotel I went out to get my bearings. The Days Inn, where I was staying, was just across the road from the Fox Theatre where the Australian team had their office and social club. The Fosters Club was in the Fox Theatre, and that was next to where Alan Jones was broadcasting for 2UE. You could see him doing his show from the street through the big window.

Inside the club, Fosters had set up lots of television sets and a hospitality lounge where athletes could meet up with their parents and where VIPs could relax, and this was the place where I was supposed to look after sponsors' guests in my official role for the AOC. When I finally got there I did actually look forward to my role and undertook it quite seriously. I soon met up with old friends, including the Managing Director of Carlton & United Breweries, Nuno D'Aquino, Raelene Boyle, lots of people from SOCOG who were there as observers for the 2000 Games, and several parents of our team members. It took almost no time to get into the swing of things. On the corner of the same street there was a little restaurant that had been taken over by some of the Australian supporters, and we christened it 'the RSL'. That's where we'd all head if the Fosters Club had closed for the night. The owner of the restaurant had imported Australian beer, wine, pies, Vegemite, and lots of other iconic Australian fare, and it became the major meeting place while we were in Atlanta. He had heard the Australian team had claimed the Fox Theatre as their head-quarters which had given him the idea for the restaurant.

I did go out for the first few nights and, to be honest, further blotted my copybook by having a few beers. At the RSL on the second night everyone got me up on the table and introduced me to the Manager: 'This is Dawnie Fraser...' and so on. Then we all sang 'Aussie, Aussie, Aussie! Oi, Oi, Oi!', a theme the soccer players had given us in Barcelona which is now used everywhere. It was fun and lovely to be among all those excited people, but I felt such a dead heartache over Zac and I couldn't talk to anyone about it. I wanted Dawn-Lorraine to be there so that I had someone who would understand. Maybe it seems crazy that there I was at this very exciting time of my life and at the centre of it all, and I could only think about Zac. To me my dogs have been closer than most people, so it was the same sadness as losing a close friend or family member.

As usual, there was a lot of competition between officials and organisers—who's got what, what am I missing out on, that sort of thing—all looking to see what the others are doing, and there I was with this amazing accreditation where I could go anywhere, and with a driver waiting for me twenty-four hours a day. The athletes were fine, as were the coaches, but the officials were asking, 'Where'd you get that pass?' I'd just say, 'Oh, it's just the pass I've been given.' Then they'd ask, 'Can we give you a lift back from the pool?' and I'd say, 'My driver is waiting. Can I give you a lift?' And so it went on. It was a very awkward but exciting situation.

Unfortunately, my driver, Kathleen, was the driver from hell. Absolutely gorgeous and great fun to be with but couldn't drive to save herself. She had a big heart and a lousy sense of direction. More often than not we'd be heading up one-way streets the wrong way—and this was her home town! Other times she'd say, in her Southern drawl, 'Dawn, just call me when you're ready to be picked up.' And I'd say, 'What's the phone number Kathleen?' And she'd say, 'Dawn, I don't rightly know.' Even when the phone rang in the car she didn't know which button to use to answer it. Other times she'd ask me if I wanted coffee and cream and I'd say, 'Just black thanks, Kathleen.'

'Oh Dawn,' she'd drawl, 'you really should have something in that coffee.'

Kathleen lived with her mother only five minutes from the Days Inn but she was always late to collect us. She'd call from home and say she'd be there in five minutes but that usually meant fifteen. I'd always sit in the front with her and wouldn't let anyone else have that seat. I didn't mind how many people piled in the back but that front seat next to Kathleen was mine. I'd watch in amazement as she ran up onto footpaths, and every now and then she'd exclaim, 'God, Dawn, someone put that kerb there yesterday, I swear.' I loved her from the very beginning.

During the Games some of the swimmers and their coaches asked for me to come and talk to them to help prepare for their swimming but that met with great opposition from an official Athlete Liaison Officer, who told me in no uncertain terms to keep my nose out. When I tried to explain I'd been called for I was told to mind my own business. It was hurtful and slightly awkward but in the end it was the swimmers who counted and as some of them wanted my advice I continued to provide it.

The day before the opening ceremony I was called to a rehearsal. By then Dawn-Lorraine had arrived and I'd had a chance to talk about Zac and now felt a bit better. Dawn-Lorraine wasn't allowed to come to the rehearsal with me because of the heavy secrecy surrounding the event. Kathleen drove me almost right up to the stage, through several security checks, before I was met and taken to the green room where the athletes who were to take part in the opening ceremony were gathered. None of us knew about each other up to that point. When I arrived I was introduced to a man by the name of Lamar, who was stunningly attractive, and the woman who had first written to invite me to participate.

There in the green room were Bob Beaman, the world-record-breaking Olympic gold medallist long jumper, who I had met so many years before at the 1968 Olympics; Leon Stukelj, the Slovenian gymnast and oldest living gold medallist; the Cuban boxer Teofilo Stevenson; the great gymnast Nadia Comaneci; Carl Lewis; Greg Louganis, the diver; and Mark Spitz.

We were told roughly what would be expected of us and how we would be described in our introductions, and then we did the walk through rehearsal twice. That was all we were told before being driven back to our hotels.

A day or two before the opening ceremony Billy Payne, the CEO of the Games, phoned to say there was a place in the torch relay, sponsored by Coca-Cola, on the morning before the opening ceremony, and would I like to run in it? Even though I didn't drink their product I thought it was a very nice gesture from Coca-Cola and I accepted. I also told them I wasn't a runner and asked if I could have a very flat part of the course so I could walk comfortably. They said I could run in front of the Days Inn and past the Fox Theatre, which was about a kilometre. I told them I didn't think I could run that far, and apart from anything else it was extremely hot in Atlanta and I was really feeling it. They reassured me that I could just run as far as I felt comfortable and then someone in the bus would get out and take over. That all sounded fine and I agreed I would run.

When the day for the run came round it was hotter than ever and the relay was running behind schedule. All of us who would be running that morning were taken by bus to wait at a church, from where our bus would set out. We had about an hour to wait because of the delay, and were sitting around on the steps of the church drinking water and trying to keep cool when a very large lady came out to walk down the stairs. She tripped over on the stair where I was and landed on my leg, and she couldn't get up because she'd twisted her ankle. I kept calling out, 'Please get her off my leg,' but I couldn't move and it felt as though my kneecap was twisted right around. Eventually they lifted the lady off me and she had hurt her ankle quite badly. I hung on to the stair rail and pulled myself up because I felt I should walk around and get some movement back into the knee. Kathleen, my driver, was running around very anxious because it was the church where she worshipped, and she wanted someone to give me a blessing, which I agreed to in order to keep Kathleen happy. At that moment I would have agreed to anything, the pain was so bad. Eventually I was helped inside to a cool room and my knee was strapped under my supervision because I knew exactly how it should be done. I did feel a bit better and eventually the bus arrived and we all climbed in.

We had to drive a couple of kilometres back down the road to meet the previous bus and there was a lot of talk about how it was all running behind and we had to get moving. That meant that our batch of runners was faced with a hill when we'd been promised flat ground. I was sitting on the bus watching my knee get bigger and bigger, and I started to panic and tried to take the bandage off because I felt as though it was cutting off the circulation. Unfortunately no one had any scissors and I couldn't get it off. Then an official came through the bus to ask me to get out and do my bit of the run. I looked out the window at the hill I had to tackle and said I couldn't possibly run and that I was due to run a different section. I was told that unless I ran then I wouldn't run at all and I said, 'Fine, I won't run.' Then a bloke climbed out and had a go before saying it was too much and that he wanted someone else to take over. I kept refusing and he was pleading with me, 'Please run for a little bit.' I wouldn't do it, though, because the hill was very steep by that stage and I knew I wouldn't make it. Eventually there were only three of us left who hadn't had a go, and looking at the others I thought I was probably a bit younger, so I got out and started to run. Just at that point the street took a sharp turn upwards and around a corner. Great timing Dawn! Somehow I made it and then I just said, 'I can't possibly go any further. I'll have another go a bit further up.' If only people could have seen what was going on behind the scenes! It was bedlam.

A police car came up just as I handed the torch over and the driver told me to get in. 'Come on, we'll catch up with the bus,' they said. With that I got in and explained that my daughter and lots of friends were waiting to see me run outside the Days Inn. They drove me down and we caught up with the bus just as the Mayor of Atlanta, who was also on the bus, was saying, 'I'm not going to run with it. I was told I could walk.' I joined in and said I wouldn't run either, but the officials kept saying we couldn't walk, we had to run.

Eventually we were outside the Days Inn and I just got out when I saw all my friends and grabbed the Australian flag and ran all the way down to the Town Hall at the end of the street behind the torchbearer. Somehow, as many Australians reading this will now know, when you get hold of that torch or participate in the relay in some way and the crowd is cheering, the adrenaline just flows through you and you keep going.

Poor Dawn-Lorraine had been put in the wrong spot to watch for me and had missed me passing. She ended up crying all the way down the street to meet me. By the time we got back to the hotel we were both emotionally exhausted and my knee was the size of a balloon. I knew I had to get ready for the night so I had my knee iced and I rested for the afternoon. By the time I was getting ready for the opening ceremony I wanted to participate despite everything. The excitement of a new Games had grabbed me and I was feeling full of anticipation again.

Kathleen brought the car round into the little turning circle at the back of the hotel to collect us on the night, and left it there while she came into the foyer. The security guard told her it couldn't stand there and that he'd have to move it, but her response was that the car had been 'sanitised' and she could leave it standing wherever she wanted and no one could touch it. A sanitised car is one that has been thoroughly prepared security-wise, after which the driver breaks the seals on the doors and from then on is the only one who can drive it or even open it—and what's more, they should never leave it.

That night on the way to the opening ceremony Kathleen got lost as usual. We ended up in a dirt carpark miles from anywhere in what appeared to be quite a rough area. She suggested we get out and walk, but I refused, so she drove on a little further and we found another carpark full of accredited cars. Once again we were told we couldn't stay there and Kathleen was given instructions about where we were supposed to go. Next we found ourselves on the wrong side of a freeway and when I said, 'Kathleen, I think we've gone the wrong way,' she calmly replied, 'Dawn this is the way they told me to go.'

We found that most of the main roads around the stadium had been blocked off by then and time was starting to run out. It had been arranged that we should get there an hour and a half early so we could be taken to our box, have something to eat and relax before the big moment. Unfortunately that flew out the window as Kathleen ploughed on, knocking into security barricades and telling police her car was sanitised so she could go on. At one point a policeman had his face pressed up hard against the windscreen trying to see who was inside and what was going on. I just sat there frozen in the end not saying a word but watching it all happen like some strange film.

From the previous day I remembered that the stadium was half an hour's drive down the freeway and that we had taken the number two exit, but when we got there the exit was closed. So Kathleen tried the next exit ten minutes further on and it was closed too. Then we tried the next and the next and I knew by then we'd passed the stadium several kilometres back down the road. When I pointed this out to Kathleen she just said matter of factly, 'I know, Dawn, but I can't get off the freeway.' By then I'd started to see the funny side and began to giggle and then to laugh and laugh hysterically. Kathleen passed about eight roadblocks, and at each of them she was given instructions she'd ignore.

When finally we arrived at the main gate Kathleen was in a lather of sweat. I told her we'd meet her back there half an hour after the closing ceremony. The gorgeous Lamar then magically appeared to take us to our seats, which were completely fantastic with a full view of the whole stadium, and we could see some of the Australian officials and VIPs a long way down to the side craning to see where we'd been taken. Behind me there was a small child who kept kicking my seat and I turned around to ask him to stop doing it because I didn't want to get my suit dirty before I went up onstage. In fact I had to ask him several times, and became quite annoyed in the end and told the adults he was with, in very clear terms, that he was to stop kicking my back.

Finally I was taken backstage by Lamar and security, but I hadn't taken a lot in because I'd been too excited. All nine past Olympic athletes had to assemble in a tunnel that led out into the arena and up onto the stage. At that point we still didn't know what order we were to go in. Then the order was read out and I was to go up first. I just thought, 'A for Australia, that's logical,' but someone who shall remain nameless said, 'That's not right, I have more medals,' which took a bit of the shine off. Still, it was such an overwhelming moment that I quickly forgot what had been said. I was talking to Nadia and Carl while we waited and the excitement was building. I realised I was about to be watched by hundreds of millions of people around the world. Outside we could see thousands of flashbulbs going off and the noise was fantastic. We watched from the tunnel as all the participating athletes marched around, and then finally the red carpet was rolled out for us, and I walked across the track, through the athletes and up the stairs onto the stage. I was very nervous.

We were being presented to the new Olympians as an example of what had gone before and it was a wonderful feeling to be part of that honouring of past athletes. It was all a bit of a blur and finally we were led off and back up to our seats. People applauded as I walked to my seat and that felt great too. When I got back to my seat Dawn-Lorraine was waiting and I realised that earlier I had ticked off the grandson of Jimmy Carter, the former President of the United States. Now they all apologised for the incident and Carter introduced himself. I said, 'Now you know why I was so concerned about my suit.' They all clapped me and got my autograph, which just about capped off the night. I settled back into the moment and basked in the glory and honour of it all.

Back in the green room where we went for a drink afterwards, the athlete who had complained in the tunnel about our order of appearance quizzed Dawn-Lorraine on how she'd got her excellent accreditation. It seems there are people like this in every country.

We managed to find Kathleen without any hassles this time and we went back to the Fosters Club with the torch that I'd had in the relay. Coca-Cola had made sure it was brought to me during the night and I took it back to share with all the other Australians who were very happy for me. Later we went to the RSL, which was so packed you couldn't move. Everyone wanted to buy me a beer and I got up on the table again and everyone cheered. We passed the torch around and talked about what it meant to travel to the Games and be part of this atmosphere. It was a magical night.

At some point in the proceedings I caught up with Kathy Watt, the cyclist, who was having a terrible time with her team and coach. I wanted to spend some time encouraging her because I felt she was being psyched out by officials after all the conflict surrounding her selection for the Games, which sometimes goes on when an athlete is very gutsy and independent. The officials can't bear not to control them, so they play mind games. It really upset me to see her in that situation, so I talked to her for quite a while and didn't get back to bed till about 2.00 a.m.

Then it all really started for me, the running from one venue to the other. Several coaches wanted me to talk to their swimmers and I spent the following Sunday night at the swimming and went back afterwards to the Fosters Club to carry out my hosting role, which I took seriously because I had committed myself to it. I stayed for a while and watched more events on the big screen and had a bit of dinner, then I went back to my hotel because I knew I had to get up early again for the swimming.

The next day I felt unusually tired when I got up. I hadn't slept much because it was so hot and I'd left all my windows open. I had a hot shower that morning, which I wouldn't usually have, and followed it with a cold one to try to revive myself a bit. The bathroom was very small; so small, in fact, that I had to come out into the bedroom to dry myself. I was sitting on the bed when the phone rang, and it was Graeme McNiece, who was the manager of swimmer Scott Miller. Graeme was concerned that Scott was a bit nervous, but he didn't have accreditation for the pool deck and wanted me to have a talk to Scott before he raced at about 9.30 that morning. It was just before eight so I agreed I'd get dressed, have a coffee and get my driver to take me to the pool.

I then lay back on the bed for a minute because I felt so hot and bothered and that's when the pains in my chest started. They were quite intense, but I managed to calm myself and call out in a normal voice to Dawn-Lorraine, who was in an adjoining room.

She came in a minute later, having just got out of the shower, and I asked her to go across to the Fox Theatre and see if she could find a doctor as I didn't feel very well.

'Well what's wrong?' she asked, her voice already sounding a bit panicky.

'Nothing, I'm not feeling well.'

'But what is it?'

'A bit of chest pain, that's all. Don't panic. Go to the Fox Theatre and see if you can find a doctor.' Well, that's the worst thing I could have said. She was out the bedroom door in a flash and I had to call out to her to put some clothes on or she would have been in the hall nude.

In the foyer Dawn-Lorraine ran into Kathleen, who was standing with Nicki Vance, the doping control expert with the Australian Sports Drug Agency. She said, 'There's something wrong with Mum!' and ran on to the Fox Theatre to look for a doctor. There she found Patsy Trethowan, the Medical Program Manager with SOCOG, who was in Atlanta as an observer. By the time Patsy arrived in the room, with Dawn-Lorraine close behind, Nicki and Kathleen were already there. There were only two small lifts in the Days Inn, and when they couldn't get one fast enough everyone had rushed straight up seven flights of stairs and in through the door that Dawn-Lorraine had left ajar.

I was still lying there with just a towel around me, and the girls tried to keep me quiet and calm. Next six big paramedics came in, by which time you couldn't see the other side of the room for people. I looked at the girls and said, 'I have first choice because I'm the sick person.' I was trying to joke my way out of the situation because by then I was scared. Actually the room was so crowded with so many busy people that I was feeling very claustrophobic.

The paramedics gave me some oxygen, wired me up for an ECG and asked me what the pains were like. When I told them I was an asthmatic I was given an injection and taken out on a stretcher to the ambulance and off to hospital. The ambulance driver was radioing through that they were bringing in a suspected cardiac arrest patient, and although I was sedated I knew by then what was happening. Dawn-Lorraine followed the ambulance with Kathleen and was allowed to come into emergency when she arrived. I asked her immediately to phone the family at home to let them know that I was all right in case they had heard about it through the media. Ever since my parents found out about my arrest in Adelaide and my swimming ban through the media I have been fanatical about letting my family know news about me before they hear it elsewhere.

Dr Ted Monitz, a cardiologist, came in to look at me quite quickly. He didn't know who I was but he assumed I was an Australian diplomat because of all the fuss that was going on around me. He told me he thought I'd had a cardiac arrest and that I probably had a blocked artery. He was reluctant about operating because he didn't want to take responsibility for an Australian diplomat. Dawn-Lorraine explained who I was and that made it even worse for him.

Eventually he put the dye through my arteries and did an angiogram to show me on the video monitor where the blockage was. I felt pretty deflated because I'd always believed my heart was strong and it had carried me through so much over the years. A stent was put in to inflate the artery, and although it is a simple operation I was a bit fearful of it. Dr Monitz was fabulous, though, and kept assuring me I would be all right.

Unfortunately, when I'd settled back down another doctor came in and, mistaking me for a different patient, proceeded to do an internal physical examination. I politely said, 'That's not where I hurt and I think I'll be fine, thank you,' at which the doctor backed away immediately. Dr Monitz was pretty embarrassed when he heard about that little episode. As soon as Dawn-Lorraine came in I told her what had happened and we had a good laugh about it, as you do in those ghastly situations. I was then taken to my own ward to recover and kept under tight security around the clock because media were trying to get a photo of me in hospital. The whole story had leaked out because Alan Jones had been sitting in his window broadcasting when the entourage had left the hotel.

I was so tired I wasn't concerned about missing the Games, except for Susie O'Neill's and Kieren Perkins' races. I tried to get the doctors to let me out of hospital for those, but there was no way that was going to happen. It turned out I'd had a very severe attack that had damaged a quarter of my heart. I was very frightened when I learned that, and knew that from then on my life would have to change. I also realised that all my inability to cope and my tiredness over the previous weeks had been a build-up of the heart condition, and that the extra stress I was feeling had tipped me over the edge. When I now look at photos of the torch relay in Atlanta I can see that I don't look at all well, and my doctor in Australia, who saw the televised images of me running, felt at the time that there was something wrong.

When I was having the heart attack I did think I was going to die. I sort of travelled down that tunnel towards the bright light that you hear people talk about but I then gathered strength and backed away again. I wasn't ready to die. I was away from most of my family in a foreign country and I hadn't made any plans for my will, so I fought back and survived.

I spent seven days in hospital and I was looked after wonderfully. The nurses would massage my feet and back every day because I couldn't move from the bed, and Dr Monitz visited twice a day to check on me. I ended up receiving faxes from children all over Australia wishing me well—one day I had more than three thousand—and the hospital rigged up a special fax machine in my room. Everyone was very kind and concerned. Doctor Brian Sandow and Dr Larkin from the team were great. John Coates, the Chef de Mission of the Australian team, came in to see me and make sure I was all right. We don't always see eye to eye but I appreciated what he did because he must have been very busy without having to visit me in hospital.

I was finally released into the care of Dawn-Lorraine and Kathleen, along with Patsy from SOCOG, and I was told by Billy Payne to keep the car and driver for as long as I needed them. As we passed the basketball stadium on the way back to the hotel I could hear the 'Aussie, Aussie, Aussie' ringing out and I begged to be allowed to go in for just a minute. I went into the back of the stadium and discovered it was the Russian women's team playing the Aussies in the quarter-final, and we ended up in the front row with all the team supporters. I had Dawn-Lorraine holding one wrist and Patsy holding the other trying to take my pulse rate. Then I saw one of the Russians hit Michelle Timms, the Australian captain, and I jumped into the air and yelled, 'You get up there, Timmsy, and belt her one!' and everyone was saying, 'Sit down, Dawn. Don't get excited.' The Aussies ended up winning in extra time, but I'd had to leave by that point because I was so pumped up.

Dr Monitz felt I should really return to Australia immediately but we had booked to go on a Caribbean cruise following the Games and decided to stick with that plan. The doctor agreed that as long as I didn't exert myself I should be all right. Lying back in the sunshine, sleeping and reading a book was surely more restful than the usual demands on my time back in Australia. I spent the rest of the Games sitting at the Fosters Club watching the events on television, but I'd missed the swimming and was very disappointed about that.

The cruise was for seven days, and I was pleased to find the doctor onboard was a locum from Australia. I told him about my condition and what had happened and that made me feel safe. A few days into the cruise, though, I started to get the pains again and when I went to call the doctor and Dawn-Lorraine I found they'd gone off shopping on one of the islands. When they came back I was moved down to the little hospital in the bowels of the ship, where I felt very paranoid and claustrophobic. I was drifting in and out of a very strange feeling and I kept thinking the ceiling, which was wood-panelled, looked like coffin lids. I think it possibly had something to do with my terrible experience on the ship in Balmain years earlier. It was creepy, and I just couldn't wait to get back into the fresh air. The ship's captain had a verandah off his cabin with a lounge bed on it and that's where I stayed during the day for most of the cruise. I was very dejected and I kept thinking, 'I'm so far from home. I don't want to die here.'

Finally it was time to fly back to Australia and we were very happy to find we'd been upgraded to first class by Qantas because of my illness. As soon as I heard we were an hour from Sydney I breathed an enormous sigh of relief. Singo had arranged for me to see Dr Paul Roy, an eminent cardiologist, and I felt safe and secure back in my home town. What had happened to me was a big wake-up call. I was placed on a strict diet and I had to educate myself about what I could and couldn't eat and what I could and couldn't do. Of course doctors don't want you to do anything much, but in the end who can obey the no cleaning, no vacuuming rule. I certainly can't afford housekeepers. I was careful about the stairs in my house, though. Walking up them took my breath away and I had to take it more easily, but going slowly for the first time in my life took a bit of getting used to. None of it mattered, though, because I was home, and there had been a few moments when I thought I might never see it again.

By December that year I was unfortunately back in hospital. Not only had I continued to vacuum my house, but I had been stripping wheat on my farm at Barellan. (No one told me not to strip wheat!) While I was out in the paddock I was gripped by chest pains and I panicked. I admitted myself to Griffith Base Hospital, where I'd been earlier in the year with what I then thought was asthma. From there, after a few days, I was transferred to St Vincent's Hospital in Sydney. It turned out to be angina this time and my doctor had a serious talk to me about over-exertion, stress and not panicking over chest pain. I had begun to think every chest pain meant I was going to die and I needed to take control of that situation. My doctor explained that unless I could control my adrenaline and learn not to panic I would be always going backwards and forwards to the hospital.

In a magazine interview I did at the time, I said I wanted to live to be a hundred, and while I think that was said in a moment of extreme optimism, there is a part of me that so much wants to enjoy a long and peaceful phase in my life, preferably on my farm. My desire to be on the land and close to the earth is very strong. I want to watch the seasons turn over and the animals being born. By the end of 1996 I felt I'd had enough wake-up calls to get a grip on my health and start to really think about fulfilling those desires.

16

THE OSCARS
OF SPORT

We all have dreams and plans for the future, and as I get older I notice a lot of those plans are about escaping the city or having a complete change of lifestyle. Often, though, we get too caught up with present demands and obligations to really pursue those dreams. My life in the years following the Atlanta Games was as action packed as ever, and the farm continued to be a place to go to in between the other commitments. It was a time of great involvement in sporting committees of one kind or another, and looking back over those years I realise that if I'd retired after Atlanta, as I'd half planned to do, I would have missed so much that has only recently come to fruition.

It hasn't all been beer and skittles, though. During my time on the Board of the National Australia Day Council some years earlier I met Professor Fred Hollows, the great eye surgeon, and he suggested I come in and get my eyes tested at Prince of Wales Hospital in Sydney, which I did. He felt my eyes were pretty good for my age but he also prescribed some reading glasses and said I should come back for annual check-ups. I became good friends with Fred and his wife, Gabi, and we did some charitable work together.

In the summer of 1997 I'd been coaching the kids at Barellan for a week and had then gone on to the Masters Games in Hawaii. At Barellan I'd had some slight irritation in the corner of my right eyelid, which developed into a fairly intense stinging. By the time I was in Hawaii, the pain had become so strong it felt like a razor blade was cutting into my eyelid. As soon as I returned to Sydney I went back to the Prince of Wales to have the problem assessed. Fred had died in the intervening time, and I saw a Professor Coroneo, who picked up that I had some skin cancers on my eyelids. He thought they were probably caused by the reflection coming off the bottom of the pool during all those training years when I didn't wear goggles, as well as general exposure to the sun, as I'd rarely worn sunglasses. It turned out that I had second stage cancer on my right eyelid. The cancers had to be removed surgically, and as I write this book it looks like I will have to go back in and have another one removed. I can't imagine coping with losing an eye, and I feel incredibly lucky and grateful that Professor Coroneo caught the cancer in time.

Just a few months after this Dawn-Lorraine organised a fantastic sixtieth birthday party for me at One World Sport, a venue at Sydney's Darling Harbour full of interactive sports-based video games and decorated with sporting memorabilia. We sent out invitations created by Singo to my very, very close friends only—which amounted to 385 people—and almost every one of them came along, even though for many it meant travelling interstate and long distances. Although I say 385 very close friends tongue in cheek, after my long and mixed career I do know an awful lot of people well, and I did in fact invite that number. Some of my very oldest friends from the days of growing up in Balmain came along and, most importantly, all of my brothers and sisters, and their partners and children, who I put up at a hotel across the road so they wouldn't have to find their way home afterwards.

Everyone was instructed to dress as their favourite sportsperson (but not as me!). I went as a racing car driver because I had the full outfit from participating in the Grand Prix celebrity race the year before in Adelaide and cars were still a passion of mine. Carlton & United Breweries donated all the beer because I'd helped in the Fosters Club in Atlanta, and any beer left over was to go to One World Sport because they'd kindly given us the venue, although I doubt there was much left to give them.

It was a great party and went till about 4.00 a.m. In the end it became very rowdy and wild, with everyone dancing on the tables and carrying on. By then I'd exchanged my racing driver's jump-suit for football shorts and T-shirt and had a few dances up on the stage. I felt loved and cared for by my friends and grateful that I was there to see my sixtieth after the events of the previous year. The cake was amazing, in the shape of a gold cup with me swimming through waves on the top, together with dolphins.

The next day all of my family came down to my hotel room to watch me open my gorgeous presents, and it was then that my sister Heather remarked how marvellous it was that our consid-erate hotel had put all those complimentary little bottles of drink in the fridge, which she'd packed up to take home. Rosie agreed and said she'd done the same. So when it came time to check out I had to pay for the entire contents of two mini-bars as well as the rooms. Still, I didn't mind. There was no way I would have been the happy sixty-year-old I was without the love and support of my family.

This same thought was going through my mind about a year later when my most cherished family member, Dawn-Lorraine, had to have a very serious operation on her neck as a result of the car accident she'd been in back in 1995. I was feeling very stressed by the whole situation as the two of us are very close and we both knew the operation involved a certain amount of risk. I was also feeling very tired and rundown. Ever since the two heart attacks I'd been conscious of how my weight had ballooned and how much I needed to get fit, and though I'd succeeded in losing weight at times, it just kept coming back on. So I put myself on a vitamin supplement that also promised weight loss. By this time, nearing the end of the 1990s, my public life had expanded as much as my waistline and the two weren't unrelated. I often found myself at cocktail parties and dinners where I was guest speaker, or appearing for this board or that committee, and I'd eat what was put in front of me. Added to that, I still caught up with my friends and watched the Balmain Tigers play football every weekend, both of which always involved a few beers.

Once I was on the self-prescribed vitamin supplement I started to lose an enormous amount of weight. Dawn-Lorraine was still in hospital following her operation, and every afternoon when I visited her I would fall asleep in the chair next to her bed. I couldn't stop myself from dropping off almost as soon as I sat down. I'd also start raiding her room for chocolate, orange juice and even lemonade, which I never drink. I was desperate for anything sweet.

Daily I began to feel a little worse and a little more rundown. In a matter of about a month I'd lost 15 kilograms, which was just too much, so finally I went to my doctor who picked up on what it was almost immediately. She arranged for a blood test, which confirmed I had diabetes. This came as a shock, and I suddenly realised I had a strange kind of prejudice against the condition. I think it had to do with the idea of injecting yourself and my feeling that it was unclean to use needles. To those of you who know about diabetes it will sound bizarre and completely wrong, but I do think it is a misunderstood disease and I misunderstood it more than most. I even felt I had been somehow unclean during my life and that I was being paid back for it. Through visiting a diabetes specialist and a dietitian I eventually learned more about the problem and was relieved to find I could cope with it using tablets rather than injecting myself with insulin. I was told my stress had helped bring it on and now I try to avoid stress as much as I possibly can—although I rarely succeed.

Dawn-Lorraine's operation left her in considerable pain and quite unable to cope on her own, which is the most important reason why I couldn't go off and live on the farm: I felt strongly I needed to be in Sydney for her. We have come to realise over the last few years of rehabilitation that she will always have to live in pain and may need an even more difficult operation in the future. This has taken its toll on both of us. As you will have gathered, we are unusually close for mother and daughter, and in many ways too close; however, we really only have each other and have been through so much together that we've grown into a particularly co-dependent relationship. As one journalist put it, we 'fight all the time but can't bear to be apart'. It is hard for other people to understand but in the end it only has to work for us. Of course I want to see her happily married with children, and I certainly want grandchildren, and I know it will come. There have been proposals over the years but she will need someone very strong to stand up to her to make it work.

Having decided to stay put for the time being I also began to look at renovating my Balmain home. I'd made some minor alterations in the period after Gary left, when I received some money from two court settlements, but after thirty years the house really needed some work. People who have moved around in their lives probably can't understand the depth of a lifetime attachment to a house. I can't imagine not owning the house because I just have to walk through the front door to feel safe. A few times over the years I have seen vivid images of my father in the house and I have a strong feeling he's still there. I'm not the kind to believe in ghosts but his appearance a couple of decades ago and again recently was strikingly clear and very convincing!

I had some plans drawn up to create a new bedroom and bathroom, as well as to extend the back of the house and renovate the kitchen. It took a marathon two years to have the plans passed by council because the renovation meant adding height to the terrace and it no longer matched the one next door. We moved out in 2000 for work to begin and we're still not living there as I write this down over a year later. Every step of the renovation has been a struggle, and of course all the experts have weighed in to tell the media I am destroying a piece of Balmain's heritage. I have tried to renovate the terrace in keeping with the original style, adding the wrought iron lace work to the extension and having both terraces painted in heritage colours. Personally I think it looks great but many activists in the area seem to disagree. It makes me laugh that all these recent arrivals in Balmain now feel free to comment about every issue going. Their comments and letters about my house have always included some reference to who I am rather than just commenting on the building itself, which is annoying. By all means state your opinion about the renovation but don't single me out for special mention. I'm all for preserving the original character and heritage of the area and it's something I've often fought for, but it is also a place where some of us have lived all our lives and surely our needs count for something? Perhaps those who are so concerned about the area should turn their attention to helping the old and frail people in the community, who are being left behind and overwhelmed by the radical changes that have taken place. These people are part of the heritage too but I don't see much evidence of that aspect of Balmain being preserved as property prices soar and increasing local shop prices force many people out. I can't help but think that the main motivation of so many who hide behind the heritage argument is simply to maintain the value of their own properties. To me, the value of my property is not so much in the bricks and mortar but in the decades of memories and in my sentimental attachment to the house where I was born and grew up.

Just when all of the renovation arguments were coming to a head I joined New South Wales Planning Minister Andrew Refshauge at the Dawn Fraser Pool, where a press conference was held to announce that the 118-year-old baths were being placed on the State's heritage list and could never be demolished or radically altered. You can imagine what a field day the press had over that one, drawing comparisons with my house renovation and saying I'd destroyed some heritage there but now I was glad the baths were being heritage listed. During the 1990s I had often campaigned to get the baths cleaned up and cared for, and now it was finally going to happen.

•

To balance out all the little things that had been going wrong, one of the best things that has ever happened to me came along around this time, and that was being nominated for Female Swimmer of the Century in the Athlete of the Century Awards, to be presented by the World Sports Academy in Vienna. I hadn't even known about the awards until I received a phone call from the organisers to explain that I'd been nominated by a world jury headed by Juan Antonio Samaranch, the President of the IOC. Eleven other women had been nominated in the category and we'd all been invited to attend the award presentations in November 1999. Six fellow Australians were to go as well. They were Betty Cuthbert, Mick Doohan, Heather Mackay, Margaret Court, Sir Donald Bradman and Rod Laver. The nominations had been made and voted on by more than ten thousand journalists around the world, with a shortlist chosen by the jury. I certainly didn't expect to win, especially as in Atlanta Kristina Egerszegi of Hungary had finally equalled my record of three swimming gold medals over three consecutive Olympic Games. However, I gratefully accepted the invitation to fly first class to Vienna with my daughter for the presentation ceremony. Almost twice a week between the initial invitation and boarding the flight I received a call to check that we were still coming. This constant attention was taken by Dawn-Lorraine to mean that I was perhaps the winner, but when we finally spoke to other nominees they all remarked they'd also been struck by the level of care they'd been given from the beginning. To say the whole awards program was very well run is an under-statement. It seemed like a fairytale as we flew in luxury to the other side of the world to be met by a barrage of photographers, reporters and minders. After being briefed thoroughly about the awards, Dawn-Lorraine and I took off to visit dear friends Andraz, Duska, Jozica and Poldi in Slovenia for the week leading up to the big night. The organisers didn't really want us to go but we convinced them we'd return at the appropriate time and took off in our hire car. It was the first time I'd ever seen snow falling and I kept begging Dawn-Lorraine to get out and have a snow fight with me. I kept pinching myself as a reminder to take it all in, being here in the snow in Europe and about to attend the World Sports Awards.

When we arrived at our destination I was very sad to learn that the Slovenian gymnast Leon Stukelj, who had been onstage with me at the Atlanta opening ceremony, had died. Our friend Andraz was himself a Slovenian silver medallist from the Atlanta Games, and I attended Leon's funeral with him the next day. Leon was the grand old man of Slovenian sport and his funeral was moving and sombre.

Following the funeral we had a wonderful week with our friends, who were exceptionally good hosts, before heading back to Vienna.

Our accommodation in that beautiful city was at one of its grandest hotels, next to the Vienna State Opera House where the awards ceremony was to take place. The Austrian organisers were relentless in their hospitality, calling regularly to see if there was anything they could do for us. I was assigned a minder, Christian, whose first task was to usher Dawn-Lorraine and me off to the fashion house Escada to be fitted for gowns to wear on the night. I tried on so many outfits I was almost driven to distraction. I was too big for their clothes and besides, I already had a perfectly tailored outfit from my friend Trent Nathan, who makes all my business and special occasion outfits. There were cameras everywhere we went and I wasn't too keen on coming in and out of changerooms in front of them. Let's face it, changerooms are terrible at the best of times, let alone with a bevy of reporters and cameramen in tow. At least we weren't trying on swimsuits.

We finally made a choice and later that day, together with a couple of the other athletes, we were the special lunch guests of the famous Sacher Hotel. Dessert was, of course, Sacher Torte, and the whole meal was magnificent.

Later we had our hair and make-up done at a salon in the centre of town. When I walked in I found myself among the likes of Janet Evans, Fanny Blankers-Koen and Nadia Comaneci. Cameras followed our every move, and for the first time that day I felt excitement start to build and little butterflies flitting in my stomach. Back at the hotel it became apparent that despite all the alterations my outfit still didn't fit me properly, so I happily went back to my Trent Nathan pants and jacket. Now I was comfortable. Tailors and dressmakers rarely take the width of my shoulders into full consideration when fitting me, whereas Trent knows exactly what I like.

All dressed up and on our way down to a photo shoot in the hotel prior to the awards ceremony Dawn-Lorraine drove me mad.

'I feel sick. I'm so nervous. Are you nervous? How do you feel? You look calm. I feel sick. Why are you so calm?'

'Shut up, Dawn-Lorraine. Of course I'm nervous. I just know how not to show it.'

Then we burst into nervous laughter and had just managed to compose ourselves as the lift doors opened and we were off and running for one of the most memorable nights of my life.

First of all we were taken to a room with all the other nominees for a photo shoot and then by security guards past hordes of autograph hunters and media to the Imperial Hotel across the road, where all the nominees were given an award simply for being nominated. We were introduced to Juan Antonio Samaranch, after which we had a bit of time to chat with each other and, because we'd also been given a poster, everyone was trying to get autographs. Dawn-Lorraine kept badgering me to get the autograph of the great soccer star Pelé. I kept hanging back because he had such a large crowd around him but Dawn-Lorraine being Dawn-Lorraine kept pushing me forward. When I got close he stopped what he was doing and gave me a big hug before signing my poster and asking for my autograph on his. It was incredible to look around the room and see Nadia Comaneci, Bob Beaman, Nikki Lauda, Carl Lewis, Alain Prost, Janet Evans, Betty Cuthbert and so many more great athletes all crowded into one room. It really did present itself as the best time to get everyone's autograph before the night was under way, but the problem was everyone else had the same idea and people were queuing for mine too. One particularly special moment was when a lovely young lady came up and introduced herself as Kristina Egerszegi. I already knew who she was, and that genuinely surprised her. I congratulated her on equalling my 35-year-old record, and she told me she'd always admired me, so it was a very pleasant encounter and we happily exchanged autographs.

I had been instructed that my car would be the second last to leave from the front of the Imperial Hotel to the Opera House and Muhammad Ali's would be the last. Gradually the room emptied out and then it was my turn. As we got into the car it had begun to snow lightly and people were calling out my name, which seemed very strange in a foreign country so far from home. It was truly like being in a fairytale. When we arrived at the Opera House—only half a block away—we stepped onto the red carpet and could not believe the roar of welcome from the crowd. 'This is the closest we'll come to an Oscars of sport,' I thought to myself, as flashbulbs went off in all directions. The security was quite intense and Christian walked very close to me, making sure I was well protected. We were ushered into a private room for pre-awards drinks and hors d'oeuvres. I was chatting with Pelé and Muhammad Ali as well as trying to find Heather, Betty and Rod. It was quite crowded and everyone in the room was buzzing with anticipation. When we were finally shown to our seats I found myself sitting near the front on the aisle. This brought new butter-flies to my stomach but I remained composed. Not Dawn-Lorraine though.

'You wouldn't be here if you didn't have a chance, Mum. Look where we are, Mum. Maybe it's you. Maybe you're going to win.'

I just wanted to gag her. She was making me so nervous I couldn't even think straight. I started to gaze around to try and take my mind off the whole event. Two rows down I could see Pelé and his wife, then Carl Lewis just in front with his partner. Across the aisle was Nadia Comaneci and her agent, and in front of Nadia was the great man himself, Muhammad Ali, with his daughter. Oh well, it didn't exactly take my mind off things but it did occur to me that here was little old Dawn from Balmain among the biggest names of sport from the century in a room that could only be described as opulent.

Dawn-Lorraine then decided she wanted to take some photos, first of me with Carl and then of me with Pelé. Sometimes I just go along with my daughter to keep the peace, so I had to get up and be arranged in the shots. Just as she was instructing Pelé and me to smile, from where she was kneeling on some empty seats in front, someone tapped her on the elbow to ask her to move. Instead of turning round, she just waved them away and said firmly without looking back, 'Would you mind waiting a minute, please!' Pelé and I looked stunned but she didn't pick up on our shocked faces. Finally, when the photo was taken and Dawn-Lorraine went to move, she saw Juan Antonio Samaranch politely waiting in the aisle with his wife before taking his seat. He didn't bat an eyelid and graciously waited for Dawn-Lorraine to extricate herself, but I wish I could have captured the look on Dawn-Lorraine's face. It was priceless.

The awards ceremony finally began and I was grateful for the dimmed lights to gather my thoughts and breathe steadily. Alain Prost, the French Formula One racing driver, was the first winner for motor sports and he made a very humble acceptance speech— which made me realise with a bit of a jolt that I hadn't even thought about a speech. Next, the ball sports categories saw Heather Mackay and Margaret Court miss out to Steffi Graf, who hadn't been able to attend the awards. In the men's category Don Bradman and Rod Laver both missed out to Michael Jordan, and that made me feel I wouldn't win in my category either because I'd been sure Rod Laver would take that award. He was such a fine tennis player and had done so much for his sport since. When the women's athlete category was announced Dawn-Lorraine and I crossed everything we could for Betty Cuthbert, but Nadia Comaneci was announced the winner. Any shred of hope I had up to that point now disappeared. I felt the Australians were being overlooked, so I sat back more comfortably just to enjoy the night. I thought Carl Lewis would win the men's athlete category and indeed he did. I love Carl and believe he was the right choice, but I am also close to Dick Fosbury, who revolutionised high jumping by going backwards over the bar—the 'Fosbury Flop' it was called—and a little piece of my heart held out for him.

Carrying the torch in Atlanta, 1996.

At my 60th birthday party with good mate John Singleton, 1997.

Speaking at the Australia Post launch of the Olympic Legends stamp series, 1998.

Playing the violin in a thousand-year-old restaurant in Slovenia prior to travelling to Austria for the World Sports Awards.

Being honoured as Female Swimmer of the Century at the 1999 World Sports Awards in Vienna.

(Above) Standing: Mark Spitz, Dawn Fraser, Jean-Claude Killy, Alain Prost, Nadia Comaneci and Carl Lewis. Sitting: Pelé and Muhammad Ali.

(Middle) Onstage next to Muhammad Ali.

(Below left) With Carl Lewis.
(Below right) With Pelé.

On tour in Dili, East
Timor, at the beginning
of 2000.

At the opening of Dawn
Fraser Avenue,
Olympic Park,
Homebush, 2000.

Meeting Nelson
Mandela at a
conference for
the World
Sports
Academy,
Monaco, 2000.

Meeting the
Queen in
Sydney, March
2000. We're
laughing
because I'd had
to race from
having lunch
with her at the
Olympic
Superdome
back to the
Aquatic Centre in time
to greet her.

With Jon
Henricks at the
2000 reunion
for past
Olympic
swimmers at
the Tobruk
Memorial Pool.

The Torch Relay 2000.

(Top) With Murray Rose at Uluru for the official start of the relay, the day the torch arrived on Australian soil.

(Right) Sydneysiders turned out in their hundreds of thousands to see the final stages of the relay. Carrying the torch down Sydney's George Street on the night before the opening ceremony was a great experience. It was an emotional moment as I handed the torch over to Murray.

The Opening Ceremony.

(Below) In the dressing-room at the Olympic Stadium before the final lap of the torch relay.

(L-R) Me, Raelene Boyle, Shane Gould, Shirley Strickland, Debbie Flintoff-King and Betty Cuthbert (foreground).

At the beach volleyball with Sir William and Lady Deane.

At the swimming with Chelsea Clinton.

Passing the torch to Shirley Strickland.

At the closing ceremony with Matthew Dunn.

(Left) The post-Games dinner hosted by Juan Antonio Samaranch. (Below) With Cathy Freeman.

With Dawn-Lorraine.

At the Laureus Awards with Louise Sauvage, who received the World Disabled Sportsperson Award.

Carl's speech inspired me. He said how humbled he was to be in the present company, and he talked about his poor beginnings. He said that if he could make it anyone could if they really wanted to, and from my perspective I agreed wholeheartedly with that sentiment.

When the women's water sports category was announced Dawn-Lorraine started crying. I sometimes can't believe I have such an openly emotional daughter when I've tried all my life to maintain such a strong public face. I had to hold her hand very tightly and when my name was read as a nominee, along with Kristina, Janet Evans, Birgit Fischer and Franziska van Almsick, my heart nearly jumped out of my body. Carl's partner turned round and told Dawn-Lorraine to stop crying or she'd start us all off. By then she wasn't just weeping quietly, though, she was completely wracked with sobs.

Then Michael Gross said those magic words: 'It is the one that came the longest way. Dawn Fraser,' and then, as I've already said, everything seemed to dissolve around me and I just sat glued to my seat. I made my speech—somehow the words arrived when I needed them—and then Mark Spitz was announced in the men's water sports category. Winter sports followed, and then the two most obvious winners of the night were announced: Pelé in soccer and Muhammad Ali in martial arts.

Later all the winners were asked to come up to the stage, and even though Muhammad Ali had walked to the stage unassisted and made his speech without any help or prompting, he now looked to me for a steadying arm, which I was pleased to give.

The rest of that wonderful night passed in a bit of a blur. There was a dinner in three rooms in the Opera House for eight hundred guests. We sat at a table with two other winners and their partners, Jean-Claude Killy, a downhill skier from France, and Alain Prost. We had our three amazing crystal trophies in the middle of the dinner table—which didn't leave much room for ice buckets.

I couldn't take my eyes off mine, and I still gaze at it in wonder even now. It reflects the light beautifully and sends patterns all over the walls and ceiling when the sun shines into the room. It makes me very happy.

All night people came over to our table to congratulate us and the mobile phone rang every other minute with calls from Australia. Our friends from Slovenia also rang because they'd just watched the ceremony on television. I did a few quick interviews with Australian journalists before really getting into the celebrations. Dawn-Lorraine kept saying how wonderful it was to be at a table with two such great sports stars and then added each time, 'And also you Mum.'

Later we went to a private party at a nearby nightclub, and I started to get nervous about Christian carrying the trophy because he was a bit tipsy. As he carried it down the stairs he kept saying the stairs were moving. I wonder why? Eventually Dawn-Lorraine went back to the hotel with him to leave the trophy there because they didn't trust leaving it with anyone, not even the security guards. Eventually I asked Christian to take me back to the hotel too because I'd more than had enough. I lay in the dark for a long time enjoying the moment and reflecting on the twists and turns in my life that had brought me to that point.

It's interesting to reflect on the different categories and awards that were part of that night. Many of those present had played sports that were sponsored or had been paid to play their sport. As everyone knows, international tennis, basketball and soccer stars are paid millions. The swimmers in my day weren't, and perhaps of all those on the stage I was the one who had come up through their sport without any sponsorship whatsoever. This made my award all the more satisfying when I later thought about it. That's not to say the others hadn't struggled. Every single one of them had endured an enormous amount of hardship to get to where they were, and that sacrifice is necessary to reach an elite level in sport no matter what you do. In the end it's as much about sacrifice, pain and disappointment as it is about medals, glory and victory.

We spent a couple more days in Vienna before flying out to Cancun in Mexico for a conference I had to attend for the World Olympic Medallists Association, of which I am Vice President. The association had been formed predominantly by past gold medallists when it was announced that Athens would host the Games in 2004. The idea was to recognise Athens as the home of the Olympics and to get as many past medallists to attend as possible, as well as to spread the word generally about the Athens Games: a sort of homecoming for the Games really.

I didn't want to ship my trophy home from Vienna, so I decided to take it with me to Mexico: a decision that presented its own unique problems. It was in a specially designed case, which I padded with clothes, and then I bought a special little trolley to wheel the trophy onto the plane as hand luggage. Of course everyone wanted to have a look at it because they'd seen it on television and that meant unwrapping it often and having my photo taken with it as we went through security checks at airports. And I wouldn't put it on the hand luggage conveyor belt and so had lots of arguments about taking it through the electronic security with me. The alarm went off every time and I'd have to unwrap it again and that would start another round of photo taking. Eventually on our way back to Australia on Lauda Air the trophy had its own seat next to me. Then we arrived in Australia and security there wanted to see it too, and so it was unwrapped all over again at the airport and there were more photos taken before we could escape.

Unfortunately we weren't able to head home to Balmain because the renovations were under way and we went instead to stay with Dawn-Lorraine's best friend Narelle and her husband Frank. Our friends have been marvellous putting us up since the work started on the terrace and we will always be grateful to them. But I hope by the time this book is published that the trophy has found a permanent home and I am sleeping in my own bed!

Back in Sydney I was given a special reception at the Town Hall by the Lord Mayor Frank Sartor, at which I was given the keys of the city.

•

My award in Vienna has led to another new and exciting part of my life. I was not long afterwards invited to become a member of the Advisory Board of the World Jury for the World Sports Awards Foundation. It was formed after the initial awards ceremony in Vienna and is largely funded by the Austrian Government. Every year I am to be part of the panel that makes the final selection of nominees for the various categories. We also raise money from the awards dinners, which is then given to establish sports activities in Third World countries. All the athletes who had won in Vienna were invited onto the board, although not all accepted. The next awards were held in London in January 2001. Apart from the serious side of what we were doing, it was great to meet Roger Moore and Buzz Aldrin who attended the awards as special guests.

After I returned from Vienna in 1999 I was also informed about the establishment of another new awards program called the Laureus Sports Awards, which are held annually. The Laureus Sports Awards are sponsored by DaimlerChrysler and Richemont and I was invited to be part of what they call their World Sports Academy. We first met in 2000 in Monte Carlo, and Nelson Mandela attended that meeting to discuss with us the need for funding of sport in Third World countries. It was a great thrill to meet him, especially in such a small group. The meeting was also to plan the role of the academy for the future.

I enjoy being a part of the academy and contributing to their decision-making process about the winners of their awards. The categories include World Sportsman of the Year and World Sportswoman of the Year, World Team of the Year, World Newcomer of the Year and World Comeback of the Year. Over two hundred journalists form the panel that nominates candidates from all sports, then a team of auditors collates their nominations before we members of the academy cast our final and deciding votes. The Board also chooses an Alternative Sportsperson of the Year and an Athlete of the Year with a Disability. The founding patrons name the Lifetime Achievement Award and the Sport for Good Award.

The Sport for Good Award is another aspect of what we all hope to achieve through the Laureus Awards and a meeting I attended was to discuss how the money raised, which is considerable, will be spent. As with the World Sports Awards, it will be directed towards Third World sporting projects. One project, nominated by one of my academy colleagues, aims at increasing the number of Aboriginal children involved in organised sport in Western Australia. Another program I have since put forward is to equip children in East Timor with swimming goggles and kickboards to use at the two pools in Dili, which I visited in early 2000. I was asked by Channel 7 to go to East Timor to inspect the devastation after Indonesian troops occupying the island had withdrawn. I had no idea what to expect but I saw a Third World country in crisis up close for the first time in my life, and it made the sports awards' sponsorship for Third World countries even more important to me when it came about. What I saw was completely shattering.

Being a part of both these world sports organisations, as well as the Australian Sport Industry Awards, is a joy for me because I have long wanted sporting organisations to have a direct connection to encouraging young athletes. If the money can find its way into worthwhile projects for the really needy in Third World countries then that's all the better. I have been to so many dinners in my lifetime where the money raised seemed to be ploughed back into the organisation, while young athletes attached to the organisation were struggling to get themselves proper training and equipment, so it is really uplifting to see some good being done at a grassroots level.

17

THE FIRST LADY
OF THE GAMES

Aussie, Aussie, Aussie!

I have always said that Melbourne was my best Olympic Games and the gold medal I won there the sweetest of all my victories. A large part of that was competing in front of a home crowd. Leading up to the Sydney Games, I heard some past Olympians remark to the current crop of competitors that it was a shame their chance to participate had come when the Games were in Australia. I have to completely disagree with that view because there is something brilliant and spine tingling about having a home crowd cheering you on. As exotic as it is to compete overseas, it can also be very unsettling, and I think you have your best chance of a medal at home.

When in 1991 I was invited to join the Bid Committee for the Sydney 2000 Games, along with people such as Rod McGeoch, John Coates and John Valder, I was very excited to be part of the process. I felt that to have the Games here in Australia would be excellent for all of us, not only for the economic upturn and sporting facilities that would result, but in bringing us together as a nation and developing our pride. And I hoped that ultimately I'd be involved in putting the whole show together. My term in State Parliament had come to an end and I was keen to sink my teeth into a new project.

All along we were quietly confident about Sydney winning the bid because we had a truly great proposal. I had participated in many of the bid meetings and had really thrown myself into every aspect of it, so I was disappointed when I wasn't invited to attend the presentation of the bid in Monaco in 1993. At first I wasn't aware that a decision had been made to exclude me, and when I eventually found out I didn't know why the decision had been made. No one said anything to me, although I heard via the grapevine that certain people in powerful places had said they didn't need old athletes hanging around. Clearly it had been decided, at some point away from my hearing, that I would neither assist in the presentation of the bid nor be invited to attend as an observer. Then again, perhaps nothing was decided and I just never came into the equation. It became obvious that every man and his dog had gone over. Admittedly some were self-funded, but I wasn't spoken to about that possibility so I stayed behind.

I understand one of the many arguments put forward in favour of the Sydney bid was that Australia was one of the few countries with an unbroken attendance at the Modern Olympic Games. Having played a large role in making sure we got there in 1980, when Moscow was boycotted by many other countries, I would like to have had an opportunity to go to Monaco. As so often in the past, I felt that I was being kept at arm's length. I think there is an attitude of 'Dawn has her uses' and clearly this wasn't going to be one of them. It is difficult to deal with, because I want to be part of the Olympic family and I love working with the athletes, but on the other hand I feel I often have to put my pride aside or eat humble pie more often than I would like to.

I spent the night of September 23rd, 1993 at a televised 'bid evening' party down at the former overseas passenger terminal in Sydney, which is now used as a function centre. It was a fantastic night as we waited till 4.21 a.m. to hear if we'd been successful. I was with some other ex-athletes from the committee who also hadn't been invited over to Monaco and we all souvenired bid flags from around the party room. When the announcement was made I, like the rest of the enormous crowd that had gathered down at the harbour, was ecstatic. The party was a forerunner to the wonderful atmosphere we would enjoy during the Games in 2000, with everyone feeling excited and friendly and revelling in a sense of community pride and spirit. It was also the beginning of a long rocky road to 2000 for myself and many others connected in various ways with the Games.

•

Back in 1991, before Sydney had even won the bid, I was contacted by a man who had what I thought was a wonderful idea for raising money for our 2000 Australian team. His proposal would also bring a sense of involvement and excitement about the Olympics to every part of Australia. Tim Konz was an average family man who had big dreams about sending a convoy around Australia to fundraise and also to increase awareness about the Games. He needed someone with public popularity, a high profile and a link to the Olympic movement to be at the helm of the convoy, and he approached me. He said to me, 'What are you doing in 2000?' I said truthfully, 'Nothing.' And that's how we got started on what would become a major project over the next seven years.

Tim owned five FJ Holden cars that he usually rented out for weddings. He wanted to take these immaculately restored FJs, paint them the colours of the Olympic rings, and make them part of his convoy to tour all the small towns in the bush and all the bigger cities leading up to the Games. That was the germ of an idea, and there was much more to it by the time we were finished with it several years later. The FJs were the first cars to be manufactured in Australia and were widely regarded as iconic and very important pieces of Australiana. We started to approach potential sponsors, and everyone from AOC officials down was impressed with our concept.

From that point we talked about it often and started to develop a much firmer model for our convoy. By 1995 we had approached the AOC formally, and both Tim and I had met their marketing and fundraising people. We were then referred to the Sydney Organising Committee for the Olympic Games (SOCOG) to try to take the concept further. We found out that the AOC couldn't really fundraise, other than to hold dinners for which tickets could be sold, and that the real control of fundraising had been handed over to SOCOG.

We next met with John Moore, the Licensing Manager at SOCOG, in mid-1995 to see if they would be interested in joining with us to run the convoy. The whole idea had now taken on a life of its own and we thought we would do it for a charity even if SOCOG decided against it. But our first preference was to fundraise for the Olympic team, so we offered SOCOG first right of refusal. We had approached Ric Birch, the maestro who has orchestrated so many opening and closing Olympic ceremonies around the world, to help put the convoy together. Ric and his company, Spectak, developed a substantial forty-eight-page document which outlined every aspect of the convoy, including the route it would take around Australia. They did it for free simply because Ric loved the concept so much.

In the document Ric agreed that Spectak would orchestrate the convoy from the original concept, through all the logistics of production and planning, to management of the actual tour. There would be parties, picnics, parades, dinners, displays and souvenirs all travelling around Australia for a period of six months. I was to travel the whole distance but we were going to get athletes and ex-Olympians to join me for short parts of the tour. Everyone who saw the plan was enthusiastic and excited, including General Motors Holden, whose marketing people flew to Sydney from Melbourne to talk to us within a day of hearing about it.

At that point SOCOG told us they could not give us a yes or no for quite a few more months while they were sorting out sponsorships. We immediately wrote explaining we couldn't wait because it would take two years to plan and put together, and if they couldn't give us a response we'd press on independently. But at a luncheon John Coates advised me to wait until sponsorships were in place, and so we resigned ourselves to putting things off a little longer. By this stage it looked on paper as if we could earn around twenty million dollars for the Australian team through the convoy. John Moore again expressed excitement about SOCOG adopting our convoy and working with us, and said it would be further discussed in Atlanta. He also expressed interest in using the logo we'd developed for the 'Ozzie 2000 Convoy'.

Our next contact at SOCOG was Di Henry, the General Manager of the Torch Relay, who said the idea was great and suggested a meeting to decide whether the convoy could fit into either the 1997 flag tour or the torch relay prior to the Games.

But once again months went by before a meeting was organised, and even then John Moore and his offsider failed to turn up. I was by then very concerned that our ideas were being taken by SOCOG, and that we were being deliberately fobbed off. At the meeting Di had asked if SOCOG could use parts of our concept—meaning me and the cars—for the flag tour the following year. We said no. It seemed they wanted to strip our convoy of all its aces.

In early 1997 I wrote again to John Moore, asking for a final decision and pointing out that the venture had now been on the drawing board for six years. A month later I received a response. I was thanked for my patience. I was invited to be part of SOCOG's marketing program (no details were given and nothing eventuated) but he was sorry he had to say 'no' to the convoy concept as they were 'already struggling to cope with the enormity of the SOCOG torch relay'. I was asked to please stay in touch and could 'we please do more together?'.

I never heard from him again. The AOC continued to appear enthusiastic but they were relatively powerless on the marketing front as SOCOG controlled all the rights. So we went on our merry way to approach GMH direct, but around that time GMH became an official sponsor of the Olympics and unfortunately that closed that door to us because SOCOG could dictate the terms of how GMH would be involved.

I feel that perhaps our convoy became SOCOG's 'Olympic Journey' that was rolled out in 1996 and which I believe was a pale version of what we could have done under the direction of Spectak and Ric Birch. Finally we had to accept that it was too late, we didn't have our sponsor and we didn't have the support of SOCOG, which was a major stumbling block. I had believed in the project wholeheartedly and had turned down many excellent offers to participate in advertising deals leading up to the Olympics because I had remained committed to the convoy. And part of that commitment was because of the continual encouragement we had received over a period of years from the AOC and SOCOG. In the end we had to cut our losses and take it on the chin!

•

In 1998 I was asked to be the Attaché for the Sydney Olympic team, which I was quite pleased about because I felt it was an opportunity to work with the athletes and help make their Games work for them. It also meant I could become part of the Team Organising Committee and could see how the Games were coming together, although, as it turned out, I was never given the chance to get involved in any significant decision-making. I was also asked to be an Athlete Liaison Officer for the equestrian team, the swimmers and the women's water polo, and I was very pleased as these were three areas where I'd had quite a bit of experience and where my greatest interests lay.

Next SOCOG approached me to participate in the torch relay and I accepted happily. I was thrilled in October 1999 when I received a letter from Di Henry stating, 'You will have the honour of carrying the Olympic Torch at the Sydney Opera House on Thursday, 14 September 2000. The Sydney Opera House is on Day 99 of the Torch Relay's 100-day journey around Australia.' I couldn't think of a better place to run with the torch. It would be by the water, which I felt was appropriate for me, and I'd be in that beautiful place, which would obviously be highlighted on the evening before the Opening Ceremony. I was indeed honoured.

But in July 2000 I received a second letter with my uniform, saying, 'You will have the honour of being a Torchbearer on Day 99, Segment 201... Starting in Sydney you will carry the torch along George Street from Bridge Street and finish at Martin Place.' I felt some mistake had been made, and my assistant called SOGOG to point out that I had perhaps received the wrong letter. We couldn't get on to Di Henry, who was the signatory on both letters, as she was by then actually on the torch relay tour, but we were assured that it would be checked out and someone would get back to me.

Before anyone called me, however, things unfortunately started to escalate. A friend of mine and IOC member, Phil Coles, had rung to say his torch relay position had been moved from Bondi Beach, where he is a member of the North Bondi Surf Club, to some back streets of Bondi. Like me, he had been very excited about his position and had told people. I tried to cheer him up, and I commiserated and said I'd been moved too. Before I knew it, the media had got hold of the story. They also knew that the positions of several other well-known athletes had been changed.

Certainly I was disappointed by the apparent change but I was also resigned to it. I just felt embarrassed that I'd told my family and friends I'd be carrying the torch at the Opera House when now I wouldn't be there. However I was portrayed in the media as being outraged by the circumstances. I was bombarded with phone calls for interviews, in which I confirmed I'd been moved but hadn't yet heard back from SOCOG. The whole thing was escalating and I was very worried that I looked to be whingeing and whining when in fact I was very busy writing this book, working for my sponsors and really couldn't be bothered with the whole matter.

Then things took a slightly strange turn for the worse. Before I received any explanatory or apologetic phone calls from SOCOG, Olympics Minister Michael Knight went on radio and television news to say no one had been promised a particular place in the relay so there were no grounds for complaint.

That's when I became angry. It was one relatively minor thing to have your position changed and another entirely to look like a liar on national television. My daughter was angrier than me and she rang the Minister's office to make a very strongly worded complaint. Quite soon after, Michael Knight called me and I was able to tell him about my original letter. He didn't really believe I'd received a letter, so I read it to him over the phone. He asked if he could send someone to collect the letter, and I said not to worry, I'd fax it, which I did. He was stunned that I had the letter and his words were, 'Well, that's not ambiguous, is it?' He offered me my original place back, but I genuinely didn't want to displace someone else and I said a public apology would be adequate. I didn't care about the position any longer and only wanted the matter cleared up in the media. Mr Knight admitted in the media that some letters had gone out earlier, but there was never a proper public apology made, and at my own instigation I did not return to my original position at the Opera House. Phil, however, was restored to Bondi Beach, which was quite right.

Michael Knight also told me in that phone call that there were plenty of other things coming up with regard to the opening ceremony and that there would be 'other things' for me to do. Only he and John Coates, he said, would know who would light the cauldron and no decision had yet been made.

The issue of the torch relay and the lighting of the cauldron had come to haunt my life a few years earlier when people began to ask on a daily basis whether I thought it would be me. The speculation continued to intensify to the point where I thought I'd tear my hair out if I heard the question one more time. Even if I knew I was going to light the cauldron, why would I tell? Still it went on relentlessly day in and day out. 'Are you lighting the cauldron, Dawn?' or even more impossible, 'Do you think you'll light the cauldron, Dawn?' How could I win that one? If I said 'Yes' I was being egotistical, presumptuous and setting myself up for a big fall. If I said 'No' I was being falsely modest and basically commenting on something I knew nothing about. It was also one of those situations where everyone knew someone who knew someone else who knew it was going to be so and so who'd light it, and they'd do it by this method or that method... On and on it went.

Of course I would be lying if I said that at that stage I didn't want to light the cauldron. It would be the biggest honour I could imagine. Just thinking about it gave me goose bumps. I felt I had a fair chance because I had the greatest number of Olympic achievements in Australia, and also because almost every part of the media had called for me to light the cauldron after I was named World Female Swimmer of the Century. Yes, I definitely wanted to light it, and a little part of me deep inside kept that hope alive right up until the night before the opening ceremony. Another little part of me, however, whispered that they would never choose me in a million years.

I had actually been told a few years earlier by Ric Birch, who I'd say would have to have known at that point, that I wasn't the one who would be lighting the cauldron. He told me I wouldn't like to light it anyway, because of the way it was going to be lit. But even when I was told point blank like that by someone I trusted, I still thought, 'Maybe he's just trying to put me off. How could he know, anyway?'

In June 2000 I was lucky enough to be chosen by Channel 7 to go to Uluru in the Northern Territory to watch the Olympic flame arrive on Australian soil. I didn't run with the torch, and was there chiefly to do some interviews and commentaries for Channel 7, but it was an extraordinary experience. As my presence wasn't crucial and I was feeling very exhausted at the time, I almost turned the opportunity down. But I'm so glad I went because it was one of the most memorable and significant moments of the entire year. Seeing the torch being lit was like a culmination of all that had gone before and the start of all that would come; a quiet moment or a lull in the general frenzy which had been building up for years and would soon burst into full throttle. Just this quiet passing over of the flame by Sir William Deane to the Aboriginal tribal elders, who lit the torch from the flame and handed it over to Nova Peris. It was so simple compared to the rest of the hoopla but deeply moving. It was very cold, very quiet and almost eerie. About sixty Aboriginal children had journeyed by road for nine hours to be at this historic event. Watching them as they watched this simple little ceremony was one of those moments when everything is stripped away and you think, 'So that's what it's all about.'

•

On the day of my own torch run, which was the 99th day of the 100-day countdown to the Games, I was called into the office by the Chef de Mission, AOC President John Coates, who informed me that the IOC President, Mr Juan Antonio Samaranch, wanted me to be his special guest at the opening ceremony because his wife was unable to attend due to illness. I was told I would be the First Lady of the Olympics. As you can imagine, I was a little bit stunned by this invitation. It isn't exactly a role I would ever have imagined for myself. I'd had my clashes with the IOC and been quite vocal at times, plus I was still very much focused on the lighting of the cauldron, and my first thought after being told of the invitation was, 'Well, I won't be lighting the cauldron then.' I gratefully accepted, and then said something like, 'So I guess that counts me out of lighting the cauldron.' To which he replied that it didn't necessarily mean that. He said no one knew who would be lighting the cauldron except he and Michael Knight.

No doubt my reaction sounds terribly ungracious, but in fact the two roles weren't related in my mind other than the fact that you couldn't do both. I was actually very pleased to be invited to accompany Mr Samaranch in the Presidential Box, but I also kept thinking it probably meant I couldn't march with the team either. And to some extent I've reached the stage where whenever I'm offered something like this, a part of me does a quick analysis: 'Are they throwing you a crumb here, Dawn, or is this a genuine invitation? Are they just trying to keep you happy and out of their hair here, Dawn, while they get on with the main game?'

Mr Samaranch then held a press conference to inform the media of his invitation to me. He said he had asked 'the most popular athlete in Australia' to be his partner the next evening. By this stage, though, I was busy in the village, distracted by what had taken place that morning and feeling pretty fraught by the developments that seemed to be sweeping me along, and over which I had no control.

Later that day I received a phone call from the AOC to say I would be required at Stadium Australia that night at about 10.00 to rehearse the opening ceremony. My heart leapt into my throat: perhaps I would be lighting the cauldron after all. I then realised I would be unable to attend the concert performance by the internationally renowned tenor Andrea Bocelli, who was performing at the Opera House. I had asked my friend Brad Cooper to arrange tickets for me and agreed to meet him there, but had warned him I would be wearing my torch relay outfit as there wouldn't be time to change. That didn't really matter because in Sydney at that time you could wear the torch relay uniform anywhere and not be out of place—it was like taking a little bit of the Games with you. I was really disappointed to miss out on Bocelli, although I wouldn't have missed the opening ceremony rehearsal for the world. I felt I was being carried along on a tide of organisational details about which I knew nothing until a short time before. I felt powerless, excited, a bit feverish and completely beholden to the powers that be.

I had been told I was to travel into Sydney for the torch relay in the early evening with Pat Rafter who was also a torchbearer. Pat, a lovely man, would be running at the Opera House and we were to catch a water taxi together from the wharf at Homebush Bay. It was impossible to travel into the city by car because the crowds were reportedly already enormous and most streets had been blocked off to private vehicles. I'd been in the village all day working with the athletes and had only just enough time to change into my uniform before joining Dawn-Lorraine and my security person, Paul, who would go with me to meet Pat and his minder at the wharf. It had already been quite a day: an invitation to go on a date with Mr Samaranch, an instruction to go to an opening ceremony rehearsal, and now the torch relay which I was really looking forward to despite all the early hitches. I was a little apprehensive about the crowds and was very glad I had Paul with me. Memories of the chaos at the Atlanta relay were running through my head and I wanted to avoid another experience like that. Halfway up the harbour, however, our water taxi broke down, which wasn't especially promising, and we were stranded with little time left. It was going to take fifteen to twenty minutes to get another one to us, so Paul, thinking quickly, rang the water police, who came and took us all into the city just in time.

Carrying the torch in front of all those happy, cheering people in my home city was a great experience, although the crowds were surging forward and it was a bit hairy for a few moments. I thought about Uluru and how far the torch had come to arrive here in the heart of Sydney. The contact could not have been more powerful, just as it had been in Uluru. I stopped to let children touch the torch, and for a moment even did a swap with a little girl who had made one out of cardboard and cellophane. Eventually I had an emotional hug with swimmer and old friend Murray Rose, to whom I handed the flame with a, 'Go and enjoy yourself mate!' Murray and I were part of the sequence that culminated in the great golfer Karrie Webb lighting the community cauldron at the Sydney Town Hall.

As soon as I was finished with the torch relay we were out of there. Paul, Dawn-Lorraine and I were escorted by police to a quiet street nearby from where the hire car drove us down to the Regent Hotel, where all the IOC delegates were staying. I had a quiet dinner with some friends and then hurriedly got myself over to Homebush.

When I arrived at Stadium Australia I was ushered into a room and found myself with Raelene Boyle, Betty Cuthbert, Debbie

Flintoff-King, Shane Gould and Shirley Strickland. We looked at each other slightly bemused but also excited, wondering which of us would light the cauldron. One of the directors of the opening ceremony then explained to us how the relay in the stadium would honour the legendary women athletes of Australia, and exactly what part each of us would play. Still we weren't told the name of the person who would take the torch and light the cauldron. We all talked about it and speculated on who it might be. Raelene said she knew who it was because of her television job with Channel 7, but she wouldn't let on. I think I knew by then that it wasn't going to be me, and to say I didn't mind would be a lie. I was let down, hurt, sad, and disappointed after the years of speculation that had gone on around me. Still, it was never going to be anyone's right to light it, and there was nothing I could have done to help my cause, so I couldn't have any regret. It wasn't going to be me and I had to accept that decision and get on with it. I wished I'd known earlier, and I wished I hadn't had to endure the years of conjecture, but that's not how it works.

We did a rehearsal that evening which lasted for a few hours and we were fitted with our uniforms, given our shoes and underwear and shown our positions on the track around the stadium. We each walked the course we'd take the following night and then wearily departed.

My instructions for meeting Juan Antonio Samaranch prior to the Olympic Games opening ceremony were that a car would pick me up from the village and take me to a specific gate at the Stadium, where I would be met by Mr Samaranch and his minders. I got there a little early. Paul was with me and we were told to wait until they were ready. Mr Samaranch arrived on time with his security people and all the most senior Olympic officials from Australia, including John Coates and Michael Knight, and their wives. Even though everyone was hovering, Mr Samaranch pulled me aside and we had a few quiet, private words. He thanked me for accepting his invitation at short notice and explained that his wife was very ill. I knew that she had been unable to come to Australia due to her illness, but now he told me she had just been taken to hospital. I expressed how sorry I was to hear that, and then we talked about how we were looking forward to the evening. I was struck by his strength under the circumstances and I wished for his sake that he didn't have to be there. He had put his position ahead of his family but planned to go home as soon as he could to be by his wife's side.

We talked together quite a bit throughout the ceremony. I asked him if he needed any help in working out some of the particularly Australian references in the opening ceremony, for instance the use of galvanised iron in the sequence about early rural days, but he had in fact read the program notes and had been well briefed beforehand. He did say that he thought it was truly a wonderful opening ceremony with some nice surprises in it, and while I know he has sat through many opening ceremonies in his time, he genuinely seemed to be very impressed.

I loved it all. I thought it was superb and Ric Birch deserves all the accolades he received. It represented so many aspects of what makes Australia unique for me. I thought the old tin sheds and the people running out with the loos on their backsides, the Victa mowers and hills hoists were inspired, and to think I'd complained to Pop all those years before about the old back-yard dunny! Now it was being honoured before a world audience and I was sitting up there, the First Lady of the Olympic Games. I wondered what Pop would have made of it all. I told Mr Samaranch that we were well known for our redback spiders on the toilet seats. He thought that was very amusing but it's probably exactly the sort of thing that certain other people dread me saying! At least Pop would have known I hadn't really left my past behind and was still calling a spade a spade.

Eventually it was time for my part in the lighting of the cauldron, and I got up and excused myself to Mr Samaranch. I hadn't told anyone that I would be playing a part, but a lot of people saw me leave, and for weeks and months afterwards I was told, 'When you left the Presidential Box, Dawn, I knew you were going to do something in the ceremony.'

When we were waiting to go onto the track for the final stage before the lighting of the cauldron I was watching from the bunker beneath the stadium and Cathy Freeman ran in wearing her opening ceremony costume. I said hello to her and she gave me a kiss before saying, 'I'm in a hurry, I have to go.' I then thought, 'It's Cathy.'

As I stood there in the dark I listened to the addresses of Michael Knight and Mr Samaranch, and then the Games being officially opened by Sir William Deane. Mr Samaranch concluded his speech by diverging from his script to say in his particular broken English, 'I thank Dawn Fraser to be with me tonight.' That was touching and I appreciated the gesture very much, at that moment more than ever.

I was disappointed to read later that John Coates had made a trip to Los Angeles in June to see Cathy and ask her to light the cauldron. This meant that when Michael Knight and John Coates had both reassured me that no one else knew who would be lighting the cauldron and that they hadn't made a decision yet, at least one other person did know and that was the crucial person. I have heard other quite credible sources say that they knew too. One of Cathy's mentors has told me she was aware of the choice, as have certain people who put the ceremony together. I don't know if they really knew or not, but Cathy certainly knew. I like Cathy very much and I don't want to take anything away from her. It's always the officials not the athletes who complicate things. Cathy was a great choice. She looked fantastic, she's young—and I'm all for the young ones coming through—and she's also a superbly talented athlete who has stood up for what she believes in despite criticism from time to time. She doesn't mind stepping on toes. For all of those reasons her role was completely fitting and I congratulate her despite my undeniable personal disappointment.

I don't remember what I felt out on the stadium waiting for the flame to arrive. Betty and Raelene took longer than anticipated, because it was apparently hard to wheel Betty's chair on the surface, and I had to start at an earlier point than was originally intended when my minder instructed me to move forward and meet them. I looked down the track and could see them coming as I stood in darkness. The crowd was very loud, but it was as if I were in my own little bubble as they came closer and we all hugged before I took the torch and held it up for the crowd. I could hear my achievements being read out in the commentary and I just started to run. I was swelling with pride and joy and I was reminded of the home crowd in 1956 when we marched into the arena. I think I floated rather than ran because it was such a buzz and so over-whelming. I handed the torch to sprinter Shirley Strickland and we embraced before she ran on to hand it to swimmer Shane Gould. Shane was making the peace sign of the dove with her hands when Shirley got to her, and then she almost bounced down the track she was so jubilant. Eventually the torch was handed to Cathy by the last bearer, Debbie Flintoff-King, and by then we were all onstage to watch Cathy run up that expanse of stairs and light the cauldron in a pool of water beneath the waterfall. It was haunting and dramatic as she held the torch out to create a ring of flame, and I felt a surge of immense pride in being Australian as I watched. The next moments were pretty terrible, though, as the cauldron stalled on its ascent to the top of the spire on which it would sit for the following fortnight, and we started to ask each other if it was indeed stuck. I was also getting a bit concerned for Cathy, because when the cauldron had bounced back down onto its stand and stayed there she had been doused with water. Later, after the cauldron had safely made it to the top and we were all standing together on the track, I grabbed a jacket from a volunteer to put around Cathy because she was so wet and cold. I started to try and warm her up by rubbing her arms because she was shivering uncontrollably, probably partly due to the cold and partly due to the intensity of having stood there for so long waiting for the cauldron to rise. It may have spoiled the tableau of us all in blue and white to have Cathy in a jacket, but it seemed pretty silly to have one of our finest athletes soaking wet in the cold night air less than two weeks before the most important race of her life.

Soon after the cauldron was lit I walked back around the arena with the other women, waving to the crowd, and went up to the Australian team in the centre of the arena to hug a few of the athletes and spend a few moments with them. Then I returned to the dressing-rooms at the stadium to find my suitcase missing. This put a bit of a damper on the evening, although I found out later it had been moved to a safer spot by security!

By the time I walked from the dungeon downstairs back up to the Presidential Box, the official party had left, and so I made my own way back to my car with Paul and we went to the apartment where I was living at Homebush next to the village. I had a few drinks with my friend Chalky and his family before heading back into the village for the night. I had to get up early the next day for the start of the swimming and nothing was going to keep me from seeing that.

•

Overall I felt our swimming team performed very well and I greatly enjoyed being with them throughout their competition. There were, of course, a few disappointments in the team but those who wanted to win medals badly enough won them and those without the experience or application missed out: it's that simple to my mind. Grant Hackett's 1500 metres swim was one of the highlights for me. I had wanted him to win and thought he turned on an amazing performance. Ian Thorpe's 400 metres was a great swim, as was the men's relay. I thought Susie O'Neill's swim in the freestyle was certainly the better of her two swims, and I think that if she'd trained harder for the freestyle she would have eclipsed the world record. She had done most of her training for the butterfly and I was sad that she didn't win gold back to back because I thought she was the better swimmer but just didn't get there on the day. I thought Leisel Jones gave an outstanding performance for a fourteen-year-old. To think that she had the finesse to say to her a coach a week out that by this time the following week she was going to be famous! That's not being egotistical, that's believing in yourself and having the confidence to fulfil your dreams. To have that sort of determination at the age of fourteen, to go through the hurt and pain that it takes to win a medal, impressed me enormously. I was disappointed in a few of our medley and butterfly swimmers. I was disappointed in Michael Klim's 100 metres butterfly, but as they so often say, it wasn't to be on the day.

The day after the opening ceremony I was attending the men's triathlon when I was informed by Thomas Bach, one of the IOC members from Germany, that Mr Samaranch had been called back to Barcelona where his wife had taken a turn for the worse and was now gravely ill. Mr Samaranch had asked me to accompany him to the swimming on the following Monday night and now he wouldn't be able to attend. Very sadly, he missed seeing his wife by a few hours, as she had already passed away by the time he arrived. He returned to Sydney with his daughter, who would accompany him for the rest of the Games. It was good for her to be with her father for the rest of the fortnight and I admired their public solidarity and composure. I believe Mr Samaranch showed great strength. He had asked Thomas Bach to tell me about the memorial service that would be held for Mrs Samaranch in Sydney and naturally I attended, although something quite unpleasant happened to me at the service, which I found upsetting but not entirely surprising.

I was sitting in the front pew with Sir William and Lady Deane when a very senior IOC official came and said to me, 'You're not meant to be here, so move.' I had been taken down to the pew by the usher and would never have presumed to find my own seat in the front row. Having been shown there, however, I wasn't about to move, and certainly not to obey such an out of place order. I didn't move but someone in the next row leaned forward and said to the IOC official, 'No, that's where she's supposed to be sitting.' To think that competition and petty rivalry goes on even at something as sad and solemn as a memorial service.

I later spent an evening at the swimming with MariaTeresa, Mr Samaranch's daughter, and I was able to catch up with Mr Samaranch again during and after the Games. He held a small private dinner at his hotel, the Regent, and I was invited to attend with Dawn-Lorraine, Cathy Freeman and her lovely husband Sandy, Mr and Mrs Coates, Mr and Mrs Knight, the Gospers and some others. It was a very happy and enjoyable evening.

I had a wonderful time during the Games and attended as many events as I could. The beach volleyball was a big highlight for me, as it was for so many people. Being down there on Bondi Beach watching such exciting performances was stunning. I felt very sorry for the Brazilian women, who were the world champions. Every time I walked into the stands, one of the Brazilian volleyball players bowed to me and acknowledged my arrival, which was unbelievably humbling. The first day we arrived she threw me a T-shirt and I looked around to see who it was supposed to have gone to. Dawn-Lorraine looked at me in exasperation and said, 'Mum, I think she's giving it to you.' I was surprised and honoured. When the Brazilians beat the second Australian team Dawn-Lorraine and I had to subdue our excitement and just applaud gently and appropriately. Naturally we wanted Australia to win but I also had great respect for the Brazilians because they'd gone unbeaten for so long. Ultimately the final was a tremendous match and there was no shame for Brazil in coming second. Everyone in the stands was completely inspired and both countries were given a standing ovation for their true spirit of sportsmanship.

I also went to the boxing, which I found a bit disappointing. I believe our team had a lot of commitments with Oceania competitions leading up to the Games, but still I would have liked to see them do better. I walked into the boxing one day and the audience all started cheering. I was told later that no one knew who to cheer for between the two overseas countries competing at the time, but when I walked in they thought, 'OK, we'll go for Dawn instead.' I received warm applause quite a bit when I turned up to events during the Games. I was quite taken aback by my reception at various venues and I want to thank everyone who did that for me right here. It really warmed my heart.

One of the personal highlights of the Games was getting to know our Governor-General and his wife, Sir William and Lady Deane. They are the most charming and gracious people, and I was fortunate enough to enjoy their company on many occasions through the Games. Lady Deane kept saying, 'Please, Dawn, call us Helen and Bill,' and I'd say, 'Thank you very much but I can't do that.' I had too much respect for them. They were delightful people who involved themselves in the Games so joyfully and made everyone around them feel warm and relaxed. One night when I was their host at the swimming pool I asked them if they'd like to come down onto the deck. I wanted to show them what went on down there with our swimmers warming up and generally getting ready for competition. The two of them were truly interested in the whole spectacle of the swimming and seemed to have an almost romantic view of the challenges the young swimmers had ahead. I liked that because I still enjoy the romance of the big Olympic quest. I took them down the back stairs with their aide-de-camp and was just about to take them through the security gate to the warm-up pool when they were stopped by an official. I said, as firmly as I could but trying to smile at the same time, 'Excuse me, you can't stop these people.'

He responded, 'They don't have the right passes.'

I sidled up very close to him so I couldn't be overheard by my guests and, with an even wider smile plastered over my gritted teeth, said, 'They don't need passes. They are the Governor-General of Australia and his wife in case you haven't recognised them.'

'Oh, sorry, sorry. But they still need passes.'

I snarled, 'No they don't,' and with that I beamed at everyone and ushered them through as smoothly as I could, trying not to make it obvious that there was a problem. I doubt something like that could happen elsewhere in the world to someone of the standing of a governor-general.

All the swimmers and coaches kept coming up to be introduced and to have a photograph taken with Sir William and Lady Deane. I explained to them the different programs the swimmers were following and where they were up to in their tapering off leading up to competition. They seemed to be genuinely fascinated, and the young swimmers enjoyed talking to this wonderful couple. Every time I got an opportunity after that I would take Sir William and Lady Deane behind the scenes to show them another side of the various competitions.

Another person I spent some time with at the pool was Chelsea Clinton, the daughter of former US President Bill Clinton, who attended several sessions of the swimming with the US Ambassador to Australia. I was on the deck when she made her first visit, and she was sitting up behind me so I introduced myself. She asked me to come up and sit with her during the swimming, which I did, and we got chatting. On the evenings after that when I'd turn up at the pool she'd call out, 'Dawn! Dawn!' and wave and gesture for me to come over and sit with her. She had at one time gone out with an American swimmer and knew many of the members of the American team. I found her very pleasant company and was glad to have met her. It was probably a pretty relaxed experience for her because while she would have been made a huge fuss of in the US, in Australia we don't tend to make a fuss over our politicians' children. They are just accepted and blend in at most functions. Come to think of it, we're probably the only country where we refer to all our prime ministers by their first names— Gough and Bob for instance—and know instantly who we mean.

•

So many people who saw me constantly popping up on television during the Games have said to me, 'How did you manage it?' Well, for a start I had great drivers who took me everywhere. Every evening I would plan where I would go the next day and then brief the driver. Gary, who after the first few events became my permanent driver for the Games, would always get me very close to gates of the events so I could cut it fine. He'd always make sure he had the right accreditation on the car and even put an Australian flag on the front of the car, which was pretty cheeky because it was a privilege usually reserved for the Governor-General and the Prime Minister. But whenever we were questioned about it Gary would argue forcefully that he had Dawn Fraser in the car, Attaché to the Australian team. We didn't mean to be disrespectful, but the Australian flag got us through a few gates just in the nick of time. I didn't attend many of the cocktail parties and other official functions because, as usual, I felt my place was with the athletes, but I did get to see Cathy Freeman race and that was a great event and another highlight.

In the second week of the Games I was invited with Dawn-Lorraine to spend a few days on the *Seven Seas Navigator*, the luxury cruiser Channel 7 had moored in the harbour for entertaining VIPs during the Games. I was really still living in the village, but all my ALO work was just about wrapped up. The Sydney village was excellent as far as Olympic villages go, but it was wonderful escaping to the luxury of the ship. I had signed a contract with the AOC not to do any media commentary for the duration of the Games but I assumed that didn't extend to going onboard the ship. The evenings were fun because people would come back to the bar after a great day at the Games, compare notes about what they'd seen and have a few drinks. Then we'd all settle down to watch Roy and HG on *The Dream*.

Sydney really turned it on for the duration of the Games and it was great just to walk around and soak up the atmosphere in the streets, something I would have liked to have done more of. I was very proud of my home town for doing so well and looking so beautiful. I considered it an enormous privilege to be at the centre of all that was happening and to see so much brilliant competition close up. The Olympics is still the 'biggest and best' competition going and Sydney was as good as any Games I had ever been to.

By the final day of the Games I was absolutely exhausted, and I was thinking about staying away from the closing ceremony. This was because during the Games I'd had a bit of a security scare and Paul thought it would be easier to keep an eye on things on the ship rather than at a crowded stadium.

Earlier during the Games I'd been invited to go along to a nightclub in Kings Cross one evening for the swimmers' break-up party, where the swimmer Scotty Miller was the guest DJ. Dawn-Lorraine and I had been to watch the soccer during the late afternoon with some of our friends. We had dinner at the Sydney Football Stadium Restaurant and then, because I had a driver, I decided, quite unusually these days, to go to the nightclub before we went home. The owner of my favourite restaurant and his wife and Dawn-Lorraine came too. We were very well looked after, given a great table and promptly served some drinks. I had a security person, Rodney, with me and we all had a fair bit to drink. I didn't know at the time but my security person had spotted a man across the room watching all through the night in a rather intense way. The nightclub was filled with young swimming stars but the man only had eyes for me. The music was quite loud and it was dark inside the room, and in the midst of all the commotion the man who had been staring at me walked over to our table. When Rodney stopped him, the man said he just wanted to give me a letter, which he handed over and left. When the security company looked at the letter later that night they were sufficiently concerned to step up my security and advised me not to go to the closing ceremony. It wasn't a direct death threat—I'd had plenty of those over the years and some have been dismissed by the experts and some taken seriously. This was a strange, menacing note, and when I read it myself later it seemed to have overtones of obsession. The whole incident made me feel very uncomfortable and not very confident about going out to a huge event like the closing ceremony.

The morning after this incident I received a call from my nephew to tell me my sister Heather was in hospital after suffering a heart attack. So I spent one of the last days of the Games beside her hospital bed where she was recovering. I ultimately went to the closing ceremony, but in video footage of the event I look rather disturbed and tired, and that's exactly how I felt.

•

And now the carnival is over and Sydney is busy finding uses for the buildings and sporting facilities that remain. I think it's a shame to change Olympic sites after the Games because people, including the athletes, can no longer wander around and truly remember what it was like if the places where they marched in the opening ceremony or where they won their medal are no longer there. Tourists who didn't get to attend but saw it on television can't later

have a look at the actual venue. You lose the romance and atmosphere. I can go to Heidelberg in Melbourne now and not see a
trace of the 1956 Games, or I can go to Rome and only say, 'I
think this is where the village was'. In Los Angeles in 1984, the
day after the swimming events were concluded, they pulled the
swimming pool stadium down.

The Homebush site, on the other hand, is being largely preserved
and is now known as Olympic Park, and I was lucky enough to
have one of its streets named after me about a year before the
Games. I am thrilled that the Homebush venues will largely remain
intact so that everyone can see where it all happened. I can still go
out onto the MCG and feel quite vividly how I felt marching in
the opening ceremony in 1956, and now I can also walk into the
Homebush Stadium and remember what it was like to carry that
torch round the track in my home town. Magic!

Oi, Oi, Oi!

18

INTO THE WILD
BLUE YONDER

In many ways my life has come full circle. I am back living in the house where I was born. I'm single again. And I like having a beer with my old friends, many of whom I have known for more than five decades. I follow the football and I am very involved with the local club, which I've had a connection with ever since I was a little girl and my brothers played football for the junior Codocks side in a comp run by the Balmain Football Club. Being outspoken and refusing to give in over things I firmly believe in still occasionally puts me at odds with the sporting organisations to which I am so inextricably linked, and these skirmishes make newspaper headlines from time to time. Going fast in the water is still a passion but nowadays it's on a personal water craft, and my idea of heaven is to take off into the harbour on my PWC for a few hours. I live with the latest in a line of much-loved German shepherds, and Conrad is a beautiful boy with the most exquisitely padded paws and distinctive head markings you will ever see on a dog.

These are the common threads that have bound my years together, seeing me through many troubled times and keeping me on the roller-coaster ride that has been my life. Above all there have been family and friends. My brothers and sisters have remained at the centre of my life through everything that has happened, even though our worlds have been very different. We still all talk at least once a week and wouldn't dream of not getting together for Christmas although sometimes with disastrous results, like the year before last when between us there was a broken arm, a heart attack and a dog bite. If it had gone on any longer the ambulance would have known which way to come on its own. Without my brother Ken's urging to get me driving again after the accident in which Mum was killed, or Joyce caring for Dawn-Lorraine through my darkest days, who knows where I'd be now? As a single mother I had support and care from my brother Alick, and even when he moved out he was always there for me. Heather and Dick took me in during my swimming days and let me use their bath with hot water on more occasions than I care to remember. All my brothers and sisters have exemplified the true meaning of family and I like to look after them now that they are getting older and I have the resources to do things for them.

For the many, many friends I have mentioned throughout the pages of this book—like the Stollers, Brian and Adele, Peggy and Graeme—there have been so many others I haven't mentioned. I don't want to share all my close friendships with the public because my friends for the most part are not public people and they deserve their privacy. I am very fortunate that I have had an ability to distinguish true friends from those who are interested in me for my public profile. Clearly and sadly I haven't been able to choose lovers with the same level of clarity, but I always seem to know who my true friends are and consequently I am surrounded by some especially good ones. I keep up with my primary school friends Jill Hericks and Marilyn Moss, and I know that if we don't see each other for a few months we can always pick up where we left off. If I was bankrupt and needed a meal they would be the first ones to say come on over. And don't forget I've had a chance to test that particular theory. My dear friend Rhonda Gardiner tells me, much to my pleasure, that it also works in reverse. Although my male friends are more numerous I have a circle of great girl-friends who have stood by me through everything and certainly know more about everything than the men!

I've known Rhonda for more than forty years. Neither of us can remember exactly how we met, but we've shared lots of good and bad times. I can remember one night at the Riverview when we'd all had a bit to drink and started talking about what we would like to have been. Rhonda, who is very leggy, said she would like to have been a ballet dancer if her legs hadn't kept growing. I laughed and said something about her two left feet, which prompted her to get up, go outside and start pirouetting on the silent cop on the road outside the pub. Just then a Greyhound bus came down that narrow street and I had to crash tackle Rhonda to save her life.

We were both great supporters of the Balmain League side and when Balmain was in the Grand Final in 1969 we both went round with some of the local boys painting tiger paws all over the place, including, under cover of darkness, the wall outside the Sydney Cricket Ground. Boy did we celebrate together that night when Balmain won. First stop was the Riverview, where I rode a child's bicycle around the bar, then we took off to the Leagues Club. I went missing for a while, and Rhonda says I eventually appeared out of a cupboard riding on an electric floor polisher.

Another time I went to dinner at the home of Rhonda and her husband, Terry, with some other great friends, Paul Broughton and his wife. They came and collected me in their brand new BMW and drove us over the Iron Cove Bridge to Rhonda's place. Rhonda's brother was there that night and he suddenly looked up and asked, 'Why is there a rooster in the tree outside the bedroom where I'm going to be sleeping tonight?' Rhonda explained that it belonged to the next-door neighbours and made all sorts of terrible noise in the early hours of the morning. Later that night, as Paul backed down the driveway of the house, Rhonda's brother threw the rooster through the car window. There was a lot of loud squawking and feathers flying, and I quickly came up with the idea of taking the rooster to the house of a friend in Rozelle who kept chickens. I had to keep the rooster under Paul's coat to stop the noise and when we got to Rozelle I grabbed it out at the last minute and threw it into my friend's chicken coop. It made so much noise that we had to take off really quickly, by which time we were all laughing hysterically. The next day my friend from Rozelle came into the Riverview and explained in great detail how some stupid bastard had thrown a rooster over his fence. He said it had chased his chickens and made so much noise that it had woken all the neighbours and everyone was complaining. I believe he kept the rooster in the end and it took Paul Broughton weeks to get the feathers out of his new BMW.

Rhonda and I have had our differences over the years but we can always sort them out and speak openly if we have a problem with something the other one has done. Rhonda has been a great aunty to Dawn-Lorraine, and even sat on the step of a Chinese restaurant with her to eat dinner when she was little because I'd sent Dawn-Lorraine from the table for playing up.

John Chalk and Dickie Hunt have been constants in my life, too; friends from Balmain that I really trust and still see regularly.

Dickie, an ex–State rower from Balmain, is of course the clown who brought the snow to the Riverview, and Chalky, an ex-yachtie, is now President of the Balmain Football Club, where I am on the Board, and the Chairman of West Tigers. Recently we worked together on the Balmain–Wests merger, something that I championed for the survival of the club, but which was also an emotional wrench. Chalky and I have known each other for more than forty years. I enjoy having a beer with Chalky more than with anyone else, and in many ways he is like family.

Bev Whitfield, who won a gold medal in Munich for breast-stroke, was one of the greatest friends anyone could ever have. I loved her very much and her death in 1996 really hit me hard. Jack Stanistreet was a wonderful friend to me before he moved back to Hobart to be with his family and we lost touch. Singo, of course, doesn't need another mention, and nor does John Marriott, who is always there for me too. My country friends have become a great part of my life, and will even more so as I spend more time there. Conversely, though, one of the reasons why I love going to the farm is because I have no immediate neighbours. That probably sounds strange coming from a city girl who has lived in a high-density suburb all her life, but as I grow older I find I like solitude and peace more and more. Perhaps it's because I've led such a crowded and busy life.

Brad Cooper has been a brilliant friend in more recent years and he kindly put me up for months while my home was being renovated. When Tammy did her swim in Manhattan, Brad, who had an interest in the St Moritz Hotel opposite Central Park, put me up free of charge in the hotel's penthouse, which was absolutely glorious and filled with Louis XIV furniture. I came to know Brad's mother, Pat, as well while I was in New York and I have remained close to her. They both came to a cocktail party I threw for Tammy after her swim, to which we invited the Australian Ambassador in New York at the time, Michael Baume. I love Brad's flamboyance and generosity. Although he is very wealthy and successful he never puts on side, and I like that. Even without all the trappings, he would still be brimming with ideas and suggestions about fun things to do.

I realise I have been attracted to flamboyance all my life. Gary was flamboyant, and so are Dickie, Rhonda and Singo. I see a bit of it in me, too, when I look back at images of myself hamming it up on swimming blocks, giving the media cheek and swanning off planes in ridiculous dark glasses during my Olympic years. That sort of behaviour spices up life—as long as you can laugh at yourself and know when you're really bunging it on.

There are several other friends I haven't spoken about who are just as important to me and some of them are just as flamboyant, but to name every one and all the great times we've had together would require a second volume.

As soon as this book is published I plan to take off around Australia with friends, following the old cattle trails. I want to see as much of the country as I can and take a good, long hard-earned break. I'm taking my own 4WD car that my sponsor Nissan has specially prepared for me and plan to meander off on my own when I want to. I can't remember having this sort of absolutely pressure-free time since my two-day trek from Adelaide to Sydney on my motor scooter in 1959. It's been a long time between drinks, as they say. Speaking of which, we're going to take some good red wine and camp out in the open as much as possible on our journey. At other times we'll stay at nice hotels and motels. I'm lucky enough to stay at the best hotels for my work—I even had a baby grand piano in my two-storey suite when I was in Bali for business recently—so camping outdoors has a far greater appeal at this point, although I'm sure a hot shower and a proper bed will beckon every now and then. I think overall the journey will take about six months, and I have no intention of leaving the mobile switched on, that's for sure.

I have just started to play golf again and intend to try get my handicap down to nine again to keep up with Rhonda, who is already there. In February 1999 I had a game with Greg Norman when we were fundraising for the Australian Olympic team, and although I was nervous and hit a few terrible shots, I found I could still play a passable game. I've been playing a few corporate days for Nissan, and that too has made me keen to take it up again.

The next Olympic Games come around in 2004, and I'm hoping that I will be invited to Athens to work with our athletes, health permitting. I will be sixty-seven, and even though I'm against some of the older officials I think ex-athletes still have much to offer. I would never want to be a hindrance or a burden, but while I can get around I want to go on working in this area. I had hoped, up until quite recently, that I would be offered a proper serious role with the AOC, or, even more ambitiously, with the IOC. I'm not sure what it could be, but I guess something along the lines of an ambassadorial role would be perfect. I like fundraising and whipping up enthusiasm for events and causes. Part of me, however, doesn't want to be involved any longer because I have grown tired of the politics taking up as much time as the development of sport. As well as this, I have had to wait too long since that lunch many years ago after David McKenzie died when I was told that if I stood back for the time being the job would come up later. Along the ever-busy grapevine I have heard that certain people in high places will never allow me to take up such a role because I cannot be relied upon to vote in an appropriate way and help make up numbers if I don't believe in something. Basically, I'm too unpredictable and it makes people nervous. I am not, and never have been, a 'yes' person.

Meanwhile, I have plenty to keep me busy. I'm now in my third year of a three-year term on the Board of the Sydney Cricket Ground Trust. I always wanted to be a member of the Sydney Cricket Ground but as a single mum I wasn't able to join because the fee was beyond me. To be asked by the then Minister for Sport and Recreation in New South Wales, Gabrielle Harrison, to become a member of the Trust was a dream come true. I find the monthly meetings very interesting and have been made very welcome by the rest of the Board. I'm now on the Homebush Aquatic and Athletic Committee as well as on the Maintenance Committee for the Sydney Sports Ground and the Cricket Ground Trust. I find it fascinating to see how the grounds are run and I am learning the finances of the organisation.

I am careful about what I take on. I get offered a lot of opportunities to join boards and committees but I only work on those where I think I can make a difference and those that really interest me. I am the patron of the Cerebral Palsy Sport and Recreation Association in New South Wales and I am patron of the Wheelchair Sports Association in Victoria. I have always taken an interest in supporting disabled athletes, and most recently worked as an Athlete Liaison Officer at the Sydney 2000 Paralympic Games. Each year I give a Dawn Fraser Award for the most outstanding male and female athletes in the Cerebral Palsy Sport and Recreation Association. Just working with these people who really have a hard time in life pulls you up short and makes you realise how bloody lucky you are. It is also a thrill to do something that is really appreciated by the recipients, who don't otherwise get very much from the system.

A couple of years ago Sport Industry Australia, which used to be the Confederation of Australian Sport, asked me if they could name an award after me, and I agreed but it has taken a while to work out the criteria. The award was presented for the first time in March 2001 to Karrie Webb, the superb young golfer from Brisbane who has won just about everything before her around the world. The night I presented that award, at a presentation dinner in Adelaide, was the night after Sir Donald Bradman died. There we were in his home town establishing a new sporting award, and it occurred to me that new, young, talented sportspeople will always come through and achieve as the older ones start to pass into memory.

Having had a few heart attacks and scares with my health I have thought about dying, and I would be lying if I said I wasn't afraid of old age and death. I want to be around to see my daughter establish her life with a loving partner, and I would love some grandchildren. I adore children, and although my daughter is dearer to me than my own life, I regret that I didn't have more, especially having come from such a big family myself. I would have liked Dawn-Lorraine to have a sibling, although her friend Narelle fills that role better than a sister might have. I guess it would have meant forgoing other aspects of my life which have been especially fulfilling, and I don't really believe in looking back with regret. I have tended to move forward and live in the present and future rather than dwell on the past—which is probably just as well given what I could have spent the rest of my life regretting.

In 1998 I received an Order of Australia (AO) in recognition of my contributions to the environment, sport and disabled sportspeople. Despite receiving an MBE in 1967, along with numerous other awards from overseas, this truly Australian honour had eluded me for years, so I was very pleased to receive the Order of Australia when it came. Recognition in my own country is more important to me than anything else.

I continue to try to work hard for my sponsors Nissan, FAI Home Security Systems and, more recently, Kellogg. Through Kellogg, I have become involved in the junior surf lifesaving movement. It is very community based these days and I enjoy getting down there on the beach and mixing with the kids, parents, grandparents, aunties and uncles. Once the kids are trained in surf lifesaving they can put so much back into the community and I believe the program helps to make them responsible citizens. At the same time, it bothers me when I see kids being pushed and shoved into doing it. When left alone to learn and participate at their own pace these children do better. They're not naturally aggressive towards each other, and can be encouraged to work well together as long as they're given the chance. Even when competing they have to learn to respect their opponents and those around them organising the competition.

I get a lot out of my time spent with the nippers but taking part in those sorts of activities often presents a particular problem for me—in fact it's one that impinges on every part of my life because I have such a recognisable face. If I go to a surf carnival and a nipper comes up and asks for my autograph I can't possibly say yes, because I'll be asked for thousands more in a day and that's not what I'm there to do. Besides, I can't possibly be fair in a situation like that so it's better to say no to all requests.

There are other times when I'm out having an intimate dinner with friends, and someone will come up to our table just as we're about to eat and ask for an autograph and a photograph. It even happens in my neighbourhood, where I'm a pretty familiar figure. I shop for a few old people in my area and sometimes I'll say to one of the old ladies, 'I'll just duck down the street and buy you some lunch, love.' I've been known to come back three hours later with a cold pie! Sir Donald Bradman dealt with it by guarding his privacy fiercely and by becoming something of a recluse, but I'm a very gregarious person and couldn't possibly take that path.

The other thing I find difficult about being asked for my autograph is the way people come up close and touch me. Physical contact with strangers is something I've been uncomfortable with for a long time. Maybe it has something to do with being assaulted years ago, or maybe it's because of the menacing letters and death threats I've received throughout my life—they don't exactly make you feel open and trusting of strangers. I get very jittery when someone I don't know approaches me in a crowd with something concealed in a bag. Having anything pushed in front of me encroaches on my space and makes me very anxious, especially when I'm in crowds. People constantly give me T-shirts to sign with a hard surface underneath and I find myself wondering what that hard surface is. I have developed a habit of stepping back if I don't know what I'm being confronted with and just saying I can't sign today. Of course if a kid comes up wearing a T-shirt they'd like me to sign I'm happy to do it. I know there's just a little body under the T-shirt and that's OK.

People send literally hundreds of packages a week with precious things for me to sign, most of them without return envelopes. Some come to me via various sporting organisations with which I don't have any connection. The trouble is, as I'm far from retired yet, I don't have nearly enough time to respond to all these things. I end up getting letters asking why I haven't returned precious memorabilia with my signature, and sometimes I haven't even seen the object they are asking me to return. It can get very embarrassing.

Sir Donald Bradman spent a large part of his life keeping up with his fan mail, and I applaud his efforts and dedication, but because I'm still such an active person, helping to fundraise, speaking to hundreds of groups a year and acting as a patron to so many different organisations, I just don't have the time. I do, however, happily give my autograph on appropriate occasions at appropriate times, and perhaps if I get anywhere near Sir Donald's age before he died I will sit at home and answer my fan mail, but I doubt I'd have his patience!

By talking about the issues and problems I have with being well known, I hope it doesn't sound as if I'm complaining about the Australian public. I have been treated exceptionally well over the years by the Australian people and I love my fellow countrymen. There's nothing better than being overseas and hearing, 'G'day, Dawnie. Howya going?' It was the public at the airport in Adelaide after I was first banned in 1961 who lifted my spirits, and it was the Australian public in Melbourne in 1956 who helped me win at and enjoy my best Games ever. When the ASU were really getting at me I was always treated well by the people on the street. Connecting with the public and being supported by the public has been a cherished part of my life for which I owe a lot, and in that sense I hope to be able to continue to serve in many useful ways for many years to come.

For now, though, as I get ready to head off into the sunset and travel around our beautiful country, Dawn-Lorraine and Conrad beside me, I'm looking forward to vast open spaces, pearly white beaches, star-filled skies, rugged mountains and rainforests. My beloved country. This will be the fulfilment of a dream that first formed when Donnie gave me that globe pencil sharpener for Christmas. I look forward now to a promising future, having reflected deeply, and often painfully, on what has gone before and having realised it has been in so many ways, one hell of a life, and I'm still here smiling.

ACKNOWLEDGMENTS

When I finally decided I wanted to write my autobiography I knew I would need some help piecing my life story together and getting my words down on paper because it was such a daunting task to undertake in any year, let alone that of the Sydney Olympics.

Originally my daughter, Dawn-Lorraine, was going to write the book with me because I felt I could tell her painful and difficult things from my life in a way I couldn't tell them to anyone else. Unfortunately Dawn-Lorraine became unwell early on and has spent considerable time in hospital during the past year, making it impossible for her to take on the enormous job of completing the book by the deadline.

At that point I asked my agent, Deborah Callaghan, if she would step in, even though that wasn't what she thought she was getting herself into when she first helped me find a publisher for my book. Thankfully, however, she agreed. Together we taped my words and those of friends and associates over many, many months before beginning the process of writing. Deb gradually wrote the story from the tapes while I checked and rewrote what she'd written, and so on until the words were exactly as I wanted them to be.

While we were working on the book Dawn-Lorraine was there for me as much as she could be, helping to keep other parts of my schedule running, prompting my memory, and reading several drafts of what you finally have before you. I couldn't have done this without her love and support, not to mention the endless cups of coffee, lunches, and the surprise birthday party she prepared while my story was being taped and written. Thanks, Gidg!

My agent, Deb, worked tirelessly on the book when she herself had just become a new mother. She put up with the good, the bad and the ugly and still kept coming back for more. I couldn't have completed the book without her and I thank her for sticking with it when the going got tough. Thanks to Rory and Rosie, too, for sharing her with me.

My mate John Singleton has helped me through some very difficult times and has been a wonderful friend for so many years. I am honoured that he has written the foreword for this book and I am deeply touched by his words. Thanks for everything, Singo.

I also want to thank a few special people in my life who help me keep everything going along smoothly:

Trent Nathan is one of them. He makes all my business and evening clothes and when I wear them I always feel especially well dressed and comfortable. The past year has brought with it quite a few special dress requirements and Trent has always managed to give me what I have needed. He is also a dear friend and, somewhere along the line, we're related.

Brad Cooper invited me to stay with him for several months while my house was being renovated and much of the book was taped in the glorious surrounds of his home. I always felt welcome and I greatly value our friendship and business association.

John Chalk, a mate for many years, was as rock solid as ever during what has been a very demanding time for me as well as for him. He was always there to share a beer or two and be a saving familiar face and comforting shoulder.

There are many people who have helped me by sharing their memories and answering fact-checking questions. I thank them all for their generosity and patience. Rose, Joyce, Heather, Ken, Chookie and Alick helped enormously and put up with endless phone calls seeking out little details from our lives: 'Are you *sure* no one can remember the cocky's name?' and 'Who *is* that man in Rosie's wedding photo?'

Phil Coles, a good friend, particularly helped by loaning me his meticulously kept scrapbooks from the time of the Moscow Games, as well as filling in blanks on all things Olympic.

Rhonda 'Gard' O'Connor told tales from our friendship of more than forty years and so did Adele and Brian Johnson. I'm glad you were all as crazy as me.

Dr Alan and Joan Stoller helped me reconstruct the period of my life when they came to my rescue, and I will never, ever underestimate what they did for me back in 1964.

Harry Gallagher was taped on several occasions and I was delighted to find that we agreed almost all the time on the facts of our intricately entwined careers!

Jon Henricks, Harry Gordon, Jan Andrew, Stuart Alldritt, John Devitt, Sue Hogan, Vena Murray, Tammy van Wisse, John Singleton, John Chalk, Ruth Everuss, John Marriott, Col Joye, Howard Toyne and Tim Konz were all interviewed for the book. Thank you all.

Jack Gandy and his wife, Joan, served the best seafood lunch and helped me remember the details of some distressing parts of my life as well as some great times in the Jet Bar. Thanks, Jack and Joan.

Sue Hogan needs special mention for bringing her exceptional research skills to the project and tracking down some almost impossible to find documents, as does Penny Chalk for transcribing the tapes. Stuart Alldritt responded quickly and graciously when called upon to check records, and I thank him.

Thanks to my sponsors, Leon Daphne of Nissan Australia, Mohamed Elsarky of Kellogg, and Brad Cooper from FAI Home

Security, for their ongoing support and for working around my book-writing schedule. I look forward to our continuing relationships.

Many of the photographs on these pages were taken by the late Ken Rainsbury who I adored as a friend and who was a wonderful photographer. His son, Ken Rainsbury Jnr, kindly allowed me to use the photographs in the book. Thank you both. Roslyn Donnelly, an old friend from Adelaide, also sent photographs from the late 1950s which appear here and brought back many happy memories when I first saw them.

I also thank the rest of my family, all my nieces and nephews and cousins, who are not mentioned above, for their support over the years and the special part they have played and continue to play in my life.

Finally I want to thank Lisa Highton and Mary Drum at Hodder Headline for believing so strongly in this project, as well as their team, Fiona Lincoln, Pauline McGuire, Romina Chapnik, Dianne Murdoch, Brett Woods, Jo Matches and Andy Palmer, for all their dedicated work in bringing my book to life!

With great trepidation I now hand it over to you, the reader. Enjoy!

Dawn Fraser, AO, MBE, JP
April 2001

BIBLIOGRAPHY

Around Balmain, The Balmain Association, Sydney, 1986.

Australia's Olympic Century, Pan Macmillan Australia, Sydney, 1998.

Clarkson, A., *Lanes of Gold: 100 Years of the NSW Amateur Swimming Association*, Lester-Townsend Publishing on behalf of the NSW Amateur Swimming Association, Sydney, 1990.

Fraser, D. & Howard Murdoch, L., *Our Dawn: A Pictorial Biography*, Sally Milner Publishing, Sydney, 1991.

Fraser, D. & Gordon, H., *Gold Medal Girl: The Confessions of an Olympic Champion*, Lansdowne Press, Melbourne, 1965.

Gallagher, H., *Memories of a Fox*, Wakefield Press, Adelaide, 1998.

Gordon, H., *Australia and the Olympic Games*, University of Queensland Press, Brisbane, 1994.

Gourlie, W., *Gourlie's Corner: Growing Up in Balmain* (eds. Kath & Val Hamey), The Balmain Association, Sydney, 1992.

Knox, K., *The Dawn of Swimming*, Stanley Paul, London, 1962.

Lawrence, J. & Warne, C., *A Pictorial History of Balmain to Glebe*, Kingsclear Books, Sydney, 1995.

1937 Born 4 September 1937

1941 Learns to swim, aged four

1943 Starts Birchgrove Primary

1945 Joins Balmain/Leichhardt League of Swimmers

1946 Attends first swimming carnival, Broken Hill

1949
- Starts Riverside then Leichhardt secondary school
- Joins Balmain Amateur Swimming Club
- Banned from taking part in amateur races

1950 Reinstated as amateur by ASU

1951
- Meets Harry Gallagher (HG)
- Starts training with HG
- Brother Donnie dies, aged 21

1952 Leaves school, starts work at clothing factory

1953
- Melbourne Winter Championships
- '53/'54 first State Championships (NSW) at North Sydney

1954 National Championships, Melbourne

1955
- First gold medal at Nationals in Adelaide
- Moves to Adelaide to train with HG
- '55/'56 State Championships (SA)

1956
- National Championships in Sydney (two world records)—makes Olympic team
- Melbourne Olympics (two gold, one silver, two world records)

1957 First overseas trip, to Honolulu for competition, tours US

1958
- National Championships, Melbourne (two world records)
- Empire & Commonwealth Games, Cardiff (two gold, two silver, world record)
- Travels through Europe attending French & Dutch championships and visiting Germany & Austria

1959
- Gets hepatitis
- National Championships, Hobart (two world records)

1960
- National Championships, Sydney (three world records)
- Gets engaged to Ken Robinson
- Rome Olympics (one gold, two silver)

1961
- National Championships, Brisbane
- Subject to unofficial ban from international competition
- Helms Award USA
- Returns to Sydney to care for Pop Fraser, who dies at Christmas

1962
- National Championships, Melbourne
- Ban is unofficially lifted
- Commonwealth Games trials—breaks the minute for 100m freestyle (59.9)
- Commonwealth Games, Perth (four gold)
- ABC Sportsman of the Year
- Babe Zaharias trophy for Female Athlete of the Year

1964
- National Championships, Sydney (world record 58.9)
- Nana Fraser killed in car accident
- Buys Balmain house
- Trains in Townsville, helped by Stumpy Lawrence
- Gets engaged to Gary Ware
- Tokyo Olympics (one gold, one silver, world record), 3rd successive gold for same event (100m freestyle)
- Flag incident
- Australian of the Year Award

1965
- Marries Gary Ware, honeymoon in Tahiti
- 10-year ban on return
- Inducted into International Swimming Hall of Fame, Florida
- Dawn-Lorraine born 15 December

1966
- Tours Japan for Sterling Swimwear
- Separates from Gary Ware

1967
- Takes up coaching at Prince Alfred Park Pool
- Awarded MBE

1968
- Divorce final
- Mexico Olympics (DF invited and does unofficial swim in close to gold medal time)
- Wins action against Bill Berge Phillips
- ASU ban lifted
- Wins action against the *Sun* newspaper

1972
- Visits International Swimming Hall of Fame, Florida, for dedication ceremony
- Munich Olympics

1975
ABC Award for Australia's Best Sportsperson for the Last 25 Years (1951–1975)

1976
- Montreal Olympics
- Starts Dawn Fraser Cheese Shop

1978
- Becomes licensee of Riverview Hotel

1979
- Premiere of *Dawn!*, film made by Joy Cavill

1980
Campaigns against Malcolm Fraser's plan to boycott Moscow Olympics—visits as guest of USSR

1981
Awarded IOC Silver Order at Baden Baden

1983
Accident at Riverview, breaks neck, loses lease on pub

1984
- Los Angeles Olympics—attends with John Singleton
- Balmain Baths renamed Dawn Fraser Pool

1985
- Masters Games, Toronto
- First Australian woman to be inducted into the American Women's Sports Foundation Hall of Fame
- Inducted into the Sport Australia Hall of Fame

1986
- Attends World Masters Swimming Championships, Tokyo (1 gold, 5 silver)

1988
- Attends North Queensland Games
- Elected as Independent member for Balmain to NSW State Parliament
- Seoul Olympics—attends as Ambassador for the Australian Bicentennial Authority
- Voted Australia's greatest female athlete

1990
Declared a National Living Treasure

1991
- Loses seat in State Parliament
- Elected to Board of NRMA

1992
- Barcelona Olympics—attends as Athlete Liaison Officer
- Buys property near Barellan in the Riverina

1995
- President of Sport Australia Hall of Fame
- Testimonial lunch

1996
- Undiagnosed first heart attack
- Atlanta Olympics—DF in torch relay—second heart attack

1998
- Awarded AO
- Diagnosed with diabetes

1999
World Female Swimmer of the Century Award, Vienna

2000
- Resigns as President of Sport Australia Hall of Fame
- Sydney Olympics—DF part of torch relay/opening ceremony
- Declared First Lady of the Sydney Olympics; Attaché to Australian Olympic Team

2001
- Karrie Webb wins inaugural Dawn Fraser Award at Australian Sports Awards
- *Dawn: One Hell of a Life* published

DAWN FRASER'S SPORTING ACHIEVEMENTS

- 30 Australian championships; 27 individual world records; 12 relay world records
- **Eight Olympic medals** *Four gold*: Melbourne, 1956 (100m freestyle, 4x100m freestyle relay); Rome, 1960 (100m freestyle); Tokyo, 1964 (100m freestyle) *Four silver*: Melbourne, 1956 (400m freestyle); Rome, 1960 (4x100m freestyle relay, 4x100m medley relay); Tokyo, 1964 (4x100m freestyle relay)
- **Eight Commonwealth medals** *Six gold*: Cardiff, 1958 (110yds freestyle, 4x110yds freestyle relay); Perth, 1962 (110yds freestyle, 440yds freestyle, 4x110yds freestyle relay, 4x110yds medley relay) *Two silver*: Cardiff, 1958 (440yds freestyle, 4x110yds medley relay)

YARDAGE/METRIC IN SWIMMING

At the general meeting of FINA during 1968 all reference to yardage distances in swimming competitions was annulled. Only metric distance events are now sanctioned and for record performances all applications must therefore be submitted for metric measurement. Yardage records set in 55-yard pools prior to 1968 are retained and recognised. Most yardage pools where national, State and international competition took place prior to 1968 have been altered to provide metric length, i.e. 55 yards reduced to 50 metres.

During the years that Dawn Fraser was competing in 55-yard pools she established both world records for yardage and metric distance in the same race; e.g., if the world record for 100 metres freestyle was, say, 1:02.30 and the world record for 110 yards was, say, 1:03.00 and Dawn's attempt or competitive swim in a 55-yard pool was timed at 1:02.10 then she would be awarded a world record for the metric and another for the imperial distance! So the time was better than both the metric and yardage records.

The many references to yardage or metric distances in *Dawn* throw up what appear to be anomalies. Generally pools in Europe have always been metric but many English-speaking countries, e.g. Australia, were yardage. The Olympic Games have always been metric except for some events in 1896.

The only metric pool in Australia during the Fraser era was the Valley Pool in Brisbane. The 1956 Melbourne Olympic Pool was constructed 55 yards long, but a false end was placed temporarily to make the length 50 metres for the Games. Afterwards the false end was removed to maintain 55 yards.

Stuart W. Alldritt
Life Member and Australian Selector
Honorary Records Office of Australian Swimming

PHOTO CREDITS

(DF = Dawn Fraser)

Jacket
Front cover: DF after winning her third consecutive gold medal in the 100m freestyle in Tokyo (DF); back cover: DF at the Sydney Olympic torch relay (DF); back cover flap: DF at the World Sports Awards (DF); spine: DF at the Sydney Olympic opening ceremony (News Ltd).

Endpapers
A selection of photographs by Ken Rainsbury Snr.

Chapter openers
1. DF at World Sports Awards (DF); 2. DF aged three (DF); 3. Donnie (courtesy of Channel 7 Australia); 4. DF with Mum before setting off for the Melbourne Olympics (Ken Rainsbury Snr); 5. (L–R) DF, chaperone Dot Quinton, Unknown, Lorraine Crapp and Mickey Rooney in the middle (DF); 6. DF in the pool (Australian Picture Library/ Corbis); 7. DF with Pop Fraser (courtesy of Channel 7 Australia); 8. DF with Rajah (DF); 9. DF on winners' podium, Sharon Stouder and Kathy Ellis (courtesy of Channel 7 Australia); 10. SMH headline (Ken Rainsbury Snr); 11. DF returning from Florida for a dedication in the Swimming Hall of Fame, 1973 (The Fairfax Photo Library); 12. Riverview Hotel, Balmain, 1960 (Noel Butlin Archives Centre, Australian National University, Tooth & Co Ltd, N60/Yellow Cards. Item reproduced courtesy Residual Assco Group Ltd); 13. Independent candidate DF voting at the NSW elections, 1988 (DF); 14. Kerry Packer and DF at the Testimonial lunch (DF); 15. DF on torch relay, Atlanta, 1996 (DF); 16. DF at World Sports Awards, Vienna, 1999 (DF); 17. DF with Juan Antonio Samaranch (DF); 18. DF (DF).

Picture section 1 (between pages 52 and 53)
p1 DF; p2 DF; p3 DF; p4 (top) The Balmain Association Inc., (middle and bottom) Photographer Hugh Ballment, Sydney Tramway Museum; p5 (top) courtesy of Channel 7

Australia, (bottom) DF; p6 (top) DF, (middle) courtesy of Channel 7 Australia, (bottom) DF; p7 (top) courtesy of Channel 7 Australia, (bottom) DF; p8 (top left and far right) The Herald & Weekly Times Photographic Collection, (bottom left) DF.

Picture section 2 (between pages 148 and 149)
p1 DF; p2 (top left) The Herald & Weekly Times Photographic Collection, (top right) DF, (bottom) DF; p3 DF; p4 DF, p5 DF; p6 DF; p7 (top) DF, (bottom left) Arch Fraley Collection, (middle right) Ken Rainsbury Snr, (bottom right) DF; p8 (top left) Ken Rainsbury Snr, (bottom) DF, (middle right) DF.

Picture section 3 (between pages 196 and 197)
p1 (top) courtesy of Channel 7 Australia; p2 (top) DF, (bottom left) Ken Rainsbury Snr, (bottom right) WA Newspapers; p3 The Fairfax Photo Library; p4 (top left and right) DF, (bottom) courtesy of Channel 7 Australia; p5 courtesy of Channel 7 Australia; p6 (top left and right) courtesy of Channel 7 Australia, (middle) The Herald & Weekly Times Photographic Collection, (bottom) DF; p7 DF; p8 DF.

Picture section 4 (between pages 292 and 293)
p1 DF; p2 DF; p3 DF; p4 (middle left) courtesy of Channel 7 Australia, (top and bottom) DF; p5 (top) DF, (bottom) Identity Studio Pty Ltd; p6 The Fairfax Photo Library; p7 (top) DF, (right) Papillon Studio, (bottom left) DF; p8 DF.

Picture section 5 (between pages 356 and 357)
p1 DF; p2 DF; p3 DF; p4 DF; p5 (top) Laureus World Sports Awards, (middle and bottom) DF; p6 (top) DF, (middle and bottom) reproduced with the consent of the International Olympic Committee; p7 (top left) Allsport/Getty Images, (bottom left) Eric Gaillard/Reuters, (right) DF; p8 (top and right) DF, (bottom left) Laureus World Sports Awards.

Unless otherwise acknowledged, the pictures in this book come from the personal collection of Dawn Fraser. Every effort has been made to source copyright holders; however, the publishers would be pleased to hear from any unacknowledged source.

INDEX